TOTAL BROOKSIDE

ACKNOWLEDGEMENTS

The author would like to thank the following
for their help in the preparation of this book:
Phil Redmond; Andrew Corrie, Dianne Musker,
Steve Byrne, Dorothy Andrew and Angela
Mocroft at Mersey Television; Sir Jeremy
Isaacs; Bill Dean; Steven Pinder; Michael
Starke; Claire Sweeney; John Whitehall

TOTAL BROOKSIDE

The ULTIMATE Guide
to the ULTIMATE Soap

GEOFF TIBBALLS

EBURY
PRESS

First published in Great Britain in 1998

1 3 5 7 9 10 8 6 4 2

Ebury Press
Random House, 20 Vauxhall Bridge Road, London SW1V 2SA

Random House Australia Pty Limited
20 Alfred Street, milsons Point, Sydney, New South Wales 2061, Australia

Random House New Zealand Limited
18 Poland Road, Glenfield, Auckland 10, New Zealand

Random House South Africa (Pty) Limited
Endulini, 5A Jubilee Road, Parktown 2193, South Africa

Random House UK Limited Reg. No. 954009

A CIP catalogue record for this book is available from the British Library

ISBN 0091864917

Design by Dan Newman

Printed and bound in Great Britain by Mackays of Chatham plc

Papers used by Ebury Press are natural, recyclable products made from
wood grown in sustainable forests

Contents

Introduction

by Phil Redmond

We launched Mersey Television on 10 August 1982 and 16 years later, we almost seem to have come full circle in terms of issues and social concerns. It's all about people and much of it is connected with employment and re-skilling for the digital age as we come towards the millennium. For example, what do we do about training structures for a large workforce which might not have the necessary skills? In 1982, Brookside was talking about re-skilling for the shift from old manufacturing industries into the service sector so the comparisons are there to be drawn and I find that fascinating.

Over the past few months, we've also been re-tuning the programme, introducing new characters like the Shadwicks who represent the shift in emphasis. Greg Shadwick served his time on the maintenance gangs at Cammell-Laird, but now he is self-employed and wants to control his own destiny. And his wife Margi is a trade union representative in the food processing industry so we have characters who will take part in some of the debates which are currently affecting the country, such as: What are New Labour going to do about health, welfare and education? and Where is the money going to come from for welfare to work?

'When we started out, we had the Collinses, the Grants, the Huntingtons and the Taylors as the four elements of society on the Close. The Collinses represented the management capitalist leg; the Grants represented the trade union movement; the Huntingtons were a young professional couple; and the Taylors represented the black economy – Gavin and his cookers. Now we've got the same range. The Farnhams represent the enterprise culture; the Shadwicks represent the unions; Ollie and Eleanor are the professionals; and Jimmy's still being a scally with his forged teaching certificates. We're going back to our roots.

Certainly, in the near future, Brookside is going to be concentrating much more on issues and the major concerns of society rather than looking at the minutiae of sexual activities! Sensational storylines will definitely be rarer in future. Part of the reason we've brought in the Shadwicks is to reflect the traditional 2.4 children of family life. Until recently, we'd been looking at a lot of the dysfunctional issues in society – single parents, second-time marriages and so on – but towards Christmas we'll be looking to bring in another 2.4 traditional family unit. The Farnhams were our solid family, but then with Patricia leaving and the children being killed, they became almost as dysfunctional as the Dixons and Corkhills. The Shadwicks – with one son and two daughters – provide the family base that we need. Greg is a good character because everyone comes into contact with a builder at some stage while Margi takes us on to the factory floor again, which is an area we've been missing for some time.

I think we need characters to represent the out-of-town shopping culture, multiplex cinemas and large appliance stores. One idea we're looking at is to have a postman – someone who can be out early and home early – with a wife who might work in a large, 'white goods' electrical warehouse.

As Brookside has done over the past 16 years, it will continue to re-examine important issues like health, education and crime. As a contemporary dramatist, I'd always wanted to examine social issues. A social issue is only such because it affects a great number of people. Talk to anyone whose child is suffering setbacks in education through illiteracy and you will hear of the stress, the sleepless nights, the loss of self-esteem, all of which can lead to bulimia, anorexia, even drug taking. So nobody can tell me that illiteracy is a dry subject. There is a lot more mileage left in it yet. You can pull any issue out of the air like that and you'll get the same thing, and that's what interests me as a storyteller. And that is the foundation on which Brookside's success has been built.

The Birth of *Brookside*

Not a lot of people know that *Brookside* would never have seen the light of day but for Sir Harry Secombe. In 1972, Phil Redmond had been working as a quantity surveyor for five years but was beginning to get itchy feet. His mind went back to some comedy sketches he'd written with a mate at their Merseyside comprehensive school and he decided to give up his job and go on the dole to see whether he could make a living as a writer. He gave it six months, and the only thing he sold was a comedy sketch to Harry Secombe for a series the ex-Goon was doing for Yorkshire Television. Nevertheless, the sale gave Redmond the impetus to carry on for another three months, at the end of which he was approached to write a script for the *Doctor in Charge* series for LWT. Phil Redmond was on his way.

As further commissions followed – notably for two ATV series, *The Squirrels* and *The Kids from 47A* – Redmond mulled over an idea for a drama serial set among residents on a new housing estate. In 1973 he submitted an outline of his proposal to the five major ITV companies and to the BBC, but they all turned it down. At the start of 1981, Redmond saw his chance again with the imminent arrival of Channel Four. Furthermore, by then he had the hugely successful *Grange Hill* to his name. He was someone to be taken seriously.

In January 1981, Jeremy Isaacs, former Programme Controller of Thames Television and then the founding Chief Executive of the new Channel Four, addressed a gathering of would-be independent producers in London. Among his audience was Phil Redmond. Isaacs recalls:

> After I had spoken, I bumped into a young man with designer stubble and sneakers. It was Phil Redmond. I'd never met him before but he struck up a conversation with me by asking me if I objected to strong language on television. I said that I didn't and he said he thought he might have something for me.
>
> At that stage, I don't think I was looking for a soap opera but I was certainly looking for strong drama which would hold an audience. David Rose, who was in charge of fiction at Channel Four, and I were very impressed by Phil and by what he had achieved with *Grange Hill*.
>
> I remember going to a party that Phil gave at which he wrapped himself in a cloak of Liverpudlian patriotism and told me that if you were born in Liverpool, you couldn't in those days work in television and still remain in your native city. What Phil was saying was that if we set him up to do this series in Liverpool, it would provide jobs for Liverpool people working in TV instead of them working in London or abroad. As a result of the birth of Mersey Television, a very substantial number of jobs were created, year in, year out, so a new industry was added to Liverpool's capacities.
>
> Of course, unless we had believed in the integrity, the strength and the grittiness of what Phil was offering us, we wouldn't have done it. The impetus to acceptance was first of all a recognition on our part that a twice-a-week soap

opera could be a valuable – not to say essential – part of the channel's output which, incidentally, would free us up to spend almost all the rest of the money that we had to spend on fiction and films for TV. There was the conjunction of this perceived need on our part and also our recognition that Phil was the boy to do it. I have never hesitated in my belief that it was the right judgement and it has been one of the best vindicated decisions from the early days of Channel Four.

Isaacs was also impressed by Redmond's idea of buying six houses to form a permanent set – an idea which dated from his days as a quantity surveyor. Not only did Redmond calculate that the houses would soon pay for themselves, but he knew that they would provide greater authenticity than any studio set. In order to maintain a degree of control, he wanted a cul de sac and settled on a development on Lord Sefton's estate. The cul de sac he chose had a brook running next to it. Hence *Brookside*.

Redmond gave the builders a profile of each of the show's main characters and had the houses tailored to meet the characters' various needs. 'The site was built in four months,' remembers Redmond, 'and all the houses were delivered by crane from the factory. One day, you'd go and it was just the framework, the next day a house would be there!'

So the notion that, instead of creating studios which we didn't have and which we weren't surprised to hear that he didn't have or want to use, we should build houses and then make them the set for *Brookside*, was an added and compelling piece of ingenuity. We thought, that's a good idea – it will be more convenient and it will save money.

However I have to say it took more time and trouble to negotiate the *Brookside* contract than to write the first 50 episodes! It was horrendous. We were determined to get value for money, while Phil and his colleagues were as tough a body of negotiators as you could ever hope to meet. But the justification on Channel Four's part for so tough a bargaining stance was very simple: these monies represented a large chunk of what was going into the independent sector and we had to explain and justify our decision, not just to the public but to the rest of the independent sector. And since I had made it a policy issue to spread our commissions as widely as possible, every major decision had to be something we were completely comfortable with in order that we could look all the other independent programme makers in the eye.

When I saw the first episode of *Brookside*, I thought it was OK. But the camera-work in the early episodes was not the most distinguished you'd ever seen and the sound quality was appalling. I don't think that had anything to do with Liverpool accents, I just think that with shooting at a great pace while walking along the street or running up and down the stairs in one of those semis you've built as a set, you run into problems. In the early weeks they must have been under colossal pressure. The programme did have teething troubles and it is hugely to the credit of the basic strength of the idea and of the professionalism and determination of Phil and his team that they were able to overcome the difficulties of the first few weeks.

A particular bone of contention – at least among the media – was the amount of swearing on *Brookside* in the early days. One week's tally on the whole of Channel

Four came to 173 swear words, a figure which led the *Sun* to label it 'Channel Swore'. According to Isaacs:

> Phil was all for naturalisation in speech because it would strengthen the thing dramatically – and so was I. But I hadn't appreciated before the channel started that the IBA, as it then was, would be so determined to stick to precisely the same guidelines regarding language for Channel Four as were applied to ITV. I thought they would give us an easier ride – a little more leeway – and they did, but not before the nine o'clock watershed. So there was a discussion and we had to tell Phil to tone down the language. Phil wisely saw that the essential characters of *Brookside* lay in its understanding of human nature and experience rather than in swearing, and that no matter how naturalistic swearing is, it could be sacrificed. So I think it was very sensible of him to cut his losses immediately and agree to abide by the new rules.
>
> John Whitney, the Director-General of the IBA, actually wanted *Brookside* taken off. He said it's not good enough and it's never going to be good enough, so you should get rid of it. And I think it's possible that in a hugely profitable and highly funded broadcasting organisation such a decision might have been contemplated – although it would have been wrong in my view – but there was no way that Channel Four could scrub *Brookside* in its first 18 months because it had nothing to replace it and we didn't have the funds to buy a replacement. So I said to John: 'There are things you might not like about it, but these will get sorted out. This is already a series with a very strong appeal.'
>
> *Brookside* was certainly not without controversy in those days. Ricky Tomlinson, who played Bobby Grant, had been a member of the Shrewsbury Two. He had once been a 'son of Trot' agitator and had gone to jail for that and, given that the channel had problems persuading people that, although radical and outspoken, it nevertheless tried to hold a political balance, this was a stick that newspapers used to beat us with. But Ricky Tomlinson was – still is – a very good actor. And Sue Johnston, as Sheila Grant, was utterly exceptional. Week in, week out, she gave one of the really remarkable television performances of our day – a most moving piece of acting which gave strength to the whole series.
>
> I've always been proud of *Brookside* and always hoped that Phil understood how much I admired him for what he's done. During my time at Channel Four, *Brookside* at its best provided a mainstay of the Channel Four schedule by attracting a loyal audience, many of whom organised their Saturdays, as well as weekdays, around the programme. It offered solidity in its appeal and also fulfilled the channel's remit by being distinctive in its character and different from what might have been seen on other channels.
>
> It was different because it had a Liverpool feel to it; and different because it had a sense of grinding poverty against which people were struggling – even though there is considerably worse housing in Liverpool than on Brookside Close! Working-class realities never seemed far away from the storylines and characters and it had a strength which derived from its understanding of family relationships and its frankness in dealing with them. The storylines also managed to give a sense of what life was like, and the problems which people were facing in one of Britain's great cities which had fallen on hard times

compared to its 19th-century pre-eminence.

Yet, as the years go by, *Brookside* seems less remarkable and more a part of the scene; its plots having been emulated by other soaps. It's the soap opera quality of *Brookside* that has survived rather than its distinctiveness. It doesn't matter how outrageous you are when you start, you move towards the centre and the centre moves towards you. But without *Brookside*, the likes of *EastEnders*, *Coronation Street* and *Emmerdale* wouldn't be the programmes they are today.

Brookside fans are renowned for their dedication. Some are so loyal that they have modelled their homes – although not, one hopes, their lifestyles – on those of their favourite characters. When residents of an estate in south Bradford were asked how they wanted it to look, they unanimously opted for a series of cul-de-sacs in the style of Brookside Close, complete with patios. The design department at Mersey Television regularly receives requests from fans wanting to know where they can purchase certain items seen on *Brookside* – the Corkhills' front door, the Corkhills' bedroom wallpaper, the Corkhills' lounge wallpaper, the picture in the Corkhills' living-room, the Corkhills' light shade, the Corkhills' curtains, the Corkhills' cabinet and even their bed linen. The Farnhams are equally popular with requests for, among other items, their crockery, wine glasses, wallpaper, window blinds and duvet cover. Bev's kitchen chopping board was similarly coveted. Even a Kinks poster on Peter's bedroom at Julia's did not go unnoticed and letters were soon coming in from eagle-eyed viewers wanting to buy one. Wherever possible, the design department helps out. When a 12-year-old boy with a collection of 209 beer mats requested some from Bar Brookie, they sent off a selection, and when someone who collects passport photos asked for one of Nat Simpson, it was duly despatched.

One of the keenest *Brookside* fans is 28-year-old Samuel Hope who has modelled his London home partly on 10 Brookside Close.

I've been watching *Brookside* regularly since the Corkhills moved into No. 10 and I've been fascinated with the house ever since, mainly because of the bad luck which seems to befall whoever moves in there. When Sheila moved in with Billy, I managed to match up their green wallpaper with something similar in my front room. I redecorated when the Jordaches came but then, when Jimmy and Jackie bought the house, I wrote to Mersey and have managed to get the same lilac wallpaper as the Corkhills have in their lounge. I did try to find their net curtains, but they were too expensive, and their velvet curtains, but they were made specially. And since I probably won't be spending the rest of my life here, it seemed a lot of trouble to go to. However, I did manage to get hold of the same white plaster angel figures as Jimmy and Jackie. On a trip to Liverpool, I also found the shop where they bought the flowery picture which hangs over the Corkhills' fireplace, but I passed on that one. I have tried to obtain a tape of the backing music used in the hair salon and the pizza parlour, but they're not available.

My favourite characters used to be Rod and Tracy because they were the same age as me, but since they've left I suppose Julia is my favourite. The episode I remember most was the police raid on No. 10 during Jimmy's days as a drug dealer. Somehow it was typical of all the terrible things that have happened in that house, but that bad luck hasn't put me off.

John Whitehall

Although he has only said a few lines in *Brookside*'s 18-year history, John Whitehall is one of the show's most familiar faces. For, among his many walk-on parts, Whitehall had the honour of playing the milkman who spoke the first-ever words on *Brookside* back in 1982.

'I'm known as the *Brookside* milkman,' says 55-year-old Whitehall. 'I was actually working as a milkman at the time, which was why Phil Redmond cast me – for authenticity – as well as being a professional singer.

I remember doing that opening scene at 7.30 in the morning. A dog licked some yoghurt off the wheel of my float and I shouted at it to get off. The original idea was to get the dog to wee up the float. We even had some aniseed to encourage it, but it didn't work.

In all, I've done about 20 episodes as the milkman, never saying much more than 'Good morning', including the 1,000th episode in 1991. By then, I was teaching snooker in Tokyo but they tracked me down. It was a nice surprise. The last time I was the milkman was at the Free the Jordaches prison campaign.

In the early days, there were three regular extras – the milkman, the postman and Mickey Starke as the window-cleaner. Of course, Sinbad has since gone on to be a major character. Mickey's a mate and so was Ricky Tomlinson who played Bobby Grant. He suggested a storyline where the milkman turned out to be Sheila's long-lost lover but it didn't materialise.

I've done well out of *Brookside* over the years in a variety of characters. I've been on the committee of the British Legion and on the magistrates' committee with Annabelle Collins. I've walked past the shops, been a taxi driver, a furniture removal man and been on a picket line.

Whitehall (real name John Smith) is a man of many talents. 'I've appeared in *Boys From the Blackstuff* and *Brideshead Revisited* and I played a cop with Rod Steiger and Anthony Perkins in the film *The Glory Boys*. As a qualified snooker teacher, I was shot co-ordinator on *Give Us a Break* (which starred Paul McGann and Robert Lindsay) and I also played the referee in that. I teach boys at a Liverpool snooker club and among my pupils is Rod Lawler, recently ranked 24th in the world. I've taught him since he was 12. What with that and my extra work, life's never dull!'

The First Episode

The very first episode of Brookside was transmitted at 8pm on 2 November 1982, the opening night of Channel Four. What follows is a facsimile of the script.

BROOKSIDE

EPISODE ONE

WRITTEN BY: PHIL REDMOND

T.X.:   2 NOVEMBER 1985

OMNI: 7 NOVEMBER 1985

CAST: BOBBY GRANT   Ricky Tomlinson
           SHEILA GRANT   Sue Johnston
           BARRY GRANT   Paul Usher
           DAMON GRANT   Simon O'Brien
           PAUL COLLINS   Jim Wiggins
           ANNABELLE COLLINS   Doreen Sloane
           LUCY COLLINS   Katrin Cartlidge
           GORDON COLLINS   Nigel Crowley
           ROGER HUNTINGTON   Rob Spendlove
           HEATHER HUNTINGTON   Amanda Burton
           GIZZMO HAWKINS   Robert T. Cullen
           DUCKSIE BROWN   Mark Birch

DAY:
TIMESPAN: 7.00am to 2.45pm

PART ONE: SCENES 1 to 27
PART TWO: SCENES 28 to 44

COPYRIGHT 1985 BROOKSIDE PRODUCTIONS LTD.

Sc.01.01 (EXT) BROOKSIDE ESTATE DAY 7.00am

EARLY MORNING - A MILK FLOAT BUMPING

OVER UNFINISHED ARTERIAL ROAD.......

IT TURNS INTO ONE OF THE CLOSES.....

MILKMAN HAS RADIO IN CAB....

CUT TO:

Sc.01.02 (INT) HUNTINGTON'S BEDROOM DAY 7.00am

CLOSE ON DIGITAL CLOCK/RADIO/LIGHT -7.00AM.

A CLICK AND ALARM SOUNDS...AN IRRITATING BUZZ AND

FLASHING LIGHT.

CUT TO:

Sc.01.03 (INT) BROOKSIDE ESTATE DAY 7.05am

MILKMAN GOING FROM DOOR TO DOOR.

CUT TO:

Sc.01.04 (INT) BEDROOM OF LARGE DETACHED HOUSE (DAY)
7.05am

CLOSE ON A "GOBLIN TEASMADE" AS IT CLICKS INTO LIFE
AND WATER POURS FROM KETTLE INTO TEAPOT.

SOUNDING ALARM.....7 05AM..

CUT TO:

Sc.01.05 (EXT) BROOKSIDE ESTATE DAY

MILK FLOAT MOVING FURTHER ALONG ROAD.

CUT TO:

Sc.01.06 (INT) GRANT'S BEDROOM (DAY) 7.10am

CLOSE ON A "BIG BEN" REPEATER ALARM...........7.10AM.

THE ALARM CLICKS....GOES OFF AS A HAND DROPS INTO
FRAME TO KILL IT BEFORE IT CAN ATTACK ANY FRAGILE
NERVES....

CUT TO:

Sc.01.07 (EXT) BROOKSIDE ESTATE (DAY) 7.10am

MILKMAN REACHES LAST HOUSE AND TURNS BACK TOWARD HIS

FLOAT — TO SEE A DOG WITH ITS LEG UP AGAINST

WHEEL.........

1   MILKMAN: Get out of it....Go on.

TAKES A KICK AT DOG WHICH BARKS AT HIM. TWO ST.

BERNARDS ACROSS FENCE ALSO BARK.

                    CUT TO:

Sc.01.08 (EXT) WIRRAL DAY

OUTSIDE VIEW OF LARGE HOUSE WITH "SOLD" ACROSS "FOR

SALE" SIGN.

                    CUT TO:

Sc.01.09 (INT) BEDROOM IN LARGE HOUSE DAY 7.15am

BACK TO THE GOBLIN TO SEE THAT THIS IS THE COLLIN'S

BEDROOM IN HOUSE THEY ARE SELLING TO MOVE TO BROOKSIDE.

IT HAS OBVIOUSLY BEEN VERY COMFORTABLE, MERGING ON

LUXURIOUS WITH FITTED WARDROBES, EN SUITE BATHROOM,

W.C........BUT NOW IT IS FILLED WITH CARDBOARD BOXES

AND PACKING CASES.......

WE PULL BACK TO SEE <u>ANNABELLE COLLINS</u> PACKING SUITCASE.

SHE LOOKS TO WINDOW WHEN SHE HEARS HEAVY VAN STOPPING.

<u>CUT TO:</u>

<u>Sc.01.10 (EXT) O/S LARGE DETACHED HOUSE DAY 7.30am</u>

AN OLDER STYLE DETACHED HOUSE....

THERE IS A "Y" REGISTERED ROVER 3500 IN DRIVEWAY..AND

A FOR SALE BOARD WITH "SOLD" ACROSS IT, IN GARDEN...

A FURNITURE REMOVAL VAN JUST STOPPING OUTSIDE....A

COUPLE OF GUYS OUT AND OPEN UP BACK READY TO START

LOADING...

WE SEE <u>ANNABELLE</u> WALK FROM BEDROOM.

<u>CUT TO:</u>

<u>Sc.01.11 (EXT) BROOKSIDE ESTATE DAY 7.30am</u>

MILK FLOAT TURNING FROM ARTERIAL ROAD INTO BROOKSIDE

CLOSE.......WHERE OUR SIX HOUSES ARE SET

<u>CUT TO:</u>

<u>Sc.01.12 (INT) GRANT'S BEDROOM DAY 7.30am</u>

CLOSE ON BIG BEN REPEATER ALARM......7.30 AM. A CUP
OF TEA IS PLACED NEXT TO CLOCK...AND WE PULL BACK TO
SEE <u>BOBBY GRANT</u> - FULLY DRESSED - SIT ON BED AND
ATTEMPT TO WAKE HIS WIFE <u>SHEILA</u> BUT SHE DOESN'T WANT
TO BE WOKEN....

1   <u>BOBBY</u>: Hey, there's a cup of tea there....Come on.

BUT SHE DOESN'T WANT TO KNOW - TURNING AWAY FROM HIM -
TOWARD WINDOW - SHADED BY HEAVY CURTAINS..........HE
GRINS, BUT HEARS MILK FLOAT BOUNCING AROUND OUTSIDE
ANDCROSSES TO WINDOW...AND WE SEE THEIR ROOM ALSO HAS
BOXES STACKED AGAINST WALL.

<u>BOBBY</u> PULLS CURTAINS BACK.....CONFIRMS IT IS MILK
FLOAT BRINGS A GROAN FROM SHEILA, AND SHE TURNS AWAY,
PULLING THE COVERS OVER HER HEAD..........

2   <u>BOBBY</u>: Come on love you said <u>you</u> wanted to be at
Tesco's early this morning.

1   SHEILA: That was last night.

HIS GRIN BROADENS AS HE GOES OUT OF ROOM - BUT THEN

COMES BACK......GRABS BED COVERS AND PULLS THEM OFF

BED....THEN HURRIES OUT....

2   BOBBY: (SHOUTS) Come on!

3   SHEILA: Bobby!!!

SHE RETRIEVES BEDCLOTHES ANGRILY AND LIES DOWN AGAIN.

CUT TO:

Sc.01.13 (EXT) BROOKSIDE CLOSE DAY 7.45am

MILKMAN WHISTLING, WALKING AWAY FROM FLOAT TOWARD No.

2 - THE HUNTINGTON'S. THEIR "Y" REGISTERED CITROEN IN

DRIVEWAY.

HE PUTS ONE PINT OF MILK, ONE PINT OF ORANGE JUICE AND

TWO YOGHURTS BY THE DOOR.......

RADIO - SAYING SATURDAY, AS HE TURNS AWAY.

CUT TO:

Sc.01.14 (INT) HUNTINGTON'S BEDROOM DAY 7.30am

WHERE THE DIGITAL ALARM RADIO IS PLAYING AWAY... BUT
WE PULL BACK TO SEE NO SIGN OF LIFE FROM THE TANGLED
DUVET COVER ON A MATTRESS PLACED DIRECTLY ON
FLOOR...........

THE BEDROOM IS ALMOST DEVOID OF FURNITURE SAVE FOR A
RATTAN ROCKING CHAIR, WHICH IS IMPERSONATING A CLOTHES
HORSE AND A GLASS AND RATTAN BEDSIDE TABLE UPON WHICH
THE ALARM IS DOING - OR ATTEMPTING TO DO ITS STUFF -
WITHOUT MUCH SUCCESS.....UNTIL

1   HEATHER : (O.O.V.) Turn that bloody
      thing off.........(NO RESPONSE - SO A SHARP MOVEMENT
      UNDER COVERS. O.O.V.) Roger!

      A GROAN FROM ROGER AND A GROPING HAND COMES FROM UNDER
      COVER, FINDS CLOCK...CAN'T QUITE REACH SWITCH...SO HIS
      HAND FOLLOWS ELECTRICAL FEED BACK TO WALL SOCKET -
      PULLS IT OUT/FLICKS SWITCH.

2   S/FX RADIO: Saturday morning and with the time just
      reaching.......

      RADIO DIES..SO DOES CLOCK...ROGER'S ARM RETREATS UNDER
      COVER.

THERE IS A SLIGHT MOVEMENT BENEATH COVERS AS "THE
BULGES" SEPARATE AGAIN SILENCE FOR MOMENT AS THEY
DRIFT BACK TO SLEEP AND WE..........

CUT TO:

Sc.01.15 (EXT) BROOKSIDE CLOSE DAY

MILKMAN PUTS EMPTIES ON WAGON. BOBBY COMES TO FRONT
DOOR AS FLOAT MOVES AWAY.

1   MILKMAN: Morning!

CUT TO:

Sc.01.16 (INT) GRANTS KITCHEN DAY 8.00am

SIMILAR TO BEDROOM IN THAT IT IS BEING USED BUT BOXES
OF STUFF STACKED HERE AND THERE....NO-ONE ON SET
BUT.......

1   BOBBY: Sheila you up yet

THEN BOBBY COMES INTO KITCHEN, BIG GRIN ON HIS FACE -
THINKING ABOUT HER REACTION TO HIM PULLING COVERS
OFF....SWITCHES ON TRANSISTOR...FINDS RADIO FOUR...AND
PUTS MILK IN FRIDGE...TAKES OUT A COUPLE OF EGGS,
BACON, SAUSAGE ETC TO START PREPARING

BREAKFAST...MOVES TO WORKTOP NEAR COOKER...LOOKS IN

DRAWER FOR SOMETHING — NOT THERE...LOOKS IN OTHERS,

THEN CUPBOARDS...CAN'T SEEM TO FIND WHAT HE IS LOOKING

FOR...STARTS RUMMAGING IN BOXES..BUT STILL CAN'T FIND

IT......GOES OUT TO LIVING ROOM.

CUT TO:

Sc.01.17 (INT) GRANT'S BEDROOM DAY 8.00am

SHEILA HAS NOW REGAINED COVERS AND WRAPPED HERSELF IN

THEM IN CENTRE OF BED. BOBBY COMES IN — GRINNING

AGAIN WHEN HE SEES HER.

1   BOBBY: Aren't you up yet, Sheila?

2   SHEILA: Yes. Didn't you see me out in the garden
     rearranging the stones.

BOBBY SITS ON EDGE OF BED.

BOBBY Oh come on, love. Shop'll be closed by the
time you get up. Listen have you unpacked the egg
whisk that thingeymejig?

3   SHEILA: Why?

4   BOBBY: Becaue I'm starting the decorating today and
     want something to mix the paint with.

SHE TURNS TO LOOK AT HIM - NO TRACE OF SARCASM IN HIS
VOICE...

5 <u>BOBBY</u>: I would like to scramble a couple of eggs.

6 <u>SHEILA</u>: Use a fork. (SHE SETTLES BACK INTO BED)

1 <u>BOBBY</u>: (RAISING EYES) Are you getting up or not?

2 <u>SHEILA</u>: In a minute.

HE RAISES EYES - EXITS...BUT RETURNS A MOMENT LATER
WITH A WET FACE CLOTH...DROPS IT ON HER FACE, THEN
BEATS A HASTY RETREAT AS SHEILA IS UP AND THROWS
FACECLOTH AFTER HIM

3 <u>SHEILA</u>: Oh, Bobby!

SINKS BACK ONTO PILLOWS.

<u>CUT TO:</u>

CONTINUOUS

<u>Sc.01.18 (INT) HUNTINGTON'S LIVING ROOM DAY 8.15am</u>

<u>ROGER</u> SIPPING FROM A COFFEE MUG AS HE STANDS LOOKING

OUT OF WINDOW ACROSS CLOSE AT THE <u>GRANTS</u>....HE IS IN

HUSH PUPPIES, CREW NECK SWEATER AND JEANS WITH A

CREASE DOWN LEG. THE ROOM IS FURNISHED LIKE THE

BEDROOM - I.E. WITH NOT MUCH...HABITAT COUCH AND

CHAIRS, COFFEE TABLE, SMALL 13" - BUT COLOUR -

T.V..HI-FI GROUND FLOOR FITTED CARPETS.....FLOORBOARDS

EVERYWHERE ELSE IN HOUSE....AFTER A MOMENT, <u>HEATHER</u>

COMES IN WEARING JEANS, BOOTS AND THICK SWEATER...SHE

IS NOTICEABLY IRRITATED.

1   <u>HEATHER</u>: Have you seen my bag anywhere?

2   <u>ROGER</u>: I don't know how they can afford those petrol

     guzzlers.

3   <u>HEATHER</u>: Roger. I don't want to know how many cars

     they have.

4   <u>ROGER</u>: It's not the cars Heather, its the problems

     we're going to have with the parking.

5   <u>HEATHER</u>: (IGNORING REMARK) Look, have you seen my

     bag?

6   <u>ROGER</u>: Are we going out or not?

HEATHER HESITATES..."COUNTS TEN"....THEN EXITS........

ROGER BLISSFULLY UNAWARE OF HER IRRITATION,

SHRUGS...ANOTHER CONSIDERED LOOK ACROSS AT

GRANTS...THEN EXITS......

CUT TO:

CONTINUOUS

Sc.01.19 (INT) HUNTINGTON'S HALLWAY DAY 9.00am

ROGER OUT TO A ROW OF COAT HOOKS ON WALL BEHIND

DOOR....TAKES DOWN A PADDED JACKET AND IS PUTTING IT

ON AS HEATHER COMES FROM KITCHEN, NOW WITH BAG AND

PULLING ON HER COAT......

1   ROGER: You got it then?

HEATHER JUST LOOKS AT HIM FOR STATING OBVIOUS - THEN

PASSES TO FRONT DOOR......

2   ROGER: Oh, have you locked the kitchen door?

3   HEATHER: (THROUGH TEETH) Yes.

GOES BACK TO CHECK KITCHEN DOOR FOR HIMSELF......

CUT TO:

CONTINUOUS

Sc.01.20 (EXT) O/S HUNTINGTON'S DAY 9.00am

HEATHER OUT AND STRAIGHT TO DRIVER'S DOOR...SHE
RUMMAGES IN BAG FOR KEYS...FINDS THEM, UNLOCKS DOOR
BUT AS SOON AS SHE OPENS IT THE HORN SOUNDS...CAR
FITTED WITH AN ALARM.....

SHE GRINDS HER TEETH...TAKES KEYS AND GOES TO FRONT OF
CAR AND TURNS ALARM OFF WITH KEY...AS ROGER COMES FROM
HOUSE, MAKING SURE HE HAS CLOSED DOOR PROPERLY BEHIND
HIM....AUTOMATICALLY GOES TOWARD PASSENGER - WHEN
THEY'RE TOGETHER - HEATHER DRIVES......

1   HEATHER: Is it absolutely necessary to put that
     thing on outside our own front door?

2   ROGER: Can't be too careful these days.

     SHE JUST GLARES AT HIM AS SHE GETS INTO CAR......

3   ROGER: (GETTING INTO CAR) What's wrong with you?

4   HEATHER: Roger....as much as I detest shopping this
     is the only day that it can be done. I did not plan
     to stay in bed until mid-morning....

1   ROGER: You said turn the thing off.....

2   HEATHER: The radio, Roger. Not the

clock.......(STARTS ENGINE)

HE DOESN'T SAY ANYTHING UNTIL SHE STARTS TO REVERSE

CAR....

3   ROGER: Seat belt.....

IT IS ALMOST TOO MUCH FOR HER......BUT SHE GRABS SEAT

BELT, FASTENS IT...AND DRIVES CAR OUT OF DRIVE.   THEN

OUT OF CLOSE......

Sc.01.21 (EXT) O/S COLLINS DETACHED HOUSE DAY 12.00pm

GUYS ARE JUST FINISHING LOADING THE VAN. LUCY AND

GORDON ARE IN BACK OF ROVER....PAUL AND ANNABELLE COME

OUT OF HOUSE.....WALK TO CAR - PAUL TO DRIVING SEAT,

ANNABELLE TO PASSENGER....AS THEY ARE ABOUT TO GET IN

THEY BOTH STOP AND LOOK BACK AT HOUSE, BACK AT EACH

OTHER - THEY DON'T SPEAK - THEIR FACES PORTRAY THE

MISERY AND REGRET AT LEAVING......THEY GET INTO

CAR....AS IT MOVES AWAY NEITHER LOOK BACK......

FURNITURE VAN MOVES OFF FOLLOWED BY ROVER.

CUT TO

Sc.01.22 (EXT) BROOKSIDE DAY 12.00noon

BOBBY'S CAR IN AND INTO "DRIVE" OF THEIR
HOUSE...SHEILA OUT OF PASSENGER DOOR, BOBBY FROM
DRIVER'S...GOES TO BOOT..WHICH HE OPENS TO REVEAL
ABOUT EIGHTY BULGING PLASTIC BAGS...THE SHOCK OF
PAYING FOR WHICH STILL HASN'T LEFT BOBBY...

1   BOBBY: Bloody 'ell, are you sure you got enough here
     Sheila? You don't want to feed the starving hordes of
     India while you're at it this afternoon?

2   SHEILA: (TAKING KEYS FROM BAG AND GOING TOWARD
     HOUSE) It's not like having the shop at the top of
     the road anymore, is it?

3   BOBBY: No...it's like having one in the bloody boot
     of the car.

     HE FOLLOWS....

     NB BARRY'S JAG. PARKED ON PARTRIDGES DRIVEWAY

                    CUT TO:

<u>Sc.01.23 (INT) GRANT'S LIVING ROOM DAY 12.05pm</u>

<u>SHEILA</u> OPENS DOOR, AND IN...<u>BOBBY</u> FOLLOWING...

1   <u>SHEILA</u>: I can't be carrying stuff home like I used
     to. Not out here I can't. We'll just have to do it
     weekly.

2   <u>BOBBY</u>: Weekly?!

     CONTINUOUS

     <u>BARRY</u> IS SITTING AT TABLE IN JEANS AND SWEAT SHIRT -
     READING NEWSPAPER AND POLISHING OFF TOAST AND BACON
     BUTTY.

3   <u>BARRY</u>: Alright, ma!

4   <u>SHEILA</u> : Oh you're up are you?

     <u>SHEILA</u> IN AND DUMPS BAGS ON KITCHEN WORKTOPS.
     AS...<u>BOBBY</u> FOLLOWS IN...

5   <u>BOBBY</u>: We can't eat all <u>this</u> every week?

6   <u>SHEILA</u>: We don't...the kids do. Especially Gannet
     here.

BARRY JUST GRINS AND CONTINUES EATING AND
READING.....BOBBY GOES BACK OUT TO CAR.....

1   SHEILA: (DISAPPROVAL) And what time did you get in
last night - or was it this morning.

2   BARRY: Nah...haven't been to bed yet.......

3   SHEILA: Huh...that wouldn't surprise me. It's a
wonder you remembered where we'd moved to.

BARRY REFUSES TO BE DRAWN. CONTINUING READING PAPER
BUT SMILING AT HIS MOTHER'S "NAGGING".

4   SHEILA: I don't suppose the other two are up yet, are
they?

5   BARRY: Damon is.

6   SHEILA: (NOW MOVED TO FILL KETTLE NOTICES PILE OF
DIRTY DISHES IN SINK) So I can see.... Where is he?

7   BARRY: Went out before.

BOBBY NOW RETURNS WITH REST OF BAGS.

1   SHEILA: That lazy madam's still in bed.

2   BOBBY: (WINKS AT BARRY) Must take after her mother then.

SHEILA IS UNPACKING THE PLASTIC BAGS......BOBBY STARTS TO MAKE TEA WHEN KETTLE BOILS......

3   SHEILA: Now here....I know you like to give the roosters an early call, but I've never stayed in bed past eleven o'clock in my life. Especially when I was her age. Always had too much to do....like helping me mother around the house every now and then.....

4   BARRY: Aye....we know and you never had any shoes on your feet...

SHE JUST CLIPS HIM ROUND BACK OF HEAD, PICKS UP TOILET ROLLS/SOAP/SHAMPOO AND EXITS.....

BOTH BARRY AND BOBBY MORE AMUSED BY HER CARRYING ON......

5   BARRY: What's up ....soap powder gone up or something?

6   BOBBY: You want another cup?

1   BARRY: (YAWNS) No thanks......aarrghh! I'm knackered.

2   BOBBY: I thought you were supposed to be the super-athlete around here.

3   BARRY: I am. A knackered super-athlete...going to Anfield this afternoon?

4   BOBBY: (NODS) If I can get out of the unpacking. Who are you playing?

5   BARRY: You should know, it's your bloody factory I play for.

6   BOBBY: I only introduced you to Ted. I'm not the Chairman of the supporters club.

7   BARRY: Broxbourne Metals.

8   BOBBY: Broxes? They shut down last month.

9   BARRY: (NODS) They're thinking of renaming the team the SS Eleven and making the dole their social club.

1   <u>BOBBY</u>: (SHAKING HEAD) Me dad worked at broxes for a while. Been going about a hundred years they had.

2   <u>BARRY</u>: Looks it, the state it's in. We've got the contract to rip it down next month.

3   <u>BOBBY</u>: Christ....they didn't waste much time.

4   <u>BARRY</u>: (SHRUGS) More money in the steel holding the place up than the metal they used to knock out.

5   <u>BOBBY</u>: (TUTS - THEN) Lack of investment that was. Our place'll be going the same way if they're not careful.

6   <u>BARRY</u>: I thought you'd been bailed out by that government grant?

7   <u>BOBBY</u>: So did we...(SHRUGS) We're putting the pay claim in on Monday and they've already got a dose of the Michael Edwardses.

1   BARRY: (STANDING) Well try to keep them going until
      the end of the season – we're in with a chance for
      the Association Cup this year. (MOVES TO DOOR)
      Still, if your place did go under there's so many on
      the social now, we could organise an inter–dole
      league. (GRINNING) "give the unemployed something to
      do". It's a wonder Heseltine hasn't thought of that.

2   BOBBY: Don't worry – he will.

      THEY BOTH GRIN – BARRY EXITS....

      BOBBY POURS TEA.........

                        CUT TO:

Sc.01.24 (EXT) BROOKSIDE ESTATE DAY 12.30pm

COLLINS'S CAR WITH FURNITURE VAN BEHIND.

BOTH TURN INTO ESTATE......

CUT TO:

Sc.01.25 (EXT) BROOKSIDE CLOSE DAY 12.30pm

VAN FOLLOWED BY CAR.....PAUL PUTS CAR STRAIGHT INTO
DRIVEWAY.....MEN GET OUT OF CAB AND GO TO BACK OF VAN.

THE COLLINS OUT OF CAR, LUCY, GORDON AND ANNABELLE
STAND LOOKING AROUND AT REST OF HOUSES, AS PAUL GOES
TO DOOR....FIDDLING WITH KEY.

1   ANNABELLE: I thought the Site Agent was supposed to
     be here to "welcome us to our new home".

2   PAUL: (JUST GIVES A CYNICAL LOOK — THEN) C'mon.....

     AS THEY TURN TOWARD HOUSE, HE MANAGES TO OPEN
     DOOR...BUT JUST AS HE IS ABOUT TO GO THROUGH DOOR — HE
     STEPS BACK, PARTIALLY IN SURPRISE AS THREE GUYS AND
     TWO GIRLS — ALL ABOUT 14/15 COME CHARGING DOWNSTAIRS...

TWO PUSH PAST HIM, FOLLOWED BY ONE OF THE GIRLS, WHILE
OTHER GUY AND GIRL GO OUT OF BACK.

3   PAUL: What the.....

IT IS ALL OVER IN A MATTER OF A SECOND OR TWO - WITH
NO SIGN OF THE KIDS - OR WHERE THEY WENT....

PAUL IS ABOUT TO GO AND LOOK, WHEN ANNABELLE TAKES HIS
ARM.

1   ANNABELLE: Paul...It's an empty house...there's not
much they could have done.

IT IS WITH RELUCTANCE THAT HE NODS ACCEPTANCE OF THE
FACT AND TURNS BACK.

2   PAUL:Let's go and see then.

HE LEADS THEM INTO HOUSE.....

CUT TO:

CONTINUOUS

Sc.01.26 (INT) COLLINS' KITCHEN DAY 12.40pm

ANNABELLE AND PAUL IN.......

BOTH NATURALLY DEPRESSED BY THEIR MOVE DOWN MARKET.
ANNABELLE OPENS AND CLOSES A FEW DRAWERS. PAUL STARES
OUT OF WINDOW. BOTH LOOK AT EACH OTHER.

1   ANNABELLE: We'll be alright.

2   PAUL: Will we?

SHE DOESN'T ANSWER.

Sc.01.27 (INT) COLLIN'S LANDING DAY 12.35pm

WHILE PAUL AND ANNABELLE GO INTO LIVING ROOM/KITCHEN,
LUCY AND GORDON GO UPSTAIRS...

1   GORDON: Lucy.

THEY BOTH STARE AT THE STATE OF ONE OF THE ROOMS.

2   LUCY: (CALLS) Mum! Come and look at this!

THERE IS JUST ENOUGH CONCERN IN HER VOICE TO MAKE PAUL
AND ANNABELLE HURRY OUT OF ROOM.....

                    CUT TO:

<u>Sc.01.28 (INT) GORDON'S BEDROOM DAY 12.45pm</u>.

FAIRLY TIGHT SHOT OF <u>LUCY</u> AND <u>GORDON</u> NEAR

DOOR.....EXCHANGING A "WAIT FOR IT" SORT OF LOOK AS

THEY HEAR MOTHER AND FATHER COMING UP STAIRS......

1   <u>ANNABELLE</u>: (O.O.V.) What is it, darling?

LUCY JUST NODS INTO ROOM....AS PARENTS COME UPSTAIRS.

FACES REGISTER IN DISGUST....AND WE WIDEN SHOT TO SHOW

THE FLOOR LITTERED WITH PAPERS AND BEER CANS...AND

WALLS COVERED IN GRAFFITI..

<u>PAUL</u> LOOKS ABOUT TO BURST A BLOOD VESSEL AS HE WALKS

IN TO EXAMINE ROOM PROPERLY.

2   <u>PAUL</u>:   Bloody...Bloody little hooligans!

3   <u>GORDON</u>:   I suppose this is my room?

THEY ALL LOOK THOROUGHLY CHEESED OFF.....

<u>END OF PART ONE</u>

Sc.01.29 (EXT) BROOKSIDE ESTATE DAY 1.00pm

A PART OF THE ESTATE STILL UNDER CONSTRUCTION...AND IN
ONE OF THE HALF BUILT HOUSES THE THREE GUYS AND TWO
GIRLS WHO TOOK PART IN THE EXODUS FROM THE COLLINS'S
ARE TRYING TO DECIDE WHAT TO DO NEXT.....

ONE OF THE GUYS...."GIZZMO HAWKINS IS KEEPING WARM BY
SWINGING MONKEY-FASHION BACKWARD AND FORWARD ACROSS
CEILING JOISTS.....

THE TWO GIRLS, DAWN AND FAY ARE LINKED TOGETHER AGAINST
NOVEMBER AIR...WHILE THE TWO REMAINING GUYS "DUCKSIE"
BROWN AND OUR VERY OWN DAMON GRANT ARE AT
"WINDOWS".......

1   FAY: See anything?

2   DUCKSIE: Nah..must have jacked it in...(TURNS AND
     HUDDLES DOWN BELOW WINDOW) Friggin hell, nearly lost
     me bottle then.

3   DAMON: Nearly? You had your brown kecks on all the
     way.

4   DAWN :   What are we going to do now? I'm freezing.

1   DUCKSIE: I could warm you up...

SHE IGNORES HIM AND LOOKS TO DAMON - HE APPEARS TO BE
NATURAL "LEADER" - HE JUST SHRUGS......

2   DAWN: Well I'm not staying out here in the freezin'
cold...(TO FAY) You comin'?

FAY NODS AND THE TWO GIRLS PICK THEIR WAY ACROSS THE
UNFINISHED FLOOR...AND OUT OF THE HOUSE...

GIZZMO DROPS FROM CEILING JOISTS..

3   GIZZMO: Reckon we'll ever get anything from those
two?

4   DUCKSIE: You won't.

5   GIZZMO: "Piss Off"!   (TO DAMON) What time we going
to the match, Dame?

6   DAMON: (SHRUGS) Dunno. See what time me old fellahs
going, and see if we can cadge a lift off him.

7   GIZZMO: Rocket......

1   <u>DUCKSIE</u>: (TO DAMON) What are we going to do about the house, like?

2   <u>DAMON</u>: Not much we can do, is there, dickhead.

3   <u>GIZZMO</u>: (LAUGHING) We should have stayed, you know, been squatters, like...(TO DUCKSIE) Got any ciggies left?

4   <u>DUCKSIE</u>: Nah..comin' over the shop to get some.

5   <u>GIZZMO</u>: It's pissin' miles away. (TO DAMON) Whatja have to move up here for anyway? Pissin' useless, it is.

6   <u>DAMON</u>: Me ma wanted her own house. They're not all deadheads like your mum and dad, you know.

WITH THAT HE CLIMBS OUT OF WINDOW....

OTHERS AUTOMATICALLY FOLLOW AND HEAD ACROSS ROAD.

<u>CUT TO:</u>

Sc.01.30 (INT) GORDON'S BEDROOM DAY

GORDON IS STARING OUT OF WINDO, SORRY FOR HIMSELF.
LUCY JOINS HIM.

1   LUCY: If you're expecting any sympathy from me you
      can just forget it.....welcome to Brookside, kids.
      Purgatory, here.

2   GORDON: You don't have to dramatise it.

3   LUCY: God, I'm gonna go crazy here......I always
      thought Dad's career was psychological warfare.

4   GORDON: It wasn't his fault he got the bullet, was it?

5   LUCY: Wasn't it?!

6   GORDON: Of course not. It was part of a
      rationalisation scheme.

7   LUCY: Yes, but if you rationalise anything, you get
      rid of the dross, don't you? My favourite bit
      (IMITATING FATHER) Tomorrow is the beginning of the
      rest of your life. (THEY LAUGH BITTERLY)

      LUCY SHAKES HER HEAD AND AMBLES OUT.

                    CUT TO:

<u>Sc.01.31 (EXT) BROOKSIDE CLOSE (DAY) 1.30pm</u>

AS <u>DAMON</u>, <u>DUCKSIE</u> AND <u>GIZZMO</u> COME INTO CLOSE AND
TOWARD <u>DAMON'S</u>....

THE PANTECHNICON IS NOW HALF-EMPTY. <u>ANNABELLE COLLINS</u>
IS WALKING DOWN BACKBOARD WITH A BOX. <u>PAUL</u> IS NEAR
THEIR FRONT DOOR WITH CUSHIONS IN HIS ARM.....

1   <u>ANNABELLE</u>: ...don't really know. I'm sure I put it
      in with the kitchen things....Paul, are you listening?

      SHE TURNS TO SEE THAT HE ISN'T, BUT IS WATCHING <u>DAMON</u>
      AND CO GO UP PATH AND ROUND TO BACK OF No.5..

2   <u>PAUL</u>: That's the hard-faced little buggers.

3   <u>ANNABELLE</u>: Are you sure?

4   <u>PAUL</u>: Of course I am.

5   <u>REMOVAL MAN</u>: Where do you want this, love?

6   <u>ANNABELLE</u>: Oh..er..down...no upstairs in the front
      please..

1   PAUL: I've got a mind to go over there and....

2   ANNABELLE: Please, Paul... (CONSCIOUS REMOVAL MEN MAY HEAR) You don't know for certain it was them.

3   PAUL: They nearly pushed me over for God's sake.

4   ANNABELLE: It might have been the first time they were in the house.

PAUL LOOKS AT HER...THINKS IT'S UNLIKELY......

5   ANNABELLE: Please....Not on our first day, darling.

HE IS RELUCTANT TO LET MATTER DROP..BUT LUCY COMES FROM HOUSE TO BREAK THE MOOD.

6   LUCY: I've found it.....(HOLDS UP KETTLE)

7   ANNABELLE: Oh good!

LUCY GOES BACK INTO HOUSE, ANNABELLE GOES IN AFTER HER AND HE ALLOWS HIMSELF TO BE DRAGGED IN.

CUT TO:

CONTINUOUS

<u>Sc.01.32</u> (INT) <u>COLLINS'S KITCHEN</u> <u>DAY</u> <u>1.45pm</u>

WHERE <u>GORDON</u> IS ALREADY PUTTING OUT CUPS ETC...<u>LUCY</u>

TAKES KETTLE TO SINK...TURNS ON TAP, BUT NO WATER...AS

<u>PAUL</u> AND <u>ANNABELLE</u> ENTER...

1   <u>LUCY</u>:   Oh..there's no water....

PAUL COMES ACROSS AND TURNS TAP ON AND OFF....TO CHECK

FOR HIMSELF....WHICH BRINGS A LOOK AND RAISED EYES

BETWEEN <u>LUCY</u> AND <u>GORDON</u>.

2   <u>PAUL</u>:   Must be switched off.

3   <u>LUCY</u>:   Turned off.

4   <u>PAUL</u>:   Sorry?

5   <u>LUCY</u>:   You turn off water you switch off electricity.

6   <u>PAUL</u>:   Really!?

OBVIOUSLY HE IS IRRITATED BY <u>LUCY'S</u> PEDANTRY..AS HE

OFTEN IS......BUT HE LOOKS IN CUPBOARDS ETCFOR STOP

COCK.......... FINDS IT UNDER SINK AND TURNS IT ON

WE SEE WATER GUSHING FROM WALL UPSTAIRS WHERE TOILET
HAS BEEN REMOVED.

PAUL IS STARTLED BY THE REMOVAL MAN'S VOICE FROM
UPSTAIRS.

REMOVAL MAN COMES RUNNING DOWN STAIRS.

1   REMOVAL MAN: (O.O.V.) Turn your water off, boss.
It's all over the shop up here....

PAUL DIVES INTO CUPBOARD, TURNS STOPCOCK OFF, THEN
HURRIES UPSTAIRS...

LUCY GIGGLES.

                    CUT TO:

                    CONTINUOUS

Sc.01.33 (INT) COLLINS'S LANDING DAY 1.45pm

REMOVAL MAN IN BATHROOM WHERE THERE IS A POOL OF
WATER... IT IS WHERE THE TOILET SHOULD BE BUT ISN'T
AND THE PIPES HAVE BEEN SAWN THROUGH.........

1   REMOVAL MAN: (FINGERING PIPES) You did bring a

spare didn't you?

2   PAUL: Right, that does it!

PAUL CHARGES DOWN STAIRS.....

CUT TO:

CONTIUOUS

Sc.01.34 (EXT) O/S COLLINS DAY 1.45pm

PAUL OUT OF FRONT DOOR....AND OFF TOWARD GRANTS....

CUT TO:

Sc.01.35 (INT) GRANT'S KITCHEN DAY 1.45pm

DAMON, DUCKSIE AND GIZZMO ARE SPACED ABOUT IN THE
KITCHEN...DAMON MAKING HIMSELF A SANDWICH..

BOBBY THEN COMES FROM LIVING ROOM.

1   BOBBY: Alright, lads.

2   GIZZMO: Alright.

3   DUCKSIE: Alright.

4   DAMON: Alright Dad.....You going the match this
    savvy, Dad?

5   BOBBY: I expect so, why are you?

6   DUCKSIE: Yeah.

THERE IS A KNOCK/RING AT FRONT DOOR.

7   BOBBY: (LOOKS AT WATCH) Don't leave yourselves too
    late for that bus now, will you.

LADS ALL A BIT CHEESED......

                        CUT TO:

CONTINUOUS

Sc.01.36 (INT) GRANTS LIVING ROOM DAY 1.50pm.

BOBBY TO FRONT DOOR.

BOBBY Karen? You out of that bathroom!?

HE REACHES DOOR, OPENS IT AND AS HE DOES, PAUL COLLINS
STEPS INTO HOUSE.

1   PAUL: Where are they?

BOBBY IS TAKEN BY SUPRISE, BUT ONLY FOR A MOMENT
BEFORE......

2   BOBBY: Aye, aye Pal. What's your game? where are
     you going?

AND HE GRABS PAUL'S ARM AND SWINGS HIM BACK THROUGH
DOOR AND INTO PATH.

                    CUT TO:

                    CONTINUOUS

Sc.01.37 (EXT) O/S GRANTS' DAY 1.50pm

PAUL COMES STUMBLING OUT OF DOOR TO STEADY HIMSELF UP
AGAINST THE WALL.

BARRY DASHES OUT.

1   BOBBY: I don't know who you are, Pal; or what you
         are but carry on like that pal and I'll spread you all
         over that wall.

     EVEN IN HIS FURY, PAUL CAN SEE THAT HE WOULD BE NO
     MATCH FOR BOBBY....ESPECIALLY AS BARRY, MATERIALISES
     AT DOOR..

2   BARRY: What's happening here?

3   BOBBY: Ask him.

4   PAUL: It's not me you should be asking — it's the
         three hooligans who came into this house.

BOBBY PASSES HIS EYES IN A "Not again" GESTURE — THEN COMES AND CALLS

1   BOBBY: Damon! You and the dynamic duo. Get out here now!

ANNABELLE ARRIVES.

2   ANNABELLE: Paul!

3   PAUL: They were inside when we arrived..the place is littered with rubbish. Graffiti on the walls. And now the bathroom has been vandalised......

DAMON, DUCKSIE AND GIZZMO, ARRIVE IN TIME TO HEAR THIS...

4   DAMON: We never bust nothing.

5   PAUL: Well what's happened to the toilet?

6   DAMON: How should we know?

7   BOBBY: Shut up. (TO PAUL) You accusing them of thieving?

1   ANNABELLE: I don't think my husband is

exactly....(saying that)

2   PAUL: It's obvious, isn't it.

3   BOBBY: No it bloody well isn't.

4   PAUL: It is to me.

5   BOBBY: It isn't to me.

BARRY STEPS BETWEEN THEM.....

6   BARRY: Alright..alright...(TO DAMON) You been

inside there.

7   DAMON: Only messing about and..

8   BOBBY: Have you?

9   DAMON: (SHRUGS) Suppose so.

IT IS MORE HIS MANNER THAN THE ACT THAT ANGERS BOBBY -

AND HIS HAND FLASHES OUT AND CRACKS DAMON ROUND HEAD.

10   BARRY: (TO PAUL) What's wrong?

1   PAUL: The whole house is flooded. When I turned the
water on....

2   BOBBY: (TO DAMON) Have you been messing about with
the water.

3   DAMON: No.

4   BOBBY: I'm warning you, Damon.

5   DAMON: I haven't. (TO OTHERS) Have we?

OTHERS SHAKE HEADS.

6   GIZZMO: We may have done the graffiti and that,
like. But we never bust nothing...straight up.

IT IS NOW THAT SHEILA COMES OUT...

7   SHEILA: What's going on?

8   BOBBY: That's what we're trying to find out.

9   PAUL: I've told you what happened.

1   BARRY: Hold up...let's shoot across and have a blimp
     come 'head.

     HE STARTS TO GO. BOBBY TURNS TO BOYS...

2   BOBBY: Get inside. I'll sort you out later.

     HE FOLLOWS BARRY...PAUL AND ANNABELLE EXCHANGE A
     LOOK....AND PAUL FOLLOWS THE TWO MEN...

                       CUT TO:

 Sc.01.38 (INT) COLLINS'S LANDING. DAY 2.00pm

     BARRY IS LOOKING AT PIPEWORK AS BOBBY AND PAUL
     ARRIVE....

1   BARRY: More than vandalism, this is.

2   PAUL: I'm sorry I don't er...

3   BARRY: Either a cash flow crises or a Sunday special

     PAUL LOOKS BLANK......

4   <u>BOBBY:</u>   Done on a Sunday afternoon when the shops are shut.

PAUL NODS........

5   <u>BARRY:</u> And probably in some little old lady's bathroom extension by now...(WINKS) paid for by a corporation grant... this where the graffitti is?

HE GOES INTO <u>GORDONS</u> BEDROOM...

1   <u>PAUL:</u> Yes..but I'd prefer it if you'd er.......

BUT <u>BARRY</u> COMES OUT.....

2   <u>BARRY:</u> Nah couldn't have been our Damon, dad. He always spells bollocks with only one "L". (GRINS).

3   <u>BOBBY:</u> Alright... thats enough of that.....c'mon.

<u>CUT TO:</u>

CONTINUOUS

Sc.01.39 (EXT) O/S GRANTS DAY 2.10pm

AS <u>BOBBY</u> AND <u>BARRY</u> CAN BE SEEN COMING FROM <u>COLLIN'S</u>
AND HEADING BACK TO THEIR OWN HOUSE. <u>SHEILA</u> AND
<u>ANNABELLE</u> COME OUT OF <u>GRANTS</u>...<u>ANNABELLE</u> CARRYING TEA
POT.

1   <u>ANNABELLE:</u> ...tends to jump the gun at times.

2   <u>SHEILA:</u>   Don't they all, love. But...don't forget. I
     meant what I said.

3   <u>ANNABELLE:</u> Thats awfully kind of you.

4   <u>SHEILA:</u> (TO BOBBY) How was it?

     <u>BOBBY</u> JUST LOOKS AT <u>ANNABELLE</u> AND GOES INTO HOUSE.....

5   <u>BOBBY:</u>   (O.O.V.) Damon !!

6   <u>SHEILA:</u> (PULLS FACE) Er...I'd better go.

     SHE GOES AFTER <u>BOBBY</u>......

                  <u>CUT TO:</u>

<u>Sc.01.40 (EXT) GRANTS' BACK GARDEN DAY</u>

<u>DAMON</u> DIVES OUT FOLLOWED BY <u>DUCKSIE</u> AND <u>GIZZMO</u>. THEY
SNEAK ALONGSIDE OF HOUSE TO STREET.

<u>CUT TO:</u>

<u>Sc.01.41 (INT) GRANTS' FRONT DOOR DAY</u>

<u>BOBBY</u> RUSHES OUT PAST <u>ANNABELLE</u> AND <u>SHEILA</u>. <u>SHEILA</u>
FOLLOWS HIM.

1   <u>BOBBY</u>: Damon!

2   <u>BOBBY</u>:   Come here!....

<u>BARRY</u> COMES FROM GARAGE WITH A LENGTH OF HOSE
AS.........

<u>DAMON</u> SLINKS ACROSS....EXPECTING A BELT...BUT
SURPRISED WHEN...

3   <u>BOBBY</u>:   You three planning on a lift to the match?

4   <u>DAMON</u>:   Er.....yeah.

5   <u>BOBBY</u>:   Got your money?

1   <u>DAMON</u>:   Er.......yeah..

2   <u>BOBBY</u>:   Let's see.

THEY ALL TAKE OUT MONEY - SHOW HIM.....HE TAKES IT
FROM THEM.

3   <u>BOBBY</u>:   That should be enough.

4   <u>DAMON</u>:   (SUDDENLY SUSPICIOUS) What for?

5   <u>BOBBY</u>:   To buy some paint and brushes to clean up your
mess.

6   <u>DUCKSIE</u>:   What?

7   <u>BOBBY</u>:   Now.(TO DAMON)   Get in! And you two. Home.

8   <u>DAMON</u>:   Ah-hey, dad

9   <u>BOBBY</u>:   Now.

THEY HESITATE FOR A MOMENT - BUT ONLY FOR A MOMENT -
BEFORE EXCHANGING A LOOK.

<u>DAMON</u> GOES INTO HOUSE - OTHERS WALK AWAY

BOBBY JUST LOOKS AT ANNABELLE..AND AT TEA POT.

1   ANNABELLE: Er...I'd better take this before it goes cold.....(SHE "SMILES" AND TURNS TOWARD OWN HOUSE).

2   BARRY: Hang on.....At least I can get the water on for you.

BARRY GOES OF WITH ANNABELLE.....

3   BOBBY: (RAISES EYES) Bloody hell.

4   SHEILA: She seems nice enough.

5   BOBBY: Not her fault she married a divvy.

6   SHEILA: No....look at me....You really going to make them pay for paint!.

7   BOBBY: They messed it up didn't they...

8   SHEILA: I said they could use our bathroom if they wanted.

BOBBY LOOKS CHEESED....ABOUT TO SPEAK.....BUT.......

1   <u>SHEILA</u>: You can't expect them to be without a toilet, Bobby.

2   <u>BARRY</u>: Great offer that is. We can't even get Karen out of the bathroom. What chance do they have.

<u>BOBBY</u> AT LAST MANAGES A CHUCKLE...

<u>SHEILA</u> AND <u>BOBBY</u> INTO HOUSE.....

<u>CUT TO:</u>

<u>Sc.01.42 (INT) COLLINS' KITCHEN NIGHT 2.30pm</u>

<u>BARRY</u> HAS PUT FLEXI-HOSE FROM PIPE TO BATH.

1   <u>ANNABELLE</u> : Er..I er..don't know how to thank you er....

2   <u>BARRY</u>: Barry. S'alright. I'll pick one up from the site on my way home

3   <u>BARRY</u>: (GETTING UP) That should keep you going till you get on to the site agent on Monday.... Although you'll have to keep your legs crossed until seven tonight

4   <u>ANNABELLE</u> : Er...yes.

THERE IS AN AWKWARD SILENCE...HE FINISHED WHAT HE CAME
TO DO - THE CULTURAL GAP.

5   <u>BARRY</u>:   Right then... I'll er...

HEADS FOR DOOR....

                 <u>CUT TO:</u>

                 CONTINUOUS

<u>Sc.01.43 (INT) COLLINS'S HALL   DAY   2.30pm</u>

<u>BARRY</u> OUT.

<u>ANNABELLE</u> FOLLOWS HIM WITH <u>SHEILA'S</u> TEAPOT.

1   <u>ANNABELLE</u>:   Don't forget this......

2   <u>BARRY</u>:   Ta.

<u>PAUL</u> COME IN WITH SMALL PIECE OF FURNITURE

3   <u>BARRY</u>:   You can turn on now, if you want

<u>PAUL</u> JUST LOOKS - ALMOST CONTEMPT - <u>BARRY</u> PRICKLES BUT
RESTRAINS HIMSELF...EXCHANGES A SMILE WITH ANNABELLE.

4   <u>ANNABELLE</u>:   I'll er...remember that.

5   <u>BARRY</u>:   Right then...see you.

     HE EXITS......

                    <u>CUT TO:</u>

                    CONTINUOUS

<u>Sc.01.44 BROOKSIDE CLOSE DAY 2.35pm</u>

     AS <u>BARRY</u> COMES FROM <u>COLLINS'S</u>...TO SEE THE <u>HUNTINGTON'S</u>
     CITROEN PARKED DOWN CLOSE AS PANTECHNICON BLOCKING
     DELIVERY.

     HEATHER AND <u>ROGER</u> WALKING TO HOUSE WITH A LOT OF "
     GEORGE HENRY LEE" BAGS.

     ALTHOUGH <u>ROGER</u> IS MORE INTERESTED IN THE <u>COLLINS</u>
     HOUSEHOLD...AND SLIGHTLY WORRIED BY WITNESSING <u>BARRY'S</u>
     EXIT.

1   <u>ROGER</u>:   God, you don't suppose they're friends of
     theirs, do you?

2   <u>BARRY</u>: How do folks!

     THE <u>HUNTINGTON'S</u> "SMILE" AND GO TOWARD OWN HOUSE.

     <u>ROGER</u> IS STILL LOOKING TOWARD <u>COLLINS</u>.

                    <u>CUT TO:</u>

Sc.01.45 GRANTS' LIVING ROOM DAY 2.35pm

TIGHT ON DOOR AS <u>SHEILA</u> COMES IN WITH CUP OF TEA...IN
ONE HAND AND TWO EMPTY MILK BOTTLES IN OTHER BUT SHE
STOPS IN DOOR.....SOMETHING IN ROOM "DISPLEASING"
HER....SHE PUTS TEA AND BOTTLES DOWN ON SIDEBOARD AND
EXITS.

CUT TO:

Sc.01.46 GRANTS LIVING ROOM DAY 2.45pm

CLOSE ON DOOR AS <u>SHEILA</u> COMES IN CARRYING WET TOWEL.
PULL BACK TO SHOW <u>BOBBY</u> ASLEEP IN CHAIR. <u>SHEILA</u> PICKS
UP TEA, CROSSES AND STANDS OVER <u>BOBBY</u> THEN DROPS TOWEL
ON HIS FACE.......

<u>BOBBY</u> COUGHS AND SPLUTTERS INTO CONSCIOUSNESS.

1   <u>BOBBY</u>:   What'd...what'd you do that for?

2   <u>SHEILA</u>:   (GIVES HIM CUP) Thought you wanted to go to
     the match. Coffee?

SO SAYING SHE GOES BACK TO KITCHEN
<u>BARRY</u> LAUGHS AND HEADS FOR FRONT DOOR

CUT TO:

Sc.01.47 O/S GRANTS DAY 2.45pm

DAMON PERCHED ON JAG. BARRY COMES OUT.

1   BARRY: You're a right dickead you, aren't y'?

2   DAMON: Don't you start. (BARRY THUMPS HIM)

3   BARRY: I'll give you more than that!

4   DAMON: I've had melecture for the day.

5   BARRY: (INDICATES COLLINS') What did y'go an' do

     that for, eh?

6   DAMON: I never knew no-one was gonna move in today,

     did I?

7   BARRY: You knew someone was gonna move in there,

     didn't y'? Imagine what me Mam'd have said if she'd

     moved in......You didn't nick the bog, did y'?

8   DAMON: They got the money for the paint, didn't they?

9   BARRY: I'd have made you paint it yourself...Anyway,

     look, take that in will y'? (HANDS HIM TEAPOT) I'm

     goin' down to the Swan for half an hour, see if I can

     get them a bog.

<u>BARRY</u> GOES TO GET IN CAR. <u>DAMON</u> JUMPS DOWN.

1   <u>BARRY</u>: Go on, get in!

<u>DAMON</u> GOES TO HOUSE.

<u>BARRY</u> SQUEEZES JAG OUT AND PAST REMOVAL VAN AS <u>PAUL</u>, <u>LUCY</u> AND <u>GORDON</u> STILL HEAPING MORE FURNITURE INTO THE HOUSE...

WE SEE <u>ROGER HUNTINGTON</u> STANDING ON HIS DOORSTEP "CHECKING ON THINGS". HE GOES IN.

<u>END OF EPISODE</u>

Bill Dean

Although Harry Cross left Brookside nearly ten years ago, his memory lives on. Seventy-six-year-old Bill Dean, who played Harry, admits: 'I still can't go out without people asking about Harry. They come up to me and say, "Hello, you miserable old bugger!" And I get asked to open fêtes as Harry. They expect me to be grumpy so I play up to it at first and then they realise that I'm nothing like him at all. I'm actually a happy person and I've got two great granddaughters who are the apples of my eye and keep me young.'

Harry's story started when I went for a drink in the Sefton pub. All the Brookside cast were there and Sue Johnston said she'd always wanted to meet me. The director Chris Clough invited me for lunch and I ended up getting the part. The character was called Alex Cross at first, but I suggested changing it to Harry. I remember they brought 12 actresses in and asked me to pick a wife!

Harry was only supposed to be in the show for three months and then die from a heart attack, but the character became so popular with viewers that he was kept on. He was wonderful to play – a real love/hate character — and I did it all with a straight face. The writers used to say that Harry was the easiest character to write for.

Jimmy McGovern, in particular, wrote me some lovely scenes. When Edna died, it was terribly moving. I remember a Jimmy McGovern speech which had me speaking to Edna's gravestone. It was a very windy day and I told the director I could only do it once. The gravestones were plastic and I'd just got to the last sentence of this long speech when the stone blew over. I threw the flowers at Edna's grave and said, 'You old so and so!'

We had a lot of laughs and Ray Dunbobbin, who played Ralph, and I really gelled. Somebody said we were the Laurel and Hardy of Brookside. I still see him for a drink occasionally.

In the end, I asked to leave. The show was about to go three nights a week and Harry featured a lot. I was driving to work at 6.30 one morning in the snow and I thought, what am I doing this for at 67? But people still want to know when Harry's coming back. I'm semi-retired now, but who knows, I might go back and moan at them all for a guest appearance. After all, I still haven't been paid for the bungalow!

Brookside 1982-1998

Plot details for the entire history of the programme.

1982

The new residents of Brookside Close discover that they have been burgled ... Lucy Collins is bullied at school ... Bobby Grant has problems at work ... Son Barry is stabbed.

November

The middle-class Collins family arrive at their new home at 8 Brookside Close to find the front door already open. The unofficial welcoming party is young Damon Grant and his cronies but as they flee the scene, further exploration of the house reveals graffiti sprayed on the bedroom walls, cigarette stubs all over the place and, even more alarmingly, no toilet. Paul Collins storms over to the Grants' to accuse Damon of the theft but Damon's elder brother, Barry, persuades Paul that it is the work of professionals and builds a temporary one in lieu. Paul is unconvinced and is none too pleased when wife Annabelle volunteers him to drive the Grants to Sunday Mass.

Lucy Collins is unhappy at her new school. Not only can't she do her chosen 'A' level subjects but, as an outsider, she is targeted for intimidation. Finally she uses a hockey stick to see the bully off. Union leader Bobby Grant is equally unhappy with the management at Fairbanks Engineering and is contemplating strike action. Karen Grant has her monthly row with her mother Sheila about going to school when she's having her period. Karen

says she's not well enough to go, but Sheila won't hear of it. Karen's boyfriend Demon Duane tries to force her to have sex. When big brother Barry gets to hear about it, he takes revenge, leaving Duane and his motorbike in a heap on the road.

A pile of second-hand cookers appears in the garden of No. 10, the property of Gavin and Petra Taylor, who arrive on the Close in a large frozen-meat truck and another lorry with yet more cookers. Just when Paul Collins thinks things can't get any worse, he returns from the regular humiliation of signing on to discover that the entire Close has been burgled.

December

Roger Huntington, who lives at number 9 with wife Heather, is aggrieved because the only things stolen from his house in the burglary were his laboriously-assembled shelving unit and a lock for the back door. When someone calls at his house trying to buy one of Gavin's cookers, it is the last straw for Roger who fires off a letter to the City Planning Officer about the Brookside cooker mountain. Gavin is given a week to get rid of them. He retaliates by erecting a multi-coloured shed made from old doors. The Taylors are desperate for a baby but their love-making is interrupted by Roger testing the new burglar alarm he has bought.

Bobby's industrial action so close to Christmas is proving unpopular with the strikers' wives, who give his wife Sheila a hard time at the baker's where she works. It emerges that as many as 200 will lose their jobs at Fairbanks. Barry is followed home by a mystery motorcyclist and is stabbed in the side. He insists he doesn't know his assailant, preferring to take the law into his own hands. Damon's school report is so bad that he won't be getting a Christmas present. Nor will Roger whose parcels are stolen after a hard day's Christmas shopping. When he takes Heather to the Law Society dinner, he is disturbed to see one of the senior partners at his law firm make a pass at her.

Lucy Collins is so fed up with her parents' reduced lifestyle that she spends Christmas with friends on the Wirral. To Sheila's disgust, Bobby has to attend an emergency union meeting on Christmas Day to discuss the management's new pay offer. But he makes up for it at New Year by throwing a party. Annabelle enjoys herself there and talks Roger into helping her set up a Ratepayers' Association, but Paul feels uneasy, particularly at the amount of attention Bobby's workmate Jonah Jones is paying to Lucy. The year ends with friends and neighbours doing the conga out into the Close.

1983

Gavin Taylor dies ... Barry homes in on the widowed Petra ... Petra goes missing and the Jacksons move in to her old house ... Other new arrivals are Alan Partridge and Harry and Edna Cross ... Lucy is arrested ... Heather throws Roger out of the house after discovering he has been having an affair ... Barry and Terry Sullivan try an insurance scam ... Harry's garden gnomes go AWOL.

January

Paul Collins prepares for his first job interview in ten years, confident that his previous experience will stand him in good stead. Certain that he has got the job, he takes Annabelle out for a celebration dinner, only to receive a letter of rejection in the post.

Annabelle begins an economy drive by making Lucy's clothes. She also plans to boost the family income by becoming a supply teacher. Son Gordon is horrified at the thought of his mother giving private tuition to pupils from his school, but welcomes the prospect of extra money to pay for his school holiday.

Bobby returns to work at the end of the six-week strike, but there is unease amongst his fellow workers when only Bobby's shift are given overtime. Karen has been mounting a campaign to go on holiday with her friends. At first, Sheila had more reservations than the Sioux but eventually she backs down. While Gavin feels that he is being blamed for Petra's failure to conceive, Roger decides to join the local badminton club with Heather.

Barry catches up with his attacker, Duane, but the arrival of the police prevents a confrontation. Barry has better luck with Irene Harrison, sex-starved wife of Eric Harrison, manager of the football team he plays for. When he calls round to measure up for an extension he's agreed to build, Barry ends up in bed with Irene who thinks he measures up in every respect. Meanwhile Damon's plans to bunk off school for the afternoon with his mates Ducksie Brown and Gizzmo Hawkins and three girls from a neighbouring school are thwarted when the Educational Welfare Officer turns up. And there's trouble looming for Karen when Sheila finds a card of contraceptive pills in a drawer in Barry's bedroom.

February

A rampaging Sheila accuses Karen of sleeping around, but Karen says their doctor put her on the Pill to ease her period pains, a problem which she had not been able to discuss with her unsympathetic mother. Furthermore, Karen insists, she is a virgin. Sheila is still worried and consults a priest who tries to put her mind at rest. Petra Taylor goes upstairs to find Gavin dead in bed. It transpires that he has suffered a brain haemorrhage. Petra goes to stay with her sister, Marie Jackson.

Bobby's friend Matty Nolan learns that he will be one of the 200 redundancies at Fairbanks. When Bobby says there's nothing he can do, the two men argue bitterly. Barry finishes Irene's extension but she wants to carry on seeing him. Although tempted, Barry decides to place his relationship with his new girlfriend, Carol, on a firmer footing instead. Irene demands to see him but he tells her he's got flu. That night, she calls round and catches Barry with Carol. Irene slaps him around the face and he returns the compliment. Not surprisingly, Carol tells him she's finished with him.

Karen receives a Valentine's card from Damon's mate Gizzmo, but Gordon's hopes of being out all night at a party are dashed when Paul refuses to let him stay beyond 10.30pm. Gordon blames Lucy, saying she always puts their parents' backs up. She responds by telling him he should stand up for himself more. Roger's boss, Derek Hobbs, makes persistent advances to Heather at a dinner party. She does her best to keep her cool but is alarmed when Hobbs indicates that Roger's career could depend on her 'co-operation'.

March

Petra returns to the Close, unaware that Barry, with her husband's body still warm, is planning on asking her out. Marie has given the relationship her blessing but just when Barry gets Petra alone and is about to pop the question, Petra blurts out that she thinks she's pregnant. This rather puts a dampener on things. Petra's younger sister Michelle stays with her until she can face the world again. The memory of Gavin's enthusiasm for life gives Petra the strength to carry on and she returns to work, only to be exasperated by the 'cotton-wool' treatment she receives from her colleagues. Most sympathetic of all is her boss, Dave Simpson, but that's mainly because he fancies her something rotten. Petra thinks about getting a new job.

The Huntingtons are burgled again and Roger points the finger at Damon. But the Grants have their own problems when the Educational Welfare Officer calls to investigate Damon's absenteeism from school. In addition, Sheila is made redundant and opts to use up some of her spare time by joining Annabelle's Ratepayers' Association.

Predictably, Paul is less than enthusiastic about his wife's activities, just as he is about his son Gordon's latest interest – music. Lucy is stood up in town by boyfriend Jonathan but does Gordon a good turn by arranging for him to spend Easter with his friend Mark Gossage. Roger's parents come to stay for Easter and his dad Syd sets about tackling some of the DIY jobs which have proved beyond Roger's limited capabilities.

April

Barry and Petra are finally going out together but now Marie has a change of heart and worries that her sister is seeing too much of Barry. Gavin's friend Frank expresses similar reservations and the pair hint that, given Gavin's alleged problems in the trouser department, Barry could even be the father of Petra's baby. The Grants go to church with the Huntingtons, and Roger's dad Syd notices Damon slipping buttons and washers into the collection bag instead of the money his mum has given him. Syd threatens to reveal all unless Damon buys some candles in the church. Damon is cornered.

The eccentric Alan Partridge moves into the bungalow (No. 6) which Damon, Ducksie and Gizzmo have been using as a secret hideaway. They decide to help him with his computer equipment but become increasingly worried as he rambles on about his partner Sam. The boys are convinced he is gay and steer clear, but Sam turns out to be leggy former model Samantha. Alan is eager for her to move in with him but she values her independence too highly.

At Annabelle's request, Barry and his friend Terry Sullivan come to lay paving stones at No. 8 where Paul virtually accuses Barry of stealing them. Barry's fury is interrupted by the return of Karen who has been threatened with suspension from school for swearing at a teacher. The bone of contention was Mass, and Karen plucks up the courage to tell Sheila that she's not going to church again. Sheila is furious and Karen runs to her room in tears.

Barry's boss, Ted, confronts him at the site about taking materials for his own use and warns that a clampdown is now on. That evening, Barry and Terry sneak back under cover of darkness but Ted is waiting for them. Barry is sacked and decides to go into business with Terry, maybe with Petra as their secretary. She's not sure about their motives but realises that any new business needs capital … and, thanks to Gavin's demise, money is one thing she has got at the moment.

May

Jonah is being taken to court by his ex-wife Barbara to reduce his access to their son Jason. Shocked that his friend hasn't consulted a solicitor, Bobby agrees to accompany him to court. There, Jonah loses his temper and, with no solicitor to advise him, finds his access reduced to a meagre two hours on a Sunday afternoon. Alan asks Samantha to marry him. She turns him down but decides to move in with him. The usually work-shy Damon helps Sam clean Alan's boat – he is clearly smitten and begins gazing longingly out of the window after school in the hope of catching a glimpse of her.

To cut costs, Paul agrees to sell the Rover. He is excited at being recalled for a job interview but is then dismayed to find that the post is beneath his abilities and turns it down. On the rebound, he argues with Lucy about her recent involvement with CND. Annabelle's ratepayers' meeting attracts an audience of one – Roger – who sees little point in staying and promptly goes home. Gordon arranges to go to a concert with Mark Gossage but the latter goes alone on account of Gordon's appalling dress sense.

Petra rejects Dave Simpson's overtures and

hands in her notice. Heather and Roger argue about their evening arrangements and, in a fit of pique, she announces that she won't pick him up after work. While she is out enjoying herself with her friend Polly, Roger is run over on his way home and ends up in hospital with four broken ribs. Bobby takes Sheila to London for the FA Cup final but returns to hear confidential and disturbing news from union colleague George Williams about the possible closure of Fairbanks. Sheila dreads the consequences.

June

The black cloud of factory closure continues to hang over the Grant household. Barry decides to escape the doom and gloom by sneaking off with Petra to the TT races on the Isle of Man. Alan and Sam are going too, but Barry does his best to avoid them. Barry and Petra stay in separate rooms at the hotel, only to discover that Alan and Sam are in the room in between. So much for secrets. On the boat back, Petra starts to feel unwell and suffers a miscarriage. Caring as ever, Barry doesn't even bother visiting her in hospital.

Paul arrives for an interview at the dole office in his new Maestro. Now that he has completed a year of unemployment, it is suggested to him that he becomes a Youth Opportunities organiser. Derek Hobbs informs Roger that he will not be made a partner as soon as he had hoped. That night, Heather and Roger argue about her refusal to give up her career in order to start a family. Upset, she storms out of the house.

Lucy skips her French 'O' level exam in favour of picketing a council meeting on behalf of CND. She is supposed to be going with two friends, Janice and Fran, but when they don't turn up, Lucy joins the meeting on her own before being led away by the police for causing a disturbance. Paul, who had earlier seen her with Jonah, fears that she is at his house and it almost comes as a relief when he receives a phone call from the police station. At the station, he persuades his headstrong daughter to co-operate. She is let off with a caution and Paul acts as peacemaker when they arrive home to face an agitated Annabelle.

July

Roger has been having an affair with a wealthy, attractive client, Diane McAllister. He has always struggled to keep one woman happy so the effort of having two on the go proves too much for him. He and Heather bicker relentlessly. One day, he snaps over Heather's impulsive spending and storms out of the house. Into this emotional quagmire step Harry and Edna Cross, prospective buyers of No. 7. They quickly fall foul of Damon and his pals.

Annabelle receives a visit from Robin Tate, chairman of the District Ratepayers' Committee. They form a mutual admiration society, much to the discomfort of Lucy and Gordon. has constructed an arch for Petra, but refuses to decorate. Tey argue, and when he marches off in a huff, it reminds her of her final argument with Gavin. Terry is also fed up with Barry who still refuses to commit himself over their business partnership. Terry feels Barry should have been committed long ago. Angered by his friend's attitude, Terry volunteers to help Petra and Michelle with the decorating. Later, following another furious row with his dad, Barry calls on Petra and offers his services. She has great delight in telling him where he can stick his paint brush. Eventually he does apologise and they gloss over their differences. They go off to look at new cars, but at the showroom Petra spots a man she thinks is Gavin. She rushes up to him, realises her mistake, and runs off down the road in tears, leaving Barry standing there puzzled.

With Bobby's own job hanging in the balance, Sheila is dismayed when Teresa Nolan (Matty's wife) turns up and asks if Bobby could give Matty a loan. Sheila settles for new seat covers instead of a new sofa but refuses to compromise over the impending factory closure and urges Bobby to fight every inch of the way. But first she must appease Alan, whose car she has crashed into while practising her driving on the Close.

August

The residents are worried by reports that there is a flasher in the neighbourhood, a story given credence by the disappearance of underwear from washing lines. Naturally, Bobby's Y-fronts are left untouched. As Sam undresses, she is aware that someone is watching her from the woods. When the prowler finally makes his move, Roger rides to the rescue. Both eager to impress, Roger and Damon fight for the right to mend Sam's broken window. Roger exerts his authority but his pane proves too small and when Sam startles him, he breaks it and is forced to admit his mistake and buy Damon's glass.

Jonah tells Bobby that the factory is under 90 days' notice of closure. Alan suggests that Bobby might like to try his luck in Saudi Arabia, but Sheila is none too keen on the idea. Sheila and Bobby had hoped that they could count on Barry for a degree of financial support, but he doesn't want to know. Instead, irritated by Petra's continuing depression and by the demands of his family, he steals some money which Sheila had collected for a kidney fund and leaves for London.

Michelle and Petra go out for a quiet drink but Petra is unable to cope with the attentions of a jocular stranger and dashes distraught from the pub. Even a trip to the supermarket proves too traumatic and on her return, she packs a case and leaves home. Her car is found and a detective starts asking Michelle questions. Michelle has to face the possibility that her sister has committed suicide. The detective also quizzes Sam about the recent attack on her and asks whether there is someone who may hold a grudge against her. To Alan's surprise, she divulges details of a dodgy dancing job she once had in Turkey, the organiser of which was later jailed for a series of charges brought by the girls. Alan recovers to ask Sam to marry him again and they agree to stage a competition to see who can earn the most money within three months. If Alan wins, Sam will get engaged.

Paul acts as mediator between the warring Annabelle and Lucy and it is suggested that Lucy spend some time in France. Roger tells Heather that he's off on a business trip to Birmingham but he has extended it so that he can spend time with Diane. In town, Heather bumps into Derek Hobbs who informs her that Roger isn't in Birmingham. Nobody seems to know where he is.

September

Marie Jackson, husband George and sons Gary and Little George move into Petra's house on a temporary basis while their own house is being refurbished. Marie exercises her psychic powers in an attempt to discover her missing sister's whereabouts. Karen thinks she has spotted her in St Helens, but it turns out to be a false alarm.

Roger arrives home from his 'business trip' to a frosty welcome. Heather suspects him of being unfaithful, a fear seemingly confirmed when she finds a tie pin in his jacket. She demands to know who gave it to him but he escapes by going rugby training with Alan. Diane McAllister wants Roger to go away on holiday with her, but after much deliberation he chooses Heather for his holiday partner. But when he breaks the news to her, Heather informs him that she's cancelled the holiday. Roger tries to mend bridges but matters deteriorate when Heather and Diane come face to come in the pub. Heather passes her accountancy exams but doesn't feel much like celebrating. Roger continues to deny that he's having an affair but when Heather catches him on the phone to Diane, it's the last straw. It's Roger and out. He rushes straight round to Diane's flat but she coolly announces that she is off to Barbados the next day. Roger has lost both his women.

October

With Heather considering her future at her parents' hotel in Belfast, Roger returns to an empty house. Annabelle gives him a key and he puts some bread under the grill and dozes off. Fortunately fireman George Jackson smells the burning from next door and he and Marie extinguish the flames before too much damage is done. While Roger's dad Syd berates him about the mess he has made of his marriage, Heather is seeking the counsel of an old friend, Will Thurley. Acting on his advice, she decides to lead an independent life. When she returns to Liverpool, Syd tries to reunite her with Roger by taking them for a day out but Heather knows they have no future together.

Gordon's latest hobby, photography, is reaping dividends and he and his friend Cathy start selling framed photos in the city centre on a Saturday morning. However, Damon's prospects of finding a job look slim so Sheila asks Bobby to help. But Bobby says Damon should stand on his own two feet. At a bring-and-buy sale to save Fairbanks, George buys Paul's cardigan and refuses to sell it back to him and, somewhat suspiciously, Damon and Gizzmo are selling Barry's jeans. They turn out to be knock-off.

A reporter asks Sheila to appear on his TV programme to talk about the fight to save Fairbanks. She overcomes her nerves to put forward a convincing case.

November

Harry and Edna Cross move into No. 7. Edna antagonises the removal men, who abandon her with her belongings on the pavement, so the Collins family and Gordon's friend, Mark Gossage, give the old couple a hand. While Harry is telling Paul about his boxing medals, Mark is stealing them. When he discovers they are missing, Harry automatically blames his old adversaries, Damon and Gizzmo. The latter subsequently spots Mark with the medals and Damon and Mark square up to each other. Egged on by Harry, they slug it out in the garden. Damon wins the fight but receives a ticking-off from Bobby.

Later, when Harry's attention is diverted, Damon and Gizzmo start moving his gnomes around. Returning from the shops, Edna is amazed to see they have 'walked' into Heather's garden. The gnomes then move to the Grants'. Damon protests his innocence and when Harry catches the Jackson boys playing with the gnomes in the Close, he is sure he has found the culprits. Marie defends her lads to the hilt but makes the fatal mistake of referring to the gnomes as 'dwarves'. Harry is mortified by the insult.

Michelle gets Terry to ask her out. Hurrying for an appointment, Alan drops an important floppy disc behind a cabinet. He blames Samantha and tells her to clean the place up. With Barry's help, she retrieves the disc but spills coffee on it. Alan is not happy. Despite the efforts of Sheila and the other wives, Fairbanks closes down. Bobby is devastated and out of a job.

Meanwhile Barry plans to set fire to his Jaguar car and claim the insurance. Barry and Terry drive to the beach but, because of Terry's generosity in giving Damon some petrol for his new motorbike, there isn't enough left to burn the car. They leave the car to find some petrol, but return to find it sinking into the sands with the water rising rapidly. They try to get the car out, until Barry realises they have stumbled across the perfect way of getting rid of the car – and one for which they are completely blameless.

December

Desperate to trace the missing Petra, Marie places an advert in a newspaper. George is taken to hospital but it turns out to be nothing more than a bump on the nose sustained while playing snooker. Marie, who was beside herself with worry, is livid. She then stuns George and Michelle by telling them that she is going to lay a place for Petra at Christmas dinner. Her hopes are boosted when she and Michelle receive a Christmas card from Petra

(with smudged postmark) and learn that cheques have been cashed in Petra's name in Southport.

Sam and Alan are still not on speaking terms and he releases some of his pent-up anger by digging the garden. While Bobby and Matty are delivering Christmas hampers, Barry and Terry try selling cosmetics. At the pub they hear there has been a radio warning about the very perfume they are attempting to flog. Deciding to cut their losses, they offer to clean the pub with the perfume in exchange for drinks.

Heather heads off to Ireland for the festive period but Lucy comes home from France. She is soon bored, however, and finds a kindred spirit in Karen whose boyfriend Mike has abandoned her in favour of going to the match. Gordon gets parental agreement to attend an all-night New Year's Eve party, but before midnight Paul has to go and collect his hopelessly drunk son. The pair arrive back just in time to see in 1984.

1984

Petra is found dead at a guest house in Llandudno ... Barry and Terry fall under the influence of local villain Tommy McArdle ... Sheila is pregnant ... Paul starts a new job ... Sam and Alan get married and leave the Close ... Harry and Edna move into the bungalow and let No. 7 to two nurses and a hospital porter ... George Jackson is framed for a robbery and jailed for 18 months.

January

Edna is too embarrassed to hang Harry's long-johns on the line so she buries them in the dustbin instead. When the police arrive to check a fault with Heather's alarm, Harry mentions his missing underwear. Edna fears it is only a matter of time before Shaw Taylor is on the trail of the long-john thief.

Sheila sets up a non-registered employment agency and tells Bobby and Barry that she expects their support. Barry has been doing a rewiring job at the Jacksons' but has left everything in a mess. Never one to shirk a confrontation, Marie goes over to the Grants' to get Barry to put things right. She is fed up with his sloppy approach but Sheila stands up for her son and the two women have a blazing row in the middle of the Close. Paul arrives home from work in the middle of the fracas and calls the police. When they arrive, Edna thinks they are looking for the long-john thief, but Harry puts her mind at rest by admitting that he has found the underwear in the dustbin. Marie assumes that it was Sheila who called the police and marches over for another row which ends with Sheila vowing that she will never speak to Marie again.

Paul is encountering difficulties with some of his YOP charges and one trainee, a lad named Skelly, threatens him with violence. Paul tries to soften his attitude but fears that he has lost their trust.

Alan and Sam arrive home from a skiing holiday. A lost contract scuppered Alan's chances of winning their wager but now, to his delight, Sam asks him to marry her. He runs out into the Close screaming for joy. It is not a pretty sight. Everyone comes to investigate the commotion – except Sheila who won't join in any celebrations while Marie is around. With the impending arrival of Alan's mother, Molly, he gets Sam to move back to her flat until the wedding so that Mrs P. won't know they've been living together.

On the big day, Alan's best man lets him down and he is obliged to accept Paul's offer to act as substitute. The worst is yet to come. Sam, who has been tempted with job offers in Los Angeles, is late arriving. When she eventually appears and the ceremony begins, she is just about to say her vows when she has a sudden change of heart and runs out of the registry office. Later she explains to the shell-shocked Alan that although she still loves him, she can't marry him at the moment. Alan is hurt; his mother is livid. No sooner have the Jacksons received a letter from the council informing them that they can move back into their house than Marie has a disturbing dream followed by a visit from the police who inform her that Petra has committed suicide at a guest house in Llandudno.

February

Depressed by Petra's death (or perhaps sensing that his presence would be unwelcome), Barry opts out of her funeral by staying in bed. Marie lays the blame for her sister's suicide firmly at Barry's feet. She believes that the suicide was the result of the miscarriage brought on by Barry's foolhardy jaunt to the Isle of Man. Marie and George think about leaving No. 10 – it holds too many bad memories – but in the end they decide to stay, much to the disappointment of Michelle who wouldn't mind the place to herself … and Terry.

Lonely and suffering from an over-protective mother, Alan starts to show an interest in Heather. Annabelle has not been in the best of health and a visit to a consultant reveals that she has hyperthyroidism. Paul immediately begins to worry about the possible expense resulting from her illness. Damon is disruptive and is thrown out of class at school for spreading clingfilm on the staff-room toilets. Consequently, he gets the cane. Karen tells him he'll be in hot water with their parents and so he offers to cook tea in return for her silence.

Barry drags himself out of bed to start up a car valeting business with Terry. Harry finds a betting slip in Edna's handbag, but that pales into insignificance when he receives a visit from his son Kevin and his family. For Harry quickly realises that they are not a conventional family and is appalled to discover that his son is living with a divorcee, Sally Haynes, and her daughter Jessica. Edna had known for some time but had been looking for the right moment to break it to Harry.

March

Heather offers Sheila some financial advice in relation to the agency's accounts and finds herself at the centre of Harry's mischievous matchmaking. For when Edna invites Alan to tea, Harry makes sure that Heather will also be present. Worried by Harry's little games, Alan asks Sheila to explain to Heather that he has no romantic designs on her, but even so the evening at the Crosses' is an awkward affair. Alan manages to forget about Sam for a while when he meets an old girlfriend, Liz. While using Alan's computer, Gordon answers the phone and ends up doing a deal with Alan to share a computer contract.

Annabelle and Paul have a small win on the premium bonds. Paul plans a celebration dinner but instead they are invited to the Tates', where Independent candidate Robin asks Annabelle to be his agent in the forthcoming local council elections. Karen plans a boycott of meat in school dinners and finishes with boyfriend Mike.

After quizzing Terry about his intentions for Michelle, Marie gets the shock of her life when Davy Jones, her long-lost father, turns up. He wastes no time in getting his feet under the table but when the Jacksons try to get rid of him, he tells them that because Petra apparently didn't leave a will and he is the next of kin, the house is rightfully his. Knowing that he is susceptible to the charms of a five-pound note, they attempt to bribe him into leaving but this merely makes him more angry and he tries to throw them out. Things look black until Heather arrives and tells them that Petra had made a will after all. The house plus £2,500 a year go to Marie while Michelle receives an annual sum of £7,500. Davy doesn't hang about, pausing only to help himself to Michelle's catalogue money on the way out. It was worth it just to be rid of him.

April

Barry and Terry's plans for easy money lead them into a dodgy video deal with local hood Tommy McArdle. When things don't quite go according to plan, McArdle leaves the boys in no doubt that they owe him a favour. The Jackson twins set off in search of their errant grandfather, leaving a cryptic note for a worried Marie. Fortunately Harry spots them at Lime Street station and brings them back to Brookside Close.

Annabelle and Robin's electioneering proves stressful for both parties and they are soon arguing like husband and wife. Paul is far from sorry about this development! Michelle starts her a new job as barmaid at The Swan and invites Terry to stay at No. 10 for Easter as the Jacksons are away. Bobby is talking to George Williams about the possibility of standing for a full-time union post when Sheila arrives to ask him to do a job for the agency. Bobby is too busy so Matty agrees to do the job instead. But as Sheila and Matty leave the client's house that afternoon, Matty is stopped and accused of fraud by an officer from the DHSS. Sheila feels guilty about what has happened to Matty and Bobby argues that she should give up the agency. However, she secretly makes an appointment to see Bob Cummings about an agency job the next day. A furious Bobby comes home to find Sheila entertaining Cummings and promptly tells him to leave. This makes Sheila more determined than ever to continue with the agency. Later Sheila wins £500 at bingo and Bobby rows with Barry about his shady business deals. Sheila even finds herself lying to the police to protect her precious son.

Dorothy Tate, Robin's wife, visits No. 8 and makes quite an impression on Paul. Alan returns late from selling Gordon's computer program on his behalf, only to be accused of plagiarism. Alan takes it badly, gets very drunk and staggers out into the Close, screaming and shouting abuse at the neighbours. They are getting used to it by now. Paul receives an unexpected late-night phone call from Dorothy Tate. Robin has left her and she needs Paul to comfort her. Paul abandons Annabelle and drives out of the Close, passing the drunken Alan. The next day Alan learns that Liz was responsible for the misunderstanding over Gordon's computer program and he throws her out. Just like Arnie, she vows: 'I'll be back.'

May

Having sealed the deal on the golf course, Paul has landed a post as production manager with a subsidiary of Petrochem, a local chemical firm. Heather is also starting a new job, for which she reverts to her maiden name of Haversham, but her excitement is marred by the arrival of an odious housebuyer.

Michelle loses her job but is pleased with the way her relationship with Terry is going. Annabelle is glad of the chance to get away for a few days to visit her sick mother but she returns to a suspicious son and an absent husband. Gordon reveals that Dorothy Tate has been a frequent visitor of late, leaving Annabelle wishing that she had never gone away in the first place.

Over at No. 7, Harry suffers a severe attack of angina and his bed has to be moved downstairs. If nothing else, it gives him a different perspective on the neighbours' movements. Yet he manages to miss the best bit, for the moment he moves back upstairs, Liz and a sinister friend pay an unwelcome visit to Alan, who ends up on the receiving end of a vicious attack.

Meanwhile Bobby discovers the truth about Barry's illegal activities and throws him out of the house. But when Bobby wins the union election, he is in a forgiving mood and father and son are reconciled, even though Barry clearly has no intention of changing his ways. Bobby is keen for he and Sheila to go on holiday to Spain for two weeks, but Sheila keeps putting him off. The truth is, she thinks she may be pregnant. Finally she agrees to go on holiday, but then a secret visit to the doctor confirms her worst fears.

June

Out in Spain, Sheila is trying to pluck up the courage to tell Bobby that she is pregnant. But choosing the right moment isn't easy, especially as the Grants are subjected to regular interruptions from their new holiday friends, Ken and Doreen. Finally Sheila takes a deep breath and tells him. When he regains consciousness, he is overjoyed and they both wonder how the rest of the family will take the news, not to mention Ken and Doreen.

In his parents' absence, Damon plans to make the most of his new-found freedom and invites girlfriend Linda over for an evening of sheer seduction. But his hopes are dashed when Barry bursts in with a guest of his own. Different girl, same idea. While Alan is about to embark on a keep-fit regime, courtesy of Terry, Michelle buys a car. She is pleased with the purchase and with Terry's business acumen until Barry implies that he could have done a much better deal.

Her suspicions fuelled by Gordon's comments, Annabelle starts following Paul on a routine trip to the tailor's prior to his first day in his new job. And Heather returns from an accounting course with German measles, forcing the hasty evacuation of her pregnant house guest, Rose. Marie comes to the rescue by allowing Rose to stay at No. 10 with Michelle going next door as Heather's nurse. Rose settles in quickly, particularly when she and George discover that they share an interest in country and western music.

While George prepares himself for a pub quiz at The Swan, Marie finds herself dealing with more important matters when the twins come home school with an upsetting tale. She thinks about sending them to private school and finds a place she likes. George is not convinced. Michelle considers setting up as a beautician and Barry goes into a tool-hire venture with a woman named Celia. Judging by her business proposition and the glint in her eyes, it's not just tungsten carbide tips he's interested in.

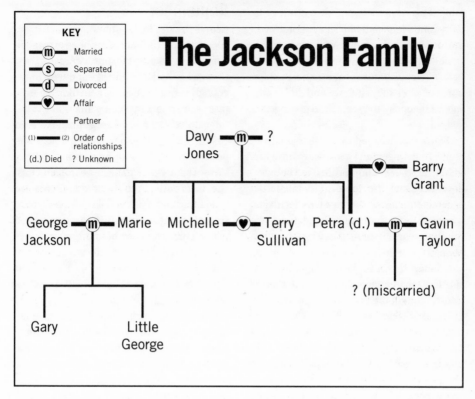

The Jackson Family

KEY

- —m— Married
- —s— Separated
- —d— Divorced
- —♥— Affair
- ——— Partner
- (1)——(2) Order of relationships
- (d.) Died ? Unknown

Davy Jones —m— ?

George Jackson —m— Marie   Michelle —♥— Terry Sullivan   Petra (d.) —m— Gavin Taylor

♥— Barry Grant

? (miscarried)

Gary   Little George

July

Following a tip-off from Gordon, Alan rushes to see Sam at the International Garden Festival, only to find her surrounded by male admirers. In despair, he turns to drink again. Harry and Edna are also at the festival with their friends Ralph and Grace Hardwick. Harry becomes suspicious when Edna she says wants to go for a walk with Ralph on her own. Could they be more than just good friends, or is Harry so repugnant that Edna would rather go for a walk with Jack the Ripper than be stuck with him?

Back at the Close, Sam is helping Alan to recover from his hangover. Both realise that they are happier together than apart but a phone call offering Alan a lucrative job in Kuwait appears to put a spanner in the works. They decide the only solution is to get married. News of Alan's impending nuptials spreads like wild fire with Harry showing particular interest in the fact that he'll be moving out of the bungalow. No stairs to climb: could be just what Harry needs.

On the day of his court case with the DHSS, Matty is relying on Bobby's support but when his friend is otherwise occupied, Matty's anger frightens both Teresa and Sheila. As Alan and Sam's wedding day approaches, half of the Close are still wondering whether it will actually go ahead this time. After one of her 'psychic' dreams, Marie is convinced that Sam won't turn up and lays a bet with Edna, so she is not a happy medium when the ceremony goes ahead without a hitch. The couple return to the Close for a final farewell and the celebrations begin. But the party comes to an abrupt halt when Sheila is knocked down by a motorbike ridden by Karen's latest boyfriend, Andrew. Sheila is taken to hospital. Her injuries are not serious but the doctor warns Bobby that there may be a risk to the unborn baby.

August

Barry wants Terry and Michelle to come in on the tool-hire business and Michelle becomes an official partner when she decides to put in £2,000. Terry is so grateful he asks her to marry him, but when they sit down and discuss the subject rationally, they choose to live together instead.

Marie is concerned when George fails to return from quenching a big warehouse fire. In fact, he is quenching his thirst at The Swan, describing the fire in great detail to an extremely interested Tommy McArdle. In total innocence, George draws a plan of the warehouse on a napkin. Barry and Terry are about to plan their evening when McArdle's henchman, Victor bursts in, demanding an alibi for that afternoon. The warehouse where George put out the fire has been raided and the haul of cigarettes and spirits runs into thousands of pounds. George is arrested and a distraught Marie turns to Annabelle for help. She drives Marie down to the police station, leaving Gordon in charge of the twins.

George is duly charged and, ignoring Paul's request to steer well clear of the Jacksons, Annabelle stands bail for him. After a week on remand, he is relieved to be home. Terry thinks they should tell George about Victor and the alibi but Barry values his own neck too highly. Crossing Tommy McArdle on a cigarettes raid could seriously damage their health. When Sheila hears about the gravity of George's case, she lets bygones be bygones and goes over to Marie to offer sympathy and support. She is staggered to learn of Barry's involvement in the case.

The other Grant offspring are also up to no good. Damon is planning a weekend in London with Ducksie and Gizzmo's new girlfriends, Yvonne and Dawn, but he omits to mention to his own girlfriend Linda that Ducksie can't go. And Karen returns from a holiday which Sheila believed was with her friends Suzi and Pauline. But in the course of their conversation it becomes apparent that Karen went away with her boyfriend Andrew.

September

George decides to do something positive and goes down to The Swan in the hope of meeting Tommy McArdle. By the time McArdle arrives, George has had a few drinks and feels brave enough to beg McArdle to help him. McArdle takes exception to having his quiet drink interrupted and beats George up. A battered George has to be helped from the pub. The police call at the tool-hire shop to verify Victor's alibi. When Michelle hears about this, she is furious that Barry and Terry are protecting Victor and not George. Terry feels suitably guilty and promises to have a word with George, but not before the latter has bumped into McArdle in the street. Tommy tells George not to make a fuss if he gets sent down – he'll look after Marie and the kids. This is scarcely comforting news.

With his court appearance looming, George is beginning to give up hope – there seems little point in protesting his innocence – but at the last minute he adopts a more optimistic frame of mind and pleads not guilty.

To show her faith in George, Edna has a little flutter on a horse called Justice For All. She thinks it might be a good omen. When the horse wins, Edna gives George and Marie her winnings. The Jacksons spend the money by having a day out at a leisure park, just to get away from it all. There, George saves a boy from drowning but his hero status is short-lived as he has to get back home to 'sign on' at the police station.

Karen celebrates her 18th birthday after Bobby has found out the truth about her holiday. For once, Sheila supports Karen but Bobby is upset and has to go for a walk. Over at No. 8, Gordon has his ear pierced and develops his interest in photography-mad Cathy.

Harry and Edna move into the bungalow, but only after he has insisted on obeying tradition by carrying her across the threshold. It does nothing for his back but everything for his pride. Acting on Heather's advice, they plan to let No. 7 to suitable tenants. They discuss the sort of tenants they would like to let the house to. Harry rules out just about everybody. Harry prepares a questionnaire to test prospective tenants and gets Edna to fill it in. She gets a very low score, leaving Harry wondering what he's married to! He takes a shine to two would-be tenants, young nurses Kate Moses and Sandra Maghie, and asks them for advice about his bad back. They pay the advance rent and leave him with the impression that the third tenant, Pat Hancock, is a girl. Harry looks forward to meeting her. Linda finds out the truth about Damon's trip to London and, telling him to grow up, finishes with him. Damon is left alone and unhappy.

October

Harry is suitably disapproving on discovering that Pat Hancock is a male hospital porter. Edna already knew but had refrained from telling Harry because she wanted to see the look on his face when he found out. She was not disappointed. Harry feels that the menage à trois gives him further justification for snooping on the tenants every hour of the day. He is particularly concerned about the old ambulance Pat drives around in. Paul is none too impressed either and, arriving home in his new company car, complains to Harry that the ambulance is lowering the tone of the Close.

Karen is considering various universities and Andrew manages to persuade Bobby to let them go to Newcastle for the weekend, ostensibly so that they can study the campus. Andrew's idea was for them to spend the night together in a bed-and-breakfast, and when Karen shatters his hopes he accuses her of being selfish and of using him.

Damon is even more despondent and tells Sheila that he is thinking of moving away to London. She talks him out of it and suggests that he start looking for a job locally by ringing round the painting and decorating firms in Yellow Pages. The apathetic response from employers does little to cheer him up.

Grace Hardwick is too ill to go on the cheap holiday which she and Ralph had booked and so Ralph asks Harry and Edna whether they would like to go instead. Harry jumps at the chance when he realises how cheap it is and persuades Sheila to keep an eye on his properties.

George's trial is not going well. The barman from The Swan (now in McArdle's pay) and the warehouse security officer both give damaging evidence and Marie's only hope appears to be a favourable horoscope in the evening paper. Michelle criticises Terry for his failure to help George, and Terry tries to persuade Barry that they should tell the truth about the false alibi they gave to protect Victor. Barry refuses and assures Terry that George is bound to get off. On the second day, George himself takes the stand but he is so nervous that his testimony is jumbled and the prosecuting counsel has little difficulty in ripping it to shreds. Barry and Terry finally realise that George is in deep trouble and try to do a deal with the police which will lead them to McArdle and save George's skin. But the police are more interested in using the lads' statements to nail the real criminals than in saving the innocent George. Barry and Terry feel they have been conned by the police. George is found guilty and sentenced to 18 months in prison, 12 of which are suspended. And Barry and Terry know that they must face the wrath of Tommy McArdle.

November

Barry and Terry are in hospital following a beating from McArdle. Terry is in a particularly bad way and is in intensive care. To make matters worse, the police are hovering around, wanting some answers. But Barry is saying nothing. Concerned about the future of the tool-hire business with two of its biggest spare parts in hospital, Celia visits Barry and expresses her annoyance that he hasn't come clean with the police. She adds that it would have been fairer if it was him in intensive care, rather than Terry.

At the ante-natal clinic, the doctor is worried about Sheila's blood pressure and wants to bring her into hospital for a few days. Bobby attributes it to the stress caused by Barry's bit of bother. Bobby decides it's about time he had a heart-to-heart with his son. He tries to be reasonable but becomes infuriated by Barry's attitude and ends up hitting him, upon which Barry's mood changes from one of defiance to one of despair. Sensing that he has no future and no friends in Liverpool, Barry decides to move away from home and make a fresh start.

When her boss, Joyce Harrington, gives her the task of auditing the books at an amateur operatic society, Heather decides to take Dr Stuart Griffiths, whom she met at the nurses Hallowe'en party, to the society's current production. Pat is worried because his prized human skeleton has gone missing and makes no bones about his relief when Paul stumbles across it at No. 8. Back from holiday, Harry wastes no time in letting himself into the nurses' house to have a good snoop around. He starts talking to the figure sitting in the chair with its back to him and it is only when he gets no reply that he realises that he has been conducting a conversation with Pat's fully-dressed skeleton. Harry reckons they're up to black magic.

Grace Hardwick dies and Ralph accepts Edna's kind offer to come and stay for a while. Much to Harry's annoyance, he immediately starts re-decorating the living-room. He also suggests that Edna should open a credit account at the bookies. Harry reckons she's backed a loser with Ralph.

December

Barry is starting out as a shop-fitter – a job which will take him all over the country. Although not everyone is sorry to see him go, he manages an emotional farewell. Unbeknown to Harry, Edna quickly falls into debt with her bookies' account. She attempts to recoup her losses but the bookie refuses to accept her bet and she is given seven days to settle. In an effort to raise the money, Edna tries renting out their garage to Paul and

Annabelle. As her debts continue to mount, she receives a letter threatening legal action and decides the only solution is to pawn her engagement and wedding rings. Finally she confesses all to Harry who hits the roof. He hasn't got far to go – it is only a bungalow. Harry blames Ralph who has now moved on to re-decorating the kitchen. Feeling guilty that it was his idea in the first place, Ralph offers to pay off Edna's debts.

While Bobby's new union role places him in opposition to Paul, Annabelle has set up a catering business from home. An exploding casserole is just a minor hiccup. With the impending award of a maintenance contract at the factory, Paul is besieged with seasonal 'gestures of goodwill' from interested parties. This annoys him to such an extent that he decides to award the contract to the one firm which hasn't sent him an enticing gift.

Stuart Griffiths falls foul of Heather by assuming that she will sleep with him. She feels he is taking her for granted. Michelle starts to show an interest in Pat, causing a rift between her and Terry. Pat makes the house a no-smoking zone, to the irritation of Sandra who is put under further pressure when she gets a call from her estranged husband, Ian Maghie: he has met another woman and wants a divorce. Sandra refuses to give him one.

The Jackson twins are sent home from school early for fighting and Marie receives a letter from the school welfare officer who is concerned about their behaviour and attendance record. Marie resolves to help get George out of prison and, with the help of journalist Rick Sexton, launches the Free George Jackson Campaign. But will anyone want a free George Jackson?

Sheila plays a Christmas Day trick on Bobby by pretending that she has gone into labour. The Grants get a surprise visit from Matty and Teresa Nolan, dressed in Eastern clothes and leading a donkey. Barry is with them – but not as the donkey. Meanwhile Harry, already in high dudgeon about Ralph's flashing Christmas tree lights, is convinced that he's having a heart attack. It proves to be nothing more than a pin prick from the new shirt he has been given.

1985

Sheila gives birth to baby Claire ... Bobby has a vasectomy ... Marie is forced to give up her campaign and moves out ... Kate Moses is shot dead in the siege of Brookside Close ... Edna Cross dies ... The Corkhills move into number 10 ... Heather meets architect Nicholas Black.

January

Paul has a meeting with Bobby to discuss the awarding of a maintenance contract at the factory and assures him that there will be no redundancies. Sheila gives birth to daughter Claire at home and Bobby is so moved by the experience that he changes his attitude towards a sexual harassment case he is dealing with. He is now on the side of Cheryl Potter, the girl who resigned after being groped by workmate Gerry Dwyer. Bobby persuades Dwyer to apologise to Cheryl and everything is settled amicably.

To Paul's acute embarrassment, Annabelle takes up jogging. More worryingly, he is accused by Colin Peterson, the new union convenor at Petrochem, of taking a bribe of a year's free food in return for the maintenance contract. Kate discovers that Pat is involved in a fiddle selling food to patients and when she finds a 'pre-op' patient, who should be eating nothing, tucking into a Chinese takeaway, she threatens to report Pat.

Sandra's husband turns up on her doorstep, demanding a divorce. When she says no again, he hits her. Pat rushes downstairs and throws him out whereupon Ian threatens to sue for divorce, citing Pat as co-respondent.

George loses 28 days' remission for being

involved in a prison fight even though it wasn't his fault. Marie's hopes are raised when the campaign to free George receives considerable publicity in the local paper, but then she is visited by a police officer who advises her against continuing the campaign – for George's own good. Undeterred, she plans to lobby a government minister on his arrival at the airport and his helicopter lands on the slogan 'Free George Jackson' painted on the tarmac. Meanwhile George is involved in another fight and Tommy McArdle warns Marie's fellow campaigners to back off.

February

Paul tries in vain to persuade Colin Peterson to accept an extra pay rise for the men in exchange for a peaceful implementation of the maintenance contract. The general manager, Brian Palmer, makes Paul reveal details of both his and Annabelle's bank accounts in order to refute the bribery allegations. Paul also discovers that his own secretary has been passing information to Peterson.

Heather buys a used car off an old flame, Don Summerhill, and Sandra gets a visit from Hina Narayan, the Asian woman who wants to marry Ian. Hina explains that unless she can marry soon, she will be forced to leave Britain. Sandra considers this to be emotional blackmail. Window-cleaner Sinbad flogs Karen's boyfriend Andrew a cheap watch. Andrew doesn't want Karen to go away to university and is also jealous at the amount of attention Pat is paying her. In an attempt to win back her heart, he gives her the cheap watch. Karen rejects both the watch and him.

Damon and his friend Neil Wilson start selling bin bags from Claire's pram, but business is slow until they encounter a Mrs Bancroft who gives Damon the distinct impression that she wants him for more than just his bin bags. On his next visit, she asks him to follow her upstairs, during which time the pram is stolen. Sheila is already depressed following the birth so losing the pram does little to lift her spirits. And there is another shock in store when Bobby suggests having a vasectomy.

Across the Close, Terry and Michelle move in with Marie. Terry starts up the car valeting service again and Michelle attends dancing classes. McArdle warns Marie in person to stop the campaign but Marie and her friend Betty Hughes press on and deliver a petition to Downing Street. They return to learn that Little George has been accidentally shot in the eye by an airgun pellet while playing in the woods. Marie is angry at an article by Rick Sexton which suggests that Little George was injured because she was neglecting him by being away in London. Following the article, she receives a spate of hate mail. George absconds from prison but, after phoning Marie about his son's condition, he is recaptured.

March

Heather is working on a new account at Curzon Communications. She takes an instant dislike to the chief accountant, Deaken Mathews, but finds company chairman Tom Curzon a different matter altogether. The devious Mathews clearly has something to hide and manages to have Heather removed from the review of the firm, apparently because of her 'unprofessional relationship' with Mike Harrison, one of the Curzon accountants with whom she had become friendly. But eventually word gets back to Tom Curzon that Mathews had Heather removed because she refused to go out with him.

Sheila is becoming increasingly depressed. She admits to Annabelle that she resents the baby and blows her top when Bobby conducts his union meetings at home. She is also suspicious of Bobby's friendship with union colleague Janet Hanson. Marie offers to baby-sit for Sheila, but while the baby is being looked after by the Jackson twins, a small boy scratches her face. The twins keep quiet about it but Sheila spots the scratch and interrogates Marie, who is unable to offer a plausible explanation.

Pat has got a singing date at a club but Kate won't go because the club operates a colour bar. When Sandra questions her, Kate gives her a few home truths about racism in Britain. However, Karen and her friend Susie are hitting the town. Pretending to be French, they go to a disco where they meet two boys, Danny and Steve. Andrew turns up – just in time to see Karen indulging in a spot of entente cordiale with Danny.

Marie gets a letter from George urging her to give up the campaign and then a stranger hurls a brick through the window. It is the final nail in the coffin and she decides to move to Leeds so that she can be nearer to George who will now have to serve the whole of his suspended sentence in the wake of his escape. A 'For Sale' sign goes up outside No. 10.

Terry becomes jealous of Michelle's dancing instructor, who calls himself Richard de Saville. The two men have little in common: Terry thinks a slow tango is a refreshing drink. Paul rides the storm at work but is shaken by the news that Gordon has suddenly left home and gone to stay with Lucy in France. Annabelle receives a visit from Mrs Duncan, the mother of Christopher Duncan, one of Gordon's school friends. She tells a stunned Annabelle that she suspects that her son and Gordon have been having a homosexual relationship.

April

Without explanation, Heather is put back on the Curzon review. She is about to celebrate by leading Don Summerhill up to bed when Mrs Summerhill knocks on the door, having obtained Heather's address from the car showroom. Don had forgotten to mention that he was married. Heather feels utterly betrayed. She cheers up when Tom Curzon sacks Deaken Mathews and asks her out. Against her better judgement, she accepts. Before long, he is inviting her for a weekend in Portugal.

Marie prepares to move out while Michelle argues about her right to the house. Marie and the twins depart, but Michelle stays put. Marie finally heals the rift with Sheila and gives her a silver locket for Claire as a parting christening gift. Following the christening, Sheila gets away from it all by spending a few days with her sister, Margaret Jefferson, in Basingstoke. Karen and Andrew finally go their separate ways – but only after they have slapped each other in a traditional Brookside farewell.

Without telling Paul, Annabelle takes on a part-time cleaner, Carol Thompson. Edna and Ralph put an accumulator bet on six horses. The first five horses come in and their winnings total £10,000, which is the betting shop's limit on payouts. When they try to claim their winnings, the bookie, Billy Mac, points out that the bet isn't over because the sixth horse has still to run. In the event, the sixth horse falls so the bet fails, but Harry, suddenly galvanised into taking an interest in his wife's hobby, thinks it is unfair since they had no chance of increasing their winnings even if the sixth horse had won. When Harry learns that Billy Mac made £3,000 by 'laying off' bets on Edna's accumulator, he daubs the front of the shop with paint in protest.

After abandoning plans to send Kate a kissagram for her birthday because the cost was so prohibitive, Pat hits upon the idea of starting up his own singing telegram service. His first booking is for a 'gorillagram' at a children's party and he persuades Damon to be the gorilla. Damon finds more meaningful work as a painter and decorator on a YTS scheme. Meanwhile Pat is due to collect Sandra from the hospital after her shift but he comes away from a kissagram booking to find that his ambulance has been stolen. In his absence, Sandra accepts a lift from radiographer Jimmy Powell who attacks her on the way home. Sandra escapes and when Pat arrives at the hospital in a taxi, she accuses him of encouraging men to attack women. Later Pat lashes out at Powell, breaking some equipment in the process, and is suspended.

May

Pat refuses to involve Sandra in his disciplinary hearing, even though he risks losing his job. Pat is duly sacked and also learns that his ambulance has been written off. Afterwards, Pat and Sandra enjoy a romantic dinner together, but it is mainly so that she can give him some hard advice about getting his act together.

Harry makes a complaint against bookmaker's Tattersall's, a firm owned by Tommy McArdle, and is offered £1,500 to forget about the whole thing. The wily old fox refuses and holds out until McArdle offers £4,000. Returning from the Post Office after collecting her pension, Edna is mugged and, although not seriously hurt, she is badly shaken and rendered virtually housebound. A few days later, a large basket of fruit arrives with a note from Tommy McArdle telling her that the mugger has been dealt with.

Terry is becoming increasingly frustrated at the amount of time Michelle is spending with 'Richard de Saville', who is better known locally as ex-brickie Albert Duff. In the end, he accuses her of having an affair with the man who sews his own sequins. Terry is offered a job in one of McArdle's clubs but doesn't want to tell Michelle. She in turn has been offered a dance job in Tunis with Richard. Each is suspicious of the other.

Sheila returns refreshed from her sister's but isn't ready to resume sexual relations with Bobby. Annabelle discovers that food is missing from her freezer in the garage and questions Carol about it. Carol pleads innocence. When redundancy notices are issued at Petrochem, an angry Bobby confronts Paul on his doorstep. Paul, in commanding mood, deflates the big bag of wind. The Petrochem workers subsequently go on strike, widening the rift between the two neighbours.

June

Terry goes to McArdle's club to say he no longer wants to work for him, but one of the villain's henchmen, Raymond, tells him that McArdle has been arrested and accuses Terry of being the informant. In terror, he rushes home and discovers that Michelle has been to bed with Richard de Saville. Terry broods around the Close for a few days before finally flipping when Michelle, after being ditched by tricky Dicky, attempts a reconciliation. Deciding that their bed must be destroyed to purge the memory of her sleeping partner, Terry hurls it out of the bedroom window and stabs at it with a knife. Wisely, Michelle concludes that their relationship is over and joins the Jacksons in Leeds.

Meanwhile Carol catches Sinbad raiding Annabelle's freezer. In return for her silence, he agrees to clean the Collinses' windows for nothing. Annabelle is pleased with Carol's handling of the situation. Sinbad begins to build a bonfire with all the rubbish collected from the residents, including Terry and Michelle's double bed, but the fire gets out of control and the Fire Brigade are called out.

Bobby is keen to end the strike at Petrochem as support seems to be crumbling. He is equally enthusiastic about having a vasectomy, but Sheila is against the idea on religious and moral grounds. Nevertheless he decides to go ahead and explores the possibility of having it done on the NHS, only to hear that the doctor requires Sheila's consent. He eventually finds a clinic that will perform the operation, but it means going private. He reasons that it's not that expensive – just a snip, really. Arriving home feeling sore and groggy, he tries to keep it from Sheila but when he attempts to climb a ladder, he is left doubled up in pain. Sheila is determined to get at the truth and Bobby's confession results in a row which is furious even by Grant standards.

July

With battle-lines still drawn and Sheila sleeping in Claire's room, Damon does his best to reconcile the warring factions. Despite Damon's valiant efforts, the mood remains one of undisguised hostility and Bobby and Sheila even discuss separation. Sheila consults a priest and Bobby talks to Janet Hanson who reveals that she is pregnant and leaving her job. Gradually the iciness between Bobby and Sheila begins to melt until a full thaw takes place and they set off on holiday together. Damon is overjoyed, although Karen is more interested in her new student boyfriend, David, whom she met in the unlikeliest of pulling places – the library.

Tom Curzon invites Heather to go to crown bowling with him – a bit of a comedown from Portugal – and there she is introduced to his father, Jim. Things are getting serious. She arranges to go out to dinner with Tom on his birthday, but when he cancels at the last minute she decides to drop off his card anyway, only to see him leaving with a young lady on his arm and a smile on his face. It turns out to be his secret daughter Rowena.

Kate, Sandra and Pat spend a day at the Alder Hey Hospital Fête, where they meet a disturbed character by the name of John Clarke. He immediately recognises Kate as one of the nurses on duty when his mother died at the hospital. Clarke is obsessed by his mother and seems to be blaming Kate and the other nurses for her death. Kate says it was nobody's fault, she was simply too ill to be saved – and Pat, acting the diplomat for once, succeeds in ushering the girls away before the argument gets too heated. But Clarke isn't finished. He finds their address and calls on Sandra when she is alone in the house. She is reluctant to let him in but he insists that he merely wants to apologise for his behaviour the other day. He appears perfectly calm but is in no hurry to leave and suggests a cup of tea. Sandra feels uncomfortable with him and is mightily relieved when the others return home.

However, Clarke's mood then turns ugly and when Pat tries to throw him out, Clarke pulls a gun on him. With the trio held prisoner, Harry knocks on the door to inform them that he is putting their rent up. Realising that the best policy is to get rid of Harry as quickly as possible, Pat agrees unreservedly to the increase. Harry can hardly believe his luck – he must try rent increases more often. Kate is the only one who appears able to get through to Clarke, but just when there seems a chance of a peaceful solution, Pat blows everything.

Despite the curtains being drawn all day, the only neighbour to be suspicious is Annabelle. At first, Paul plays down her worries but finally he becomes convinced that something is wrong and notifies the police. Meanwhile at No. 5, Damon and Neil Wilson are preparing a seance with three girls, Ruth, Wendy and Camilla. When the police arrive, Damon thinks he has been rumbled, but they are there to evacuate the Close.

August

At a boarding house, the residents watch the siege on television. Camilla embarrasses Damon by telling a reporter about the seance. Over at the nurses' house, Kate finally persuades the increasingly deranged Clarke to release Pat and Sandra. While the police are trying to ascertain whether the gun is real, Clarke's mood suddenly changes and he prepares to shoot himself. Kate attempts to stop him. Three gun shots ring out across the Close. The police enter cautiously and discover the dead bodies of Clarke and Kate.

Sandra and Pat are horrified, thinking that they should have done more. Pat, in particular, blames himself for Kate's death. As life returns to normal, the press are hovering in search of stories about the siege. Harry seems tempted by the offers of money while Damon has a lot of explaining to do to his parents after they read Camilla's wildly exaggerated account of the seance. Terry allows Pat and Sandra to stay at No. 10 where a persistent reporter persuades them to talk to him. Pat gets annoyed by his questions and assaults him when he won't leave. At Kate's funeral in London, Pat and Sandra are upset when Debbie, Kate's sister, snubs them. Pat again expresses his guilt over her death.

Damon and Neil take photographs of

Sheila, Karen and Claire and secretly enter them for a mother and baby competition in the Gazette. Sheila hears that she has won but Damon discovers that the winning photo was the one of Karen and Claire. He doesn't relish having to tell his mum the truth. Paul and Annabelle's holiday plans are wrecked when their travel company folds. They decide instead to borrow Carol's tent instead and go camping, but Paul clearly doesn't know the ropes.

While Harry is out, Edna, who had earlier been found wandering aimlessly, collapses and the chip pan ignites. Discovering Edna lying on the floor, Harry panics and runs for help. Terry saves the day but Edna has suffered a stroke and is unable to speak. Harry refuses to put her in a geriatric ward and, with no other bed available, vents his frustration with the NHS on poor Sandra. Realising he has gone too far, he apologises. Sandra thought hell would freeze over before she got an apology from Harry Cross. Despite Harry's attentive nursing, Edna has a relapse and is admitted to hospital. He becomes very down-hearted as she fails to respond to treatment.

September

The shared tragedy of the siege has brought Sandra and Pat closer together. She goes for a break with her mother in Glasgow but finds that she is desperately missing Pat, so when he turns up, saying that he was missing her too, she is overjoyed until her friend Fiona starts making a play for him. After eventually consummating their relationship, Sandra and Pat return home to find Harry in their house, but their anger turns to sympathy when they hear that Edna has died.

Ralph is making the funeral arrangements and Annabelle is preparing the funeral tea but, even in the depths of despair, Harry is proving a hard task-master. The last straw is when the vicar thinks Ralph is Edna's husband. Missing Edna terribly, Harry pays Annabelle £25 for the tea. Paul discovers that it actually cost £56.

Heather begins to have misgivings about

Tom. Not only doesn't his father Jim know that he has a granddaughter, but Tom hurts Heather when he hints that his involvement with her could jeopardise the impending flotation of Curzon Communications. At least Heather knows where she stands in the great scheme of things.

Karen's romance is progressing more smoothly and, in order to be near David, she has chosen a degree course in media studies at Liverpool University. Sheila and Matty also set about improving their minds by enrolling on a further education course. Terry moves in with Sandra and Pat but is unable to shift all his property because Pat doesn't turn up with the van. So the new owners of No. 10, the Corkhills, arrive to find Terry's possessions still inside and respond by dumping them on the front lawn.

Sandra is feeling the strain of being the only bread-winner in the house, prompting Pat and Terry to set up a van hire business with a £2,000 loan from the bank. But the new set-up gets off to a shaky start: three definitely proves to be a crowd. Pat and Sandra never have any time to themselves with Terry around and, in frustration, she ends up locking Pat out of their room, forcing him to sleep on the sofa.

Julia Brogan, Doreen Corkhill's mother, fills Ralph in on the shady past of Doreen's husband Billy, and young Rod Corkhill becomes infatuated with Heather. Rod's sister Tracy persuades Billy to let her go on a school skiing holiday to Switzerland, even though they can't really afford it.

October

Pat and Sandra come to an agreement: if he hasn't made a go of the van hire business in three months, he'll look for a proper job; and she will give up smoking for the same period. When Damon gives Karen an expensive book for her degree course, she rightly suspects that it is stolen. She is anxious to get off to the right start at university and makes it clear to David that she wants to go her own way, but she is unsettled by the self-assurance of middle-class Pamela.

It quickly becomes apparent that Billy Corkhill has more fiddles than the Liverpool Philharmonic. He has forgotten to 'unfix' the electricity meter at his mother-in-law's and when Julia is caught by the meter reader, she faces prosecution. When her electricity is switched off Julia is forced to rely on candle-power, but after a small fire Doreen takes pity on her and invites her to stay at No. 10 for a while. Billy is overjoyed ... not! He then puts up some tasteless window shutters which antagonise Paul and Annabelle so much that they decide they contravene the conditions of the ground lease. Billy's next home improvement is a burglar alarm, but that goes missing, taken by Karen and Pamela on their way back from a late-night party. Discovering that her precious new alarm has been stolen, Doreen is all for calling the police until Billy reluctantly admits that it could be 'knock-off'. Rod's second love (after Heather) is Everton FC and he commandeers the front bedroom from Tracy so that he can compete with Damon's Liverpool posters across the Close.

Lucy Collins returns from France and announces that she has an interview for a translator's job in Liverpool. Tom Curzon is entertaining important clients and wants to give them the impression that he has a wife, so he asks Heather whether she would mind being 'Mrs Curzon' for the evening. When she refuses, Tom asks her to marry him for real. Now that her decree absolute from Roger has arrived, she is free to contemplate Tom's proposal. She consults her mother, thinks about it long and hard, decides that's a good enough reason and accepts. Heather and Tom plan their wedding reception but he insists that he's not going to invite his daughter, Rowena. He then rushes off to America on business, leaving Heather to finalise the wedding arrangements.

November

Julia is heavily fined for fiddling her electricity meter and receives a warning from Doreen about gossiping to the neighbours about the family's history. Even when Billy arranges for Julia's electricity to be reconnected, she doesn't take the hint about moving back home. Eventually she goes off in a huff after Doreen as good as accuses her of stealing from her Christmas turkey fund (in fact, the culprit was Rod).

Lucy is having an affair with a married man, James Fleming. As a result of his influence, she thinks the translator's job is as good as hers, but her confidence proves unfounded. He partly redeems himself by getting her a secretarial post at the office where he works, but she was expecting something better. Paul and Annabelle have been worried by Lucy's erratic timekeeping, but all is forgiven when she reveals that she has a boyfriend. Annabelle is ready to start ordering the bridesmaids' dresses.

Tracy has also got a mysterious boyfriend – a fact which appears to be causing problems at school, for Rod arrives home one day with a black eye after defending Tracy's reputation. Perry Mason would have struggled to defend Tracy's reputation.

Before setting off for a break with Ralph at the Blaenau Ffestiniog railway in Wales, Harry draws Jim Curzon's attention to the name Rowena on Heather's list of wedding guests. When Jim asks Heather about the mystery guest, she reluctantly confesses that Rowena is the granddaughter he never knew he had. Jim confronts Tom, who in turn argues with Heather over the fact that she has broken her promise to keep Rowena's existence a secret. In a bid to make amends, Tom takes Heather to see the house he has bought and offers her a job with Curzon Communications. After resigning from Hamilton Devereux, however, she is perturbed to find that her new job is little more than a sinecure. Heather's mum senses that all is not well and advises her daughter to think very carefully before making another marital mistake. Heather realises that marriage to Tom won't work and calls off the wedding. Back in her old job, she is driving through the city when the MG Midget in front of her brakes too quickly and she runs into the back of it. The driver is architect Nicholas Black.

December

Damon's painting and decorating job takes him to an up-market residence where he spots workmate Gerry Blake stealing an ornament. When Damon remonstrates, Blake tells him to keep his mouth shut. Even when Damon is suspected of the theft and suspended, he doesn't 'grass' on his colleague, insisting that he can sort it out himself. Sheila decides to take matters into her own hands and confronts Blake, threatening to reveal the truth unless the vase is returned. Damon is duly reinstated.

Karen is distracted by her new university friend Pamela and, instead of writing an essay for her tutor, goes off to town with Pamela to buy a Walkman. When Karen panics because she is behind with her work, Pamela arranges for fellow student Guy Willis to lend Karen an essay. In exchange, he asks for a date.

Pat and Terry win a delivery contract from Mike Henty of the fruit machine company Hentytainments. Via Harry and Ralph, who are fielding phone calls while Pat and Terry are out to avoid waking Sandra, the boys receive a booking in Wrexham. They also receive a visit from Vicki Cleary of the van firm which used to have the Henty contract. It is not a social call and she accuses Pat and Terry of adopting unfair tactics and stealing her business. The trip to Wrexham proves a waste of time – the address doesn't exist – and when they are sent off on further wild goose chases, they fall out with their geriatric secretarial staff. Who can blame them, considering that Harry thinks Pitman's shorthand is a mining injury. Later they discover that Vicki Cleary is behind the skullduggery and, to add insult to injury, their van is vandalised during the night. Certain

The Corkhill and Grant Families

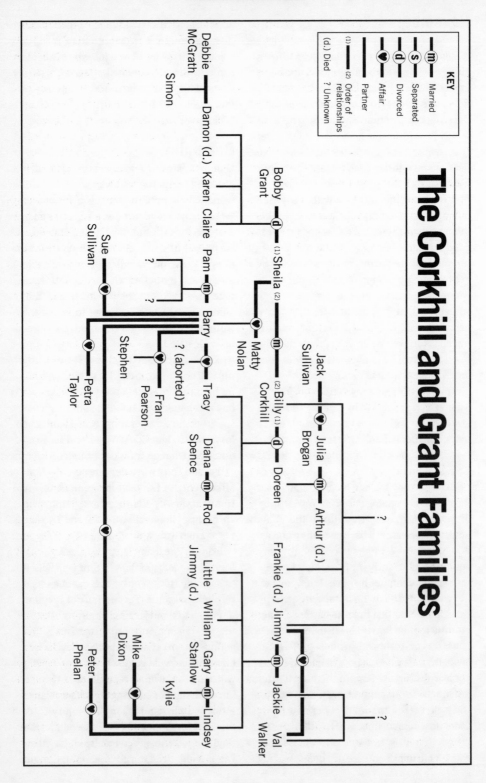

that the Clearys are responsible, Pat advocates strong-arm tactics; Terry is more cautious.

Just as he is making headway with Vicki, Terry finds himself playing host to Barry's heroin-addicted ex-girlfriend, Jane Smith. She is so desperate for money to buy heroin that she offers Terry her body in exchange for £20. Terry politely declines.

Sinbad sells a bargain turkey to the Close. Its name is Trevor and it's still alive. Sheila refuses to kill the bird but Harry appears perfectly willing to do a hatchet job. To Sinbad's relief, however, Trevor emerges from the bungalow with feathers intact. Billy crosses a picket line at his factory, to the fury of Bobby, who has organised the picket and there is to support the strikers.

1986

Billy is charged with assaulting Tracy's geography teacher ... Heather marries Nicholas Black ... Six months later, he is dead ... Sheila is raped ... Teresa Nolan commits suicide ... Gordon's gay friend, Chris, comes to stay ... Sandra finds a new man and leaves the Close ... Pat and Terry go to Barbados ... Heather returns to Ireland.

January

Heather and her friend Joyce are in the middle of decorating when they are interrupted by a visit from Nick Black, who says he has heard nothing about the insurance claim for the damage to his car. Heather gives him a cheque, but it is wrongly dated, giving Nick an excuse to call round again. This time he offers to help with the decorating and will stay up all night to finish it off. Heather and Joyce come down in the morning to find that Nick has been as good as his word.

On the work front, Heather discovers that

her liaison with Tom Curzon has gone against her and that her new boss, the slimy Keith Tench, thinks her attractiveness is a liability to the company. Lucy's friend James comes for dinner and Paul and Annabelle immediately suspect that he is married. When they mention this to her, she coolly tells them that she knows he is and that they should mind their own business. An anxious Paul goes to see James, who reveals that he tried to end the affair but Lucy wouldn't let go.

Rod is suspended from school for attacking a teacher, Peter Montague, after seeing graffiti about Tracy which read: 'Tracy Corkhill gave Monty a Swiss roll.' Pat and Sandra are fed up with Jane and decide to tell her to leave, but before they can do so, she vanishes, taking some of their valuables with her. After catching Joe and Eddy Cleary sabotaging the van outside a cafe, Pat and Barry plan to end the van war by force, despite Terry's opposition. They beat up the Clearys (Vicki's brothers) and then Barry goes to the Clearys' yard and smashes up a van. Alas, it doesn't belong to the Clearys.

With the binmen on strike, Damon and Neil borrow a rat – Marilyn – to photograph in a pile of rubbish, in the hope of selling the picture to the papers. Pat and Terry start clearing away the rubbish from the Close with Sheila's blessing, but she in turn incurs the wrath of Bobby, who tells her she is helping to break the binmen's strike. When Damon and Neil lose Marilyn, Barry gets a gun and shoots her.

February

To thank Nick for the decorating, Heather invites him for a meal and he arrives with his youngest son Adam in tow. Heather likes the boy and, while relegated by Keith Tench to conducting a small audit at a feminist printers' workshop, meets Nick's lesbian ex-wife Barbara.

Julia reveals that she saw a love letter from Tracy to someone called Peter, and Tracy eventually confesses that the teacher mentioned in the graffiti is named Peter. Concerned that Tracy is having an affair with this teacher, Billy and Doreen try to discuss the matter calmly. When they finally hear from Tracy that the rumours are true, Billy storms off to school and thumps Montague. That's Billy's idea of calm. Billy is arrested and when Tracy briefly runs away from home, Doreen accuses Billy of driving her out with his violent over-reaction to the whole affair. Afraid to go home and face her father, Tracy meets Doreen in a park and makes it clear that she was very much a willing party with Montague. Billy agrees to keep quiet in court as to why he hit Montague, in order to prevent Tracy's name being dragged through the mud.

After pretending to be Bobby in order to obtain a loan for £1,500, Barry does a vanishing act, and Harry puts an advert for a companion in the personal columns. Despite her promises to the contrary, Lucy is still seeing James. She tells Annabelle that James is leaving his wife and that they are getting married. Paul has another meeting with James, who assures him he has no intention of leaving his wife. When Paul tells Lucy, she refuses to believe it. James still can't bring himself to drop Lucy so she marches round to his house to tells his wife, Penny, about the affair. Big mistake. James throws her out and, humiliated, she returns home and locks herself in the bathroom. She finally emerges and goes into work, only to be sacked.

March

In court, Billy pleads guilty but is considered unco-operative and is sentenced to three months in prison. Doreen protests and shouts out about the affair with Montague. Billy is released on bail, pending an appeal.

Harry and Ralph sift through the replies to Harry's advert and agree that Madge Richmond sounds the best candidate. Harry posts his reply to Madge but still feels disloyal to Edna. They arrange a meeting at the Walker Art Gallery but a nervous Harry approaches the wrong woman and annoys her. Meanwhile

Ralph, who has gone along for moral support, meets Madge and gets on famously with her.

A letter arrives telling Bobby he owes £1,500 to a loan company. Sheila assumes that Barry is somehow responsible and, fearing that her beloved son is in trouble and might go to jail, stops Bobby from phoning the company. The money arrives to pay off the loan but Sheila and Bobby are worried about how Barry came by it.

Sheila has a college tutorial at home where Bobby's jealousy of tutor Alun Jones becomes apparent. She snaps and says the only people who could be having an affair are his mate Matty and divorcee Mo Francis. Bobby implies that Sheila is paying more attention to the course than to Claire and later confronts Matty about Mo. Matty eventually admits it is true, but swears Bobby to secrecy, even from Sheila. When Teresa asks her about Matty, Sheila feels guilty about not voicing her suspicions. She thinks her friend has a right to know.

Karen interviews Paula Yates for the university magazine as part of Rag Week and is finally persuaded by Guy to stay the night. However she is unable to have sex and goes home depressed. Confident that he would be kept on at the end of his YTS, Damon also returns home desolate after learning that, despite good references, he is being released.

While Terry and Vicki are growing closer, Pat and Sandra seem to be drifting apart. The showdown comes when Sandra comes home with a handsome colleague, Dr Tony Hurrell, thereby thwarting Pat's plans to take her out for the evening. To Sandra's acute embarrassment, Pat behaves like a spoilt brat and has a little temper tantrum.

April

Delighted that Lucy seems to have got over James, Paul and Annabelle are horrified to hear that she is off to France again to sell videos with Barry Grant. After her departure, they discover a load of stolen shampoos in her room. Having agreed to go on holiday to

Torquay with Ralph, Madge is alarmed to hear that Harry will also be coming along for the ride. To appease Madge, Ralph says he will try to find a suitable companion for his friend. Harry's eyes light up at the prospect of a few days in Torquay with Heather but his jaw drops with the grim realisation that his escort is to be Julia Brogan.

Damon is also bound for Torquay, in search of a job. With no money to his name, he ends up sleeping rough. There are different priorities in the rest of the Grant household. Bobby is preoccupied with a union dispute at Bragg's while Sheila worries whether to tell Teresa that she thinks Matty is having an affair. Bobby strongly advises Sheila to keep her nose out. Sheila decides to have a word with Mo, and when Matty finds out, he offers the same advice as Bobby. Sheila is particularly annoyed to learn that Bobby knew about the affair. She then offers sanctuary to battered wife Sally Dinsdale and her children, which prompts Bobby to tell her that she finds time for everyone except her own family. Sheila receives an anonymous threatening letter and a nasty phone call and wonders whether Matty is trying to warn her off.

Nick tries to defend Heather in front of her boss, Keith Tench, but does so with such vigour that the conversation ends in a scuffle. When Heather discovers what has happened, she throws Nick out. Pat and Terry are tipped off that they are being watched by the DHSS. Confined to barracks by Doreen, who blames her for Billy's predicament, Tracy becomes so lonely that she starts phoning Chatline and running up big bills. Billy wins his appeal and Doreen celebrates by going on a shopping spree. When she gets back, he tells her he has been sacked.

May

Billy tells Bobby that he has lost his job. Bobby advises him to go to the union but warns him that the lads won't support a scab. With Billy jobless, Doreen's answer is to get a new credit card and stock up for the millennium. So the

last thing Billy needs is a visit from brother Jimmy with a pile of 'hot' bricks to build a garage.

When Teresa asks Sheila if Matty and Mo are having an affair, Sheila rubbishes the idea and quickly changes the subject. Over the next few days, Sheila receives a number of silent phone calls, but it turns out to be Damon, who has been having trouble getting through. Guy and Karen have also finally been connected, and she is delighted that she has overcome her fears and lost her virginity. Paul, who lost his during rationing, is made redundant following a take-over. He expects at least a phone call from the MD, Brian Palmer, but instead merely gets one from the transport manager requesting the return of his company car.

Madge accepts the challenge of a lifetime and promises to teach Harry to drive. She'd have more chance of success with Mr Magoo, and Harry is soon annoyed when he makes a fool of himself behind the wheel.

Sandra is spending an increasing amount of time with Tony Hurrell on a secret investigation of a leading surgeon at the hospital, Mr Cribbs-Baker, whom they believe has been carrying out unnecessary operations in the private wards for his personal financial gain. The pair meet regularly at No. 7, to the exclusion of Pat who is becoming consumed with jealousy.

Heather and Nick are reunited and she accepts his offer of marriage. But she is worried about the reaction of his two older children, Ruth and Scott. Her fears are not unfounded, for when the youngest son, Adam, is knocked down by a car while walking to Heather's after his cricket match finishes early, Ruth and Scott seize the opportunity to blame Heather.

June

Dinner guests have suggested to Annabelle that she should apply to be a magistrate. She warms to the idea but becomes alarmed when Paul, with time on his hands, gets involved in plans for a road safety blockade. She fears that his law-breaking activities will jeopardise her chances. She accuses Paul of turning into a vigilante but Paul responds by persuading Harry and Ralph to join his lollipop army.

Rod stuns the Corkhill family by announcing that he wants to join the police. He could double Merseyside's clear-up rate just by starting on his own doorstep. Billy is bitterly opposed to the idea, but Doreen is all in favour and refuses to let Billy sleep with her until he discusses it properly. For some reason, Billy gives in.

Pat accuses Sandra of having an affair with Tony Hurrell. When Pat demands proof of her love, she goes to sleep in Kate's room but memories of Kate come flooding back and she returns to Pat for comfort. Karen tells Sheila that she saw Matty and Mo together and also reveals that there have been further sinister phone calls to the house. Learning that Matty is going to leave her, Teresa has a showdown with Mo at college. Bobby is shocked by the separation and admits that he was wrong. Sheila won't give up without a fight, however, and makes one last attempt to get through to Mo. After confessing that she sent the threatening letter, Mo sees sense and tells Matty it's over. Meanwhile tutor Alun Jones renews his efforts to persuade Sheila to attend a weekend course.

Heather and Nick are married at a registry office. Nick's laid-back pal, Charlie Dawson, is best man. The omens are not good. Adam tells Heather that his father and Ruth keep secrets between them and, after not receiving a wedding invitation, Harry sourly predicts that the marriage won't last.

July

Billy is offered what appears to be a good job as maintenance supervisor by Julian Tyler, a forthright businessman who has no time for trade unions. Ralph is coerced into giving Harry a driving lesson but would have felt less terrified on the Cresta Run. While trying to teach Harry the basics of clutch control, Ralph hears a furious row between Pat and Sandra.

Pat hits her before storming off.

Sheila learns that Ken Dinsdale, husband of battered wife Sally, has been behind the anonymous phone calls. Then she has to face an irate Matty who accuses her of turning Mo against him. When Matty becomes aggressive, Damon, back from Torquay, has to throw him out of the house. Sheila's tutor, Alun Jones, is also becoming dangerously obsessed with her. He arranges to meet her in a pub but, instead of discussing course work, he begs her to go away with him. Although she turns him down, he won't take no for an answer and is still pleading with her when Matty barges in and, seeing them together, accuses Sheila of hypocritically having an affair with her tutor. Sheila denies it, but the besotted Jones claims that they're in love. Sheila has had enough and gets into a taxi but Matty jumps in beside her and continues his tirade of abuse. Near the Close, she stops the cab and gets out, ready to walk the rest of the way home. She has barely gone 100 yards when she hears someone call out her name. Before she can react, a coat is thrown over head and she is dragged into some bushes and raped.

The immediate police suspect is Pat, who has scratch marks on his face following the row with Sandra and was picked up for being drunk and acting suspiciously. When Pat's alibi is confirmed, the police arrest Matty instead. Teresa is convinced he is guilty.

August

Hearing that a man has been charged with Sheila's rape, Teresa jumps to the conclusion that it is Matty. In fact he is on his way home after being released but all he comes home to is a suicide note. While Teresa is drowning herself in the Mersey, the cab driver confesses that he raped Sheila, which at least spares her the ordeal of having to give evidence. At Teresa's funeral, Matty and Sheila are reconciled and Bobby expresses his remorse, feeling that he could have done something to save her. To add to his woes, he has been suspended by his national executive for

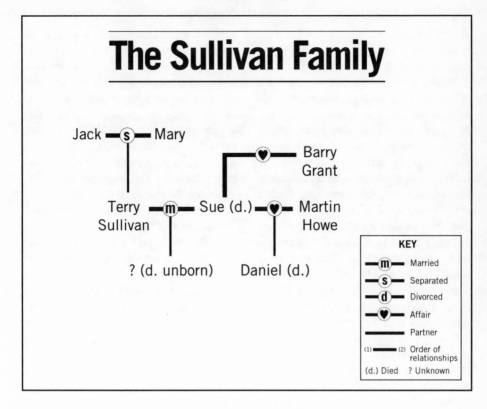

The Sullivan Family

Jack —(s)— Mary

(♥)— Barry
Grant

Terry —(m)— Sue (d.) —(♥)— Martin
Sullivan   Howe

? (d. unborn)   Daniel (d.)

KEY

—(m)—	Married
—(s)—	Separated
—(d)—	Divorced
—(♥)—	Affair
——	Partner
(1) ■■■ (2)	Order of relationships
(d.) Died	? Unknown

supporting the unofficial strike at Bragg's.

Pat goes to the football club to watch Terry train but finds the sight of Andrea Parkin infinitely preferable. Although she is married, she chats him up and implies that she is definitely available. Terry warns that she is a man-eater, but Pat can only dream about scoring in extra time. Annabelle buys Paul a bike but he won't admit that he can't ride it and gets young Adam to give him lessons. Annabelle's worst fears about the road safety blockade materialise when Paul and the organiser, Kathleen Monaghan, are arrested there. However, at her interview with the Clerk to the Justices, she is relieved to learn that Paul's aberration won't affect her chances of becoming a magistrate.

Paul and Annabelle breathe a collective sigh of relief when Gordon returns home from France with a girl, Cecile. Just as Paul is about to suggest a lads' night down at The Swan with a few beers and a game of arrows, Cecile

reveals that Gordon has been her brother Pierre's lover. *Sacre bleu!*

Against Heather's wishes, Nick has insisted on keeping his flat. While she is away on business in Hong Kong, the shifty Charlie informs Nick that the flat has been burgled. Their behaviour indicates that they have something to hide. Nick agrees to allow Charlie to move into the flat.

September

Back from Hong Kong, Heather is dismayed to find the omnipresent Charlie getting in the way of her reunion with Nick. Nick lies to her about how little he has seen Charlie in her absence but his deception is unmasked when she stumbles across Charlie's cheque book. She begins to wonder whether the two men are gay, but Charlie laughingly denies this. After much badgering, Ruth eventually decides to let Heather in on their little secret. She takes Heather to the flat where Nick is about to take the heroin he'd been waiting for. He overdoses, leaving Charlie to dispose of the evidence while Heather and Ruth go in the ambulance with the unconscious Nick.

Billy puts his car up for sale. First the battery is stolen and then the vehicle is stripped down to its shell. The thieves leave the furry dice. Tracy has taken up modelling, for which she buys expensive ball gowns which the family can't afford. Terry locks Pat out in his underpants when Andrea calls. He is forced to borrow a pair of flares from Heather and, understandably, Andrea makes him change before seducing him. To her, flares are definitely a sign of distress. Pat then asks Sandra to move out, claiming that he is inhibited by her presence. He thinks nothing of making love to Andrea while Sandra is downstairs. Sandra doesn't think much of it either but she refuses to move out.

Having been warned off the Cribbs-Baker case, Tony Hurrell calls to say his farewells before leaving Liverpool but instead he and Sandra end up in bed, forced together by Pat's petulance. Sandra tells Pat that it was only desperation after Kate's death that brought them close and she leaves for good … with Tony. Karen and Guy rent a grotty flat together (much to Bobby's disgust) and Damon meets a new girlfriend Gail on the Mersey Ferry.

Delighted that his daughter-in-law, Sally, is pregnant, Harry insists that she and his son Kevin accompany him to the cemetery where he tells Edna about their grandchild. Gordon and Paul argue about homosexuality but Paul defends his son against cleaner Carol who is afraid of catching AIDS from Gordon. Gordon's gay school friend, Christopher Duncan, comes to visit and, to Paul's surprise, he enjoys his company and a shared interest in cycling. Paul still finds it difficult to talk openly about homosexuality but gets a chance to practise when the *Gay Times* is delivered to the Corkhills' by mistake. Paul finally admits to an amazed Billy that it is Gordon's.

October

Nick's ex-wife, Barbara, fills Heather in on his drug history and urges her to get out of the marriage while she can. But when Nick regains consciousness, Heather says she will help him. In return, he promises never to take heroin again, but Charlie is soon back supplying him. After catching Nick rifling through her wallet, Heather seeks Barry's advice. He too tells Heather to kick Nick out, before she ends up on heroin herself.

Annabelle makes a mess of her first training session to be a magistrate and is mercilessly criticised by Rod who plays the defendant. Next it is Rod's turn for his police interview – a nerve-racking experience as he worries what skeletons they will uncover in the Corkhill family closet. Billy is finding Tyler a demanding boss and gets fed up with Tracy asking for money for her modelling course. In anger, he makes the cardinal sin of breaking his bleeper. When Billy refuses to go into work, Doreen heads for the shops but is refused credit at a supermarket. She returns home to find Tyler brow-beating Billy and tells him what he can do with his job. Pat and Terry take in a new tenant, Gill, who is deaf and lip-reads.

Sheila is having nightmares about the rape and is scared to be left alone in the house. Although Bobby has put a chain on the door, any knock can send her into hysterics. On one such occasion, Barry, thinking she is being attacked, breaks the door down. He thinks he knows the best cure for his mum's problems and secretly arranges for Tommy McArdle to have the rapist, Dutton, beaten up. McArdle agrees in exchange for a favour. The favour is a trip to Barbados for Pat and Terry. Bobby admits to Sheila that he is unable to respond to her sexually. He can't help thinking of the rapist and is also jealous of Barry.

November

Pat and Terry's task is to accompany dear old Mrs McArdle, Tommy's mum, to Barbados. They think she is senile – a few pages short of a pension book – but she is craftier than the two of them put together. From the moment she leaves a parcel in the airport locker, it is obvious that she is acting as Tommy's courier. Terry is a mite suspicious but Pat thinks the job is easy money and is much more interested in Avril, the Bajan tourist guide. Pat thinks about staying over in Barbados just to be with Avril, but she tells him it wouldn't work. On the way back, Mrs M collects an envelope, conceals it in a case and gets Terry to carry it through customs.

Gordon wants a motorbike but Paul intends spending his annuity on himself. Money is in short supply over at the Corkhills', where Tyler's men repossess Billy's car and Doreen has to persuade Billy not to get up to his old tricks with the 'leccy' meter. They sign for a loan, using the house as security. Rod wants the house spotless for the Police Inspector's home visit the next day. In particular, he wants no sign of Uncle Jimmy. Awaiting the outcome of Dutton's trial, Sheila is angry and upset to hear that it has been postponed because Barry had arranged for him to be beaten up. Now her ordeal must be prolonged.

Nick steals Heather's ruby pendant and comes home high. He has been sacked by the council and needs to take some heroin to relieve the stress. He offers Heather some to try, so that she can understand. She refuses and asks him to leave.

Pat and Terry return to the Close to find that Harry wants them out so that he can install Kevin, Sally and his future granddaughter, but when Harry broaches the subject with Sally, she says no. He rounds on her and she goes into labour. The baby is born prematurely. Harry is full of remorse and wills the baby to live.

December

Harry's grandchild is christened Harriet but her condition deteriorates and she dies, leaving Harry to blame himself for upsetting Sally. Charlie blames Heather for Nick's disappearance and decline. He says that Nick

coped until he met her. Then a policeman calls with news that Nick has been found dead on a bench in Sefton Park. After identifying the body, she pledges Barry to secrecy and leaves on the next boat for Ireland. Charlie tries to find a place on the Close where he can stay for Christmas but when Barry finds him, he throws him out on his ear.

At the Corkhills', the phone and the electricity are cut off and the TV is repossessed. Billy is consequently possessed and rants and raves about the family's overspending. By way of a change, Tracy is in a bad mood. With no money coming in, her catwalk career is in tatters and she has been obliged to sell her ball gown and sign up for a YTS hairdressing scheme instead. On her first day, she arrives late and, in her own inimitable style, manages to rub the salon owner, Shelley Rimmer, up the wrong way. Billy tries to rent a TV for Christmas but learns that the Corkhills are listed as bad payers. There is a little festive cheer – but not much – for Rod when he meets a new girlfriend, Kirsty Brown, and later apprehends burglars in the empty No. 9.

Following a food poisoning scare, Annabelle decides to give up catering but starts her first day as a magistrate. Jack Sullivan, Terry's dad, could be a future customer as he is running a Christmas hamper scam. When Harry hears Jack boasting about the fiddle, Jack has to give him four hampers to pay for his silence. Sheila has taken a dislike to Damon's pushy girlfriend Gail and now Damon reaches a similar conclusion and dumps her. It's the end of the road too for Karen and Guy. Moving in with him has proved a disaster and now she wants to change courses and go to London. Sheila says she must follow her instincts and not allow herself to be trapped.

1987

Harry unmasks Madge Richmond as a gold-digger ... Bobby and Sheila make a pilgrimage to Rome ... Newcomers Jonathan Gordon-Davies and Laura Wright are married ... Billy finally goes over the edge ... Damon is fatally stabbed in York ... Laura has a nasty shock ... The Rogers clan move into No. 7

January

Brookside Close witnesses the biggest evacuation since Dunkirk. Karen goes to London, leaving Bobby hurt because she didn't discuss her decision with him, and Barry also does his familiar disappearing act. Desperate for work, Billy gets a job in Tunbridge Wells, having finally arranged for the electricity to be reconnected legally. Rod starts out at Police College, after promising to be faithful to Kirsty, and Ralph and Madge head off on holiday to Spain. This last departure is not without rancour. Harry has become suspicious of Madge who seems to have more birthdays than the Queen and, even though he claims to have lost his voice, he tries to warn Ralph off her. Ralph won't listen. Love may not exactly be blind for Ralph but it is certainly in need of an eye test. When Harry confronts Madge about her birthday, she tells him he confused her and threatens to expose the truth about the illness he faked in an effort to ruin their fun.

Sheila is also planning to get away from the Close on a spiritual trip to Rome as part of her recovery process from the rape. Bobby thinks it's too expensive, but Sheila says she'll go on her own and, to Bobby's horror, gets a part-time job at The Swan to pay for the trip. Bobby hears of an asbestos problem at Billinge Chemicals and is convinced there's a cover-up. Damon falls for schoolgirl Debbie McGrath

and Pat and Terry advertise for another new tenant. They end up with two kiln builders, Mike and Mick, who, because they work opposite shifts, will use the bed alternately and pay extra money. It seems like an ideal arrangement until they discover that Mick comes complete with irritating habits and a noisy pet macaw and Mike is a serial womaniser. Meanwhile Tracy wants to pack in her hairdressing job – it's not as glamorous as she thought – and Doreen is tempted to the sales by Julia. It's reassuring to know that the Corkhill women are standing by Billy in his hour of need.

February

While out for a ride, Paul rescues a drowning puppy. Annabelle says it can only stay for a day or two until it can be taken to the RSPCA, but Gordon and Paul become quite attached to the dog and Gordon builds a kennel in the garden. However, the dog, which Paul has christened Lucky, steadfastly refuses to set paw inside the kennel and prefers to foul Sheila's path. Paul has to clear up the mess. Gordon and Christopher get the idea of making money from furniture restoration.

Bobby is still worried that the asbestos problem will cause job losses at Billinge Chemicals and is taken to meet a worker, Don Crawford, who is dying from asbestosis. Bobby is moved when Don asks him to make sure that his death won't be in vain and resolves to bring in the inspectors. The factory is closed down and irate workers accuse Bobby of being a member of Militant Tendency.

Frustrated that the continual presence of either Mike or Mick is curbing her love life with Terry, Vicki tells him that he must get rid of them. Meanwhile Pat and Terry keep the existence of Mick a secret from Harry so that he doesn't want more rent. Ralph and Madge return from holiday engaged. Madge is sporting an expensive ring but Harry spurns the presents they have bought him. Determined to expose Madge, Harry sneaks a look at her driving license which confirms that her birthday is in July, not January as she had claimed. Ralph is unimpressed by the evidence and anyway Madge comes out with a heart-breaking story to explain why she no longer celebrates her birthday on the right day. But, by now, Harry is like a dog with a bone and lays a trap by placing an ad in the lonely hearts column. Among the replies is one from Madge. Heavily disguised and using an assumed name, Harry meets her and accuses her of being a gold-digger. Madge confesses that there are other men in her life and agrees to call off the wedding with Ralph. When she tells Ralph that she wants to end their engagement, she concocts a yarn about grieving for her late husband. As she departs, Harry makes sure she leaves the ring behind.

March

Trying to help Ralph get over the loss of Madge, Harry hides the holiday snaps from Spain when they arrive. Ralph finds them and accuses Harry of being spiteful and jealous. He decides to leave. However, he returns on discovering the truth about Madge from Julia. From the sale of contents at Heather's house, Terry buys her double bed so that he can ask Vicki to move in. The ever-watchful Harry monitors its arrival.

At The Swan, Pat has met Fran, Ellie and Trish, an all-girl band who want to hire a van. Pat is only too happy to oblige. Mike and Mick's departure leaves Terry fretting about the rent but Pat is only interested in acting as the girls' roadie.

Gordon and Christopher fulfil a fantasy by rushing out of a restaurant without paying but, returning to the Close in a stolen car, they run over Lucky. When Paul discovers that Lucky is dead, he vows to catch the culprit. Gordon doesn't own up and gets annoyed by Christopher's flippancy as Paul buries the dog. Paul comes to the conclusion that Pat killed the dog and, despite Gordon's pleas, takes revenge by videoing Pat and Terry's activities and reporting them to the DHSS. While Annabelle is worrying over a letter about her mother, Gordon is desperately trying to pluck up the courage to confess to Paul. After Gordon tells Pat and Terry what his father has done, Pat confronts Paul and is only prevented from doing physical damage by Gordon's sudden admission that it was he who killed Lucky. Disgusted with the pair of them, Annabelle goes to her mother's in the Lake District. She returns to be greeted by a large banner erected by Pat to tell the world that Paul is a DHSS spy.

Unsurprisingly, Tracy is sacked from her hairdressing job for dyeing a girl's hair rainbow-coloured and being rude to her mother, and Billy, after a visit from Doreen to his caravan hovel in Tunbridge Wells, returns home none the richer. The ever-helpful Jimmy suggests a fake burglary to make money on the insurance.

April

Bobby gets the hump when Matty tries to persuade him to accompany Sheila to Rome. He says everyone sees things from Sheila's point of view and ignores his feelings. Emotions escelate – Damon threatens to leave home and Sheila threatens to tear up the tickets – before Bobby finally backs down and agrees to go to Rome. The holiday starts badly as old resentments resurface but when Bobby hears that Don Crawford, the asbestosis victim, has died, he is able to put things into perspective. For her part, Sheila realises the enormous implications of a split with Bobby. Better able to understand themselves and each other, the pair are reunited.

Yuppie solicitors Jonathan Gordon-Davies and Laura Wright arrive at No. 9 and start decorating. Laura is looking forward to moving in but not to all the fuss and expense of the impending wedding. And Jonathan is unhappy about the presence of Laura's younger sister Joanne who seems to be making herself too much at home.

Harry decides to sell No. 7 so that he can live for today and informs Pat and Terry of his intentions. Vicki moves in but sees no future for her and Terry unless he gets Pat out of the house and the business.

Doreen persuades Shelley the hairdresser to give Tracy her job back but, with money too tight to mention, Billy goes along with Jimmy's plan to burgle the house in order to pay off the mounting debts. Jimmy wants to make it look authentic, so when Paul and Annabelle return from collecting her ailing mother, Mona Harvey, they find that their house has been burgled. Jimmy then times his raid on No. 10 to coincide with Rod's passing out parade. Typically, Jimmy goes too far and leaves the place in a mess. While Doreen is in a state, Billy makes out a false insurance claim. Jimmy offers Billy the proceeds from the sale of the stolen goods from the Collins burglary, but Billy refuses and insists that Jimmy retrieves a brooch with sentimental value for Annabelle. The burglary has made Mona more confused than ever. She thinks Paul is not only trying to poison her but is also after her money. Nevertheless Annabelle wants her to stay on a permanent basis. Paul thinks she would be better off in a home.

May

Debbie McGrath's father goes to the Grants' to tell Damon not to see Debbie any more. Damon tries to sort it out himself and gets annoyed when his parents take over. At Sheila's request, Damon invites Debbie round. He is confident that she will meet with approval, but when she has gone Bobby and Sheila both say she is too young for him. Debbie thinks her dad would like Damon more if he had a job so he finds work as a door-to-door salesman.

Jonathan and Laura argue about her intrusive family, especially her dad Geoff, and about the guest list for the wedding. With Laura already having second thoughts about her new home, she and Jonathan drive into a large hole which has just appeared on the Close. Mona writes to her son Teddy on the Wirral to complain about Paul but, on her way

to post the letter, it gets blown into the hole and she falls in after it.

Although Pat continues to lose Terry money, Terry can't bring himself to sever the partnership. Fed up with his indecisiveness, Vicki sticks to her threat and walks out on him for good. Pat tries to muscle in on the girls' band, to the annoyance of Trish and Ellie. He says if they don't let him join, they'll lose the van. They are left with little option but to let him become their backing vocalist. On his way back from a repossession job, Pat is forced by the hole to drive over Billy's front garden. Near boiling point because he thinks everyone is dumping on him from a great height, Billy storms out ready to thump Pat, only to discover someone has beaten him to it. He got a smashed nose courtesy of the repossession job.

With no money coming in, Billy decides to sell the items which he and Jimmy had stashed in the loft from the fake burglary but when he forgets to lock the door and Doreen walks in, she discovers the truth. While the 'stolen' goods are being hidden from Rod's gaze, the kindly policeman allows Annabelle to drive over Billy's garden whereupon an irate Billy parks his car to prevent anybody else abusing his property. Doreen pours out her troubles to her dentist boss, Howman, who offers to lend her money but indicates that she could repay him with her body – not a bad deal since it's worth marginally more than her mind.

June

Doreen is keeping secrets from Billy. Not only hasn't she told him about Howman's generous offer, but she has hidden a letter from the building society announcing the commencement of legal proceedings. Tracy has managed to find an equally morose boyfriend, Jamie Henderson. They can't afford to go out until Rod offers them a sub if she'll iron his shirt. Naturally Tracy refuses, but Jamie says he'll do it. Having burnt Rod's shirt, the pair run off.

Telling Billy that Howman has invited the

staff out for a meal, Doreen goes to Howman's hotel room, apparently ready to lay down her first instalment. But once there, she can't bear the thought of hands which spend all day in other people's mouths touching her body and she throws the money at him and runs home to Billy. Perhaps he should have worn his surgical gloves … Chez Corkhill, Doreen tells Billy she's lost her job and that she nearly slept with Howman for money. Before Billy can react, she shows him the repossession letter from the building society. Billy responds by driving maniacally over the neighbours' lawns. At the end of his tether, he decides to resort to crime to clear his debts and asks Jimmy to use his underworld contacts. Jimmy is worried about what his brother might be getting himself into but, seeing how upset Doreen is about the repossession, agrees to do what he can.

On Pat's debut with the band, he upstages them and Ellie storms off. Damon packs his job in. Mona remains distrustful of Paul and critical of Annabelle. The only one she can relate to is Gordon. She even offers him her wedding ring. Paul's attempts to make Mona realise that Gordon is gay fall on deaf ears, but when she eventually twigs, she takes the news in her stride. Ralph takes an interest in the occult and arranges for a medium, Mrs Bailey, to hold a seance in the bungalow. She appears to contact Edna who is sending betting tips from the grave, but Harry and Ralph back the wrong horse. And Laura postpones the wedding so that she can concentrate on an important deportation case. Jonathan is not amused, but that's nothing new.

July

Christopher sees Mona's house in Kendal as a potential source of income and secretly rents it out to Ralph for a holiday. Ralph makes the mistake of mentioning it to Julia who promptly invites herself along, but when Gordon finds out, he angrily demands the rent money. On his return from the Lakes, Ralph shows Paul and Annabelle his photos and they recognise Mona's house. Discovering that Christopher arranged the whole thing, they suggest that Gordon should stop seeing him.

Damon does some painting work for Jonathan Gordon-Davies, but his standards don't match those of DIY bore, Laura's father Geoff Wright, whose insistence on decorating the house is driving Jonathan to distraction. Mr McGrath fixes up Damon with a job in Ipswich. Damon knows it is a ploy to force him and Debbie apart. Damon says he'll take the job, but will continue to see Debbie. Pat takes over as the band's manager while Terry gets on well with their latest tenant, Alison. Pat thinks she could be a prostitute. Harry decides to try and buy out Pat and Terry and offers them £100 to leave. They reject the money but Pat implies that he might reconsider if the price was right.

Doreen gets a selling job but Billy is annoyed that she has had to buy a new suit for work. On her 40th birthday, Billy, as agreed, doesn't buy her a present but Rod and Kirsty send a huge bunch of flowers which shows up Billy's poverty. Meanwhile Tracy steals a key so that she and Jamie can use the sunbed at the hairdresser's and Rod finally makes his first arrest – an elderly shoplifter. It's not exactly Lord Lucan but it's a start.

August

Bobby gets his first AIDS case at work. The victim, Stan McHugh, wants to keep his job but doubts Bobby's will and ability to fight the prejudice of the rest of the workforce. To prove a point to the personnel officer, Bobby invites Stan to tea in his own home and eventually summons the courage to tell Sheila what he's done.

Pat blows his chances with Fran by trying to double-cross the other two girls. The band split. Gene, a local villain, offers Billy a 'job' as getaway driver on a supermarket raid. It is to take place on the same day as Jonathan and Laura's wedding for which a huge marquee has been erected across the adjoining gardens. Jonathan presents Laura with a wedding gift she'll never forget – a 40ft-high inflatable gorilla – and at the reception Billy talks to as many people as possible in order to establish his alibi before slipping away unnoticed to join the rest of the gang.

The robbery is a bungled affair. Unable to wrench the cash case from the manager, the gang stab him and bundle him into the back of the car where he gets a good look at Billy, the only one not wearing a balaclava. To underline the point, Gene carelessly orders 'Billy' to drive off. Billy roars through the streets until the rest of the gang decide to give up trying to open the case and run off, leaving Billy with his bleeding passenger. Billy wants to run off too but can't leave the manager to die and so he drives him to the nearest hospital and dumps him at the main entrance.

Back home, Billy waits for the police to knock on his door. Gene also anticipates Billy's arrest and, to ensure his silence, mugs Tracy. When she subsequently spots Billy with Gene, Tracy realises something is going on.

September

Harry's offer of £500 is sufficient to make Pat leave the Close. If only the residents had known earlier, they could have had a whip-round. Alison expresses an interest in buying the house. Sinbad pinches tiles off the lawyers' roof and then offers to fix it for them. He tries the same trick with Paul until Geoff Wright catches him out. Billy is behaving more suspiciously than usual and Doreen says that unless he tells her everything, she is leaving. Passing up the opportunity, he chooses to tell her all about his involvement in the robbery. Not unreasonably, she thinks he has ruined Rod's career and says she wishes now she had slept with a dentist. Billy slaps her round the face and she walks out on him. So he needn't have told her after all!

Blissfully unaware that his father is an armed robber, Rod gleefully announces that the police have picked up the rest of the supermarket gang and it will only be a matter of time before they catch up with the driver.

This cheers Billy up no end and it is somehow appropriate when Tracy and Jamie paint her bedroom black. Doreen returns and promises to help Billy with a cover-up. Incriminated by Gene, Billy is taken for questioning and an identity parade is held. Rod thinks Gene has 'grassed' on Billy out of spite and thinks his dad will soon be released, but Doreen, who is privy to the truth, is unable to share his confidence. Yet at the parade, the supermarket manager, Riordan, fails to pick out Billy. He is released, unaware that Riordan is following him.

October

Jamie has been kicked out of his home and Tracy gives him sanctuary in the salubrious surroundings of the Corkhills' garage where they conclude that Billy was somehow involved in the attempted robbery. Just when Billy thinks he has got away with it, Riordan leaves a calling card … and it's not a special offer on pineapple chunks. Doreen overhears him trying to blackmail Billy into robbing his supermarket for him and pleads with Billy not to get involved, but he feels he has no choice.

Having eventually come round to Paul's way of thinking about Mona being put in a home, Annabelle finds somewhere she thinks is suitable. Paul tells Annabelle to be positive about it. Paul is certainly positive – positive that the old bird has to go.

Returning from Ipswich, Damon goes to see Debbie and the pair reaffirm their love for each other. Damon learns that Debbie's mother has left her father and that things are not good at home. He notices a bruise on Debbie's neck which she passes off as a sporting injury but later reveals to be a blow from her father. Damon goes to Debbie's house to face her father. An argument develops which ends with McGrath hitting Damon and throwing him out. Debbie tells Damon he shouldn't have interfered. Poor Damon is at his wits' end. Back home, after arguing with Bobby and Sheila about the relationship, Damon is visited by an apologetic Debbie. Both realise they are isolated from their parents. They decide to go off together. Sheila thinks they'll find things difficult and feels that she and Bobby have let them down.

Jonathan holds a barbecue but nearly blows both the sausages and himself sky high. Returning from work one day, he is dismayed to find handy home repairman Geoff Wright there again. This time he has come to fix a cracked light switch on the landing. After he has left, Laura, alone in the house, flicks the supposedly mended switch and receives a huge electric shock which sends her crashing down the stairs, rendering her unconscious. Visiting his daughter in hospital, Geoff tries to work out what might have caused her fall. His wife Dorothy is certain Laura will recover, but Jonathan is typically pessimistic.

November

The Wrights are put out by the fact that Jonathan has gone back to work with their daughter's life hanging in the balance. Jonathan in turn finds it hard to accept their blind faith that Laura will recover. There is a flash of optimism when Laura's hand moves but the doctor points out that this doesn't necessarily mean her brain is working. It certainly wasn't when she agreed to marry Jonathan.

Just when Terry and Alison seem to have a future together, she announces that she is going back to her husband and won't be buying the house. When Harry learns that the sale has fallen through, he issues Terry with a notice to quit. Jonathan offers to take him in as a lodger – another move which doesn't go down too well with the Wrights. Later Jonathan gets a shock from the faulty landing light switch and realises that Geoff's wiring caused Laura's accident. Despite their continued objections to just about everything, Jonathan bites his sagging bottom lip and refrains from revealing their role in the tragedy.

Billy defies Doreen's wishes and succumbs to Riordan's blackmail threat. Doreen fulfils

her side of the bargain by walking out on him. Jimmy convinces Billy that he knows enough about Riordan's own criminal activities to be able to call his bluff. At their next rendezvous, Billy tries this tactic and sure enough it works. Riordan backs off. Billy thinks Doreen will come back now that everything is sorted, but Doreen insists that she has gone for good.

Harry starts a new job as doorman at the Commonwealth and Empire Club. He revels in the power and takes great delight in ejecting Ralph when he tries to join. Even the SAS would have difficulty getting in past Harry. Barry gets a nasty surprise on discovering that his new girlfriend Ursula is also romantically linked with stuttering psychopath Sizzler. It could be c-c-c-curtains for Barry.

Sheila is cleaning the windows when Tommo, Rod Corkhill's policeman friend, knocks on the door. It is terrible news. Damon has been stabbed to death in York. Outside the mortuary, Sheila finds her grief brings her closer to Debbie. But Bobby blames Debbie for his son's death.

December

In the wake of Damon's murder, Bobby starts drinking heavily and becomes annoyed when Debbie turns up to the vigil. He doesn't want her around. Watching the funeral cortege leave, Jonathan gets upset remembering Laura as she will never be again. At the service, Father Daley describes Damon's life but Barry decides to set the record straight, warts and all.

Billy lands a job fixing fairy lights: he thinks his luck is beginning to change. Rod buys an engagement ring to surprise Kirsty but when he proposes, she deflates him by saying there is no point in getting engaged until they can afford to get married. Tracy and Jamie fall out after he makes a derogatory remark about the absent Doreen. Terry steps in as Father Christmas when his dad Jack is taken ill and, heavy with beard, chats up Jonathan's secretary, Sue Harper. He subsequently asks her out but their evening is ruined by the drunken Jack.

Chrissy and Frank Rogers arrive to rent No. 7 with their children Sammy, Katie and Geoff, known to his friends as 'Growler'. It soon becomes clear that the only thing articulate about Frank is his lorry. The Wrights continue to vent their disapproval of Jonathan's attitude towards Laura. He further upsets them by producing Laura's donor card and saying that, as the next of kin, he is prepared to agree to organ donation. Mona comes to spend Christmas with Paul and Annabelle. Christopher, who has moved in temporarily because he has given his flat to someone with AIDS, cooks the dinner and Mona reveals that the people at the home are trying to kill her. Nobody takes any notice.

1988

Laura dies … Debbie is pregnant … Sheila and Bobby split up and Sheila moves in with the Corkhills … The Collins' house is daubed with anti-gay slogans … Jonathan gets a new girlfriend … Annabelle has an affair … Sheila meets her grandson.

January

Laura is declared brain dead and the doctors want to switch off the artificial ventilator. The Wrights finally accept the idea of organ donation and, following the operation, Laura is allowed to die. Geoff Wright says accusingly that the coroner may be suspicious about Jonathan's role in Laura's death but when Jonathan gives Geoff and Dorothy the wedding rings as a keepsake, the trio become more united in their grief. However, Jonathan realises that he will have to lie at the inquest to save Geoff from the awful truth. Jonathan returns from the funeral in a strange mood. He humiliates Terry at squash before suggesting

that the pair go on a skiing holiday together, even though Terry's only experience of the sport is watching *Ski Sunday*.

Christopher is also off skiing – without Gordon. Paul, who has decided that Christopher is a bad influence, sees this is a chance for Gordon to make new friends. In the meantime, a letter arrives from Mona in which she complains about her treatment at the home. Paul dismisses it, but Annabelle and Gordon take it more seriously.

Chrissy learns that 'Growler' has been skipping school and pushes Frank to see the personnel department at work about the desk job he was promised. Personnel tell him they know nothing about any promise, but Chrissy doesn't intend giving up without a fight. Sheila is doing an Open University course which leads to resentment from Bobby who is angry at the amount of time she devotes to studying. He tries to make amends by having the house re-decorated as a surprise, but the gesture backfires when an emotional Sheila points out that the new decor has removed all traces of Damon's handiwork. Things get worse and after a night out together, Bobby mistakes Sheila's need for emotional closeness for a 'come-on' and forces himself upon her.

February

Billy and Sheila are both missing their nearest and dearest. Billy goes off to Bristol in search of Doreen while Sheila follows a boy, thinking it's Damon. When Billy returns, Tracy asks him awkward questions about the robbery. Billy lies through his teeth, but Tracy isn't wholly convinced. The Corkhills' has more guests than the Adelphi as first Jamie (sacked and nowhere to stay – again), then Jimmy (thrown out by wife Jackie) and finally Jimmy's mistress, Kathy Roach (thrown out by her husband), all take up residence.

Bobby loses his licence after being found guilty of drinking and driving. Waiting anxiously for his return, Sheila is disgusted when he arrives home late and stinking of beer after meeting up with Barry for a reconciliation pint or six in The Swan. Bobby concedes that maybe he's been too hard on Debbie. In the unusual role of peacemaker, Barry hears from Mrs McGrath that Debbie is pregnant and that her father wants her to have an abortion. Barry duly tells Sheila, who offers to help Debbie raise the baby.

Gordon's sudden departure to France presents Paul with the opportunity to ask Christopher to pack his own bags. Gordon is not away for long, however, and comes back in a private ambulance following an accident on his motorbike. Swathed in bandages and unable to move his arms, he does a passable impression of the Invisible Man. Paul is none too happy at having to nurse him and trips to the toilet prove an unforgettable experience for both parties. Eager to escape toilet duty, Paul and Annabelle visit Mona's home where the matron assures them that she is being well cared for. But shortly after arriving back in Liverpool, they find Mona on their doorstep. She has run away from the home.

Chrissy Rogers is on the warpath with a zeal which would have made the Spanish Inquisition look apathetic. Not only is she up in arms about Frank's promised desk job but also regarding the school's complaint about Sammy's new, non-regulation school coat. When Paul confiscates Growler's football, he and his mates take revenge by hoisting a chair on to the roof of No. 8. Ralph has managed to be accepted into the Commonwealth and Empire Club and now he and Harry are competing for the post of entertainment and concert secretary. When a straw poll indicates that Ralph is ahead, Harry unearths an obscure rule which forces Ralph to withdraw.

March

Harry's triumph is short-lived. During his inaugural speech, which is against women being allowed to join, Councillor Redfearn dies and the Third Light Rule is invoked. Consequently, the entire committee has to be re-elected. Club secretary Arthur Parkinson co-opts Harry into helping organise the Commonwealth Day celebration while Ralph gets lumbered with accompanying Arthur's widowed sister, Betty. Ralph does organise the entertainment but inadvertently books a male stripper. The voice of Julia Brogan nobly fills the breach and proceeds to hit the high Cs more often than Captain Cook. On the back of this, Ralph and Harry learn that they have both been elected.

With space at a premium at the Corkhills', Jimmy persuades Billy to convert the garage into an extra bedroom and Bobby breaks the news to Sheila that Debbie has had a miscarriage.

Terry becomes a fully-fledged taxi driver before preparing to set off for Austria with Jonathan. Terry's skiing gear dates back to the days of Sherpa Tenzing and so Barry lends him £300 to buy some new stuff. It certainly works because Terry soon gets off with a Canadian girl named Donna. Her friend, Cheryl Boyanowsky, is interested in Jonathan but, with him still grieving for Laura, Cheryl faces an uphill battle.

Mona reluctantly goes back to the home, but on their next visit Paul and Annabelle notice bruises which the matron attributes to an accident. Paul and Annabelle believe her but Gordon and Christopher resolve to go to the home unannounced to check things out. Their suspicions of ill-treatment are confirmed and they rescue Mona and bring her back to Brookside Close. Paul is still not convinced and, apologising to the matron, announces his intention to send her back. However, when Mona remembers the name of another woman, Molly Harrison, who claimed she was being ill-treated there, Paul agrees to track her down and uncover the truth. Molly Harrison confirms Mona's allegations.

April

While Jimmy finishes building the extension, using only materials advertised on television – *Crimewatch UK* – Rod and Jamie go to London in search of Tracy who was fed up with the crowded house – and indeed with music in general. If she took the weather with her, it would be a gloomy month in the capital. She eventually returns to a showdown between Jimmy and Kathy who, sensing that he is going back to Jackie, throws him out. Only Jimmy could get thrown out of his brother's house by a lodger!

Back from holiday, Jonathan and Terry receive a surprise visit from Cheryl and Donna, the latter eager to see the fleet of taxis Terry had told her he owned. Unfortunately Sue Harper has also called on Terry, only to leave in a huff when she witnesses the warm welcome he gives the girls. Geoff Wright is similarly aggrieved to find them staying with Jonathan and mutters darkly about having another inquest into Laura's death. Jonathan is so angry he nearly blurts out the truth, but Terry manages to stop him in time.

At Chrissy's urging, Frank goes to London to see personnel officer Anne Barber about the Liverpool desk job. She agrees to look into the matter but his prospects of promotion are not improved when he returns to the car park to find that his lorry and its load have been stolen. The police think Frank is implicated in the theft and cast aspersions regarding his relationship with Anne Barber. Frank has to reassure Chrissy that he's innocent. Although the lorry is recovered with its load intact, Frank is charged with serious misconduct. But he manages to hang on to his job.

Immersed in trying to save the apprentices' jobs at Bishop and Wardle's, Bobby proves his commitment by offering to put his wages into the strike fund. He omits to mention this to Sheila. Meanwhile Sheila has a secret of her own: she has been to see a marriage guidance counsellor. When each discovers the other's secret, the resultant bloodshed makes *Reservoir Dogs* look like a vicar's tea party.

May

Sheila and Kathy are old friends and are both in need of cheering up. Kathy suggests a night out at a club – to the fury of Bobby who refuses to babysit Claire. Sheila is determined not to bow to his threats and ropes in Billy as babysitter. When Bobby returns to an empty house, he hurls a suitcase full of Sheila's belongings out on to the Close. He then storms over to the Corkhills' to reclaim Claire, smashing Billy's front door in his anger. Meanwhile Sheila and Kathy have been followed back to Billy's by two men who tried unsuccessfully to chat them up at the club. When the men lurch on to the Close and start making a noise, Bobby comes to confront Sheila and slaps her around the face.

Next morning, at Sheila's request, Barry fixes the Corkhills' front door but Bobby then argues with Billy and breaks it again. Billy plans to retaliate by kicking in the Grants' front door but Kathy manages to calm him down. As the recriminations continue, Sheila makes a bed for herself in the study. Bobby leaves and Sheila puts the house up for sale before taking Claire to Basingstoke.

There is also a lack of harmony at No. 8 where Paul forgets Annabelle's birthday and is horrified to find Gordon and Christopher sleeping together. He can't tolerate such goings-on under his roof. The more liberally-minded Mona wants to give the boys some money so that they can buy a house together, but Paul tries to stop her. Annabelle is so fed up with all the aggravation that she goes to Shrewsbury on a magistrates' course while Mona also escapes to stay with her darling son Teddy. And Harry catches Growler Rogers hanging his gnomes.

June

Egged on by Betty Parkinson, Harry has changed his view about lady members at the club and, following a petticoat protest, her brother Arthur is forced to place the issue of ladies being allowed to join at the top of the agenda at the next committee meeting. There is still scarcely room to swing one of Tracy's mascara brushes at the Corkhills', where Rod decides to play a trick on Jamie who claims to be a very light sleeper. So it comes to pass that Jamie wakes up on a settee outside, his face painted like a clown's. Jamie gets his revenge by borrowing Rod's new leather jacket for an interview, without asking. Kirsty sees condoms in the pocket, immediately assumes they are Rod's and thinks he's seeing someone else.

Gordon and Christopher try out a new club in town but are followed by a gang of 'queer-bashers' when they leave. After a fight, the pair are charged with being involved in a fracas. Meanwhile, in Shrewsbury, Annabelle has met up again with car dealer and fellow magistrate Brian Lawrence. The two become so close that when Paul rings through to tell her about the incident with Gordon and Christopher, she is not in her room.

Sizzler has a job for Barry – he wants him to get to know a woman called Penny Riozzi. After Barry has taken her to a designated hotel room and bedded her in a personal best time, Sizzler strides in brandishing a video of their performance. He proceeds to use it to blackmail Penny in order to seize control of her husband Franco's betting shops.

Growler Rogers borrows a model which Ralph had made of the Close and passes it off as his own work. It ends up on display at school and the press photograph Growler and his pal 'Bumper' Humphries. When Ralph sees the photo, he orders the boys to bring it back and they break into the school to retrieve it. But Growler leaves behind an incriminating scarf.

July

With pressure mounting following the school break-in, Growler runs away from home. Chrissy and Frank are living on their nerves when they hear that a body has been found in Sefton Park lake but their son returns the next day with more of a whimper than a growl. Sister Sammy is worried about having to wear a brace on her teeth and takes her mind off it by joining an animal rights demonstration.

Mona returns unexpectedly from Teddy's, having discovered a dark secret about her son. Penny tells Barry that Franco has sold out to Sizzler, and now she wants the tape back. She is terrified of what Franco might do to her if he finds out about her involvement with Barry and Sizzler. Mistaken for being gay, Jamie is beaten up by the gang who attacked Gordon and Christopher. Paul finds him lying concussed and wonders what he's been up to.

Back from Basingstoke, Sheila discusses broken families with Billy. There seems little hope of a reconciliation with Bobby and, with the house up for sale, Kathy is concerned that Sheila will be left without a roof over her head. She asks Billy if Sheila can stay at the Corkhills'. What's one more? reasons Billy. But Sheila is not sure. A drunken Jimmy, kicked out once more by his wife and kids, turns up and expresses concern about the relationship between Billy and Kathy. When Jimmy sobers up and tries to apologise to Kathy for his behaviour, she tells him to get lost. Reminded of Damon by Growler's disappearance, Sheila goes to the cemetery and finds Karen there too. They talk about Damon and the break-up with Bobby. Karen encourages Sheila to persevere with her Open University course.

August

Terror at No. 8 as Paul and Annabelle receive a succession of threatening phone calls, followed by a brick through the window which injures the visiting Brian Lawrence. A nervous Mona is taken to her new home but soon settles in with her old friend Mrs Harrison and the dapper Gerald Fallon. Paul and Annabelle return to find their home covered in abusive anti-gay slogans. Paul takes another offensive phone call and deliberately provokes the people on the other end. Shortly afterwards, a blazing car is left outside the house. Blaming Paul for baiting the gang, Annabelle arranges another clandestine meeting with Brian. In her absence, the gang come back but are sent packing by the angry residents. It's all too much for Paul who insists that this time Christopher really must move out.

Penny is furious that Barry has done nothing about retrieving the video and reveals that the body in the lake was that of Franco's accountant. She remains strangely attracted to Barry and says that she'll leave Franco and move in with him. When Barry again asks Sizzler for the tape, the stuttering one gives him a job to do. If he does it properly, he can have the tape.

After a series of run-ins with passengers, Terry buys a baseball bat for self-defence. With Jonathan away, Sue visits Terry and stays the night. Later they profess their love for one another. Jonathan and his colleague Sarah Townes fly out to Calgary on a business trip but Jonathan stays on to seek out Cheryl and tracks her down to Vancouver University. He discovers that she has a boyfriend, Deburau, but when she expresses an interest in the Manchester Business School, he realises that all is not yet lost. Cheryl and Duburau are due to be married soon but she admits to her grandfather, Joe, that she is having second thoughts. Acting on Joe's advice, Jonathan interrupts the wedding rehearsal and a delighted Cheryl runs away with him.

September

At her family's holiday cabin up the coast from Vancouver, Cheryl and Jonathan mull over their future. He wants her to come to England but she needs more time to think about it. She does concede that she's not sure about the wedding which, given the manner of her departure, is probably also fairly obvious to Duburau. You don't need to be Claire Rayner to work out that a bride-to-be who flees half-way through her wedding rehearsal has got cold feet. Jonathan sets about warming them up but when the refugees return to face Duburau, he responds by pushing Jonathan into the water. Jonathan flies back to England, unsure of whether Cheryl will follow him. In fact, she's on the next flight.

Sizzler fills Barry in on the job he wants him to do. He wants control of Ma Johnson's gaming arcade and, if she won't play ball, Barry is to kill her dog and deliver its head to her. Forced to choose between Penny and the dog, Barry spares the dog. It's goodbye Penny.

Having been living in a squalid bed-sit,

Sheila finally agrees to move into the Corkhills' extension. To make room for her, Kathy goes to stay at her sister's. Tracy gets a new hairdressing job but takes an instant dislike to the manager, Gerrard. Chrissy angrily discovers that Growler is still sagging off school. He tells her he thinks he's stupid and admits that Ralph made the model. Chrissy takes him to have his eyes tested. Meanwhile Sammy starts work at a supermarket where she befriends a young Asian girl, Nisha Batra.

Tired of being a landlord, Harry decides to put No. 7 up for sale, a fact which Chrissy only discovers when she comes across details of her home at the estate agent's where she works. She and Frank try to buy the house, but Harry rejects their offer. However, scared into thinking he might have trouble selling, he tells them to contact the agent. And the affair between Annabelle and Brian is now in full swing: never have twinset and pearls been ripped off with such passion.

October

Accepted by Manchester Business School, Cheryl moves in with Jonathan. Sheila is having difficulty settling in at the Corkhills' where Jamie is proving a particular nuisance. Barry gently advises him to find somewhere else to live. Tracy gets cornered into going for a drink with Gerrard. He continues to pester her and she finds herself taking it out on Jamie. In need of money, Jamie takes to cleaning windows, in the course of which he succeeds in breaking the Collinses' sink. In a flash of inspiration, he replaces their bathroom suite with the one from the Grants' empty house where he is squatting. But when Barry returns from a trip to Birmingham and switches the water back on, the bathroom is flooded. The prospective buyer, Tom Osborne, is less than impressed.

Two doors down, Chrissy and Frank learn that Harry has turned down their offer on the house and issued them with a notice to quit. But the old devil has met his match in Chrissy and he unknowingly ends up accepting a lower offer from her, one she made anonymously. Chrissy is less successful in her dealings with Mr Jenkins, the pastoral head at Growler's school, who suggests that parental pressure may be at the root of their son's learning problems. He also mentions that Sammy has refused to perform dissections in biology.

Gordon and Christopher split up. Paul's suspicions about his wife are aroused when, after Annabelle has said she is visiting her friend Miriam, the aforementioned Miriam rings asking to speak to her. Annabelle covers up by pretending that she had been out buying Paul a surprise birthday present. She and Brian are looking forward to a weekend of lust but when Paul discovers the hotel booking, he assumes it is Annabelle's surprise birthday present for him. Annabelle has to break the bad news to Brian and, while Paul is out, summons him for a quickie. Sheila spots the pair of them kissing. Annabelle tries to explain, but Sheila doesn't want to get involved.

November

In his new capacity as shop steward, Frank, angry at the state of the drivers' toilets, deliberately blocks the sinks and loos in the executive toilets. Since the management have nothing to go on, he escapes detection and later gets a guarantee that improvements will be made: his guerilla tactics seem to have paid off. Harry boasts to Chrissy that he's sold the house and wants them packed and moved out in good time. To wind Harry up, Frank dresses the whole family up as Arabs and when Harry realises he has been tricked and that the mystery buyers are the Rogers, he stomps off in a huff.

Relieved that Gerrard is away on holiday, Tracy discusses him with workmate Nikki White. They share a mutual loathing for the man. Billy has been seeing Linda, a woman from work, totally unaware that Kathy has also set her sights on him. Julia decides to help Kathy by lying that Doreen is coming home for Christmas. Linda leaves and Sheila

starts to pack.

Annabelle asks Brian to give Gordon a job as a car salesman in his new showroom and, on his first day, Annabelle's car goes in for a service. Gordon wonders why the mechanics are sniggering until he sees 'the boss's bit on the side' scrawled into the dirt on the car and realises the vehicle isn't the only thing getting a service. After spotting Annabelle kissing Brian, Gordon confronts him. He admits they are having an affair and says that he has no intention of stopping.

Terry presents Sue with an engagement ring which she immediately takes off, claiming that she intends to change it. Her behaviour becomes increasingly irrational, especially when she is invited to dinner at Jonathan's, only to rush out of the room on discovering that one of the other guests is her old boyfriend, Martin Howes. Not for the first time in his life, Terry is puzzled, but Sue reassures him that it's him she wants, not Martin.

December

At a surprise party for his mate Tommo, Rod learns that the rest of the force think he's under Kirsty's thumb, so he asserts his independence by going off with sexy WPC Emma Reid. Later, at the station, she returns his trousers. Tracy has to stay late at work and ends up having to fight off the groping Gerrard, the man with more arms than Iraq. Trying to be helpful, Nikki tells him about Tracy's history with Montague, and so at the office Christmas party when Tracy again plays hard to get, he asks her whether she'd respond if he was a geography teacher. Tracy rushes out. When she is subsequently sacked, allegedly for poor timekeeping, she seeks advice from Sheila who tells her to take Gerrard to an industrial tribunal.

Sheila finds a flat, but Julia admits that she lied about Doreen's impending reappearance, whereupon Sheila angrily throws Julia out. Billy tells Sheila she can stay as long as she likes – he's finished with Doreen. The two grow closer and when Julia makes a snide comment about Sheila fancying Billy, Julia again finds herself propelled through the front door. Even by Julia's standards of being about as welcome in most houses as dry rot, this is something of a record.

Sinbad's Christmas scam necessitates joining forces with Barry to sell a supply of cuddly seals, but they turn out to be poisonous and one kills Ralph's dog, Rommel. Thirty have been sold to Harry, who is dressing up as Father Christmas at the club, and so he has to revert to his true persona and snatch the presents back from the children. In the middle of all the furore, he is called to the hospital to be introduced to his new grandson, Tim. The baby achieves the impossible – it puts a smile on the face of Harry Cross.

Sheila also receives a wonderful Christmas present when Debbie calls holding Sheila's grandson, Simon. She hadn't miscarried after all. In an emotional reunion, they talk about the past and their hopes for the future. Billy and Sheila finally cement their friendship with a New Year's Eve kiss. Both realise they are now ready for greater commitment.

Elsewhere, there is a distinct lack of festive cheer. Terry rescues Cheryl from a fire at Jonathan's (she was in the bath at the time) while at No. 8 Brian gives Annabelle a ring for Christmas but Paul finds it and begins to realise what's been going on. Inviting Brian round for Christmas drinks, he confronts them about the affair. They confess, but the snake slithers away, leaving Annabelle to face the music. She too bales out and Paul is left to face a future alone.

1989

Billy and Sheila become an item ... Geoff Rogers is dyslexic ... Paul and Annabelle are reconciled ... The Chois arrive on the Close ... Kirsty calls off her wedding to Rod ... A pregnant Sue marries Terry ... Ralph leaves for Las Vegas ... Sammy hits the bottle ... Cheryl packs her bags.

January

Following an incident where he made an elementary but humiliating mistake on a school banner, Chrissy thinks Geoff must be dyslexic. The school prevaricates but Chrissy won't be placated and she and Frank argue about what he thinks is her obsession over dyslexia. Geoff is put in a special unit, but Chrissy still doesn't think the school is doing enough. She wants to seek private help.

Annabelle, who has returned to an uneasy truce, finishes with Brian after he makes it clear that he doesn't want to get involved in her problems. Paul is angry that Gordon is still working for Brian, but has underestimated his son, who plans to hit Brian where it will hurt him most – in the wallet. Accordingly, Gordon peaks as a salesman by selling Brian's finest cars off at ridiculously low prices. Before Brian, twitching with rage, can sack him, Gordon resigns, satisfied with his work.

Harry becomes the hero of the hour in Betty Parkinson's eyes when he and Ralph outmanoeuvre Arthur to enable ladies to join the Commonwealth and Empire Club. To mark the occasion, Harry proposes to Betty – for a bit of companionship in their old age – but she turns him down. Harry is devastated. Following the fire, Cheryl expects Jonathan to re-decorate but she realises he is reluctant to do so because the decor reminds him of Laura. Finally she persuades him to exorcise the ghost.

After talking to Gerrard's area manager, Tracy is offered a job in Blackburn, but turns it down in favour of a date at the tribunal. And Rod has to explain away the scratches on his back to Kirsty. To show his sincerity, he proposes ... but continues to see Emma. Sheila goes off on one of her regular jaunts to Basingstoke and on her return, Billy tells her he loves her. They go to bed, only to be discovered by a furious Barry. A monumental row ensues.

February

Tracy finishes with Jamie and, unaware of the developments between Sheila and her father, asks Sheila how long she'll be staying. Billy realises he's going to have to tell her. Still pursuing her sexual harassment claim against Gerrard, Tracy hopes that Nikki will act as a witness at the tribunal, but it seems that Nikki is too scared of losing her job. Gerrard menacingly advises Tracy to drop the case. Bored senseless with Kirsty's preparations for the wedding, Rod slopes off to see Emma. When Emma drives him home, Tracy spots them kissing on the doorstep.

A private assessment shows that Geoff has dyslexia. Chrissy takes the report to Mr Jenkins who informs her that nothing can be done until the school receives the state report. Hearing this, she angrily removes Geoff from his class. She starts teaching him at home, only to find it is tougher than she thinks. The moment her back is turned, he skives off to play football. Furthermore, she learns that the Dyslexia Society does not approve of her actions in removing Geoff from school.

With Harry still dejected after Betty's rejection of his charms, Ralph tries to cheer him up by arranging a visit from Kevin, Sally and baby Tim. However, Kevin arrives alone, saying that Sally is suffering from post-natal depression and won't leave the house or let Harry go there. Harry's sense of gloom returns. Mona arrives unannounced at No. 8 and reveals that she is getting married to Gerald Fallon. The news seems to bring Paul and Annabelle back together and, after a frank and emotional scene, they realise how much they love one another. Annabelle's brother, Teddy Harvey, turns up to express his concern about Mona's forthcoming marriage, particularly the effect it will have on her will. Paul impresses Annabelle by embarrassing Teddy into leaving. At the lawyers', after being passed over for a partnership, Jonathan is considering Sarah's suggestion that they set up in practice together. Meanwhile Sue has weightier matters on her mind. She is pregnant, but confides to Cheryl that she can't face telling Terry that the baby isn't his.

March

The problems of dealing with Geoff's specific learning difficulties begin to take their toll on Chrissy who becomes increasingly snappy with all around her. Matters come to a head when Geoff, unable to take any more, storms off and locks himself in the bathroom – the first known case of a teenage boy spending more than five minutes in that particular room. When he emerges, Chrissy concedes defeat and takes him back to school. Frank feels that Chrissy's actions in singling him out have had an adverse effect on the boy, and that is confirmed when he is subjected to name-calling at school and then goes sleepwalking on the Close. Meanwhile Sammy has an admirer, Owen Daniels, but since his first visit to the house ends with him being physically ejected by the neanderthal Frank, Sammy can't be sure whether she'll ever see him again.

Gordon has another car salesman's job and reaches his target of earning £2,000 in ten weeks. He celebrates by going to a casino and, after several drinks, places a bet for the entire £2,000 on one spin of the roulette wheel. He wakes up the following morning with a sore head – £2,000 worse off. Using first threats and then emotional blackmail, Gerrard make a last-ditch attempt to get Tracy to drop her case. But Kirsty convinces her to go through with it and she gets £1,500 damages and costs, plus her job back. Kathy turns up at the Corkhills' battered and bruised. When her soldier son Sean arrives later, it emerges that it was he who had hit her.

While Jonathan and Sarah start poaching clients for their new firm, Sue tells Cheryl that Martin, her former boyfriend, is the father of the baby she's expecting. She considers abortion but can't go through with it. She becomes a byword for irascibility and, during one particularly heated argument, she blurts out to Terry that she is pregnant. Terry is delighted, but only because Sue forgets to mention that he isn't the father. From Cheryl's reaction, Jonathan guesses that Martin is the father and informs Cheryl that if Sue doesn't tell Terry the truth, then he will.

April

Cheryl finds the pressure of living in someone else's house with someone else's secret too much to take and issues Jonathan with an ultimatum – either they move out together or she goes alone. Jonathan and Sarah's first day in business is marred by the realisation that one of the accounts they have been given is about to fold. As they set about finding alternative clients, Jonathan is disturbed to see Sarah looking for legal aid work.

On her first day back at work, Tracy hears one of Gerrard's old customers bad-mouthing her and moaning about his sacking. In true Tracy fashion, she sprays the woman's face with hot water before storming out. Back home, she accuses Sheila of trying to buy her favour and lambastes Billy over his relationship with Sheila. Even though she calms down, Tracy still feels isolated at work and decides to resign. However Antony, her new boss, refuses to accept her notice and instead invites her to take part in a national hairdressing competition at Wembley.

Harry harangues Kevin about why he never sees his grandson, Tim. Kevin tries to explain that Sally is still depressed but Harry can't understand and instead announces a generous endowment policy for the child – on condition that Tim's name is changed from Haynes to Cross. Kevin refuses to accept this blackmail and beats a swift retreat. Mona and Gerald are married but are unable to accept their wedding gift – a night in the honeymoon suite of a local hotel – because they are leaving immediately for Las Vegas. So Paul and Annabelle use the suite to cement their reconciliation. Billy marks his 23rd wedding anniversary by beginning divorce proceedings and Sheila hears that Bobby has been injured in a road accident in Reading. Midway through the auction of the Grants' old house, Frank is gripped by auction fever and ends up buying it.

May

While the Rogers move into No. 5, widower Michael Choi moves into No. 7, along with sister Caroline and his young daughter Jessica. Thinking they are from Japan, with whom Harry is still at war, and fearing a kamikaze attack through the kitchen window, the old soldier promptly sends Ralph to the timber merchants to erect a 6ft-high fence. Before Ralph can go, Harry discovers that not only are the Chois Chinese, but also that Michael is a doctor. Sensing an on-the-spot cure for his many ailments, he orders the fence to be reduced to a more modest 1ft 6in.

As a result of Chrissy's appeal for Geoff's educational needs, he is to receive specialist tuition from a peripatetic teacher. Meanwhile Geoff has a trial for the Liverpool Boys area football team. It goes well, but he is embarrassed by Frank haranguing the referee from the touchline. Chrissy worries that football will interfere with Geoff's schoolwork but Frank is just relieved that the boy has been distracted from the problems of his dyslexia. Geoff makes it for a second trial where he is rejected for being too small. Frank is sick as a parrot but is then over the moon when he hears that Geoff has been offered a trial with Tranmere Rovers. It really is a day of two halves.

At Annabelle's 52nd birthday party, Gordon uncorks a new friendship with a wine merchant named Ian and Paul is pleasantly surprised when the Soldiers', Sailors' and Airmen's Families Association ask him to help out a fellow Burma veteran. As love continues to blossom, Sheila moves from the extension into Billy's room and gets a job as a school dinner lady where she helps a deaf girl pupil. She also discovers that Bobby has cut her maintenance on hearing that she is living with Billy. Terry keeps pressurising Sue into marrying him. This leads to further arguments until she finally gives in. A delighted Terry books the registry office.

Work prevents Kirsty from going on Rod's 21st birthday trip to Blackpool so he invites Emma instead. But then Kirsty manages to change her shift and decides to give Rod a nice surprise by turning up unannounced. Kirsty's surprise is not exactly what she had in mind. Seeing Rod and Emma together, she lashes out before storming off into the night. Later she humiliates Rod in front of his family by returning the wedding gifts and leaving him in no doubt that their relationship is over.

June

After interviewing for potential secretaries, Jonathan and Sarah eventually settle for Coral, although her broad scouse accent offends Jonathan's sensibilities. On returning home, he is once more urged by Cheryl to look at flats and, after an argument over the fact that he has offered to rent his house to Terry and Sue, he eventually agrees to look over a few waterfront properties. While Terry and Sue are trying to choose a name for the baby – 'Martin' springs to mind – Jonathan is delayed on the flat-hunting expedition. Tired of playing second fiddle to his work, Cheryl packs her bags and heads for the airport. Jonathan catches up with her and begs her to stay but she tells him it's all over and jets back to Canada. Selfish Sue worries that Jonathan won't vacate the house now that Cheryl has left him. When she raises the subject at an inopportune moment, he loses his cool and tells her that he knows the true parentage of

her baby. What's more, he threatens to tell Terry. When a carrier firm arrives to remove Cheryl's trunk, Jonathan notices that it is to go to a flat in Manchester. He tracks her down and begs her to give him another chance.

After winning her category at the hairdressing competition, Tracy is promoted to stylist. But there's sad news for Harry who, on a visit to Edna's grave, is alarmed to find that it has been moved, along with half of the cemetery. Out shopping, Michael Choi and a woman named Alison Gregory help an old lady who has collapsed. Despite their attempts to resuscitate her, she dies in hospital. Michael and Alison later go out together, once she has ascertained that Caroline is his sister, not his wife. And Sinbad falls head over ladder in love with Caroline.

Not content with being on the PTA, Chrissy announces her intention to stand as a school governor. The rest of the family are horrified. Frank takes delivery of his Father's Day present from the kids – a huge pile of manure for the garden. And Sinbad ends up well and truly in it.

July

Sinbad's devotion to Caroline knows no bounds and when the magician friend he had booked for Jessica's sixth birthday party does a disappearing act, our resident window cleaner provides emergency entertainment. At least he stops short of producing rabbits from a bucket or a string of chamois leathers from up his sleeve.

Harry is horrified to discover that his friend Arthur Parkinson has been commissioned to carry out the moving of Edna's cemetery. After writing to the Queen and Downing Street, Harry sets about the public humiliation of Arthur and parades outside the Commonwealth and Empire Club wearing a sandwich board proclaiming Arthur to be a grave-robber.

Cheryl forgives Jonathan but makes it clear that she is keeping her Manchester flat which she will use as a work-base. Annabelle tries to help a young offender, Louise Mitchell, who turns up on her doorstep and Gordon has a gay boss in the wine trade, Keith Patterson.

Rod endeavours to get back with Kirsty but learns that she is going out with Tommo. Sheila and Billy are about to set off to Ireland with Claire when they receive the phone call they have been secretly dreading – not the VAT man or the police, but Doreen. She's coming back. Her return causes emotions to run high. Billy wants her to go, but Rod and Tracy want her to stay. When Doreen hears that Billy and Sheila are lovers, she decides to hang around. Sheila tells Billy that if he wants her to stay, he must kick Doreen out. With Tracy as her loyal lieutenant, Doreen sets about winning Billy back and tells him that she will leave only if he says he doesn't love her in front of the kids. Sheila is encouraged by her sister Margaret to fight for Billy but when he fails to evict Doreen, Sheila walks out. Using all her feminine wiles, Doreen tries to lure him into bed, but he manages to resist – just.

August

Escaping Doreen's clutches, Billy rushes to see Sheila just as she, Margaret and Claire are about to board the Irish ferry. Sheila doesn't make it easy for him, but eventually allows him to join them. Realising Billy has chosen Sheila instead of her, Doreen prepares to leave but Tracy urges her to put up more of a fight. So she removes Sheila's and Claire's belongings from the house and changes the lock on the front door. She then tells Tracy the real reason why she left – the supermarket robbery – and both agree that Rod must never find out about Billy's involvement in the raid.

Annabelle finds herself playing host not only to runaway Louise but also to Lana Costello, an American friend of the Fallons. Lana is introduced to Ralph who shows her the sights of Liverpool. The pair get along famously. However Louise is proving quite a handful, never more so than when she discovers a pile of letters from Brian Lawrence. Annabelle immediately destroys them and

Louise promises not to tell Paul. Later she reveals that someone has been touching her at the home.

Sue and Terry get married. With the baby due, Terry decides to cut down his taxi hours and asks a friend, Mick Johnson, to take over his day shift. Stephen Choi, Michael's father, is far from happy to see Alison with his son and tries to split them up by introducing him to family friend Amy Ying. Alison is clearly envious of the interloper and keeps her distance.

Back from Ireland, Sheila listens to a bitter row between Billy and Doreen, during which details of his criminal past emerge. She finishes with him. Doreen hands Tracy a letter to give to Billy, but Tracy has a change of heart, burns the letter and instead explains to Sheila how, after the robbery, Billy drove the stabbed manager to hospital. It's hardly *Hearts of Gold* material, but it's something. Doreen still refuses to leave until Billy tells her he doesn't love her. Finally he tells her, she gets the message and walks sadly off into the sunset.

September

Sue gives birth to baby Daniel. Acting as babysitter, Jonathan mentions to Cheryl that he'd like to become a father too. This does not fit into Cheryl's career plan. She tells him their relationship isn't strong enough for them to have a baby and when he presents her with a GTi, she thinks that he's trying to buy her and makes him take it back. Annabelle realises that it is Louise's brother, Gary, who has been touching her. Paul has never been keen on Louise and when he returns from a trip to London to find her still ensconced in his home and hears about the abuse, he worries that she might compromise him. Louise then threatens to tell Paul about Brian's love letters. Annabelle slaps her.

Sheila and Billy are reunited, as are Michael and Alison. Alison says she's been offered a job in America, whereupon Michael tells her he loves her. She threatens to smile, but the moment quickly passes.

Sammy's relationship with Owen is going through turbulent waters, made rougher when her holiday photos turn out to consist almost entirely of snaps of an Italian gigolo named Luigi. Owen's jealousy becomes unbearable and Sammy throws him out. A couple of nights later, Sammy, Nisha and their friend Ronnie (short for Veronica) Williams sneak out to a club where they get chatted up by two lads called Kav and Tony. The boys drive them back to the Close where Owen is hanging around waiting for Sammy. He makes a grab for her and she screams, alerting the neighbours. Sammy is sent in; Owen is sent packing.

With Ralph and Lana staying with the Fallons, Mick Johnson moves in with Harry. It is only supposed to be a temporary arrange-ment but Harry plays the old invalid, forcing Mick to stay. When Ralph and Lana return, Ralph ends up sleeping on the couch and Harry gives Mick strict instructions to prevent any funny business between Ralph and Lana during the night. Scared of being left on his own, Harry stirs things up by warning Ralph off Lana and confiding to Lana that Ralph's only after her money. His treachery proves in vain as Ralph proposes to Lana. She accepts but shocks him by announcing that they'll live in Las Vegas. Harry looks like being left home alone.

October

Harry and Ralph aren't speaking. Ralph can't wait to get away and suggests to Lana that they bring the wedding forward. Lana tries in vain to act as peacemaker. On the day of departure, Ralph desperately wants Harry to say goodbye but he remains stubborn to the last. Ralph and Lana drive forlornly to the station and their train is just about to pull out of Lime Street when a breathless Harry rushes along the platform to say goodbye. There isn't a dry eye in the station. Even the porters stop work. Although pleased that he swallowed his pride and made the effort to bid farewell to his friend, Harry returns to a lonely bungalow. But

after a committee meeting with his dog, Monty, he decides to allow Mick to stay.

Jonathan feels betrayed on discovering that Cheryl has started using 'the cap' when it has always been him who has taken the precautions. With the incisive brain of a lawyer, he feels she could be trying to tell him something. Stephen Choi is angry to discover that Alison has stayed the night with Michael and tells his son he should be looking for a Chinese wife. The rift grows wider when Stephen learns from Jessica that Michael is planning to go to America with Alison, and Caroline returns from Hong Kong to find that Alison and her daughter Hattie have moved in. Caroline warns Alison of the perils of marrying into a different culture.

After a couple of false starts, Sammy and Owen make up. She then asks him to join Nisha, Ronnie, Kav and Tony on a group night out. Owen is wary of the two lads and has a sneaking feeling that the car they're driving is stolen. He doesn't want to get in, but Sammy persuades him. Soon the car's excessive speed attracts the attention of a police vehicle which gives chase. Tony says the car is stolen so they can't stop. Weaving an ever more erratic course, the car swerves off the road and crashes. Kav and Tony are killed, Ronnie and Nisha escape with concussion and Sammy and Owen are left in comas. Sammy soon comes out of hers but, on hearing that Owen is seriously ill, blames herself.

November

Riddled with guilt about Owen and learning that Nisha has told the police that Kav and Tony were her friends, Sammy hits the bottle with a fervour. Soon she will be able to afford another holiday abroad just by taking back her empties. Owen has come out of his coma but Sammy makes excuses not to visit him. She feels lonely and isolated. Her only friend is a cider bottle. Frank is too wrapped up in his own world to notice that Sammy is drinking or that Katie is being bullied at school by a girl named Bagga, for a report Frank has done on lorry maintenance is being used by management as an excuse to close down the maintenance department and put the work out to tender, leaving Frank none too popular with the workforce.

Paul has mellowed towards Louise and inquires about fostering her but is shocked to learn that his birthday present from her – a wallet – was stolen. He strikes a deal with her. If she will accompany him to the shop and return the wallet, he won't tell the social services. The shop manager gives her a severe lecture, at which she runs away yet again. It transpires that Paul had primed the manager beforehand, but it appears that this plan to teach her a lesson has backfired. She eventually returns, unrepentant, and produces £20 to pay for the stolen wallet. Paul immediately worries where the money has come from.

Sheila applies for a care assistant's job at the deaf school and Billy lands a contract to wire up a wool shop. When the shop owner, Mr Trevor, refrains from paying up, Jimmy decides to hasten settlement by removing the door from the shop. Trevor's sons, Carl and Rob, get the needle and retaliate by wrenching the doors from Billy's car (it was only rust that was holding them on anyway), at which Jimmy attacks the wool supplies in the shop with a fire extinguisher. The feud is rapidly developing into a full-scale vendetta.

December

Sheila awakes to find the living-room windows pasted with paper. Realising that it's not Billy's idea of cut-price, easy-to-maintain curtains, she concludes that it must represent another stage in the vendetta. Billy's perpetual financial problems are compounded when a bill for interim costs on his divorce arrives from Doreen's solicitor. Desperate to be paid by Trevor and seething at the assault on his home, he is persuaded by Jimmy to launch another attack on the wool shop. This time, the pair strip all the electrical fittings which Billy installed, an action which proves too

much for Trevor, who collapses. The sons' response is to arrange for a JCB to be driven on to the Close, dig up the Corkhills' front lawn and deposit it on the garage roof. The sons decide that enough is enough and that the vendetta must stop before someone gets seriously hurt. Shocked to learn about Mr. Trevor's heart attack and by the fact that Jimmy has taken a delivery of jumpers in lieu of half the money he is owed, Billy agrees to wait for his money. But when Barry arrives to collect the money Sheila has been saving for him so that he can buy a second-hand car for Debbie as a Christmas present, he is furious to learn that Sheila has lent the cash to Billy. The two men start laying into each other and have to be prised apart by Jimmy and Terry.

Trying to concentrate on her studies, Cheryl is irritated by Jonathan's baby talk. Hopelessly misreading the situation, he then proposes, to which Cheryl responds by announcing that she's leaving him for good. He takes that as a 'no'. There is another proposal on the Close when Caroline's shifty ex-boyfriend, James Markham, turns up out of the blue and suggests marriage.

Gordon and a colleague, Judith, set about exposing a wine fraud, but in the course of his undercover investigations, he gets arrested. He not only comes up with a convincing explanation but also manages to keep Judith's name out of it, as a result of which she is so grateful that she invites him for a meal. She can't understand why he is unresponsive to her advances – until he points out that he is gay.

At No. 5, Geoff covers up for Katie who tells him that Bagga is trying to force her to steal money. He persuades Katie to talk to one of the teachers, as a result of which Bagga is suspended. Sammy finally gets round to visiting Owen in hospital but is so drunk that she creates a scene and Chrissy has to be summoned to collect her. Chrissy demands to know why she's been drinking but Sammy, worried about the forthcoming inquest, remains defiant. Later Sammy babysits for Michael Choi and helps herself from the drinks cabinet. She gets involved in a row with Alison, who is a scientist, about animal rights and spray-paints the word 'murderer' on the side of her car. Sinbad and Jimmy plant a huge Christmas tree outside the Corkhills', but Harry guesses from a radio bulletin that it is stolen. So the pair have to return the tree to its intended destination – a local children's home.

1990

James Markham is killed in a car crash … The Chois move out … Paul and Annabelle leave the Close … Harry moves to St. Helens … Terry discovers Sue's little secret … Sheila tells Billy that Barry isn't Bobby's son … Jimmy tangles with Joey Godden … Sheila and Billy get married … The Farnhams and Dixons become new neighbours … Little Danny Sullivan is kidnapped.

January

The ill-feeling between Barry and Billy intensifies when Billy discovers that Tracy has been sleeping with Barry at Nikki's flat. Billy accuses her of trying to get back at him because he turned Doreen away. Barry helps Tracy to move out of No. 10. Still upset by Barry's hostility towards her, Sheila also has a tough time at the deaf school where she lets one of the pupils, Melanie, leave for a dental appointment without first checking her story. On hearing this, her boss, Linda Spencer, gives Sheila a dressing-down.

Partly to ease his guilt about the report, Frank joins a workers' co-operative to put in a tender for the maintenance contract. He can't bring himself to tell Chrissy and even when he hints that he'd like to be part of it, she answers with a definite 'no', reminding him that his family responsibilities must come first. This is brought home to him when he finally learns about Sammy's drunken behaviour at the hospital. His boss, Marsland, hints that they are in with a good chance, but Frank doesn't trust him. Frank is thrown into a greater dilemma when Marsland tells him that the post of Assistant Transport Manager is vacant and that he would be Marsland's choice for the job.

Sue is also feeling guilty, but her solution is to try for another baby. Her plans are put on hold, however when baby Danny is rushed to hospital with suspected meningitis. Sinbad is crushed by the presence of James Markham who seems to have everything Sinbad hasn't – class, looks, poise and Caroline. Sinbad's attempts to smarten up his act with smooth business patter end in humiliation and his offer to become Caroline's partner in her jewellery business is firmly rejected. She says James will be taking care of that. Sinbad tries to warn Caroline off James, but without success. He decides to keep an eye on James and his suspicions appear vindicated when he discovers a hoard of video nasties in the boot of James's car. However silver-tongued James manages to talk his way out of it.

February

The co-operative wins the tender at NCT and Frank is offered the post of Assistant Transport Manager, a job which would finally put him behind a desk instead of in a cab. With Chrissy still in the dark about the whole thing, Frank's loyalties are with the men and he rejects the office job. Anyway Chrissy is too busy mobilising the neighbours to fight proposals for a parade of shops near the Close.

Danny Sullivan is released from hospital, while Kathy's son, Sean, turns up at No. 10, having deserted from the army. He is in a dangerous frame of mind and attacks both Sheila and Barry. Sheila urges Kathy to turn him in before he gets in even bigger trouble and, after much agonising, she does so, leaving Sean facing a court martial. Sheila then has another unwelcome visitor in the shape of a woman called Susan Morgan who introduces herself as Bobby's girlfriend. She says she wants to marry him and wants Sheila to agree to a divorce. Then she drops another bombshell: she's pregnant.

Harry is invited to Las Vegas to be best man at Ralph and Lana's wedding. Realising he'll need someone to look after the bungalow – and Monty – in his absence, he persuades Mick to move in again. To compensate for the fiasco of the Christmas tree, Jimmy and Sinbad fix a large satellite dish to the outside of the Corkhills', assuring everyone that it's legitimate. But when the only picture they can get is horse race meetings, they realise that the dish has come from the roof of a betting shop. Angry that nobody is interested in his trip to America, a vengeful Harry reports the Corkhills' satellite dish to the council for lack of planning permission. And, to settle another old score, he does it in the name of Paul Collins!

March

Billy's determination to discover who grassed him up (Paul naturally denies all knowledge) leads to a guilty Harry offering to buy the dish for £50. Still reeling from the request for a divorce – Barry says at least she'll now be free to marry the 'tea-leaf'— a devastated Sheila learns that Bobby has had an operation to have his vasectomy reversed. There is another blow for Billy when Sheila, hit by Bobby's latest demand – for joint custody of Claire, tells him that she doesn't want to marry him. Sheila begins to feel she's losing control. She tells Billy that the courts will claim they're not fit to care for Claire because he's her fancy man with a criminal record and a house full of knock-off stuff. Billy is hurt by this – nobody's ever accused him of being 'fancy'.

Harry is fussing about what to buy Ralph and Lana for a wedding present. Mick suggests a garden gnome. Harry then compiles a list of Dos and Don'ts for Mick which runs to more pages than the Maastricht Treaty. After Harry's departure, Mick's children, Leo and Gemma, visit the bungalow. Gemma is admiring the goldfish in Harry's garden pond when she falls in and her life is only saved by the quick thinking of Geoff Rogers who administers artificial respiration.

Caroline Choi is dismayed to discover that her jewellery is being sold with fake stones. James promises to investigate and sacks one of her outworkers, who then goes to the house to protest her innocence. Caroline wavers but bows to James's pressure. But when she gets a visit from the menacing Dave Smith demanding £5,000 in gambling debts owed by James, she realises that James is up to his neck in it.

Sammy is precious and stoned. Now that she has ditched Mr Woodpecker in favour of Mr Gordon, she is in a permanent alcoholic daze. Things are so bad that Chrissy consults Dr O'Rourke. Owen is confined to a wheelchair following the accident and his feelings are understandably hurt when he realises that Sammy's drinking is caused partly by the fear that she might be stuck with a 'cripple'. After Sammy downs a bottle of gin and wets the bed, Chrissy calls on Dr O'Rourke again. He lends a sympathetic ear. Chrissy promises to return it the next day.

April

A drunken Sammy makes a spectacle of herself at Katie's school concert, but at least it drowns out the sound of Katie's trumpet playing. Chrissy sees Joe O'Rourke at the concert and he makes it clear that they could make sweet music together. He invites her to go kite flying with him – the oldest excuse in the book. Later they go to the cinema. Frank doesn't even notice she's left the house.

Mick is given the runaround by two kids and a dog, the final insult being when Monty goes missing. Mick sets food in a trap, but merely ensnares a tiny kitten, and when Mick suggests a ride around to search for Monty, Leo insists the kitten must come too. The kitten promptly disappears behind the dashboard, forcing Mick to dismantle the entire car. Once he has done so, the kitten reappears – it wasn't trapped in the car at all – and Mick is left with the task of putting it all back together again.

Eager to get pregnant again, Sue continues to leap on Terry with gusto, forcing him to tell Mick he can't do his night shift in the taxi. But trouble is looming when they hear that Jonathan is putting the house up for sale so that he can buy out his business partner Sarah. Jonathan gives Terry first option on the house, along with a lecture about his negative 'working-class attitude'. Terry is furious that Jonathan seems to have forgotten that he promised him a home for ever after he saved Cheryl's life.

Tracy has a new admirer – a young customer named Liam Riley who is so besotted that he comes in for a haircut about three times a week. Tracy is flattered, unlike Barry, whose temper is even shorter than Liam's hair. Sheila remains in a quandary over her relationship with Billy. She is about to leave him for good when she realises how much she has to lose. Instead, in a remarkable U-turn, she agrees to marry him. Over at No. 8, the dreaded Lucy returns and immediately makes life more miserable than usual for Louise.

At the Chois', Michael refuses to give James the £5,000 he desperately needs and when Alison remonstrates with James over his shabby treatment of Caroline, she is hurt in the ensuing struggle. James flees in Caroline's car with the intention of selling it. On the run from Smith and his cohorts, James is killed in a car crash in Aberdeen. The police suspect it was murder. Caroline receives a letter from him, posted just before his death, and concludes that, despite the fact that he had attempted to destroy her business, he did love her really. She decides to leave Liverpool.

May

With Mick growing increasingly flustered at the prospect of Harry returning to a Monty-less bungalow, two lads turn up with what appears to be Monty. The dog certainly looks like Monty, but seems to think its name is Harry! Harry's homecoming proves a traumatic experience. Leo has been rearranging the gnomes and when Harry wakes to find one of the little chaps in his bed, Mick thinks that things can only get better. They don't. Gnomes are missing and broken, ornaments have been moved, the pond is ruined and, worse still, his beloved 'Monty' bites Harry on the nose. When 'Monty' gives birth to pups, it dawns on Harry that the hound is an imposter.

Michael and Alison leave the Close bound for Boston, Massachusetts, and Sinbad installs himself in the house. Stephen Choi appoints him official caretaker and when Chrissy calls with some prospective tenants, she finds Sinbad and Jimmy sipping tea. To deter buyers, who would leave him without a roof over his head, Sinbad lags the hot water tank with kippers. The pair also take the opportunity to order items from the Chois' catalogue – under Michael's name.

Sue is plunged into depression when she discovers she's not pregnant, and starts drinking heavily. Meanwhile Terry proves powerless to prevent a group of drunks from avoiding paying the fare. The last one out of his taxi turns out to be a dummy from Lewis's!

Lucy's sojourn in France has done nothing to improve her demeanour. She is as catty as ever and gets her claws into Louise when the latter accidentally shrinks Lucy's favourite jumper. In an effort to impress her, Louise tells her about Annabelle's affair with Brian Lawrence, but the outcome is that Paul argues with Lucy and feels betrayed by Louise. When Louise then cuts her arm, Lucy suggests it was self-inflicted, a plea for sympathy. Louise then runs away again and is caught stealing from a supermarket. Paul and Annabelle finally decide against adopting her and announce that they are moving to the Lake District.

Liam's pursuit of Tracy continues apace. With no hair left to cut, he takes her for a pizza and tells her he loves her. Tracy tries to cool it down, but he lurks outside the salon awaiting the opportunity to present her with an engraved bracelet. As he is about to lock lips with her, good old Barry arrives on the scene and sends him packing. But Liam is nothing if not persistent and comes back for more, this time armed with a pile of travel brochures and plans for a life together in sunnier climes. In frustration, she blurts out the truth – that she's pregnant. He then throws himself off the roof of a building.

June

Blocking out all thoughts of her pregnancy and Liam's demise, Tracy is pleased to be invited by Antony to become senior stylist in his new shop. Her enthusiasm is tempered when Billy tells her that she won't be able to fulfil her dreams at the salon with a baby to look after. Feeling that everyone is trying to organise her life, she goes off and has an abortion, to the anguish of Barry, the father, and Sheila, who is devastated that Tracy could kill her grandchild. Barry is quick to blame Billy for Tracy's actions.

Colleagues Judith and Gordon are embarrassed after spending the night together and Lucy, who is making a play for Jonathan, wastes no time in winding her brother up. But she hadn't bargained for Gordon's reaction as he sounds off at her, telling her that she doesn't know the first thing about genuine friendship. She is so taken aback that she accepts an offer to manage a restaurant in France and leaves the Close shortly before her parents. Meanwhile Judith gives Gordon a key to her flat so that he can stay whenever he wants. Their embarrassment now gone, they discuss a business partnership.

The new improved Sammy is off the booze and back with Owen. Her happiness is in stark contrast to dad Frank who, worried about the dangerous use of sub-standard engine parts, decides to leave the co-op. Marsland refuses to give him his old job back, causing Chrissy to fear that they will lose the house.

Following a disastrous barbecue which leaves the place looking like a bomb site, Sinbad and Jimmy are evicted by Stephen Choi. Consoling himself in The Swan, Jimmy spots dome-head Joey Godden, the man who murdered brother Frankie, and launches into a frenzied attack. Jimmy is angry at Billy's lack of interest in being revenged on Godden and reminds him of the promise they made at Frankie's funeral. Billy eventually agrees to go and tell Godden to keep his distance but Godden laughs it off, leaving Billy humiliated. Afraid that Sue might get depressed again at not being pregnant, Terry opts to take a sperm test. When he learns that he has a sperm count to match his IQ – low – he is not a happy man.

July

Having discovered that he can't have children, Terry corners Sue and demands to know who Daniel's father is. Her response is weak and he throws her out of the house. She tries to drive away in his taxi but he drags her from the vehicle and roars out of the Close, leaving Sue in a bedraggled heap. On his return, Terry sets about erasing all memories of Sue and Daniel from the house, stripping the wallpaper in Daniel's bedroom and burning Sue's belongings. Barry says Sue got what she deserved and reminds Terry that at least he knew Daniel, albeit for a short time, whereas Barry's baby by Tracy never even lived. Terry wonders who the real father is and the malicious Barry answers that it must be Jonathan, someone whom he has always regarded as stuck-up.

When Jonathan arrives back from a trip to London, Barry can't wait to throw the first punch. In the course of the struggle, Jonathan manages to convince Terry that he isn't Daniel's father. He says it's Martin Howes. Sue eventually admits that Martin is the father but says he doesn't know. She tries to patch things up with Terry, but an embittered Terry responds by snatching Daniel. Sue is terrified that Terry has taken him out of the country and accuses Mick and Barry of a cover-up. Sheila tries to comfort her, but there is a real fear that Terry might have harmed himself and the baby. Terry returns but treats Sue with

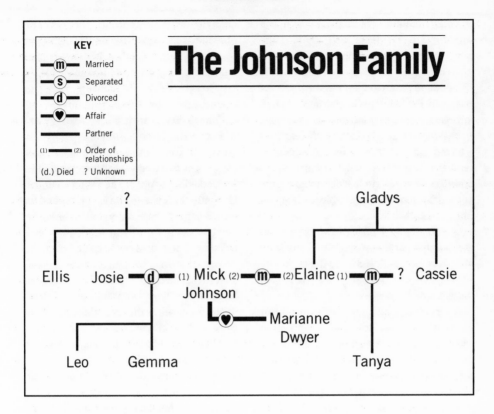

The Johnson Family

KEY
- —m— Married
- —s— Separated
- —d— Divorced
- —♥— Affair
- ——— Partner
- (1)———(2) Order of relationships
- (d.) Died ? Unknown

disdain and cruelly taunts her that he could take Daniel from her at any time.

While Harry is visiting his son Kevin, Mick's estranged wife Josie comes to stay at the bungalow for a few days. Mick doesn't like the way she brings up the kids but they still fancy each other.

Sammy goes to Blackpool on a course for hotel chambermaids, a decision which leaves Owen concerned that they'll drift apart. Katie is not just environment-friendly, they are practically engaged, but when she goes to investigate a polluted river nearby, she falls in and is taken ill. There is no joy for Chrissy either: she learns that she is being made redundant at the estate agent's. Should she accept the receptionist's job which Joe O'Rourke has offered her? Ignoring everyone's wishes, Jimmy goes looking for Godden and ends up in hospital. And with the wedding approaching, Sheila thinks she ought to let Billy in on her little secret – that Barry isn't Bobby's son. Billy is relieved to know that they have both made mistakes in their lives.

August

Billy warns Jimmy to stay away from Godden – one dead brother is enough. All he wants is a quiet wedding, but Jimmy realises the chances of that are slim when he takes delivery of a wreath bearing the message 'Billy and Sheila – R.I.P.' While he tries to hide the wreath from the happy couple, Jimmy discovers another wedding hitch – the cake bears the names 'Mavis and Derek'! With a flair for organisation reminiscent of Frank Spencer, Jimmy also forgets to book the wedding cars, and when Billy's car runs out of petrol, he is left with a last-minute dash to get to the registry office in time. To everyone's surprise Jimmy catches the bouquet – the last thing he caught was a rash – and, carried away by the romance of the moment (plus the need for a bed), he proposes to Kathy, even though they're both still married. Kathy eventually agrees to live with him. Terry steers well clear of the celebrations and files for divorce.

A few days after the wedding, Billy stumbles across Godden's wreath in the extension. He seeks out Godden and asks him to forget the past, but Godden won't play ball. As he drives off, he tries to run Billy over. Billy is forced to agree with Jimmy that Godden is certifiable. Scared witless, Billy decides that it's time to confess his criminal past to Rod in the hope that Rod might be able to lean on Godden 'unofficially'.

Broke and cold, Sinbad takes to sleeping in the Collins' garden shed. When his little primus stove tips over during the night, the shed catches fire, but Sinbad survives to tell the tale.

After splitting up with boyfriend Tony for the umpteenth time, Josie Johnson moves in with Mick. He says he's sick of her using him as a shoulder to cry on and only wants her if she's prepared to make a definite commitment to him. Josie says she's definitely staying this time.

Chrissy gets a job promoting Romanian goats' cheese and Sammy leaves to start permanent hotel work in Blackpool without saying goodbye to the over-protective Owen. Frank lands a job as Assistant Transport Manager with Lichem – at 43, he knows it could be his last chance – but, after going on a spending spree, he is promptly sacked for unsatisfactory references.

September

Frank is convinced that Marsland is to blame for his losing the job, but he learns that Marsland's reference merely commended his tireless commitment as shop steward. Geoff and Katie are appalled to learn that Chrissy has got a new job – as school secretary.

Harry summons Mick to St Helens and tells him that he is planning to stay on there and wants to let the bungalow to Mick on a long-term basis. He sells a delighted Mick the furniture for £100. Max and Patricia Farnham move into No. 7 with son Thomas and live-in nanny Margaret Clemence and Max wastes no time in wrongly accusing Geoff Rogers and Bumper Humphries of theft. Barry offers Terry the chance of easy money by joining him in his latest venture, warehouse parties, but when he realises it is illegal, Terry wants nothing to do with it.

Rod asks DC Jaundrill to have an unfriendly word with Godden and the reply comes back that Godden will forget the feud if the Corkhills stay out of The Swan and British Lion pubs. Billy is living on his nerves and for once is happy to have Barry around the house. Barry revels in Billy's fear when a parcel is delivered, but it turns out to be nothing more sinister than the wedding album. Billy is almost goaded into revealing the truth about Barry's father. Jimmy and Kathy go for a drink in The Swan where they are joined by cousin Don. Suddenly Godden walks in. A fight breaks out, leaving Don dead and Billy, who rushed to the scene, in hospital.

Doreen turns up at the funeral and succeeds in irritating Sheila who tells Billy that the violence must stop. She then overhears Doreen advising Jimmy to 'get Godden before he gets you' and a full-scale row ensues during which Doreen claims she only has to crook her little finger and Billy will come running. Sheila knows better and throws her out. Doreen asks Tracy to come with her to Bristol but Tracy refuses and tells her to keep away. Jimmy and Billy decide to sort Godden out once and for all, but realise they are out of their depth when Frankie's tombstone is 'delivered' through the front door. Billy concludes that the safest place for Sheila, Claire – and himself – is well away from the Close and so the three head for Basingstoke, uncertain as to whether they'll return. As soon as the car goes, Barry determines to end the feud his way. He stakes out Godden's house, shatters the patio door with one blast of a shotgun and, holding the gun to Godden's throat, warns him to keep away from the Corkhills. Godden gets the message.

The Crosbie and Farnham Families

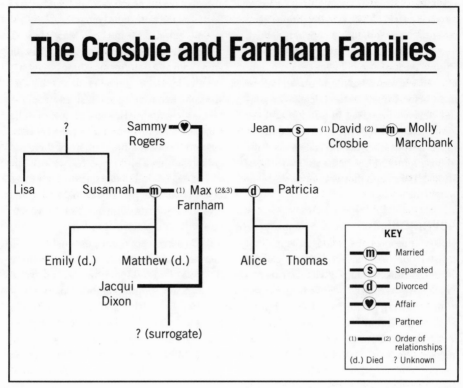

Sammy Rogers ♥ — Susannah ─m─ (1) Max (2&3) Farnham ─d─ Patricia

? — Lisa, Susannah

Jean ─s─ (1) David (2) Crosbie ─m─ Molly Marchbank

(1) Max Farnham ─d─ Patricia

Emily (d.)   Matthew (d.)   Alice   Thomas

Jacqui Dixon

? (surrogate)

KEY

─m─	Married
─s─	Separated
─d─	Divorced
─♥─	Affair
───	Partner
(1)───(2)	Order of relationships
(d.) Died	? Unknown

October

The Dixons – Ron, DD and their children – land on Brookside Close and immediately start to ruffle feathers. The front garden is piled high with junk and hostilities break out with their next-door neighbours, the Farnhams, when Ron Dixon parks his Tesco on wheels – the Moby – in their drive. Nanny Margaret, who gave Ron permission to park there, is caught in the crossfire. Patricia demands an embargo on buying from the Moby – then unknowingly eats a packet of biscuits bought there. The youngest of the Dixon clan, Tony, proceeds to wreak havoc with his mates Togga and Benno while teenager Mike Dixon comes between Sammy and Owen. Owen tries to break up the cosy arrangement by barging into the house and presenting Sammy with a bottle of gin – a timely reminder that she got drunk once in Blackpool and that she still needs him. Sammy is humiliated and finishes with Owen. But

there's a rare bit of good news for Frank who gets a new lorry-driving job.

Leo Johnson runs away from his new school. Mick and Josie think Leo has been subjected to racial abuse but the teacher assures him that Leo is singled out simply because he is brighter than the rest of the class. Tracy and her friend Nikki go on holiday to Rhodes where they make quite an impression on the local waiters. In their absence, Jimmy infuriates Kathy by frittering away all the money needed to pay bills. He solves the problem by pawning all of Billy's furniture, leaving Kathy to return to an empty house. They have a good laugh about it but the smile vanishes from Jimmy's face when she tells him she has had enough of his irresponsible behaviour and leaves him for good.

Sue learns that her mother has been killed in an accident. She regrets all the things she never had a chance to say to her mother and wonders whether the pain she has caused Terry will ever heal. The situation brings them closer together and, to Sue's obvious delight, Terry asks her and Daniel to move back home. The divorce is put on hold. Jonathan goes for an interview with a Japanese firm and meets an attractive woman named Helen. The job – and Helen – are based in London and the combined package proves too good an opportunity to miss. Jonathan offers to sell the house to Terry and Sue for the reduced price of £40,000. The snag is they've got just six weeks to raise the deposit.

November

Chrissy's presence at school is driving Geoff to distraction. Now that she's wearing glasses, she doesn't miss a thing – it's like having two pairs of eyes watching over him. Her latest stunt is to drag him off the football pitch because he should be working on the computer. At home, he accuses her of imposing her own frustrated ambitions on her children and pleads with her to give up the school job.

The Farnhams receive a County Court summons for non-payment of a catalogue bill totalling £1,044.55. They know nothing about it, but suspect that the debts are Josie Johnson's. When they subsequently try to do some early Christmas shopping, they are horrified to find that they are refused credit because their address is blacklisted. Patricia strongly implies that Josie is responsible and receives a kick on the shin for her trouble. Eventually they learn that Jimmy and Sinbad are the culprits.

Mike Dixon plays the big brother at school when he assaults a sixth-former, Sinnott, whom he sees talking to his sister Jacqui. Mike refuses to tell the year head why he attacked Sinnott and is suspended.

While Sue and Terry resume a sexual relationship, Mick is beaten up in the cab, leaving him in hospital with a broken cheekbone, a broken arm and a badly bruised leg. With no money coming in from Mick, Josie accepts a part-time job with her friend Marcia Barrett at the notorious Fourstar Club. When he finds out what she has done, Mick is furious.

Tracy returns from holiday full of plans for going solo as a hairdresser. Antony saves her the time by sacking her after discovering that she has been touting for business from the regular clientele. Her grandmother Julia consoles her with the promise of plenty of new customers but the first batch are three old ladies wanting a blue rinse. Tracy is suitably unimpressed. Julia later returns with three more. Two are practically bald and the luxurious head of hair on the third turns out to be a wig. What's more, they'll only pay 25p a head. When one of them steps on his brand new cassette, Rod orders the whole tribe from the house. Rod and Tommo are on undercover duty at a supermarket but Rod finds it excruciatingly boring until he is chatted up by Diana Spence. She looks familiar and he later realises that she was the pharmacy assistant who sold him spot cream. Rod hopes their relationship might come to a head.

December

Rod and Diana are going out together, but he continues to lie about his real job. He and Tommo nail the supermarket thief, Arthur, who confesses that he's also involved in dog fighting. Mike reveals that his feud with Sinnott dates back to the time when Sinnott slipped Jacqui some acid at a party, an experience which left her sick and frightened.

The only thing about Christmas that Max Farnham is looking forward to is being put in charge of the Round Table sleigh, but that dream evaporates when Jimmy and Sinbad 'borrow' it to pay off the catalogue debts. Rather than let them discover that the coveted sleigh has gone, Max is forced to take his Table colleagues out to dinner. He is so relieved when it magically reappears that this time he tethers it to a lamp-post.

Still off sick, Mick catches a burglar trying to break into the children's bedroom, chases him and knocks him unconscious. Mick feels his actions were totally justifiable and is stunned to learn that the burglar is threatening to prosecute him for using 'undue force' in defending his property.

Barry offers to lend Terry and Sue the £4,000 they need for the deposit on the mortgage. After much deliberation, they accept, but only on their terms. Sue gets a job as a trainee legal executive but Terry's dad has been sacked from his traditional role as Santa and replaced by a robot. Having made a tidy profit from the first one, Barry arranges another warehouse rave, but he double-crosses his backers, Ricky and Kenny Fisher, and escapes with the profits, including their cut. The Fishers go looking for Barry and, mistaking Sue for his wife, kidnap her and Daniel as down-payment. Barry successfully negotiates their release but the Fishers exact further revenge by locking Barry inside a meat freezer. He is finally hauled out semi-conscious by Matty and Terry, having spent Christmas Day cooped up with a stack of frozen turkeys. Barry is not one to forgive and forget. Discharging himself from hospital, he drives to London, plants his shotgun in Ricky Fisher's car and tips off the police. He returns to the Close in high spirits.

The Dixons hold a New Year's Eve fancy dress party for neighbours and friends. Against their better judgement, the Farnhams attend but are mistaken for Princess Diana and a bouncer. In the middle of the celebrations, Mike returns home, having had a bad trip on drugs. Furious at his hypocrisy, Jacqui hides him upstairs.

1991

Mick is acquitted of assault ... Ron builds a fence of doors between his house and the Farnhams' ... Geoff joins Torquay United ... Jimmy goes on an armed robbery to stitch up Joey Godden ... Sue and Daniel fall to their deaths ... On Sammy and Owen's wedding day, Chrissy leaves home ... Rod's wedding day also ends in disaster ... Margaret declares her love for Father Derek O'Farrell.

January

Julia is spitting blood. The last time she saw Jack Sullivan and Ron Dixon's dad, Cyril, they were at each other's throats, fighting over her at the New Year's Eve party. Now they seem to be the best of friends. So she is pleased when her appearance sparks off another clash between the two rivals which ends with Terry carting Jack off and Cyril claiming the prize. But before she's had a chance to 'consume' the relationship, Cyril has disappeared, leaving a note which says simply 'gone travelling'.

Jacqui learns from Mike's friend, Carl Crawford, that Sinnott spiked Mike's drink with acid. Mike and Jacqui lay a trap for Sinnott. She buys two tabs from Sinnott but just as she is handing them to Mike, the police swoop. Jacqui fears that news that she's involved with drugs could wreck her blossoming swimming career. Mike and Carl try again by spiking Sinnott's cola, a move which leads to Sinnott throwing himself through a window. Although seriously injured, Sinnott is well enough to be expelled.

Ron has always dreamed of a string of Dixons shops in the High Street (until Jacqui points out that it's already been done) so when he hears about the new shopping parade, he puts his name down for one of the shops.

The Dixon and Rogers Families

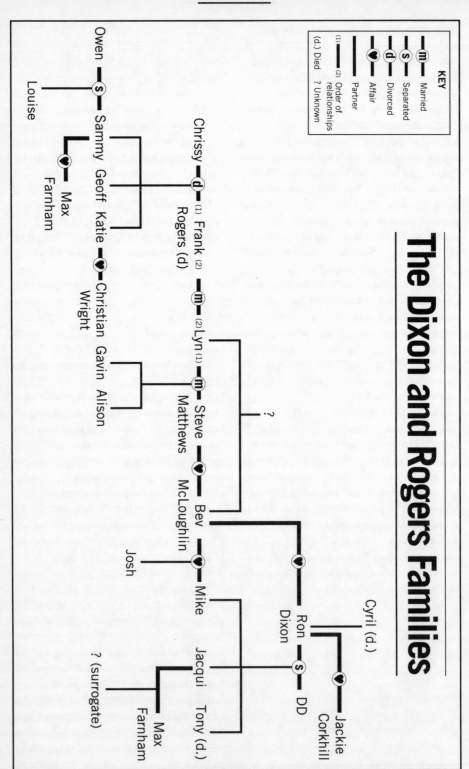

KEY

m	Married
s	Separated
d	Divorced
♥	Affair
	Partner
(1)	Order of relationships
(2)	
(d.)	Died
?	Unknown

Sammy has been on a hotel management course and returns with a new man in her life, but she's keeping the family in suspense. At least they know now that it won't be the manager of the local off-licence.

Mick and Josie return from spending Christmas in Cardiff to be greeted with a £2,500 bill for furniture bought on the store card. Mick blows his top and then learns that he is being charged for the assault on the burglar.

Preparing for an interview at the Electricity Board, Max panics when his shirt isn't ready because Margaret, fed up with being imposed upon, is on a work-to-rule. He is forced to go out and buy another one. Margaret threatens to quit unless her conditions of employment improve, but when Max gets the job (which pays £3,000 more), he and Patricia realise they can give Margaret the rise she wants. They opt to spend more time together as a family but their first evening out ends with them coming home to a delivery of ten pizzas, courtesy of Tony, Togga and Benno.

Rod and Tommo bust the dog fight, enabling Rod to tell Diana that he is a policeman and not a trainee supermarket manager. But her reaction is one of anger that he could have lied to her for so long. What else has he lied about?

February

Grounded by her parents following the drugs bust, Jacqui pleads to be allowed an hour's swimming training. DD relents but when Ron goes to collect her from the pool, he discovers she's gone to a party instead. She is so cocky when he confronts her that he slaps her face. DD is horrified. Mike and Jacqui are later given a caution for the possession of drugs.

Max and Patricia fear Thomas will pick up Margaret's Oldham accent or, worse still, sound like a character from the TV soap *Meadowcroft Park*. As the guerrilla war with Tony and his pals escalates, Max finds water-filled plastic cups on the roof of his Volvo and two bags of cement on the drive and Patricia takes delivery of 15 identical Valentine's cards.

Geoff Rogers goes on a date with beautiful classmate Paula Heneghan, but Sammy is still being coy about her new boyfriend, Tim Derby, until Frank spots him giving her a lift home and realises how old he is. A defiant Sammy points out that Tim is 39, but Frank is incensed. Reminiscing about the past, Chrissy tells her old student friend Gina about the near-miss with Dr O'Rourke and worries that Sammy will make the same mistake as her and marry too soon. On Geoff's second date with Paula, she gets drunk and becomes amorous on the doorstep whereupon her irate father appears and chases Geoff off. The next day, Mr Heneghan barges into No. 5, grabs Geoff and accuses him of taking advantage of his daughter. Remaining calm and rational, Frank head butts him. While Heneghan bans Geoff from seeing Paula again, Sammy and Tim plan a romantic week away in Nottingham.

Terry and Sue legally become home owners and Terry marks the occasion by planting a tree. To fit Sue's personality, he chooses a weeping variety with a tough bark. Although his solicitor, McGinn, advises a guilty plea with mitigation, Mick pleads not guilty and elects for trial by jury. McGinn points out the danger of racial prejudice in the jury. Meanwhile Josie, relishing the prospect of being her own boss, decides to set up a market stall with Marcia. When Rod is attacked while enjoying a quiet, off-duty drink, Tracy meets his handsome colleague, Mark Potter.

March

Geoff's apology to Roy Heneghan ends with the latter hurling a bucket of water over him. Frank is still brooding about Sammy, particularly as she has been staying at Tim's house. When she stays out for another night, he starts off about Tim's age again. Chrissy points out to Sammy that she's only 17 but Sammy reminds her mother that she was only 17 when she started sleeping with Frank. A disgusted Frank can't believe Chrissy has told their daughter such intimate details and this results in another huge row between husband and wife. Sammy prepares to go out again, but Frank says that if she sets one foot over the doorway, she's in trouble. Sammy points out that she isn't going to make the same mistake they did – that of having to get married. Katie overhears this and is upset. While Chrissy has some explaining to do, Sammy leaves home and moves in with Tim. Frank follows the lovers to the hotel where they work and demands his daughter back. He warns Tim that if he breaks his daughter's heart, he'll break him!

Tony, Togga and Benno rig the Farnhams' shed so that it will fall down when the door is opened. Margaret hears a noise and rattles the door of the shed to check that it's locked. As she does so, the shed falls to pieces. Patricia hides Easter eggs for Matthew and Emily (Max's children from his first marriage) and Thomas in the garden, but Tony is wise to this and digs them up. Max is forced to buy more from the Moby, but Ron graciously lets him have them 'on the house'.

With the court case looming, the other cab drivers have a whip-round for Mick and raise £300. Mick is suitably humbled. Nikki is working for Tracy but her attitude leaves a lot to be desired. She even makes Tracy look polite. After she loses Tracy yet another customer, she is sacked. Barry tries to rekindle his romance with Tracy, but she tells him she is going out with Mark. Barry is miffed. Terry and Sue visit a consultant who, after listening to their colourful history, informs them that they may be able to have another child. The atmosphere between Sue and Barry is reaching boiling point. She tries talking openly to him in the hope that he will understand, but he continues taking pot-shots at her reputation. Admittedly it's a pretty big target. When Terry returns, she tells him about the argument and says she can't handle having Barry in the house.

April

Patricia and Josie argue when Josie commandeers Margaret to help with party packs for her market stall. As the quarrel intensifies, Patricia kicks Josie on the shins. The scores are even. Jimmy is flogging children's clothes and tempts Josie to buy some for the stall. She pays for them by taking Mick's collection money. Terry speaks up for Mick in court and Mick is found not guilty. Despite the verdict, Mick is mixed up – he didn't think he should have been charged in the first place – and smashes a glass against the wall at his celebration party. His mood darkens further when he learns that Josie has spent the cab money.

Max realises that his new job is a mistake and hands in his notice. While Patricia is polishing up her advertising campaign for Kleen-Sheen impregnated mops, Max is putting up new kitchen units. He receives help from an unexpected quarter when Keiran, Margaret's ex-boyfriend, shows up. Margaret is less than thrilled to see him again. When they are left alone, he makes a pass at her and she screams at him to go. Max has dumped the old kitchen units at the front of the house. A council lorry comes to collect the rubbish and the driver asks Max what he wants moving. Max tells him the whole lot, at which the men also remove a pile of the Dixons' stuff. Realising what has happened, Max pledges Margaret to silence. Ron doesn't take long to put two and two together and storms round for a showdown with Max who challenges him to prove it. After a scuffle, Max pushes Ron to the floor. Ron vows that from now on the Dixons will have nothing more to do with the Farnhams and, to make his point, he builds a barrier of garish old doors between the two houses – Ron's answer to the Berlin Wall.

May

Max doesn't go over the top about the wall and merely suggests putting up a trellis on his side, while Patricia's mind is preoccupied with a job she has been offered in London. Max isn't keen on her taking it, but, as the sole breadwinner at the moment, she feels she has the right to choose. She accepts it on a month's trial, commuting home at weekends. When his ex-wife Susannah rings and says he's got to have Matthew and Emily, Max is stuck at home looking after three children. He can't wait to find work and phones his Round Table colleague, Geoffrey Fletcher, fishing for an opening.

Nikki and Tommo move into the Corkhills' and Mark Potter becomes a frequent visitor, to the discomfort of Rod who thinks there's something odd about him. His suspicions are confirmed when he witnesses Mark inflicting unnecessary pain on a small boy he caught trying to break into his car. Mark just shrugs it off. Predictably, Barry also dislikes Mark and takes great satisfaction in scratching his keys down the side of Mark's car. Convinced that Barry is responsible, Mark starts putting the squeeze on him and their confrontation ends in a vicious fight in front of Tracy. The brawl somewhat overshadows Rod's engagement to Diana.

Terry's sperm tests confirm that he is now fertile but Sue suddenly decides that she is enjoying herself at work too much and wants to wait before they try for another baby. Terry can't believe what he's hearing and when Sue suggests they use contraception, he says from now on he's going to use the best form of contraception in the world – he's sleeping on the couch!

Sammy invites Frank and Chrissy round to Tim's for a meal, but Frank vows there's no way he's setting foot inside Tim's house, so Chrissy, aware that she could lose her daughter for ever, says she'll go alone. Frank backs down at the last minute but makes no attempt to be polite and the evening degenerates into a shouting match between the two men. Frank doesn't even wait for the cheese and biscuits and attempts to drag Sammy home. But she chooses to stay with Tim. Following an awkward meal out with Tim's children – Chloe and Adam – Sammy is shocked to learn that Tim has to go away for three weeks.

Geoff is distraught at being told that Tranmere Rovers aren't taking him on. Frank rips out the Tranmere sticker from his car and cruelly asks Chrissy whether she's satisfied now because she never wanted Geoff to make a career in football. Geoff sits in the stand crying, looking out on the pitch where he dreamed he would be playing.

June

A distraught Geoff walks out of his exams – he can't see the point. Tim finishes with Sammy and tells her to 'go home to daddy'. Sammy refuses to believe that it's over but on her 18th birthday he throws her out of the house. He then drives her home and dumps her stuff on the pavement. Sammy tries to explain the incident away as just a bit of a tiff and goes round to his house, only to discover that he's changed all the locks. When he won't talk to her, she starts ranting and raving on the doorstep so he opens the door and hurls a bowl of water over her. Unwilling to take the hint, she calls on him again and this time throws a brick through his window. Chances of a reconciliation look slim.

Mark goes round to see Tracy and demands to know what Barry means to her. His mood turns ugly and he tries to rape her. In self-defence, she grabs a pair of hairdressing scissors, stabs him in the arm and charges £3.50. In the station locker room, Rod strongly advises Mark to get out of the force, and he applies for a transfer.

DD has forgotten to buy Ron an anniversary present and asks Jimmy if he could get her a garden ornament. Jimmy appears with a huge stone lion but Sinbad recognises it as the one from the orphanage. Jimmy has to take it back but in the course of doing so is arrested for theft. Jimmy is feeling particularly down: he has just learned second-hand that his daughter Lindsey is getting married. Jimmy knows that he is about as welcome at the wedding as the Vice Squad.

Never short of confidence, Mike Dixon reckons he's got what it takes to make it in the music world. He's certainly more than capable of blowing his own trumpet. His band auditions for a new singer and he is bowled over by one of the applicants, a girl named Tina. Just as he is about to move in on her, his old enemy Sinnott walks in. He is Tina's boyfriend. The two rivals end up challenging each other to a daredevil car race.

Barry is the new owner of the shops. While waiting at the site, he meets Sue and her friend from work, Fran Pearson. Later, Fran tells Sue that she fancies him. Sue says she hates Barry – and he knows it.

July

In the race with Sinnott, Mike's car crashes and he is pulled from the wreckage. He goes home and tries to pass off his injuries as the result of a fight but when he passes blood and faints, Ron takes him to the hospital. Sinnott visits him there and they make a truce.

DD hates having to cover for her friend Maria Benson who is having an affair. Ron is also placed in an awkward position as he is pals with Maria's husband, Charlie. With Max still unable to find work, Patricia has gone to London, ready to accept the job on a permanent basis. It will mean the whole family uprooting to the capital. Finally Geoffrey manages to fix him up with a job and he has to make a frantic dash to London to reach Patricia before she accepts. In fact he is too late – she has already said yes – but she turns down the job when she hears his good news. Margaret has struck up a friendship with DD's brother, Father Derek O' Farrell, and, in a bid to bring peace to the community, they set about dismantling Ron's wall of doors.

Ron's dad Cyril is back on the scene, to the delight of Julia who is contemplating marriage. But she finds out that Cyril has been somewhat economical with the truth and is in fact a bigamist – three times over.

Geoff's soccer career is resurrected when he gets a YTS placement with Torquay United. Out on the town with Margaret, Sammy spots Owen in a pub with a girl called Grace. The worse for wear, she tries to win Owen back with a kiss, whereupon Grace hurls her drink over the sozzled Sammy.

In the wake of being snubbed by his own daughter, Jimmy is vowing to look after number one from now on. His criminal activities become more daring and he takes part in a smash-and-grab raid on a jeweller's. He's got the taste for easy money. Diana is alone in the house when Arthur, the dog fight man, thirsting for Rod's blood, muscles in and holds a knife to her throat. Alerted by Julia, Rod summons back-up and the fleeing Arthur is apprehended in the Dixons' pond.

After work, Sue goes for a drink with Fran but ends up alone with another colleague, Graeme Curtis. He explains that he doesn't have much luck with women, but Sue is understanding and talks to him like a friend. Graeme gives her a lift home – a scene witnessed by Barry who, in his own charming way, accuses her of 'getting it' off someone else. He tells her that she need not have looked any further than him and forces a kiss on her. Sue snaps that he'll never come between her and Terry.

August

For the Sullivans' wedding anniversary, Sue cooks Terry a romantic meal – i.e. something with chips. But Terry still can't understand Sue's sudden change of heart about trying for another baby and the evening ends in a blazing row with Terry storming out after smashing all the plates. Sue senses that it is more than just his way of getting out of the washing-up. In need of comfort, Sue gets it from an unexpected source – Barry. They finish up having sex on the sofa. The next day, he brings her chocolates but, riddled with guilt, she punches the box with her fists, making a nasty mess of the strawberry surprise. Later she tells Terry she wants another baby after all.

When Ron expresses his disapproval of Jacqui's new black boyfriend, Keith Rooney, she calls him a racist. And Diana's father, Freddie Spence, is equally angry at his daughter's choice of partner. Discovering that Rod is a policeman, he tells her that if she doesn't ditch Rod, she's no daughter of his. Explaining the outburst, Diana reveals that her mum ran off with a policeman when she was four and since then he's hated all policemen.

Mick's no-good brother Ellis turns up out of the blue and soon proves a disruptive influence, both on his ex-girlfriend Marcia's flourishing relationship with Sinbad and on Mick's with Josie. Indeed within a few days of his arrival, Josie, who seems to pack her bags more often than Judith Chalmers, walks out on Mick and the kids and goes back to Tony. No sooner has she gone than the police come round to investigate the sale of stolen goods on Josie's stall.

Chrissy urges Frank to live a little, to 'come out of the stone age', and they have a fearful row which culminates in her telling him about Dr O'Rourke. Shattered by the revelation, Frank rejects the offer of marriage guidance and orders Chrissy to leave. She and Katie go to stay with Gina.

With the help of his mate Vinny, Jimmy is let in on a big job – an armed raid on a nightclub. Jimmy is to drive the getaway car but is horrified to see that one of the other gang members is Joey Godden. Jimmy has the engine running outside the club when the masked Godden rushes towards him clutching the bags of cash, hotly pursued by two bouncers. Godden screams for Jimmy to open the door but instead Jimmy's hand reaches across to lock it. He drives off, leaving Godden at the mercy of the bouncers.

September

Frank is uncharacteristically contrite. He is even pleased that Sammy is seeing Owen again. Eventually Chrissy realises that the situation is having a traumatic effect on Katie

and the pair return home to a tearful reunion. Frank thinks everything will now get back to normal but Chrissy tells him she certainly hasn't abandoned her ambitions: she doesn't want to be stuck in a rut.

Scared and lying low after the bungled robbery, Jimmy calls on Jackie for sympathy. Later Vinny pays him a visit and says that Jimmy's actions cost him £100,000. He adds that the word is out that Jimmy Corkhill is a liability and that he won't ever be taken on a job again.

When Patricia refuses to accompany Max to an important Round Table do, the resourceful Geoffrey Fletcher recruits Max's ex-wife Susannah to play Mrs Farnham for the evening. Patricia need never know. Feeling guilty at letting Max and the Fletchers down, Patricia suggests making amends with a barbecue. All the neighbours are invited too – even Ron – and it is he who captures the highlight of the evening on Geoffrey's camcorder when Susannah surprises Max with a lusty kiss.

Margaret and Derek are spending a lot of time in each other's company, to the concern of both DD (his sister) and Father Thornton (his boss). When Margaret turns up at Derek's youth club, he too tells her that they can't carry on meeting like this and that their friendship is dangerous.

Mick tells Terry he's packing in the cabs, Fran and Barry grow closer and Graeme Curtis is becoming alarmingly obsessed with Sue. Besides insisting on giving her lifts to and from work, he starts sending her flowers. Sue orders him to stop bothering her – or he'll regret it. Undeterred, he steals her scarf while she is out at lunch and takes a photo of her, Terry and Daniel from her desk. He then carefully cuts Terry and Daniel out of the photo, leaving only Sue. When he continues to hassle her, Sue humiliates him in front of the whole office before storming out. When she has gone, Graeme describes it as a 'lovers' tiff'. Then Fran discovers the photo…

October

Sue confronts Graeme again and calls him a creep, adding that unless he stops pestering her, she'll inform the senior partners about his behaviour. When Barry collects Fran from work, she tells him about the photo. To escape from Graeme, Sue takes a day off work, but he comes round with another bouquet of flowers and says he must talk to her. Reluctantly she agrees to meet him at the new parade of shops. Individually, Barry and Terry see Sue talking to Graeme outside the shops. Terry jumps to the conclusion that they're having an affair and storms off. While her back is turned, Daniel somehow manages to climb to the top of the scaffolding alongside the shops. Sue climbs up to rescue him but then realises that someone else is up there too. The mystery person grabs Sue but, as she backs away in pain with Daniel in her arms, she and Daniel plunge over the side and fall to their deaths on the concrete below.

Unaware of the tragedy, Terry walks on to the Close, heavily hung-over. He is unable to account for his movements and is taken in for questioning by DS Kent who reveals that Sue was pregnant. And Terry was the father. When Graeme turns up at the funeral, Terry erupts and has to be pulled off him. Barry forces Fran to tell the police about the cut-up photo, as a result of which Graeme is charged with the murders of Sue and Daniel.

Elsewhere, Jacqui demands a pair of expensive new trainers but DD says that all the spare money they've got is going towards the new shop. DD buys her a cheap pair but Jacqui refuses to wear them. Mike's first gig with Tina at the Polytechnic ends in uproar when, given something to calm her nerves by Sinnott, she starts stripping off on stage. After postponing the opening in the wake of the double death, Ron declares the Trading Post open for business. But he disowns dad Cyril after discovering his bigamous secret.

Feeling left out by Susannah's frequent visits, Patricia tries to lay down a few ground rules to Susannah about when she can see Max. Susannah hits back, telling Patricia she could win Max back any time she wants. Sammy tells Owen that she's pregnant. At first, he accuses her of doing it deliberately in order to trap him but eventually says he'll marry her and be a proper father.

November

Frank is chuffed to bits about Sammy and Owen but Chrissy is appalled. It is history repeating itself. She has been offered a place at teacher training college and intends leaving the school – and Frank – to take it. When Katie finds out, Chrissy tries to explain her reasons for going but asks her not to tell her father because it's something she must do herself. Frank accompanies Owen on his stag night and gives him the benefit of his wisdom on how to manage a successful marriage. This is rather like Sinbad addressing weight-watchers. When they get back, Chrissy tells Owen that it's not too late to back out. However, he goes through with it – and so does Chrissy. For while everyone else is enjoying themselves at the reception, Chrissy is upstairs packing her things. She takes off her wedding ring, places it on the bedside table and quietly slips out of the house.

Fran tells Barry she knows he slept with Sue and wonders what Terry would do if he knew. Mike appears carrying an expensive new keyboard which he claims is a friend's. Ron sub-lets the Moby to Jimmy, who persuades him to offer Jackie a job at the Trading Post. Julia is also interested in the vacancy and, unable to choose between them, Ron takes them both on. Jackie asks Mike to mind the shop for five minutes and, while she is out, he helps himself to £100 from the till.

Harry has put the bungalow up for sale. Barbara Harrison, the new deputy head at Brookside Comprehensive, and her husband John are the prospective buyers, leaving Mick fearful for his future. He knows that Leo and Gemma don't want to move. Father Thornton warns Derek about his 'relationship' with

Margaret and tells him that he may have to be transferred to another parish.

Diana goes for a job at a department store, but doesn't get it because she is illiterate. She confesses to Nikki but dreads telling Rod for fear that he'll leave her. Meanwhile Rod is unofficially spending a lot of time at an amusement arcade where he was recently on undercover surveillance. He is intrigued by a teenage lad, Craig, and eventually discovers that he is a rent boy. Rod is so obsessed with the case that he is unsympathetic when Diana breaks the news to him about her illiteracy. Deeply hurt, she goes back to her father. But Rod wins her round – she manages to write 'I love you' – and even her dad agrees to attend the wedding.

December

Rod's wedding day preparations are interrupted by a phone call from Craig. He's about to be carted off to Amsterdam by his pimp, Eddie, and wants Rod to come to Lime Street station to rescue him. Saying he'll only be gone an hour, Rod rushes to the scene but is beaten up in the toilets by Eddie. Diana is left stranded at the altar while Rod is lying in hospital, battered and bruised. He pleads with Tommo to keep quiet about Craig, but a security video from the arcade shows Rod handing money to Craig and he is suspended from the force for two months on full pay. Despite the hiccup at church, Diana stands by her man.

The Harrisons inform a relieved Mick that they've pulled out of buying the bungalow and are buying the Sullivans' house instead. The second shop unit on Brookside Parade has been let to hairdressing guru Kenny Roberts who installs Angela Lambert as manageress. Barry's obvious attraction to Angela leaves Fran feeling jealous.

While Julia is out the back at the Trading Post, Mike, who is heavily in debt, sneaks another £30 from the till. When Ron cashes up, he realises that somebody has been thieving from him and immediately challenges Jackie

and Julia. Both women are understandably furious and march out, leaving Ron to manage the shop single-handedly. Eventually he is forced to eat humble pie – but only because it's past its sell-by date – and apologise to Jackie and Julia. They decide to give Ron another chance. Julia then catches Mike taking £5 from the till but he offers a convincing explanation.

To take her mind off Derek, Max and Patricia fix Margaret up with a blind date – David, a young lad from the Round Table. King Arthur himself wouldn't have impressed Margaret who ends up being uncommonly rude to the poor boy. She continues her pursuit of Derek and the pair declare their love for each other. Already worried about a lump on her breast, Patricia goes to London for a presentation. It turns out to be an embarrassing disaster and, in need of comfort, she phones Max from her hotel room. To her horror, Susannah answers the phone. Back in Liverpool, Max assures Patricia that he slept on the sofa but she throws him out on Christmas Day, along with Susannah's expensive present to him. Max pleads to be allowed back, but Patricia slams the door in his face. He returns later with Susannah so that she can tell Patricia the truth, but Susannah is deliberately vague and a huge argument erupts on the doorstep. The year ends with the Harrisons moving into No. 9 and Ron discovering the body of his dad Cyril who has had a massive heart attack.

1992

Patricia has breast cancer ... Graeme Curtis is found guilty of the double murder and kills himself ... Barry learns who his real father is and confesses that he killed Sue and Daniel ... Sammy rejects her baby ... Rod and Diana marry at last ... Margaret and Derek get engaged ... The Johnsons battle against racism ... Diana accuses Peter Harrison of rape

January

Patricia is diagnosed as having breast cancer. She wants Max back and together they prepare for her operation. Afterwards, she tells him she's going to make a will. Julia accuses Mike of thieving from the till, but he twists her words, saying she is confused after Cyril's death. Mike pretends to lays a trap for the thief and gets Jacqui to put a marked fiver in the till. Meanwhile he slips another marked fiver in Julia's bag. Julia plucks up the courage to tell Ron about his devious son but Mike suggests they look in Julia's bag. Discovering the marked fiver, Ron sacks Julia, making her a suitable case for *You've Been Framed*. However, when Cyril's medals also go missing and Ron finds a pawn ticket in one of Mike's shirts, he realises that Mike is the real culprit. Ron is again obliged to apologise to Julia. He begs her to come back to work but she milks the situation for all it's worth, saying she'll never be able to forgive or forget.

DD is aghast at catching Derek and Margaret kissing on the Close. Raining fire and brimstone, DD tries to blackmail Derek and when that fails, she goes to see Father Thornton who arranges for Derek to be transferred to the Lake District. Margaret is gutted and has a ferocious row with DD, in which the two women blame each other for Derek's departure.

While Jackie agrees to take Jimmy back, Sinbad's girlfriend Marcia pushes him into tracing his real family and he discovers that he has a sister called Ruth Sweeney. Ruth is evasive and it is only later that Sinbad uncovers the truth – that she is his mother.

After spending the night with Angela and being woken by her two girls, Barry learns that Angela is separated from her husband. When Fran finds out where he's been, she threatens to reveal everything about him and Sue at Graeme's trial. Having been found guilty, Graeme is also found dead. In church, Barry confesses to a priest that he was responsible for the deaths of Sue and Daniel. Seething at Barry's continued association with Angela, Fran tells Terry that Barry slept with Sue. Barry denies it, but Terry head butts him and lunges at him with a knife.

February

With his back against the wall, Barry comes out fighting and forces Fran to tell Terry that she was lying because she was jealous. Terry doesn't know who to believe. Fran quits Liverpool and Barry cleverly manoeuvres Terry into prising a confession out of him – that Sue tried to seduce him. As a result of this chicanery, Terry thinks Barry is the only real friend he's got. With money from the sale of the house, Terry plans to open a pizza parlour on Brookside Parade.

Jimmy's son, Jimmy Junior, does his best to wreck his parents' reconciliation by revealing that when he was little he caught Jimmy in bed with Jackie's sister, Val. But Jackie succumbs to Jimmy's charms and gives him a fresh chance. Worried that she and Max haven't made love since the operation, Patricia sets about seducing him.

Josie's parents, the Christies, turn up unannounced and are surprised to find Sinbad looking after the children. They voice their concerns to Mick about Leo and Gemma being looked after by the window-cleaner but say they only want to help. He is irritated by their interfering and downright angry when they whisk the kids off to Cardiff without his permission. Sinbad proposes to Marcia via the electronic scoreboard at Goodison Park and is delighted when she accepts. Ellis tries to pour cold water on the happy news by winding up Sinbad, but ends up having cold water poured on himself.

Katie is persuaded by domineering school-friend Leanne Powell to hold a party at No. 5 while Frank is away. When Katie gets cornered in the kitchen by Billy Duncan, she runs outside and is spotted by Barbara Harrison, who promptly disbands the party. Later a horrified Frank finds a packet of condoms in someone's jacket, but Owen, prompted by Leanne, says they're his. Leanne has got the hots for Owen. However, Frank then spots the jacket on the true owner, Billy Duncan, and demands to know what's been going on. When Owen is made redundant, his mother wants him to go back to college. Frank is not in favour of the idea.

John Harrison is puzzled to find that he owes £3,000 to a certain David Hurst, with whom John and his brother Hugh's company used to do business. Calls to Hugh in Spain prove fruitless and the situation worsens when two debt collectors come to remove the Harrisons' belongings. About to fly out to Spain to see Hugh, the Harrisons are taken off the plane by Customs and Excise and informed that they are under investigation for VAT fraud. They hope their son Peter will be able to shed some light on the whole sorry business.

March

With debts to Customs and Excise of £70,000, the Harrisons have no option but to shop Hugh. Trouble-maker Leanne is still making passes at Owen and boasts to Katie that he kissed her at the bus stop. Even though Owen is totally innocent, the situation causes friction with Sammy who accuses him of preferring schoolgirls. When Owen is alone in the house, Leanne again comes on strong but

he tells her he's not interested and throws her out. She runs away in tears, her emotional exit witnessed by John Harrison. Ever ready to jump to the wrong conclusion, Frank waylays Owen who pleads with Leanne to tell the truth. Instead she states that she and Owen had sex. Hurt that Sammy chooses to believe that little scrubber instead of him, Owen goes home to his mum. It is Barbara who finally succeeds in coaxing the truth out of Leanne – that she is still a virgin. Armed with this information, Frank and Sammy do what they do best – apologise – and Owen agrees to come back. To make his day complete, Owen gets a job in Terry's new pizza parlour.

There is an outbreak of vandalism on the Close and Ron suspects that Jacqui's latest boyfriend, Darren Murphy, is the ringleader. Barbara catches one of Darren's gang stealing a school computer and when Darren spots her on the Close, he starts threatening her. Shortly afterwards, a brick is hurled through the Harrisons' conservatory. Then Julia is mugged on the way back from the pizza parlour. The gang steal her handbag but leave the pizza – it had anchovy topping.

Derek is back and promising to make a go of things with Margaret. The only problem is they have nowhere to meet away from DD's prying eyes…until Patricia offers them a 'safe house'. Just when things are looking up, Margaret's mum arrives on the Close, learns that her daughter is dating a priest and vows to split them up at all costs. Rod starts teaching Diana to read and write and says that he won't marry her until she can write out the wedding invitations. It could be the world's longest engagement.

April

Jacqui goes out with Darren and the gang and they break into a classroom at Manor Park Primary School. Messing about with a lighter, Darren starts a fire. By the time they realise what they've done, the fire has got out of control. Everyone flees in panic except for Jacqui who finds herself trapped in the smoke-filled room. Fortunately Barry happens to be passing at the time and rides to the rescue. Ron goes looking for Darren and grabs him by the throat, only to be knocked cold by Darren's dad. Ron tells him about the school burning down, but Mr Murphy covers up for his son, saying that he was working in a pub all that night. Darren's revenge is swift. A stolen car is dumped outside the Dixons' and then the Trading Post window is smashed in open defiance of the newly-formed Brookside vigilante group. Jacqui is intimidated into keeping quiet by Darren, but she begins to reconsider her position when she sees Darren bullying Tony.

Angela's estranged husband, Colin Lambert, arrives at the shops and it's soon obvious that he wants more than a haircut. In fact, he wants his wife back and, to that end, he also wants Barry out of her life. Frank meets a woman named Denise at a singles' club but the friendship fails to find favour with Katie, who sees Denise as a replacement for Chrissy. Frank, on the other hand, says there was only one Chrissy. He's not wrong there.

Margaret is anxious that her relationship with Derek should move on. She tells him that there have been many priests in similar situations, who have had to make the decision to leave the Church. However Derek is in a turmoil: he doesn't want to give up the Church or Margaret. But Margaret thinks she knows how to win him round.

May

With Derek due to return to Grasmere, Margaret seizes her opportunity and begins defrocking the priest. She gets as far as unbuttoning his shirt when he says he can't go through with it and leaves in tears. Derek goes missing until Mike and Keith find him at the top of a sheer rock face at Pex Hill where the youth club go rock-climbing. They take him back to Mike's flat where a disturbed Derek just wants to be left alone. He contemplates suicide but finally agrees to talk to Margaret in private and tells her that he's

decided to leave the priesthood.

When, following another row with Max, Ron bars the entire Farnham family from the Trading Post, Margaret tries to circumnavigate the problem by handing the shopping list to Diana and asking her to go in. Alas, Diana can't read the list. Patricia recognises Diana's difficulty and offers to help.

As one door (Angela) closes for Barry, another (Fran) appears to open, for she's back on the scene, telling him that she's pregnant with his child. But her mood is far from conciliatory and an equally angry Barry threatens her physically and tells her he wants nothing more to do with her.

Terry is proving to the have the same head for business that King Alfred had for bakery. He wanders around like a zombie, leaving all the work to his staff, Owen and Matty. So it comes as no great surprise when the pizza parlour is closed down by the health authority on suspicion of food poisoning. Owen promptly resigns and lands a job selling conservatories. He is paid strictly on commission – no pane, no gain. When a series of forged £20 notes begin to circulate, Barry discovers that the mysterious Asians who have been renting the flat above one of his shops have been printing counterfeit money, so he breaks in and helps himself to £35,000. On the way down from the flat, he bumps into Matty and Terry. Matty has a go at Barry for the way he treated Fran the other day, to which Barry replies that it's got nothing to do with Matty. Then Terry drops the bombshell. It's got everything to do with Matty because he's Barry's father!

On the run from Nawaz and his fellow counterfeiters, Barry becomes increasingly desperate. Fran taunts him about the contents of a letter Graeme sent before his death which points to Barry as the killer. Barry is scared and kidnaps her, taking her to an isolated stretch of beach. There he later tells Terry that he did sleep with Sue and also killed her and Danny. He hands Terry a loaded shotgun with the command 'Do your own justice.'

June

The Harrisons wake to find a haggard-looking Terry in their back garden, holding a shotgun and with blood on his shirt. They quickly realise that he is not delivering a pizza. Barry's jeep is found abandoned on the beach but there is no sign of Barry himself. Everyone wonders who could have had it in for Barry. Several hours later, when the list is exhausted, the police arrest Terry. Just when they are about to charge Terry with murder, Barry puts in a fleeting appearance at the station and Terry is released. When Fran and Matty catch up with him, Terry confides that the reason he didn't kill Barry on the beach was because he wants Barry to suffer for the rest of his life for what he did. Fran decides to move away and Terry has had enough of being a pizza king.

The opportunist Jimmy makes the most of Barry's absence by squatting in one of the shops. His cheapo emporium, Kowboy Kutz, threatens Ron's trade. With Owen away at his mum's, Sammy goes into labour. Baby Louise is born prematurely and her life hangs in the balance for a few days. Meanwhile Marcia breaks it to a stunned Sinbad that she can't have children.

Mick has been campaigning for the rebuilding of Manor Park Primary after the fire but, at a meeting, Marianne Dwyer of the education department puts the case for relocation. She later takes Mick to one side and reveals that a decision to close the school was made a year ago, well before the fire. Mick responds by keeping his children off school and urging other parents to do the same. Unfortunately they all bring their kids round to the bungalow with the result that Mick finds himself running a day nursery. Then Mick receives the shattering news that he is to lose his taxi because Ellis has been caught illegally driving the cab. Ellis tries to make amends by suggesting to Mick that they buy the pizza parlour off Terry, who agrees to a month's trial. Margaret and Derek plan a weekend away but Nick, the lorry driver friend of Frank's who is taking them, suffers a fatal heart attack on

the journey to London. Margaret watches horrified as Derek administers the last rites. Will he never be free of the priesthood?

July

After the seedy ritual of the singles' club, Frank finds a novel chatting-up place – a Chapel of Rest. He gets talking to Lyn McLoughlin, Nick's sister, although thankfully he refrains from asking her whether she comes here often. Lyn's brother's body has hardly been lowered into the ground when Frank ditches Denise and takes up with her.

After having sex at the Farnhams', Margaret and Derek fall asleep and fail to notice that Thomas has been sick. Mad Max accuses Margaret of neglecting her duties and Derek realises they've got to find somewhere to live. He borrows some money from Ron – a first in itself – but when DD finds out, she is furious and walks out on Ron for a week. Max wastes no time in replacing Margaret with a new nanny, Anna Wolska. Patricia is put out that he hired someone without consulting her but agrees to keep Anna on until Margaret gets back. As far as Max is concerned, Margaret is sacked.

Ron is boiling over about Kowboy Kutz, particularly when he catches Jimmy checking the Trading Post prices. With Max's firm, Fletchers, in charge of collecting the rent from the shops on Barry's behalf, Ron decides to go on rent strike until Max sorts out Jimmy. Mick goes to see Marianne to inform her that he's scrapping the campaign. He starts taking an interest in the pizza parlour and in Marianne, but inevitably supersmooth Ellis gets in there first. Meanwhile Sinbad and Marcia split up.

With Owen working hard to make ends meet, Sammy can't cope with the baby and abandons her outside the hospital maternity unit. Owen decides the only safe place for Louise is at his mum's. He wants custody of the baby and a divorce. John Harrison suffers a severe asthma attack and starts shoplifting, but son Peter returns and gets a job at a chemical plant. And Rod and Diana are married at last.

August

Their happiness is short-lived. While Diana is having her hair done, two masked men wielding baseball bats burst into Angela's salon, intent on snatching the takings. Rod, who has come to collect his wife, stumbles across the crime and attempts to block the robbers' exit but they slash him across the face with a knife before escaping in a getaway car. He nurses a badly cut eye and Diana wants him to leave the force while he still can. For her own part, Diana gets a job on the make-up counter at Lewis's. She is made up.

Sinbad and Marcia are reunited and join half the Close on a trip to Alton Towers. Also back together are Sammy, Owen and Louise. They decide that this time they'll find a place of their own and Sammy will go back to work. Frank and Lyn go camping in Scotland with the Dixons, and Ron and DD take the opportunity to stop off in Edinburgh where Mike has a five-minute film being screened at the Young People's Television Festival.

Margaret accepts a new nannying post, to the disappointment of Patricia who blames Max for letting her go. Margaret isn't happy in her new job but is delighted when Derek suggests they get engaged, even though he can't afford a ring. Patricia hands in her notice and thinks about going solo as a public relations consultant. John's shoplifting continues – a tin of sardines from Ron, cassettes from Jimmy. Is he planning to record the mating call of the sardine? When he goes into town and walks out with a video he hasn't paid for, he is arrested. He is later let off with a caution, but his shame and embarrassment is matched only by that of Barbara who worries about the effect on her job.

Terry, who is going downhill fast, has demanded £15,000 in cash for the pizza parlour. Mick thinks it's a lost cause, but Ellis won't give up without a fight and borrows the money off a loan shark. The Johnsons are back

in business, but at what cost? Discovering that his water and electricity have been cut off in a bid to oust him from the shop, Jimmy installs gas cylinders.

September

Disaster at the Trading Post! Standing in for Marcia, Julia switches off the freezers before locking up, leaving the shop flooded and the stock ruined. At first, Ron accuses her of doing it on purpose but later accepts that it was a genuine mistake. Jacqui announces that she's not going back to school; she's got a placement at a leisure centre instead.

Having had the all-clear for her cancer, Patricia is shocked to learn that she is pregnant. But Max is overjoyed, particularly when he is made a partner at Fletchers. Margaret and Derek celebrate their engagement and, after a bit of gentle persuasion from Ron, both DD and Margaret's mum give it their blessing.

Mick is pleased that the pizza parlour is doing sufficient trade to cover the £600 monthly loan. Then Ellis breaks the bad news – the payments are actually £1000 a month. In the aftermath of the robbery, Angela quits the salon, selling the franchise to Brian Kennedy who quickly appoints Tracy as manageress. Brian wants Terry out of the flat above the salon, but Terry says he has a special arrangement with Barry Grant.

Another arrival is George Webb, proprietor of the new petrol station. The beginning of his tenure coincides with the appearance of 'Strength Through Purity' stickers on the pizza parlour window. Later Webb tells Mike and Matty they should quit working at the parlour before there's trouble. Ellis is all for sorting Webb out, but Mick suggests a more cautious approach. The traders also learn that the spare unit is to be a nightclub. Ron starts dusting off his winkle-pickers. Following all the gossip about John, Barbara thinks about her future and a possible job in Chester.

Rod leaves the force because he's not prepared to take a desk job and applies for a post as a security officer. Since attending literacy classes, Diana has grown more independent of Rod and, with her new job being in Manchester, the two are drifting apart. They put the house up for sale and one row ends with Rod slapping her face and walking out after finding her with her new friend, Peter Harrison.

October

Rod doesn't return. Instead he's thinking about taking a security job in Hull. Meanwhile a couple called the Shackletons come to view the house. Anna, the Farnhams' nanny, fancies Peter and holds a party to which he and Diana are invited. In the middle of the party, Tommo arrives with another message from Rod. Unless Rod hears from Diana that night, he's taking the job in Hull. Hearing the words 'Rod' and 'Hull', Diana thinks of Emu and, additionally upset by what seems to be the end of her marriage, she rushes upstairs. Peter follows her to offer comfort and she leads him into the bedroom for some privacy. They become more intimate and start kissing passionately but when Max goes upstairs to the loo, he's shocked to see a half-dressed Diana rushing from the bedroom, shouting 'I said no.' She is pursued out of the house by a dishevelled, worried-looking Peter. Back home, Diana tells Julia what happened and Julia encourages her to press rape charges. A stunned Peter is led away by the police. He strongly denies the accusation of rape and maintains that Diana was a consenting party.

The pizza parlour is subjected to further racist attacks. Jimmy spots some men behaving badly and catches one but, just as he is about to put the boot in, Webb intervenes and the lad escapes. It turns out they had been about to throw a petrol bomb. As Ellis points out: 'We know who's got plenty of petrol.' Mick is also in deep trouble with the building society over his lapsed payments. Ellis volunteers to move in with Marianne to save rent. She demurs, so he goes a step further and proposes marriage.

In the middle of a speech to the Round Table, Patricia collapses in agony and suffers a miscarriage. Terry meets Joe Halsall, co-owner of the new nightclub. She hands Terry a mystery package which contains two airline tickets to Madrid, leaving that day from Manchester. He takes Sinbad along for the ride after Sinbad has promised not to clean the plane's windows at 30,000ft. In Spain, they are instructed to meet up with the amazing disappearing Barry, who wants to know whether it's safe for him to go back to Liverpool since he is the other co-owner of the nightclub. After getting the nod from Terry, Barry returns to discover Jimmy squatting. When Jimmy refuses to budge, Barry sets fire to the shop, unaware of the presence of the gas cylinders. A huge explosion blows out the front of the shop and puts Kowboy Kutz out of business.

November

George Webb reports the Johnsons as illegal immigrants, causing Mick to be taken in for questioning. Ron goes for a drink with George and his mates but his blood runs cold when he hears of their plans for 'the darkies from the pizza parlour'. When Ellis hears about Mick being lifted, he drives his car straight at a stumbling Webb, stopping it inches from his face. Ellis's violent tendencies scare Marianne who is not sure whether she can live with such a person. Webb retaliates by attempting to petrol bomb No. 6, but Ron spots him and disarms him, though his own arm is burnt in the struggle. Ron confronts Webb, but Webb twists things by saying that Ron is involved with the racist attacks. It's Webb's word against Ron's. Ellis is more determined than ever to get rid of Webb and, with the help of Ron and Mick, parks three vehicles outside Webb's pumps, thereby bringing his business to a standstill. Ron is persuaded to go the police, but it's not necessary as Webb has been kicked out of the petrol station on orders from above – namely Barry and Max. With a final parting threat, Webb tells Ellis about the little insurance policy he's got should they ever decide to go the police: Marianne's address.

On a lighter note, Ron is elected compère at the Legion. Derek opens a charity shop on Brookside Parade until Christmas and Patricia teams up with her old boss, Karyn Clark, to organise a charity fashion show. Barry begins to take a keen interest in the event – and Karyn. Peter tries in vain to talk to Diana, who also learns that Rod has accepted the Shackletons' offer on the house and wants her out in four weeks. Tracy feels guilty about deserting her in her hour of need, but the offer to run one of Brian's salons in Chester is too good to refuse. Encouraged by Patricia, Diana stands firm and Peter is duly charged with rape.

December

Terry has borrowed £500 from Barry but won't tell him why he needs it. Barry's curiosity gets the better of him and he follows Terry to a house in Birkenhead. He is just about to leave when he sees Fran emerging from the house, pushing a pram containing his offspring. Fran and young Stephen then spend Christmas with Terry at his flat.

Ron pursues Jackie Corkhill with the sort of enthusiasm he usually reserves for a lost 5p piece. When they fall into an impromptu kiss, she momentarily enjoys it but then worries about where it will lead. Ron knows exactly where – a weekend away at that mecca for small shopkeepers, the Harrogate Gift Fair – but Jackie declines the offer and reaffirms her loyalty to Jimmy. When Ron continues to push his luck, she walks out on her job at the Trading Post. Ron's face drops lower than his takings.

Leanne Powell is pregnant and, fearful of her parents' reaction, determined to have an abortion. With Sarah Greene as host, Patricia and Karyn's charity event proves a great success. Karyn even wins the raffle – a weekend for two in Paris – and takes Barry. Farnham Clark Associates also organise the opening of the nightclub, La Luz, on Christmas Day. The theme is a Spanish fiesta.

Jimmy, Barry's new dogsbody, knows all about fiestas – he once drove one as a getaway car.

At Patricia's suggestion, the homeless Diana has moved into the Farnhams' where she comes into direct conflict with Anna, who is going to testify on Peter's behalf at the trial. On the first day in court, Diana breaks down under intense cross-examination and Anna's evidence also weighs heavily against her. Patricia – who later receives a surprise visitor when her father, David Crosbie, turns up on the doorstep – is so frustrated that she tells Anna that if she takes any more time off to go to court, she'll lose her job. But when the trial begins to swing Diana's way, John suggests to Peter that he could plead guilty in the hope of receiving a lighter sentence. Peter is appalled that his father could even think such a thing. To compound Peter's misery, his parents move out of the Close in a hurry. The hate mail and the strain has all been too much for them. Peter feels they have abandoned him. His only hope appears to be to get Diana to drop the case. But when he tries to reason with her, she slams the door in his face.

1993

Peter is acquitted … A double wedding ends in double despair … The Jordaches move in and No. 10 acquires a body under the patio … Ron has an affair with Lyn's sister Bev … Max and Patricia divorce and re-marry … Jimmy turns to drugs and kills Frank Rogers on his wedding day … Tony Dixon is left in a coma … Katie joins a religious cult.

January

A vindictive Patricia sacks Anna. When Anna relays the news to Peter, he tells her she's probably got a good case for unfair dismissal. But Anna says there's nothing she can do because she's in the country illegally. She goes to stay at the Harrisons' where things threaten to get passionate until Peter pulls away, mindful of what happened with Diana. At the end of the trial, Peter is found not guilty. Jimmy flips when he hears the verdict and vows to carry out his own brand of Corkhill 'justice', but Barry says he'll sack him if he goes anywhere near Peter. Diana feels that she has been found guilty and, in the depths of despair, slashes her wrists.

Patricia's mother, Jean Crosbie, returns from Spain and announces that she threw David out for flirting with their Spanish maid. Patricia tries to convince her that his flirting is harmless but then Jean reveals that David also had an 18-month affair with their nanny, Sandra, over 20 years ago. Patricia is speechless.

Back from Paris, Barry demands to see his son but is powerless to act as Terry takes Sue and Stephen home to Birkenhead. Terry and Fran start to build a relationship but their romance is shattered by Barry who, discovering that he has no rights of access to his son, snatches baby Stephen while Tracy is babysitting.

With Derek planning to do voluntary work in Romania, DD needs a new life to meddle in. Her chosen subject is Leanne who is threatening to kill herself if her parents find out she is pregnant. Ron warns DD not to interfere, but he is wasting his breath. With the help of Lyn, DD arranges for Leanne to have a secret abortion. Leanne's parents, who are not the monsters she has painted, are disgusted that DD helped their daughter get an abortion and Ron also turns on her.

Marcia is still reeling from what she witnessed on New Year's Eve – a passionate kiss between Mick and Marianne. Ellis and Marianne are planning a Valentine's Day wedding and Marcia decides to surprise Sinbad by making it a double wedding. Mick is honoured to be asked to give Marcia away but less thrilled when he spots the name of Josie on Marcia's guest list.

February

On the eve of the double wedding, the two stag and hen nights collide at La Luz. With impeccable timing, Mick admits to Sinbad that he loves Marianne and thinks she might feel the same about him. Sinbad makes the mistake of confiding this to Marcia who merely redoubles her efforts to get Mick and Josie back together. Marcia dismisses Mick's declaration of love as the drink talking and warns Sinbad not to breathe a word to Marianne. But Sinbad can't stand by and see his bezzie mate hurt and tells Marianne what Mick said. When Marcia finds out, she petulantly calls the wedding off, saying she can't possibly marry someone she can't trust. She tries to patch things up the next day but Sinbad stuns her by saying they should postpone the wedding. Josie wants Mick back, but he's not interested. She says she's changed; he's heard it all before. The second wedding also falls through when Marianne leaves Ellis standing at the altar.

Realising she's been dumped in favour of Marianne, Josie tries to snatch the kids, only for Mick to throw her out of the bungalow forever. Marianne intends leaving for London but Mick finally gives in to his feelings and kisses her passionately, an act witnessed by Ellis.

Baby Stephen is returned safe and well but Terry knows the only way Fran will ever be free from Barry is to get as far away from Liverpool as she can. The Wirral just won't do. So Terry gives her a large sum of money and, after an emotional farewell, she heads for pastures new. He may have lost Fran, but he's got even with Barry.

In a rare act of generosity, DD has paid for Margaret's fare so that she can go to Romania with Derek, but Margaret backs out at the airport when she discovers that she and Derek won't be together at first. DD and Ron are still barely speaking to each other, not only because of the Leanne affair but also because she is opening a florist's shop on the parade – a venture he knew nothing about. Margaret soon receives a sad letter from Derek and is so moved by it that she changes her mind yet again and flies out to Romania to join him. After a trip to a psychiatrist, Diana comes back in confident mood. Peter tries to insist that the whole thing was a misunderstanding but she states that they both know he's guilty and he'll have to live with that. Peter is dumbfounded.

Lyn and her children, Gavin and Alison, move in with Frank and a strange new family arrive at No. 10 – the Jordaches. They seem eager to preserve their anonymity.

March

Mandy Jordache is a battered wife who has been placed by the Shackletons in a 'safe house' with her daughters Beth and Rachel. Given its history of headstones through the front door and bricks through the window, No. 10 would appear about as safe as an igloo in the Sahara, but Mandy feels secure enough … until she discovers that her brutal husband Trevor has been released from prison. It's not long before Trevor tracks them down. The neighbours all think he's utterly charming and he strives to convince Mandy he's changed by sending her flowers, but Beth in particular isn't fooled and knows she must protect Rachel from his evil ways.

Mick and Marianne are unsure how to proceed with their sudden relationship. Both feel guilty about what they did to Ellis who has sulked off to Tenerife, the honeymoon destination. Mick's happiness is marred only by heavy debts. Marianne suggests he give up the bungalow and move into the flat above the pizza parlour, but Jimmy has a better idea and tells Mick that he should get someone to burgle his house and claim off the insurance – it's an old Corkhill family tradition. Mick is understandably wary but the newly-returned Ellis thinks it's a great idea and gives Jimmy the cash to organise it.

Margaret comes back alone from Romania, Terry takes charge at the petrol station and Diana gets a bar job at La Luz which ends when she throws a glass of lager in the face of

a raucous male customer. Ron and DD try in vain to rekindle the fires of passion with a second honeymoon in Blackpool and return to find the house in a mess following an impromptu party. Ron takes his frustration out on Mike, slaps him across the face and orders him out of the house. His marriage on the rocks, Ron starts going to the Legion to forget. He perks up when Lyn introduces him to her younger sister Bev and he wastes no time in offering her the vacancy at the Trading Post. Ron feels like a born-again grocer.

April

Drenched in after-shave, Ron starts canoodling with Bev in the back room at the shop, under the guise of stock taking. Bev is flattered and eagerly accepts his suggestion of an evening at a hotel. She also wants him to find a little 'love nest' for them. While Ron is out enjoying himself, DD is languishing at home and steadily sinking into depression.

Jimmy's fake burglary goes like a dream. There was just one thing he hadn't taken into account: Mick isn't insured. Mick then gets a letter from the building society saying they want to repossess the bungalow. Angrily he throws the keys at the manager, storms out and breaks into the flat above the pizza parlour, ready to make it his new home.

With no job and no money, Anna decides that the only way she'll be allowed to stay in the country is if she can find herself an English husband. She asks Peter whether he would consider marrying her but, much as he likes her, he declines her kind offer. Max is horrified to hear that Susannah is planning to take the children to the States to live with her new actor boyfriend, Andrew. It's bad enough losing them anyway – but to an actor!

Taken in by his hard-luck stories and promises that he's a reformed character, the weak-willed Mandy foolishly allows Trevor to stay for a couple of nights. Rachel is delighted; Beth is furious. She pushes him out into the pouring rain but Mandy takes pity on him and allows him back in. Trevor

The Jordache and Sweeney Families

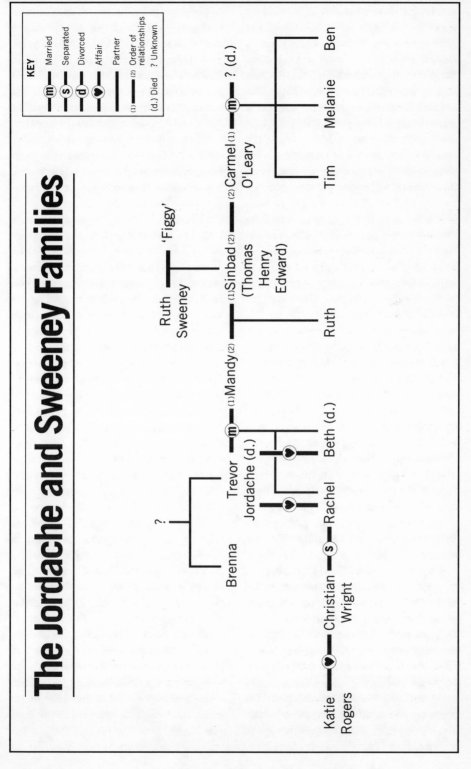

remains all sweetness and light until he learns that people on the Close have been talking about him. He creeps into Mandy's bed, grabs her by the throat and threatens that if she tells a soul, he'll kill her, the girls and then himself. He forces her to hold a 20th wedding anniversary party to present a united front, but when only David and Jean show up, Trevor blames Mandy. After the Crosbies have made their escape, Trevor accuses Mandy of spreading tales about him and punches her, leaving her in a crumpled heap on the floor. The following week, Beth arrives home to find Mandy in pain from another beating. With no sign of Trevor, Beth rushes upstairs to Rachel's room and is horrified to see Trevor and Rachel asleep together in Rachel's bed.

May

Rachel is confused about what happened but when Beth says Trevor did the same thing to her, Rachel breaks down. Mandy promises Rachel she won't ever let Trevor touch her again. With Trevor drinking heavily, Beth decides to get him out of their lives by spiking his whisky with weedkiller. It may get rid of dandelion and clover but it can't get rid of Trevor and so they decide to dissolve painkillers in his drink – the final solution. From the look on their faces, Trevor realises what they are up to and lashes out at Beth. In desperation, Mandy picks up a kitchen knife and stabs him in the back. He sinks to the floor – dead.

The next day, Mandy is in a terrible state. Beth pulls herself together, covers the body in a blanket and buys a load of air freshener to mask the smell. All enquirers are told that Trevor is in a drunken stupor. She and Mandy then drag the body into the extension, dispose of the bloody carpet tiles and knife and tell a sad Rachel that her dad has gone and won't be back. Soon the smell from the extension becomes unbearable and they decide to bury him in the garden with the help of a spade borrowed from Peter.

Sinbad, who has become friendly with the family, calls round and spots the bloody tiles and the knife in a bin bag torn open by the cat. They pretend they're digging a pond. Sinbad thinks it's best not to ask too many questions. Mandy is on the point of giving herself up but Beth stands firm. They must stick together. But Mandy's nerves are further shattered by a letter from the Shackletons, who, knowing nothing of Trevor's reappearance, say they don't think she needs a safe house any more. Mandy knows they can hardly move house with Trevor buried in the back garden.

Over at No. 7, Max refuses to sign a letter of consent allowing Susannah to take Matthew and Emily to the States. As things get heated, Andrew exits stage left and Susannah assures Max that there's no danger of Andrew ever replacing him in Matthew and Emily's affections. Husband and ex-wife seal the truce in an emotional embrace…witnessed by Patricia. Meanwhile her parents, the Crosbies, move into the bungalow. Mick proposes to Marianne but she hands him back the ring, saying she's not ready for marriage.

Having heard from Lyn about Bev's track history of wrecking marriages, Ron is beginning to have second thoughts about continuing with the affair, but he melts when she tells him she's found the perfect love nest. Then Lyn spots them kissing and confronts Bev about the affair. Brazen Bev doesn't deny it and says that Ron is leaving DD for her. But when Ron hears that their secret is out, he assures Lyn that it's nothing serious and promises to end it as long as Lyn doesn't tell DD. She doesn't need to. For coming downstairs from her sick bed, DD catches Ron and Bev mid-snog. Acting on the advice of Father Munroe, DD goes to stay in a convent. Riddled with guilt, Ron finishes with Bev. Bitter and angry, she tells him not to come running back to her when he realises he's made a mistake. To tide her over in the meantime, she fixes up a new beau – Ron's son, Mike.

June

Joe Halsall and Barry have the biggest fall-out since Chernobyl. She wants him to give up his share of the club but Barry finds an ally in the eccentric Oscar Dean who is keen on buying into La Luz and who informs Barry that Joe has been cooking the books. Still sniffing around about the murders of Sue and Danny, the police start leaning on Barry, as does Joe who gets her hired heavies to force him to put pen to paper and sign the club over to her. Always game for a spot of arson, Barry threatens to torch the place and casually mentions to Jimmy that he's done it before – to Kowboy Kutz. Jimmy knocks him to the floor. Joe summons Barry to the club and frames him by arranging for Jimmy to be knocked down by Barry's car, driven by a man wearing Barry's coat. Jimmy may have a broken arm but his mind is in full working order and he is convinced Barry was driving the car which tried to kill him. Encouraged by Joe to go to the police, Jimmy wants Barry done for attempted murder.

Joe has also been busy arranging escort work for Anna. Realising she can make more money by providing optional extras, Anna drifts into prostitution. Peter becomes suspicious about her late-night sorties and eventually rescues her after she has been attacked by a client. The next day he confronts Joe who promptly sacks Anna. She is furious with Peter for losing her the job. Against his better judgement, Sinbad offers to cover the Jordaches' incriminating mound of earth with a patio. It is a sad moment – even the concrete is distressed.

Meanwhile Bev drops the bombshell to Mike that she's pregnant. Max has relented and allowed the children to go to Florida but he soon changes his mind and flies out to the US and snatches them back. Susannah follows him to England, frosty and unyielding. Max apologises for his impetuous behaviour and they reach a compromise over the kids. Susannah then reminds him that he could have the kids all the time – provided she was part of the package. Max says he loves Patricia but Susannah points out that it's possible to love two women, a statement which leaves Max more flustered than usual. With Patricia away on business, Susannah stays the night. He plans to sleep on the sofa but has to go to her room to get something and doesn't come out again. The next morning, David spots Susannah wearing Max's bathrobe and is appalled at the way his daughter is being deceived. He threatens to tell Patricia everything.

July

Mustering the wealth of pomposity and hypocrisy at his disposal, David reveals to Patricia that Max slept with Susannah while she was away. Unwilling to hear any excuses, Patricia moves into the bungalow with her parents and instigates divorce proceedings. David has an admirer of his own – Julia Brogan – and Marianne starts a job as an Equality Officer at Grearson's where her boss is the smooth-talking Charles Weekes.

Anna goes kerb crawling but Peter follows her and ridicules her in front of the other prostitutes. To prove that she's not stupid, she throws a handful of condoms at him.

Ron is sure the baby is his, but Bev points out that it could just as easily be Mike's. Mike is still ignorant of Ron's affair with Bev until Keith shows him photos of the two of them kissing. Mike marches round for a scene and father and son end up grappling on the floor. Finally Mike walks out and tells Ron he wants nothing more to do with him. Later he starts handing out posters of the photo. Ron has a lot of explaining to do. Strangely he is relieved that it is all out in the open and asks Bev to move into No. 8. She is thrilled by this show of commitment and says yes, to the disgust of Mike, Jacqui and Tony. Lyn is none too pleased either and storms over and hurls Bev's clothes out of the window to create an Ann Summers cascade. The two sisters brawl like fishwives, their combat interrupted only by Ron's showstopping declaration that Bev is pregnant. Cue dropped jaws all round.

Trevor's sister Brenna turns up at the Jordaches' and starts asking asking awkward questions about her brother. She becomes suspicious about Mandy's relationship with Sinbad and claims that Mandy drove Trevor to violence. When Mandy tells her to leave, Brenna says she's going to the police. She won't rest until she finds out what's happened to Trevor.

Barry seems to have nobody to turn to. Jimmy gives short shrift to his protestations of innocence and Terry rejects all his pleas for help. Then comes the final blow – his arrest for the attempted murder of James Corkhill or, as he's better known at the station, No. 1456938. Oscar puts the wind up Jimmy but Joe warns him to stick to his statement or he'll lose more than his job. However, Oscar perseveres and Jimmy withdraws his statement. As the case against Barry falls apart, Joe makes her excuses and leaves. A free man, Barry cautiously returns to La Luz where he finds Oscar sitting at the desk. He reveals himself as the new owner and immediately offers Barry a 60/40 partnership.

At a rave night at the club, Jimmy throws out two scallies dealing drugs in the toilets and pockets their tabs of ecstasy. He notices that they drive off in a flash car. He later mentions this to Brian Kennedy who has a more relaxed view of drugs and encourages him to take one of the tabs. Jimmy enjoys the experience but starts spouting rubbish. Amazingly Barry is able to spot the difference and sacks him. However, Oscar reinstates him and Brian tells Jimmy that there's a lot of money to be made out of drugs.

August

Jimmy is stunned when Brian asks him to supply him with cocaine. Jimmy says he wants nothing to do with drugs but his resolve weakens when Brian entices him with a wad of readies. The lonely Terry asks Anna to escort him to a dinner dance. She comforts him but won't let him kiss her, explaining that if he wants her to stay the night, it will cost him. Terry checks his wallet and asks her to stay. As their dates become more frequent, she talks about a 'friend' who entered into a marriage of convenience. Terry expresses interest.

Although feeling threatened by Charles Weekes's interest in Marianne, Mick agrees to his suggestion to take up football coaching. After suffering a minor heart attack, Frank emerges with a new sense of priorities and asks Lyn to marry him. She gleefully accepts. Patricia orders David to change the locks so that Max can't get in. Locked out, Max loses his temper and smashes the glass in the door, vowing to fight Patricia for everything. David then waltzes off to Butlin's, Pwllheli, where he and Julia win a ballroom dancing competition as Mr and Mrs Dixon. He celebrates so much he can't drive home.

Called to identify a badly decomposed body which the police think might be Trevor, Mandy sees a way of getting the dogged Brenna off her back and lies that the belongings found with the body are Trevor's. However, after struggling through the sham funeral, she is shocked when Brenna asks for Trevor's signet ring – the one that's buried with the real Trevor in the garden! And so the loyal Sinbad, aided by Beth, has to dig up the body during Beth's 18th birthday party. Beth has passed her 'A' level science, no doubt helped by practical revision on blood flow out of the body courtesy of Trevor, and receives confirmation of her place at Guy's Hospital in London. But then Mrs Shackleton calls round with news that the Jordaches have only got another three months in the house and furthermore the trustees are contemplating building an extension which would mean digging up the patio. There's no way Beth can go to London now.

September

Beth has had no shortage of suitors since arriving on the Close – among them Mike Dixon – but the one she is really taken with is

Peter Harrison. Since they've both got so many secrets, it is a fraught relationship with more false starts than the 1993 Grand National. Eventually they get round to making love, only for Jimmy, still simmering at Peter's acquittal, to inform Mandy that her daughter is going out with a rapist. Beth quickly ends the relationship, but Jimmy isn't finished yet and breaks into the Harrisons' house and attacks Peter, saying that he'll always be there to remind him he's a rapist. This is too much for Peter who decides to leave for the Corkhill-free zone of Oxford.

Terry offers himself to Anna as the English husband she so desperately needs, but Barry takes more than a passing interest when he learns that she is paying Terry to marry her. Meanwhile Lyn's daughter Alison pleads with her not to marry Frank and runs away from home. And Geoff turns up, telling Frank he received a knock during training with Torquay and has been told to rest. But is he telling porkies?

Patricia goes on a date with Brian Kennedy but just when things look like getting intimate, she tells him about her mastectomy. He takes it badly and she wonders whether the only person who will ever understand is Max.

Mick has problems with a disruptive young footballer, Garry Salter, and with his forthright mum, Carol, who is convinced Garry is being victimised. But this pales in comparison with Mick's other headache – Charles Weekes. When Charles makes a pass at Marianne she puts him in his place, only to be humiliated by him when he chastises her over a minor error at work. Reluctantly, she joins him in Coventry on a course but, after initially apologising for his behaviour, he visits her room on the pretence of discussing work and starts toying with her knickers in her half-unpacked case. She slaps his face and kicks him out of the room. He says he'll keep the knickers as a souvenir. Marianne is frightened to tell Mick and thinks about resigning. Then she decides to report Charles for sexual harassment, but Charles gets his retaliation in first and tells

Mick that he and Marianne have been having an affair. By the time she finally gets round to telling Mick the truth, it's too late. He doesn't believe her.

October

Marianne eventually convinces Mick that Charles is lying through his lily-white teeth. Charles tries unsuccessfully to bribe Marianne into dropping the allegations of sexual harassment, only for Mick to make a mess of things by losing his temper and flooring Charles. Seizing his opportunity to wriggle off the hook, Charles brings a private prosecution against Mick who is petrified that his previous GBH case will come up. Accordingly, Marianne tells Charles she'll drop the sexual harassment charges on condition that he drops his private prosecution against Mick. Charles is only too happy to agree and while they prepare for a presentation, he starts to talk openly about his attraction to her, unaware that she is recording the entire conversation. When she plays back the tape at the presentation in front of the company management, his smug expression turns to one of horror and he rushes from the room, his career in ruins. It couldn't have happened to a nicer bloke.

The build-up to Frank's wedding is thrown into confusion by Geoff's confession that he's not injured at all – he's simply packed in football because he doesn't think he's ever going to make it. And the on-off affair between Ron and Bev looks like having an even bumpier ride now that DD is back. There is disappointment too for Terry when Anna calls off their wedding. Barry hears about this development and, still desperate for a child of his own, offers to marry Anna if she'll have his baby. She agrees.

Max has just about given up trying to win back Patricia when she exercises her female prerogative and has a dramatic change of heart. She doesn't want a divorce after all. Unfortunately she reaches this decision on the very day that her decree absolute comes through. Although Max is keen to remarry, Patricia is hesitant – but he wins her round by taking her up in a hot air balloon. Max always was full of hot air. The wedding is attended by Clive Crosbie MP and his wife Penny, Clive being David's brother. They present Max and Patricia with a cheque for £2,000 and an invitation to stay with them at their home in Banbury. But the honeymoon is marred somewhat when Clive commits suicide in his garage by means of carbon monoxide fumes.

Meanwhile Brian is lining up a major drugs deal and Jimmy, keen to be taken seriously, wants a piece of the action. Brian is putting in £30,000 and says Jimmy will need to find £3,000 – by the end of the week. Taking a life assurance policy and a bracelet belonging to Jackie, Jimmy raises the cash and nervously hands it over. Brian gives him a sample of the cocaine and assures him it will be the easiest money he's ever made. As they await the fruits of their endeavours, Brian tempts Jimmy into taking his first snort of cocaine. Jimmy is relieved when Brian tells him the deal went smoothly and hands him a jiffy bag. But instead of cash, it contains £3,000 worth of cocaine. What's Jimmy supposed to do with that?

November

The big news in Banbury is that Clive Crosbie was a kerb-crawler, as a result of which his house is besieged by the Press pack. David decrees that the most appropriate course of action is to smuggle Penny back to Liverpool, but the journalists soon discover her hideout and camp out on the Close. One, Adrian Roache (as in cockroach), even brings along Clive's favourite prostitute to meet Penny. Talking of prostitutes, Anna hears from Terry that Barry is a murderer.

Jimmy is desperate to get rid of the cocaine but Brian doesn't want to know. He tells him to hide it and bide his time. Jackie just wants her bracelet and the money from the insurance policies back and, despite Jimmy's assurances that everything is fine, she throws him out.

Jimmy even tries to sell the coke back to Brian in return for his three grand, but Brian washes his hands of him. However, the next time Brian washes his hands is in a police station as Jimmy watches him being led away by the boys in blue. Jimmy breaks out in a cold sweat and has to take a shot of coke to calm his nerves before going off to lie low for a while.

It is Frank and Lyn's wedding day – and the moment Ron has been dreading – when DD catches sight of the pregnant Bev at the registry office. DD causes a scene and young Tony chimes in, only to get a slap from his dad. Poor lad – they were the first words he'd said in weeks. Frank is thrilled that Lyn has arranged for him to drive the Rolls-Royce to the reception and Tony joins them, leaving behind a sobbing DD, an ashamed Ron and a guilty Bev. Enjoying the drive, Frank takes them on a little detour but suddenly has to swerve violently to avoid a car coming straight at them, driven by Jimmy. The Rolls ploughs into a wall and Jimmy screeches off.

Frank is dead, Tony is in a coma and the recriminations begin in earnest. Ron says Tony would never have been in the car if he hadn't hit him, for which he receives little sympathy from DD. Ron then blames Bev for everything and Katie says Lyn should never have allowed Frank to drive with his weak heart. Chrissy Rogers returns and is surprised when Lyn says she's going to carry on living at No. 5. Chrissy urges her children to fight Lyn for possession of the house. Just when Lyn thinks nothing worse can happen, Ron makes a revelation at the funeral – that Frank was over the limit at the time of the crash. And she discovers she is pregnant. In her hour of need, Katie turns to prayer and finds a soulmate in Terry's new assistant at the garage, Simon Howe.

December

The fur flies at No. 5 as Lyn and Sammy argue over the house. When they fight over custody of Frank's guitar, Lyn slips, falls down the stairs and loses Frank's baby. Sammy and Owen

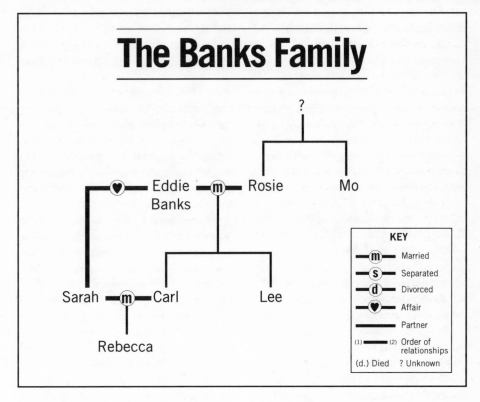

The Banks Family

KEY

—m—	Married
—s—	Separated
—d—	Divorced
—♥—	Affair
——	Partner
(1)—(2)	Order of relationships
(d.) Died	? Unknown

back down and return to their flat. Lyn subsequently puts the house on the market and agrees to split the money evenly with the Rogers children. The outlook for Tony is bleak. The doctor tells Ron that Tony is in a persistent vegetative state with no prospect of recovery. DD wants to take him to Lourdes while the ever-optimistic Ron pins his hopes of a cure on America.

Jimmy has resurfaced, wracked with guilt and taking comfort from cocaine. Hearing Ron's plans for the trip to the States, he volunteers to help with the fundraising. Ron is moved by his generosity, but says what he really wants is to get his hands on the driver of the other car … whoever he is. After a couple of near misses, Jackie finally catches Jimmy snorting coke. As she flushes it down the toilet, Jimmy pathetically explains that he was driving the car which killed Frank. On Christmas Day, Bev gives birth to baby Josh. Ron is convinced the baby is his. Having learnt

that her husband was an adulterer, embezzler and compulsive gambler, Penny naturally needs a day or two to take stock of her life. The family home has been repossessed so David insists she stays with Max and Patricia.

Anna tries to back out of her deal with Barry by going on the Pill. She feels trapped but Terry tells her there is one way out – she could always marry him after all. She agrees and promises that she won't let him down this time. However when Barry discovers the contraceptive pills, he realises he's been duped, slaps her face and phones the Immigration Department. Instead of marrying Terry, she is forced to flee the country. The wedding is arranged for New Year's Eve.

When Keith asks Beth whether he could be on with Margaret, he is baffled by her reply that he doesn't stand a chance. Beth makes it clear to Sinbad that she's not interested in lads at the moment – it's another woman she fancies. Sinbad wonders who it could be until he sees Beth catching Margaret as she accidentally falls from putting up the Christmas decorations. Eventually Beth confesses her feelings to Margaret but Margaret backs away. Katie joins Simon's religious circle, to the disquiet of Jacqui who worries about the control he already appears to be exercising over her vulnerable friend. After taking part in a fast, Katie is initiated into the group by losing her virginity to Simon.

1994

Beth and Margaret sleep together ... Tony Dixon dies ... The Banks move in ... Jimmy is sent to prison ... Mike is revealed to be Josh's father ... Patricia gives birth to Down's syndrome baby Alice ... The cult kidnap Barry and blow up No. 5 ... Simon commits suicide ... Grants restaurant opens ... Mick is arrested for armed robbery on his wedding day ... David has a one-night stand.

January

Margaret and Katie both wake up with strangers in their beds. Margaret instantly regrets choosing Keith to prove her 'normality', and tells him it was just a one-off. The mistake propels a confused Margaret into Beth's arms. She allows Beth to kiss her and they cuddle up together in bed at the Farnhams' but Margaret, afraid that tongues will wag, soon goes back to her own room. Beth opens up about her sexuality to her (female) university lecturer, Chris Myers, and the pair go to a gay pub. When Beth takes Margaret to the same pub, Margaret flees in horror.

Mandy is preoccupied by the thought that they might have to find a new home for Trevor since Rosie and Eddie Banks are interested in buying the house. Sinbad persuades them to buy the house next door instead. Trevor can rest in peace ... for now.

Meanwhile Katie's sleeping partner is Simon, but her only regret is that they didn't use contraception. Simon assures her that there is nothing to worry about and sets about welcoming another lost soul – Terry – to the fold. Mick blows it at work for Marianne by angrily reminding her that the company refused to support her over the Charles Weekes case. As a result she is transferred to Newport – the second woman Mick has lost to South Wales.

DD gets Bev alone and says she knows that Josh could be Mike's son and therefore her grandson. Bev says all she knows is that she wants Ron to be the father, but that isn't good enough for DD who demands tests to solve the question of Josh's paternity. Jimmy feeds his habit out of Tony's fund but his conscience gets the better of him and he hands the £30 to Ron. The doctor tells Ron there is no hope for Tony, and Ron starts sobbing on Jimmy's shoulder. Sinbad catches Jimmy with his hands in the pizza parlour till and hears from Jackie that Jimmy is a drug addict. Jimmy denies it and tells Jackie that he only takes drugs to give him the strength to face the fact that he's a murderer.

February

Barry catches Jimmy with drugs he's confiscated from a dealer at the club. Jimmy can't bring himself to get rid of them so Barry gives him a helping head by sticking Jimmy's head down the toilet. He comes up feeling flushed. Tony dies and Jackie promises to stand by Jimmy.

Mandy is horrified to learn that the Bankses have been gazumped and are buying No. 10 after all. There's more bad news when Roy Williams, an old cell-mate of Trevor's, turns up and demands £500 which he claims Trevor owed him. Although Sinbad tells her not to pay Williams a penny, Mandy panics when he calls again and ends up giving him £700 from the Tony fund, just to get rid of him.

Knowing he's on to a good thing, Williams comes back for more and attacks her. Terrified of being in the house alone and fearing that she will be arrested any minute, Mandy decides to take the girls away as far away from Brookside Close as possible. But at the last minute Sinbad hears that the Bankses are now buying the Harrisons' house after all so there is no danger of Trevor rising like Lazarus. Sinbad races to Lime Street and drags Mandy and the girls off the train.

Simon moves the cult into No. 5. Lyn wants to evict them but the brainwashed Katie says they're not leaving. Simon is worried that Jacqui is a bad influence on Katie and unsuccessfully tries to stop his disciple going to Tony's funeral. Derek comes over from his latest posting in Bosnia to attend the funeral, at which Jimmy helps carry Tony's coffin. Jimmy breaks down in the graveyard and unburdens himself of his terrible secret – that he was responsible for Tony's death. Mike goes for the throat while Ron stands there in a daze, unable to take it all in. Finally he tells Jackie to get Jimmy out of his sight and leave them to bury his son.

Simon is angry that Katie disobeyed his orders and decrees that she must be punished. So he comes up with the most dastardly punishment in the world – she must sleep with Terry! This is too much of a strain even on Katie's faith and she runs to seek sanctuary at the Dixons'. The atmosphere there is suitably tense, not least because DD has also been harbouring Jimmy, her son's killer. It's a funny old world, thinks Ron … or words to that effect.

March

Sinbad has taken the rap for the missing fund money and is forced to borrow from a loan shark to prevent Ron involving the police. At the Legion, Ron is upstaged by stand-in comic Ray Piper who clearly has his eyes not only on Ron's position as compère but also on Bev. Ray succeeds in reducing Ron to a bag of nerves and the latter's act goes down quickly rather than well. Ray is elected the new compère.

Jimmy has progressed to heroin and turns to burglary to fund his worsening habit. However, he learns that he won't be facing charges over the deaths of Frank and Tony – news which infuriates Ron. In a fit of rage, Ron tracks Jimmy down to the drugs house where Jimmy has been injecting himself. He finds Jimmy in a bad way, but resists the temptation to leave him to die. Instead Ron saves Jimmy's life.

Simon persuades Terry to buy No. 5 for the cult but someone beats him to it. Simon doesn't intend giving up without a fight and erects a series of barricades.

Rosie and Eddie Banks move into No. 9, followed shortly afterwards by their eldest son Carl. Jealous of Beth's friendship with Chris, Margaret decides to teach Beth a lesson by going out with Carl, but she gets a nasty surprise when Carl's wife Sarah appears with their daughter Rebecca. Before Margaret can take that in, Carl is arrested for being an army deserter. In a bid to get to know the neighbours, Rosie hosts a lingerie party which is rudely interrupted by the traditional welcome to new residents on the Close – a brick through the window. David wants to call the police, but Eddie stops him. What is he hiding? While Max considers opening a restaurant with Barry, Patricia, who is pregnant, learns that there is a slight risk of the foetus being abnormal.

April

The result of her amniocentesis reveals that Patricia's baby could have Down's syndrome. She and Max discuss abortion but, after seeing other Down's children, decide against it. Penny sells her story to Adrian Roache and is pleasantly surprised with the result until the follow-up article reveals that Clive had a long-standing mistress, Sandra Pennington, and a ten-year-old son by her. Carl wants out of the army and his marriage but he has blown his chances with Margaret who decides to join Derek in Bosnia.

Rosie and Eddie apprehensively collect

their other son, Lee, from the secure unit where he has been detained since his conviction for joyriding. He is hurt that they have been pretending that he has been at his aunt's. Lee's misdemeanours resulted in a young girl being crippled and now he is free, her family – the Kershaws – are thirsting for revenge. Rosie and Eddie know that the Kershaws were responsible for the shattered window. The vengeance escalates when a van dumps Lee, tied to a wheelchair, on the Close with the word 'joyrider' scrawled on his forehead.

Despite having a voice reminiscent of the QE2 docking at Southampton, Bev is determined to enter the talent contest at the Legion and Ray has even written a song specially for her. Ray thinks her singing could charm the birds from the trees; Ron thinks they'd drop to the ground in a state of shock. But, with more than a little help from Ray, Bev wins the contest. It could be the start of a whole new career. However, she goes off the idea when Ray reveals his true intentions, suggesting that Bev go in for topless modelling. She slaps his face and totters off on high heels and in high dudgeon.

Bar chloroform, Carol Salter has been using every method possible to lure Mick into bed. She thinks she can usurp Marianne's place in his heart but Mick puts her right about a few things: far from splitting up, he and Marianne are engaged.

Sporting a bushy beard which makes him a dead ringer for Charles Manson, Terry defends Simon and the cult to all-comers. But then he finds out who the mystery house-buyer is. It's Barry, and he wants Simon and his loony tunes out. Still on the rob for drug money, Jimmy keeps Jackie sweet by returning her bracelet. He then brings his housebreaking activities closer to home, burgling the Farnhams' and then No. 9, but Eddie returns unexpectedly and holds him till the police arrive. Jimmy's number is up.

May

Jimmy's probation officer, Paul Heery, interviews Jimmy as part of a pre-sentencing report to the magistrates. Jimmy admits that his crimes were drug-related and Jackie adds that Jimmy has been to see a drugs counsellor. He is put on methadone but still tricks Jackie into giving him money so that he can buy smack. But it seems his drug days are over when he is sentenced to nine months in prison.

Penny comes face to face with Sandra Pennington and learns that she used to be a call-girl and that her affair with Clive had been going on for 12 years. To help her get over this latest discovery, Penny seeks the services of that well-known agony uncle, Barry. Meanwhile Barry continues to lean on Simon but finds that he doesn't scare easily. Simon paints a picture of Barry to his troops as someone who has been sent by the devil and must be defeated.

Marianne's latest job is Personnel Manager at Litrotech, where Eddie Banks happens to be shop steward. But with redundancies in the air, trouble is brewing. Following further intimidation, Eddie goes round with some mates to sort out the Kershaws and, after an initial scuffle which leaves Mick with a broken arm and cracked ribs, both parties agree to call a truce.

Sinbad's mum, Ruth, has come to stay at the Jordaches' and Sinbad takes the whole family on a Bank Holiday trip to New Brighton. Beth and Chris tag along too and split up from the main bunch to enjoy a little time together. However, Rachel spots them kissing and cuddling in the car and threatens to tell Mandy. Later, David too stumbles upon their little secret and is suitably outraged. He feels the situation calls for drastic measures – perhaps a letter to *The Times*. Deep in debt, Mandy discovers that the loan has been taken over by the sinister Kenny Maguire who immediately increases the payments. Ruth feels out of place at the Jordaches' and accepts an offer to live in Australia with her brother Jake. She invites

Sinbad to go with her, leaving him to choose between Ruth and Mandy. It's a tough choice – the mother who abandoned him as a baby or a wife who killed her husband.

June

Secretly hoping that Mandy will say something to make him stay, Sinbad finally gets his reward when she admits that she has feelings for him. It may not exactly be a declaration of everlasting love but it's enough to dissuade Sinbad from ringing Qantas. Mandy is soon in need of a broad shoulder to cry on when she is coerced by Maguire into signing a new exorbitant agreement and then becomes the latest to chance upon Beth kissing Chris. Upset at her mother's reaction, Beth moves out and goes to stay with Chris.

David is still reeling from his earlier discovery and preaches about the sins of lesbianism to anyone who will listen – that is, until his wife Jean takes the wind from his sails by disclosing that she too had a female lover in her youth. And she's still got the letters. David is most put out at this news, particularly on the eve of his Ruby Wedding anniversary. Thereafter the Crosbies lead separate lives under the same roof.

Buoyed by his success with Mandy, Maguire visits the restaurant site and demands £2,000 protection money from Max. Rather than tell Barry (in case he uses the gun he carries around with him), Max pays up but immediately receives another visit from Maguire and a further demand for three months' payment in advance. Barry finally gets Max to spill the beans about Maguire and tells him to arrange a meeting with the 'jumped up loanshark'. When Maguire arrives at the site, Barry is nowhere to be found. Instead, while Maguire is in the office, Barry is pouring cement from a mixer into Maguire's car. Maguire senses that he is out of his depth with Barry and backs off. Barry gets the £2,000 back the next day and warns Maguire to stick to frightening little people in future.

Carl is supposed to be making another go

of his marriage, but instead he is secretly dating Jacqui. Delving into Mike's video diary, DD realises that Mike genuinely believes that Josh could be his. She says the only way to be certain is for the two men to take DNA tests. Bev is not looking forward to the results. Waiting for the letter to arrive in the post, she discovers an even more shocking secret – that Ron dyes his hair!

July

The tests show that Mike is Josh's father. Bev is terrified of having to tell Ron: she's sure he won't want to know her. But Jackie comes up with an intriguing solution – for Bev to get herself pregnant again, this time by Ron. Bev embarks on a campaign of non-stop sex. And she banishes all talk of contraception. After a few days, Ron hasn't the strength to resist and is so exhausted he starts dozing off in the shop.

Mandy confronts Chris at the university and threatens that, unless she stops seeing Beth, she will tell her superiors. Chris promptly shows her true colours and finishes with Beth, who returns home heartbroken.

Barry is fast losing patience with Simon and the cult. Max delivers a solicitor's letter giving the squatters three weeks to move out but Simon simply screws the letter up in front of Barry and Max. Barry says they've tried doing things through the proper channels, now he's going to do it his way and goes to the office to load his trusty shotgun. Meanwhile Terry is warning Simon not to push Barry too far because he's killed before. Barry bursts into the kitchen of No. 5 but is surprised by Simon who grabs him from behind and relieves him of the shotgun. Barry is dragged upstairs and tied up in the front bedroom with tape across his mouth. Simon says the devil is now their prisoner. While business associates and neighbours draw their own conclusions about Barry's disappearance, Simon sets about converting him. He wants Barry to sign the house over to the cult but Barry refuses and spits on the contract. Simon says if they can't have the house, no one will. He tells the group that the day of Armageddon is approaching and that Jesus wants them to move on. The promised land is Bristol. While the others go, Simon and Terry stay behind to deal with Barry. Simon intends cleansing the house with a little something he made earlier – a home-made bomb. They untie Barry but don't make it out of the house in time. The bomb goes off and the explosion blows out windows all over the Close. Barry emerges relatively unscathed but Terry and Simon are in hospital fighting for their lives.

August

Barry recovers from the blast by sharing a night of passion with Penny. He later visits Terry in hospital but Terry rejects his overtures, reminding him of what he did to Sue and Danny.

With Carol Salter in hospital, Mick kindly offers to take in her son, Garry. His presence places a strain on Marianne who finds it difficult enough having Leo and Gemma about the house. Nevertheless she and Mick finally get round to naming their wedding day. While Patricia is rushed to hospital (courtesy of Bev's driving and a police escort) to give birth to baby Alice, Rachel joins Mick's football team and proves the star player.

In prison, Jimmy is offered some smack by cell-mate Don McAteer. Determined to clean up his act, Jimmy resists at first but finally gives in to temptation when Don goes on a binge. It turns out to be Don's last hit as the following morning Jimmy finds him dead. The prison officers search the cell for drugs but Jimmy knows that Don's stash is still safely hidden in the kitchens and decides that he is the ideal man to inherit Don's drug-dealing empire.

Sinbad's got a bad back and has to wear a corset. He wonders how he's going to survive with no window cleaning money coming in until Carl offers to take over his round. However, when Sinbad is able to resume work, he discovers to his horror that Carl has set himself up in direct competition. As the war hots up, Sinbad pinches Carl's ladders, leaving him hanging on to a window for dear life. With Sarah filing for divorce, Carl is chasing anything in a skirt. The window-cleaning round provides him with the perfect opportunity to bed bored housewives but he makes the mistake of boasting about his conquests to Mike, who feels it his duty to inform sister Jacqui. When Jacqui finds out, she drenches Carl with the contents of his own bucket. Jacqui also overhears Bev moaning to Jackie Corkhill about Ron, including the fact that Josh isn't Ron's son. Jacqui forces Bev to tell Ron the truth. Devastated to learn that he is Josh's grandfather and not his father, Ron storms out and moves into the storeroom at the Trading Post…back where it all started.

September

Jackie takes pity on Ron and invites him to stay with her while Jimmy is still a guest of Her Majesty. But Jimmy is let out unexpectedly early and arrives home to find Ron with his feet under the table. Homeless again, Ron is surprised when DD of all people offers to take him in and positively gobsmacked when she suggests that he return to the marital bed. To make him feel at home, she goes out shopping for clothes which are a bit more his own age, unlike the brightly-coloured shirts he wears for Bev. Finding Ron back at home, a disgusted Jacqui announces that she's sharing a flat with Katie.

Max is doing everything he can to avoid contact with baby Alice. Citing pressure of work, he barely visited Patricia in hospital and now that she and Alice are home, he deliberately works late. When they eventually get round to discussing Alice's christening, Max can't bear to hold the baby and runs out. Later he pours out his feelings to Patricia and gently takes Alice from her arms.

Meanwhile David and Jean have patched things up but unfortunately he is impotent. With industrial unrest at Litrotech, Eddie is voted out as shop steward in favour of his mate, Joey Woods. And when Sarah and Rebecca leave for Reading, Carl suddenly starts missing them. Mick and Marianne are house-hunting but worry what will happen to Garry. Their problems appear to be solved when Greg, Garry's ex-con dad, turns up and lands Sarah's job at the pizza parlour.

No. 5 has been transformed into a bachelor pad, though Barry asks Penny to move in with him. Despite the age difference, they seem to get on well. Simon is released from hospital. He is charged with causing an explosion but is released on bail. Barry can't believe that Simon is free to walk the streets and warns him that he could murder again if he doesn't get out of Liverpool.

October

Simon is sleeping rough in the woods behind the petrol station and making a nuisance of himself on the Parade, putting the fear of God into customers and shopkeepers alike. Simon tells Terry he has no intention of going to prison; he says they're going to take their own lives in the name of Jesus. He drives Barry's car to the woods and sets up the exhaust to suffocate himself and Terry. Barry arrives to find them both unconscious. He drags Terry out and resuscitates him but leaves Simon behind to die.

With Mick and Marianne away, Greg moves his stuff into Mick's flat and throws a party, to which Jimmy is invited. Greg wants Jimmy to think about coming in with him on a job but when Jimmy is shown a sawn-off shotgun, he doesn't want to know. Rachel and Garry go shoplifting and Patricia finds the strain of work and a new baby too much and collapses during Alice's christening.

Joey Woods organises a strike at Litrotech and Carl hears that there's some temporary work going there. It means crossing the picket line and leaves Eddie ashamed that his own son is a scab. Emboldened by a night of sex, Ron agrees to make another go of things with DD … at precisely the same time that Bev returns to the Close and announces that she

wants him back. When she hears that Ron has moved back in with DD, Bev marches round for a confrontation which ends with DD's smug declaration that she and Ron are sleeping together. Later Ron tries to apologise to Bev who says she'll deliver his clothes to him personally. Sure enough, she drops them round, only for Ron to discover they are all in shreds. And while she's in the mood for trouble, Bev tells Mike that Josh is his son. From her position of power, DD pressurises Ron into agreeing to renew their wedding vows. DD enjoys rubbing Bev's nose in it and Ron feels terrible when Bev scurries off with tears in her eyes. Shocked to learn that Bev and Josh are moving to London, Ron realises he can't go through with his vows and rushes out of church to be with Bev, leaving behind a devastated DD.

November

While David mounts a campaign against wheelie bins, Max and Barry are preoccupied with the opening of their restaurant, Grants. Loyd Grossman and Lily Savage do the honours but the icing on the cake is provided by Terry who, having discovered that his mate Simon is as stiff as a stick of spaghetti, saunters into the party and loudly announces that Barry is a murderer. As Terry's mental state deteriorates, Penny (or 'Lady Penelope' as Jimmy calls her) says she doesn't want Terry hanging around the restaurant. He's not safe with a soufflé, let alone a set of steak knives.

Kenny Maguire continues to pile on the financial agony for Mandy but suggests that she could clear her mounting debts by sleeping with him. Sinbad hears that his mother has sold her house and given him the proceeds: £45,000. He plans to use the cash to buy No. 10 as a Christmas present for Mandy, but wants to make it a surprise. Bad move. For Mandy, with seemingly no end to her money worries, reluctantly decides she has little option but to take Maguire up on his generous offer.

Greg is interested to hear from Marianne

that the temporary workers at Litrotech are being paid cash in hand, news which prompts Greg to boast to Jimmy that the wages snatch he's doing the next day will set him up for life. After Marianne has resigned following allegations that she collaborated with the union, Greg and his accomplice carry out an armed robbery there. Eddie stumbles across the raid and is hit in the face by the butt of Greg's shotgun. The robbers escape but an elderly cleaning lady catches a glimpse of Greg without his rubber mask. The news of the robbery is in the papers and Jimmy knows Greg was responsible. The gang got away with just £200, which Greg swaps for money in the pizza parlour till. The only description the police have is that the gun-toting villain was local and black but when they visit the pizza parlour to interview Marianne about her sudden resignation, they are fascinated to learn that her boyfriend Mick fits the description and doesn't have an alibi. Greg, on the other hand, is relieved when Garry provides him with an alibi.

On the morning of Mick and Marianne's wedding, the police find the stolen notes in the pizza parlour till. Officers head straight for the registry office and take the would-be bride and groom away in a police car instead of a wedding car. Somehow Sinbad's best man's speech seems academic. Marianne is subsequently released but the cleaner picks out Mick at an identity parade. Charged with the robbery, Mick feels distant towards Marianne and says he'll only move house and get married when he's cleared his name. But if he does get sent down, he wants Marianne to look after Leo and Gemma. To judge by her reaction, she'd rather be banged up in Holloway.

December

Marianne is considering accepting a job in Glasgow and is furious when Mick forbids her from taking it. Mick's got more on his mind when Leo and Garry are arrested for shoplifting along with Rachel and Lee. Mick

reads the riot act to Leo and when Marianne protests, Mick tells her to keep out of it – she's no longer part of his family. Rachel and Lee run away to London while Garry, who has worked out that his father was involved in the Litrotech wages snatch, pleads with Greg to give himself up in order to help Mick. When Greg refuses, Garry tells Mick who forces Greg to go to the police station and confess. Although Mick wins his freedom, he loses the girl. Marianne tells him she's taking the Glasgow job; it just won't work between them.

Perplexed by the hold which Terry seems to have over Barry, Penny gives it to Barry straight: he's got to choose between her and Terry. He chooses Terry and the pair head off to Spain for a break, leaving Penny to lick her wounds. While Barry is away, Penny befriends the eligible Sam Martin who advises her and Max to buy Barry out. They both eye Sam as a prospective business partner until Barry returns and gives Sam and Penny their marching orders.

For David Crosbie, sex is like catching a bus: nothing for ages, then two come along at once. After finally giving in to Audrey Manners' taunts to prove to her that he's a man, he rushes home guiltily to Jean who compounds his misery by telling him that she wants to show him how much she loves him. And he won't get rid of Audrey that easily; she is well and truly smitten with her galloping 'Major' and tries to blackmail him.

Having also done the dirty deed, Mandy thinks she's seen the last of Maguire and explains away his anticipated absence by announcing that she was able to pay him off after a big win on the bingo. She even has her hair done. But she is sickened when Maguire turns up again and calmly informs her that it wasn't just a one-off arrangement – she'll need to sleep with him several more times before all her debts are cleared. Thrilled that the house deal has gone through, Sinbad prepares to put a huge ribbon around it as Mandy's present, but is stopped by noises coming from upstairs. When he goes to investigate, he finds Mandy and Maguire in bed together. Encouraged by Beth to give the relationship another chance, Sinbad goes round to pay off Maguire once and for all. But Maguire refuses to take his money.

1995

DD moves out of Ron's life ... The Jordaches go on the run ... A killer virus sweeps the Close ... Mandy and Beth are found guilty ... Beth dies in jail, Mandy is freed ... Mick is stalked by Jenny Swift ... A lottery win divides the Close ... Rosie becomes a compulsive gambler ... Jean and Mandy say farewell ... Ron suffers a heart attack ... Jackie discovers the truth about Jimmy.

January

Sinbad resolves to sort Maguire out with his fists and seeks the advice of Jimmy and Barry. The latter advises him not to mess with Maguire but Sinbad won't listen and goes round for a confrontation. When he gets there, however, he finds Maguire has already been beaten up. Barry denies all knowledge of the attack but assures Sinbad that Maguire won't be back.

Ron lets DD have Josh behind Bev's back and she takes him off to church to conduct her own private baptism – something Bev is dead against. When Bev discovers her, she snatches back Josh. Angrily, Bev tells DD she'll never see Josh again. DD is determined to find what rights Mike has over Josh, but Mike isn't interested. As far as he's concerned, Ron is Josh's father. Deeply upset, DD sells the florist's and contemplates suicide. Ron finds her at Tony's graveside with a bottle of pills in her hand and, although he manages to talk her out of taking her life, she is still insistent about leaving the Close. Bev is reluctant to move into

No. 8 but changes her mind when she sees the house sign that Ron has bought – 'Casa Bevron'. Tacky is not the word.

Mike and Beth have become good friends but he has hopes that it will develop into something more physical. He buys some flowers to woo her but they wilt dramatically when he spots her in a car kissing her latest girlfriend, Viv. He finds an able substitute in Sarah Banks who, much to the annoyance of Rosie, has moved back into No. 9 with Rebecca.

David has trouble with an old boiler – Audrey's – and the femme fatale of the over-55s moves herself into the Crosbies' where she threatens to expose David to Jean.

Eddie is puzzled by the sudden appearance of a large puddle in his back garden and reckons the water is coming from beneath the Jordaches' patio. With Sinbad and Mandy on holiday in Ireland, Eddie starts to dig up the patio himself, but Beth discovers him, angrily throws him out and frantically shovels soil back into the hole. However, Eddie is undeterred and announces that the Water Board are coming out the next day. Mandy, back from holiday, says they'll have to move the body, but when it comes to the crunch, she can't go through with it. Instead the whole family go on the run – back to Ireland. This time it's no holiday. Meanwhile Eddie mentions to Jimmy that Sinbad has got something stashed under the patio and they decide to retrieve it before the workmen do. As Eddie digs, he hits a plastic bag and recoils in horror when he finds it contains a human hand. When news of the gruesome discovery reaches the Irish papers, Mandy decides it's time to tell Rachel what really happened to her father.

February

Shaken by Mandy's confession, Rachel goes missing and is picked up by the police at Dun Laoghaire ferry terminal, near Dublin. To the relief of Sinbad, Mandy and Beth, Rachel says nothing and soon the quartet are flitting between bed-and-breakfasts faster than you can boil an egg. When she finds out that Mandy stabbed her father, Rachel slaps her face and denies that Trevor abused her.

Back on the Close, Jimmy's dog Cracker digs up a bone in the back garden of No. 10 and dog and owner become overnight celebrities. However, the bone turns out to be nothing more than an old ham shank. In Ireland, Sinbad and Mandy finally consummate their relationship, but the four fugitives are arrested shortly afterwards. Beth, Mandy and Sinbad all claim they killed Trevor single-handedly, but Sinbad slips up by saying he stabbed Trevor in the chest. Mandy and Beth stick to their stories until Mandy at last admits that they both tried to poison Trevor and then she alone stabbed him. Both are then officially charged and released on bail.

To the amazement of the neighbours, they return to the Close where Rachel says she hates them both and never wants to see them again. And she admits it was she who told the papers that Beth is gay, hence the lurid headline 'BODY IN GARDEN GIRL IN GAY SEX STORM'. The Jordaches start receiving poison-pen letters, but Mandy's main concern is being reunited with Rachel whom she desperately wants to come home. But Rachel doesn't want to know. She is staying with the Bankses which gives Rosie, angry that Sarah is dating Mike, the excuse to tell Sarah to move out. In desperation, she and Rebecca move in with Mike, Jacqui and Katie. Jacqui wants her out and Mike's not too keen on the idea either. In fact, he began to go off Sarah the moment he discovered she had a kid. He's all heart is Mike.

In her pursuit of an organic lifestyle and free-range eggs, Bev introduces a chicken which she promptly christens Kiev. Ron says it looks like a cock to him but Bev, who knows about such things, won't take it back. Barry finds one of the waitresses at Grants, Emma Piper (daughter of Ray), a tough nut to crack and Audrey Manners receives an unexpected visitor. At first, she passes him off as her long-lost brother George, but he soon puts everyone right : he's Audrey's husband, fresh back from Kenya.

March

Shiftier than a weasel carrying a swag bag, George begins selling timeshare holidays in Kenya. Eddie reckons one would make a great 40th birthday present for Rosie and willingly hands over £1,000. Rosie's party is by no means uneventful, particularly when Rachel spots Mandy and Beth and accuses them of being man-haters and murderers in front of everyone. It needs more than a bowl of Twiglets to restore the peace.

Hung-over from the party, Eddie starts having second thoughts about the timeshare business but his fears are eased when George hands him a video of Kenya. Eagerly he sits down to watch the tape, only to find it is blank. Convinced he has been stitched up, Eddie tries to contact George who is beginning to become impossible to track down.

Suddenly a mystery virus sweeps the Close. Carl is taken ill and then Garry, on his first day at work at the leisure centre, doubles up in pain and collapses into the swimming pool. Mick dives in and desperately tries to revive him but his efforts are in vain. Garry is dead. George's sales are considerably healthier than he himself is and Jean, seeing him in distress, kindly offers him refuge at the Crosbies'. His health will deteriorate further if Eddie and Jimmy, his latest victim, catch up with him. When Eddie tells Jimmy the whole thing's a scam, the pair hunt George down. Having just about mustered the strength to do a deal with Jean, George emerges from his hiding-place to be confronted by Eddie and Jimmy. They snatch the money they are owed from his jacket, but as they let him go, he drops to the ground...dead.

Audrey tells Jean that George probably died of terminal greed but it's no laughing matter when Jean too falls ill to the virus, closely followed by Audrey and young Thomas Farnham. Mick fears they've got an epidemic on their hands. As the Close is sealed off, Audrey becomes the third fatality and the health authority orders the residents to give samples. The tests show that Ron is to become a father – but the identity of the mum-to-be remains a mystery. Mandy also discovers she is pregnant.

In the midst of the mayhem, Emma proposes to Barry who promptly does a runner, giving rise to speculation that he is in financial difficulties. Tired of waiting for him to return, Emma moves out of his house. The engagement is off.

Max rushes back from a business trip to the States to be at Thomas's bedside. It's touch and go for a while but he eventually pulls through. It looks grim for Jean however. Certain that his wife is on her deathbed, David tries to ease his guilt by confessing to his one-night stand with Audrey and expressing his utter remorse over the whole sordid episode. But the next day Jean regains consciousness and tells a startled David that she heard every word he said...

April

Jean says she has no intention of forgiving David for his infidelity, to which he declares that he will do the honourable thing and leave. She makes no attempt to stop him. As it becomes clear that the killer virus was brought over from Africa by the ill-fated George Manners, the other positive pregnancy test turns to be that of a shocked Rosie.

Trying to build bridges, Mandy throws a surprise 16th birthday party for Rachel, but when Rachel learns that Mandy is pregnant, she attacks her, packs her bag and leaves. With David out of the way, Jean offers Rachel a room at the bungalow. David is soon allowed back too, on condition that he and Jean are totally honest with each other from now on. Both find that having Rachel around is like a breath of fresh air.

In Barry's absence, Carl and Jimmy are put in charge of La Luz and Jimmy exploits Carl's naivety and eagerness to make a quick tenner by using him as an unwitting courier for his drug deals. Carl also changes the club's beer supplier on the grounds that the new supplier is much cheaper. He boasts that Barry will be quids in. Jimmy has been keeping his drug money in the bathroom at home but when Jackie finds it, he not only has to do some quick talking, he also has to think of a new hiding place. He chooses Barry's loft.

Ron wants to expand into the florist's shop, but Max beats him to it and Patricia takes over, renaming it The Gift Box. Jacqui also branches out with her own aerobics classes and plans for a car boot sale.

With the trial approaching, Rachel is informed that she will be called as a prosecution witness. The letter upsets her and she tells David that it must be because of the lies Mandy and Beth told, about her dad getting into bed with her. David is suitably stunned. When their solicitor, Alison, suggests they plead guilty to manslaughter, Beth angrily replies that it was self defence and they will plead not guilty. Alison accepts this but warns her about losing her temper in court. It would play right into the prosecution's hands. Mike wants to help Beth to the point of being prepared to lie for her in court but Jacqui, who makes no secret of her dislike for Beth, threatens to tell the judge if he does. In the end, Beth says she wouldn't allow him to perjure himself but she and Mike both wonder whether Jacqui is behind the hate mail she is still receiving.

May

Jacqui's car boot sale reveals her to be a hard-headed little businesswoman. She has Leo and Lee cleaning cars, taking 25 percent commission from them, and Katie flogging herself to death serving. Ron is proud of his daughter until he notices that she's selling the same stuff as him, only cheaper. Jacqui is later sacked by the leisure centre but doesn't care; she wants to be her own boss from now on.

David is organising a VE Day street party with everyone as Forties' characters. Jimmy plans to go as Churchill until David points out it would be inappropriate in view of Jimmy's criminal record, so he goes as Hitler instead.

David had always made his father out to be a war hero but is forced to admit that he was a conscientious objector who worked down the mines – a miner not a major.

On the eve of the trial, Sinbad proposes to Mandy. She accepts – but wants to wait until after the trial when they can have a proper wedding. Brenna turns up and starts causing trouble, her arrival coinciding with a vicious card expressing the wish that Mandy and Beth may rot in hell. Brenna is particularly keen to browbeat Rachel, forcefully making the point that her mother and sister are liars and murderers who'll get what they deserve. Rachel is confused and upset. On the first day in court, Beth realises that Brenna is behind the hate mail so Mandy gives Brenna a bloody nose in the ladies'. On the witness stand, Brenna portrays Trevor as a decent, hard-working man and Rachel testifies that Trevor never touched her sexually, adding that Beth always hated him. When Beth gives evidence, she loses her cool and the prosecution succeeda in painting Sinbad as the lover waiting to fill Trevor's shoes.

The jury find Mandy guilty of murder and she is sentenced to life imprisonment plus seven years for conspiracy to murder, to run concurrently. Beth is also found guilty of conspiracy to murder and gets five years. Both intend to appeal but in the meantime David summons a meeting of the Brookside Residents' Association (BRA) to launch a campaign to free the Brookside two. A women's group also take up the case and organise a vigil.

Jacqui and Katie both take a fancy to Shaun Brookes, the boss at the video company where Mike works, but Jacqui is jealous when Katie gets in there first. Max learns that the cheap beer Carl is buying is illegal and tells him to get rid of it. When Leo has problems at school, Mick finds that his teacher, Jenny Swift, is only too pleased to help.

June

It soon dawns on Mick that Jenny is a few pages short of an exercise book. He's already found her stark naked except for his jacket draped over her shoulders and now her behaviour is becoming increasingly obsessive. She uses every excuse to be near him. What's more, Mick has been getting silent phone calls at the pizza parlour and begins to wonder whether Jenny is making them. Jenny lies to Rosie that Mick has sent her flowers and chocolates and Rosie encourages her to go for it – Mick deserves a little happiness in his life. Jenny then tells an excited Rosie that Mick has proposed, but it's a big secret … not least to Mick. Together Rosie and Jenny arrange a surprise engagement party but when Mick arrives, he angrily tells everyone to leave: there is no engagement. He tells Jenny he wants her out of his life, but she won't take the hint. Mick is forced to report her to the school headmaster and then to the police, but gets no joy. In the end, he has to resort to a solicitor's letter warning her to keep away.

Jacqui starts trying to prise Shaun away from Katie. She wants to open her own hairdressing salon and asks Shaun to lend her £2,000. She invites him round when Katie is out and goes to bed with him under the assumption that he will lend her the money. But in the morning he doesn't want to know, so Jacqui exacts revenge by stealing some valuable master tapes from his office.

Carl's beer suppliers, the Donnellys, are none too pleased when he is forced to cancel the order on Max's instructions. But they tell him he won't get his money back. Telling Lesley Donnelly he's Barry Grant, Jimmy snatches the money he and Carl are owed from the Donnellys' safe, but the Donnellys retaliate by breaking into Barry's house and setting fire to his furniture. Hell-bent on revenge, Jimmy takes Carl to the Donnellys' yard and throws petrol bombs at the vans. As the whole place goes up, Jimmy and Carl make their escape across the portakabin roof, but Carl goes back to rescue a fireman and ends up in hospital. The Donnellys agree to a truce as long as the police don't get to hear about the beer scam and Carl agrees to take the rap for Jimmy – in return for cash.

Patricia, Jean and Jackie publicise the Jordache case on the TV debate show *Loud and Clear*, hosted by Michael Parkinson, but when a darts marathon fails to stimulate much interest, they decide on more drastic measures. At the end of a prison visit to Mandy and Beth, Jean and Jackie tie all their hands together with nylon cable and refuse to leave until they get justice for the Jordaches. The women then join a protest outside the prison gates and Rachel begins to open up to the Crosbies, who start to realise that she lied in court.

July

The prison protest turns ugly and the pregnant Rosie is arrested by mistake. In serious pain, she is rushed to hospital for an emergency operation. She loses the baby and the doctor explains to Eddie that there is internal bleeding: it would be best for Rosie to have a hysterectomy. Eddie tells him to do whatever is necessary to save Rosie's life. But when Rosie learns about the hysterectomy, she is furious with Eddie and pushes him away. The only good news for the family is when Carl is freed without charge after the rescued fireman supports his story that he was just a passer-by at the explosion.

Jacqui tells Shaun he can have his tapes back in return for the £2,000 he promised to lend her. Shaun threatens to let Katie know that her best friend cheated on her but Jacqui calls his bluff and Shaun is obliged to cough up. But he gets his pound of flesh from the Dixons by sacking the hapless Mike. In turn, Mike gets back at his sister for losing him his job by telling Katie about Jacqui and Shaun. Bev starts wearing skirts around her neck and hanging around with her friend Janice in preference to the company of an old fuddy duddy like Ron.

To get away from Jenny, Mick takes the kids and Uncle Sinbad to Southport for a few days, unaware that Jenny has followed him every inch of the way. When they come face to face over a 99, she tries to gain his sympathy by fainting. Discharging herself from hospital, Jenny leaves Mick what appears to be a suicide note. He dashes round to her flat and discovers that her bedroom walls are plastered with photos of him. When he asks her why she's doing this to him, she answers that she's got a brain tumour. As Jenny continues to stalk him, Mick pays her another visit. He tells her he never loved her whereupon she threatens to throw herself over the bannister. Mick tries to pull her back but the bannister cracks and she crashes to the bottom of the stairs.

Meanwhile, as a result of the trouble outside the prison, the Jordaches are moved to another jail, in Yorkshire. David and Jean have stumbled upon some private letters to Rachel from Trevor – letters which indicate that the relationship between father and daughter was of a sexual nature. They eventually persuade Rachel to hand them over and they are passed on to Alison, the solicitor, in readiness for the appeal. But on the morning of the appeal Beth is found dead in mysterious circumstances.

August

Following Rachel's new testimony that Trevor did rape her, Mandy is freed. The post mortem reveals that Beth had a genetic heart condition. Brenna begs Mandy's forgiveness and insists on cooking her a nice meal. What Mandy doesn't know is that the evil Brenna has added poison to the soup. With the wedding approaching, Brenna bakes a cake whose ingredients could end the marriage before it's even begun. Sinbad puts the house up for sale and Jimmy sets to work on persuading Jackie to move in.

Jimmy goes to retrieve his money from Barry's loft, only to find that the locks have been changed on the orders of Barry's new house guest, Dil Parmar, who announces that he is in charge of all of Barry's business affairs while Mr Grant remains in the US. A worried Max learns from Dil that Barry plans to sell his half of the restaurant.

Ron is worried that the age difference between him and Bev is beginning to show. Already wound up by Bev's jibes, he is further humiliated when refused entry to a nightclub. Rather than stand Janice up, Bev goes in, leaving Ron to seek out the nearest Age Concern disco. To prove his youth, he plans to do a bungee jump with Max for the Alice Farnham Appeal which Patricia has set up to help Down's syndrome children. When Max takes fright at the last minute, Ron does it alone and wins the admiration of Bev. He buys himself some new clothes and struts his funky stuff at La Luz, only for his evening to be cut short by an angina attack.

Having raised the money, Jacqui opens her hair salon – Jacqui D's Style House – with her business partner, Peter Phelan, someone she met on holiday. Her judgement is open to question as Peter's first act is to take on Julia Brogan as receptionist.

Jenny undergoes counselling and moves into Mick's flat after being evicted from her place, but soon outstays her welcome. Mick tries to ease her out by going on a date with Bev's friend Janice, but this merely drives Jenny into a jealous frenzy. She goes to visit her parents in Nottingham (she had told Mick they were both dead) and steals a gun and bullets from her father's cabinet. When Mick gets back from Sinbad's stag night, she is waiting for him.

September

There are one or two hitches on Sinbad's wedding day: the bride-to-be is lying unconscious after her sister-in-law made a last, desperate attempt to poison her and the best man is being held at gunpoint by a crazed stalker. Even though the vol-au-vents arrived on time, the wedding is off. Mandy recovers, although for some reason she refuses to press charges against Brenna, but there is still no sign of Mick. The residents express their concern to PC Ian Coban who goes to the flat to investigate and is promptly taken hostage himself. As Jenny becomes ever more deranged, PC Coban is shot in a struggle and the siege only ends when armed police burst in and overpower her.

In court, Mick meets Jenny's father (the one he thought was dead) who suggests that Mick must have driven Jenny to behave so irrationally. Mick is relieved when Jenny is refused bail but he returns home to find a message from her on his answering machine telling him that she misses him and that she will see him soon. Feeling like a prisoner himself, Mick keeps his children off school in case Jenny gets to them. He becomes paranoid about everything and everyone and discovers that her father, John Swift, has hired a private detective to dig up some dirt on him.

Needing cash to buy out Barry's share of Grants, Max's bacon is saved by David, who takes out a loan on the bungalow without Jean's knowledge. When Jean finds out, she complains that his actions have ruined her chances of being able to travel. In an attempt to satisfy her thirst for globe-trotting adventure, David books a long weekend in Bath with the Golden Oldies. Jean is not impressed. Mike's chances of passing his driving test are not helped when he stops at a pedestrian crossing and Julia climbs in the back for a lift. But he's still disappointed when he fails.

Since she cannot get an apology from the hospital, Rosie commences legal proceedings. In a bid to ease the pain of what she has been through and in an attempt to forgive Eddie for his part in it, Rosie tries to rekindle her sex life. She orders skimpy lingerie from a catalogue, only to arrive home to find Eddie wearing it. She is upset, not only because you should never wear black satin knickers with a boiler suit, but also because he is mocking her attempts to make herself feel desirable again. The only bright spot in her life appears to be the new lottery syndicate they have formed with the Crosbies which, using numbers systematically selected by David, quickly produces a £10 win. Carl and Sarah make another go of their marriage at No. 5 although she insists that they sleep in separate rooms. Carl allows Jimmy to keep his drug money in the loft. Jimmy buys a cab company from Dil which he names Korky Kars. His base is a shabby caravan, but it serves as the perfect cover for his drug dealing and as evidence to convince Jackie he is on the straight and narrow.

October

Jimmy's ploy works and Jackie agrees to move into No. 10. But when he goes to retrieve his money from the loft at No. 5, Sarah catches him and thinks he's a burglar and he is forced to tell her about the deal with Carl. This is the last straw for Sarah who throws Carl out. Realising that his marriage is dead and buried, he quickly accepts Dil's offer of a job in Dubai.

Unable to stand being cut off from the outside world, Leo and Gemma run away and hide in Jimmy's caravan. At the same time, Ron has had enough of the eyesore that is Korky Kars and tows the caravan to the scrapyard. It is just about to go under the crusher when Ron spots Leo and Gemma peering through the window. He manages to stop the crane driver and takes the kids home to Mick. When Mandy starts her contractions in the Trading Post, there is no time to call an ambulance and she ends up giving birth to daughter Ruth in the Moby – at a bus stop because Ron couldn't miss the opportunity to stop and sell crisps!

Susannah is back in England following the break-up of her relationship with Andrew. Her presence unsettles Patricia who endeavours to minimise her threat by pairing her off with Dil. When Susannah announces that she has moved in with Dil – on a purely platonic basis – Max can barely conceal his jealousy. He later learns that Dil may be leaving for Dubai and fears losing the children again if Susannah goes with him. Susannah tells Max the one thing she'd stay in England for is him.

Katie is pursuing a career as a dancer but thinks she'd have more success at auditions if she lost weight. Her new look attracts the

attention of one of her fellow dancers, Christian.

David drags Jean off to Bath, leaving Rachel with strict instructions to hand the lottery stake to Rosie and Eddie. Although she forgets, the Bankses put the money in anyway and are delighted when they get five winning numbers and the bonus ball, giving them a £100,000 prize. Rachel then turns up with the Crosbies' money but Eddie refuses to accept it, saying it should have been in before the winning numbers were announced. Rosie's sister Mo is also disappointed with her cheque from the Bankses as she was expecting a bit more than £500. The Crosbies return home clutching bottles of champagne, ready to celebrate their win, only for Rose and Eddie to inform them that they closed the syndicate when the Crosbies failed to pay their stake money. David demands their share, particularly as his numbers were responsible for the win, but the Bankses offer a miserly £500. David throws the money back at Eddie and it scatters all over the Close. With David threatening legal action and the Bankses becoming social outcasts, Rosie finally gives in and hands the Crosbies the full £50,000. But the lottery win has whetted Rosie's appetite for more.

November

Certain she's on a winning streak, Rosie hauls Mo off to bingo at every opportunity and starts buying scratch cards by the dozen. If Rebecca sees two little ducks at the park, Rosie shouts 'House!' Eddie accuses her of putting bingo before her own family, an accusation which she counters by taking Rebecca into town for the day. However, Sarah later discovers fruit machine tokens in Rebecca's pocket. Eddie confronts Rosie but she lies her way out of it and says the only problem she's got is him. When he finds their account has gone down by £4,000, Eddie arranges for the money to be deposited in Mo's account, out of Rosie's grasp. As a further precautionary measure, he confiscates Rosie's cash card but she persuades Mo to withdraw some cash from the account, lying that Eddie knows all about it.

Jean and David plan to spend their winnings on a foreign trip, but whereas Jean fancies an ambitious trek, David has set his heart on the comfort of the QE2. Neither is prepared to bend and so they go their separate ways. She has hardly turned the corner than David realises what a mistake he has made in letting her go.

Another departure is Mandy who has been offered a job at a women's refuge in Bristol. Sinbad doesn't want her to take it, but has to concede that it is her vocation in life and waves her and baby Ruth a tearful farewell.

Jimmy's daughter Lindsey turns up on the doorstep, saying she's left her husband, Gary. The errant Gary follows on and Jimmy reluctantly agrees to allow him to stay.

Jenny changes her plea to guilty but Mick's relief is tempered by an outburst from John Swift who tells the Court that his daughter's life has been ruined by Mick. Jenny is subsequently sentenced to three years in prison. Sinbad and Mick agree that they both need to make a fresh start in life. So do they leave Merseyside, even move to a different part of the city? No, they move to 5 Brookside Close, all of 100 yards from Mick's old flat.

Ron feels threatened by Bev's friendship with Peter and is convinced they are having an affair, so when she suddenly proposes and asks Ron to marry her, he thinks she's after his money. In fact, Bev has resisted all Peter's advances and they have agreed to be just good friends. He thinks she has a flair for hairdressing and offers to teach her with the help of an old dummy which they christen 'Ron'. Therefore when Ron gets Mike to bug Peter's room at Julia's and hears Peter and Bev saying that 'Ron' has served his purpose and that after she's finished with him, they could bury him under the patio, the real Ron becomes more paranoid than ever.

December

Ron refuses to eat anything in case it's poisoned and gives a little of a casserole Bev prepared to her chicken, Kiev. When Kiev keels over, Ron thinks he has proof enough and he and Mike confront Bev and Peter at Julia's. The strain proves too much for Ron and he suffers a heart attack. Reports of his death prove slightly premature – although he did stop breathing for two minutes during which time he had an 'out of body experience' and met Frank Rogers – and he comes round to find DD and Bev at his bedside, arguing. Now he knows he's back in the real world. But his brush with death has had quite an effect on him. He says maybe there is something on the other side – and he doesn't mean *Emmerdale*.

Transformed from bible-bashing zombie into astute businessman, Terry has returned to the Close and ousted Dil. But he is not exactly the bearer of good tidings as far as Katie is concerned and tells Jacqui that Katie could have AIDS after sleeping with Simon. Katie comes back from a weekend away full of how she slept with Christian and the condom slipped off. At that point, Jacqui relays Terry's news. At first, Katie refuses to take a test and drops a mystified Christian. He pushes her for an explanation and eventually she blurts out that she might have AIDS. She eventually gets the all-clear but he wants nothing more to do with her and she starts bingeing on food.

The Banks's lottery money finally runs out and all the Christmas presents have to be returned. Desperate to win the money back at bingo, Rosie steals from Grants where she has got a part-time job. Lee, who also works there, discovers her stash and Max brands him as the thief.

Jimmy hands Lindsey and Gary jobs at Korky Kars but, when Jimmy is out, Lindsey innocently gives Gary the job of delivering one of Jimmy's parcels. As a result, Gary knows all about Jimmy's little sideline and wants to be let in on the operation. When Gary is followed while doing a deal, police with sniffer dogs raid No. 10. Jimmy and Gary are arrested on suspicion of possession but are released on bail. Following the raid, Jimmy's supplier pulls out, so the resourceful Gary decides they should cut out the middle man and get the gear themselves from Holland. Jackie finally cottons on that the new house has been bought with drug money, but is adamant that Lindsey must never find out.

1996

Eddie falls in love with Sarah ... Jimmy's drug dealing causes another death ... Gary stitches up Mike and Lindsey ... The Farnhams split up ... The Bankses move out and the Simpsons move in ... Nat abandons Jules on their wedding night ... Sammy is taken to court ... Sinbad gets engaged to two women...Little Jimmy Corkhill is executed by drug dealers ... The Simpsons' secret is revealed ... Bev walks out on Ron and sets fire to the house.

January

Rosie comes clean and admits that she is the restaurant thief. There is another fearful row with Eddie, at the end of which he packs his bags and seeks comfort from Sarah. Eddie tries to get Rosie to go to Gamblers Anonymous, but she still maintains she doesn't have a problem. He finds himself drawn ever closer to the sympathetic Sarah and becomes jealous of Terry, who is also clearly interested in her. Finally the inevitable happens and Eddie and Sarah end up in bed.

After his heart scare, Ron announces his retirement from the Trading Post and Bev takes over. Katie is appearing in panto with Australian soap star Shane Cochrane who wastes no time in asking Jacqui out to dinner. Meanwhile Katie's ideal meal consists of three pizzas and a trip to the bathroom to throw up. Jimmy is impressed when Shane, having heard from Jacqui about his criminal past,

approaches Jimmy for some drugs for a 'mate'. Shane enthusiastically takes up Gary's offer of free heroin and, when he misses a performance, Jacqui explains that he's exhausted, little realising that he's high on drugs. She discovers the truth when she finds a hypodermic needle and heroin in his sponge bag and tells him she never wants to see him again. A scared Gary receives a visit from local drug baron, Big Davey, who strongly advises him not to import any more drugs. Mike and Lindsey start seeing each other behind Gary's back but their secret is out when Jackie catches them in bed together.

Still in a state of shock after Big Davey's visit, Jackie tells Lindsey that the quicker and the further she gets away from Gary, the better. Lindsey is puzzled by her mum's apparent change of heart. Jimmy is undercutting Big Davey by five percent but is full of bravado, saying he'll wait for Big Davey to get in touch and negotiate. Unfortunately, Big Davey's idea of negotiation is a hail of bullets through the front window of number 10. Frightened for their lives, Jackie and Lindsey move out to live with Val (Jackie's sister) and Mike respectively. Jimmy realises he's lost everything and Ron is far from happy at having a Corkhill under his roof. Jimmy orders Gary to bin the remaining heroin, but Gary can't bear to see all that money go down the drain and sells some to Shane. But the heroin is uncut and Shane is found slumped dead in his dressing-room.

February

Jacqui vows to let the world know about Jimmy and sprays the front of the house with 'Murderer Jimmy Corkhill – Drug dealer'. Jimmy and Gary start to remove the graffiti but get fed up, leaving 'Jimmy Corkhill – rug dealer'.

Max is delighted when Grants is voted Best Restaurant on Merseyside by *Mersey Nite Out* although he is a shade miffed that the article compares him to Basil Fawlty. As a result of his new-found fame, he is asked to do an interview at a local radio station but has to borrow Ron's car to get there. On the way, he gets lost in the new one-way system and ends up being propositioned by a prostitute who thinks he's a kerb-crawler.

In the wake of their dangerous liaison, Sarah is determined to distance herself from Eddie. Lee tries to get his parents back together, but Eddie isn't interested and tells Rosie he's in love with someone else. Lee has fallen for Katie but the feeling is not reciprocated. However, when he stumbles across her stash of food, she suddenly softens and explains that she's detoxifying her body and that it's to be their secret. Pleased to be taken into her confidence, he agrees to say nothing. But when everyone gathers for the Close pancake race and Katie faints, Lee is forced to reveal that she has an eating disorder.

Gary sets out to find Lindsey, unaware that she is so close to home. She and Mike had been planning to go to Turkey but, when that falls through, they hear from Sinbad of a job going in Australia. However, Gary spots daughter Kylie watching the pancake race through the Dixons' window and asks her to let him in. Upstairs, he discovers his wife in bed with Mike. Gary snatches Kylie and tells Lindsey the only way she'll get her daughter is to go back to him. But Jimmy steps in. He has seen Lindsey suffer enough and returns Kylie to her before throwing Gary out of number 10. On Mike and Lindsey's day of departure to Australia, Gary, seemingly repentant, turns up at the Dixons' to say goodbye. He later asks Jackie to present Kylie with a farewell gift on his behalf – a teddy bear.

March

As Mike and Lindsey's plane stops off at Bangkok, customs offers search their belongings and discover a bag of heroin inside Kylie's teddy. Both are held in custody on suspicion of drug smuggling and when news of their arrest and Gary's likely involvement reaches the Close, Ron heads straight for the Corkhills'. There, Gary finds himself confronted by a lynch mob and is forced to make his escape down the drainpipe.

The Corkhills and Dixons are united in trying to free their children. Jimmy tells Ron he's really sorry and will do anything to secure the release of Lindsey and Mike, to which an emotional Ron replies that if he loses his only remaining son, he'll come after Jimmy even if it means being put away for life himself. Gary sneaks back into the house for the remaining drugs, but is captured by Jimmy and marched down to the police station. Gary makes a full confession, but is told he won't be charged: it's all down to the Thai authorities. Gary admits he only wanted to scare Mike and Lindsey – he didn't even know the plane stopped in Bangkok. To raise money for lawyers and for Ron and Jimmy to fly out to Bangkok, Gary sells the last of the drugs to Big Davey for £30,000.

Sarah decides to leave Liverpool in order to get away from Eddie. As she is about to make her exit, Eddie breaks down and confesses his love for her ... just as Rosie and Mo are coming along the path. As part of her treatment for bulimia, Katie attends a clinic and is pleasantly surprised by the counsellor, Dr Mark Smith. Baby Ruth comes to stay with Sinbad for a few days but he is reluctant to let her go back to Mandy.

It really isn't Ron's month for he is also accused by the police of kerb-crawling until closer inspection of the time and date shows that the alleged offence took place while Max had borrowed his car to get to the radio station. Max goes to the police station to clear his name but, despite his protestations of innocence, is given a caution. He pledges Ron to secrecy and seeks out Linda, the prostitute in question, to back up his story but she refuses to talk to him without payment. Unaware that he is being watched by a police patrol, Max offers her money and, before she can say 'That will do nicely', he is arrested for soliciting. He manages to keep the news from Patricia until David, back from holiday, shows her a newspaper cutting about the case. Max repeats that it has all been a misunderstanding but Patricia refuses to believe him and tells him she doesn't want him anywhere near her. Susannah, however, is infinitely more sympathetic.

April

What really galls Patricia is that Max told Susannah about the business with the prostitute before he told her. Max is truly frustrated – he doesn't know how he's going to convince a jury he's innocent when his own wife doesn't believe him. David continues to be very cool towards Max until he too is the recipient of bad news: Jean has written to say that she won't be coming home. Despite Max's pleas, Patricia refuses to support him in court and instead goes to France to see her mum. Susannah backs Max all the way and he is acquitted. Patricia comes home to congratulate him but, hurt by her lack of trust, he packs his bags and moves in with Susannah. Despite last-minute attempts at a reconciliation, Patricia leaves again for France. Max has lost her for ever.

Katie, who is staying at the bungalow with Rachel and Jacqui, sinks into a depression and locks herself in her room. Mark Smith coaxes her out and she admits that she stopped going to the sessions because she had a crush on him. He promises to help her, but on a purely professional basis. He can't get involved with a patient. Bev runs an Easter Egg promotion at the Trading Post, promising £50 in one egg. Bev knows which egg it is but when she is called away to speak to Ron in Bangkok, DD, who has returned to offer moral support, unwittingly sells the marked egg. Luckily for Bev, the egg has been bought by Katie as a present for her. So Bev gets her £50 back. Sammy reappears on the scene, drunk, saying she's left Owen, and proceeds to make an exhibition of herself.

Rosie and Eddie are drawn together by the fight for compensation against the hospital, but are shocked to receive a letter from the bailiffs with a repossession order telling them

to quit the house in 14 days. A shamefaced Rosie admits she has been gambling away the mortgage money. The hospital makes a final offer of £25,000, enough to save the house, but, knowing that £50,000 would enable them to buy the house outright, Rosie can't resist one last gamble. She blows the lot on the roulette wheel at a casino and the Bankses are left homeless. They sell off their possessions and seem set to split up, but in the end they leave the Close together, prepared to give their marriage another chance.

The local MP, James Payne, agrees to help in the release of Mike and Lindsey and a Foreign Office minister offers a glimmer of hope by revealing that in such cases, the authorities invariably prosecute one of the accused and let the other go. News comes through that one of them is being released. It is Lindsey. Ron is gutted.

May

Hearing that Mike is being charged with drug trafficking, Ron nearly has another heart attack. Any trace of goodwill towards the Corkhills evaporates as a bitter Ron and the mouthy Bev give Lindsey a hard time. Not one for sitting on the fence, Bev insinuates that Lindsey gave sexual favours to secure her release, an allegation which leads to Jackie slapping Bev's face – hard. After going on the run, Gary resurfaces and promises to tell the police everything, on condition that Lindsey comes back to him. Lindsey realises it's Mike's only hope. Gary bargains with the police to secure immunity from prosecution and now Lindsey has to keep her side of the bargain. She tries to convince Jackie – and herself – that she's going back for Kylie's sake, because Kylie needs her dad. Mike is eventually freed from jail but Ron warns Lindsey that if she really loves him, she'll keep well away from him. In the meantime she has to invent a succession of excuses when Gary wants to resume sexual relations. Mike arrives home and is devastated when Lindsey tells him she's back with Gary and that it's all over between them.

The Simpson Family

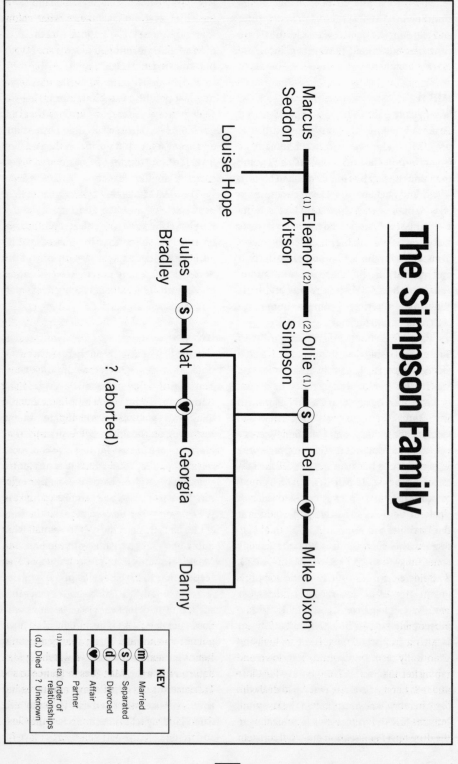

Marcus Seddon ━━━ (1) Eleanor (2) ━━━ (2) Ollie (1) ━s━ Bel ♥ ━━ Mike Dixon
Kitson Simpson

Louise Hope

Jules Bradley ━s━ Nat ♥ ━ Georgia Danny

? (aborted)

KEY

━m━	Married
━s━	Separated
━d━	Divorced
━♥━	Affair
━━	Partner
(1) ━━ (2)	Order of relationships
(d.) Died	? Unknown

Susannah turns up on Max's doorstep with Matthew and Emily in tow. Dil has stopped paying the rent on the flat and they have nowhere to live. With great reluctance, Max allows them to stay and Susannah sets about making herself indispensable. Sammy lands her dream job, as a barmaid at La Luz. She also gets a part-time cleaning job at the Farnhams'. Mick takes up weight-training with the help of Jackie's sister Val and Sinbad opens a shop on the Parade selling washing machines and cookers.

Bel and Ollie Simpson buy No. 9 and move in with their sons Nat and Danny. The latter hates life at Brookside Comprehensive where he is repeatedly bullied by a boy called Tinhead and secretly plans to educate himself at home. Nat is preparing to be married to Jules Bradley, but when his elder sister Georgia turns up he seems less than ecstatic.

June

There is clearly bad feeling between Nat and Georgia but nobody can get to the bottom of it. Nat's explanation to Jules is that he doesn't get on with Georgia's husband, Martin. Bel worries that Nat is rushing into marriage and Georgia admits that her own marriage was a mistake. To Nat's relief, Georgia says she's going back to Martin but the farewell peck on the cheek from sister to brother quickly turns to something more passionate, followed by a declaration of love. Before long, Georgia is back and her presence makes Nat unable to rise to the occasion with Jules. Sensing something is wrong, Jules confides in Georgia.

Rejected by Lindsey, Mike decides he's going to live life to the full and goes to La Luz on the prowl for a woman – any woman. Gary is becoming increasingly annoyed that Lindsey is giving him the knock-back in bed and eventually resorts to pinning her down and raping her. In terror, she runs back to the Close and tells her mum. Jackie decides to deal with Gary her own way. She phones Big Davey and informs him that Gary has been squealing to the drug squad about his underworld contacts.

Big Davey (who is well-named) promises to sort him out and asks Jackie what colour flowers she would like in Gary's wreath.

Now that Mike is back, Bev wants DD to leave. Ron tries to break it gently to DD, saying he's worried that she is falling for him again, but she finds this hilarious and reveals that her new man is on his way to fetch her. Ron feels instantly jealous. Seeing how miserable Lindsey and Mike are without each other, Ron and Jackie try a spot of matchmaking to prevent Mike leaving for America. Their plan works and the pair enjoy an emotional reunion.

Mick's interest in Val (Jackie's sister) comes to an abrupt halt when she reveals that it's Sinbad she fancies. To add to his woes, Mick hears from the Education Welfare Officer that Leo has been sagging off school with Danny. Still resenting Susannah's presence, Max suggests she and the children move into the flat above the pizza parlour. Susannah is outraged by the idea and tells Max that if the flat is so perfect, why doesn't he move there himself? In his fury, he does, thereby managing to throw himself out of his own home! But she wins him back by promising to do the restaurant books which are due for inspection. Having satisfied the VAT man, she sets about reclaiming Max. But she has a rival in Sammy who is determined to ensnare Max. One night after work at La Luz, they have a few drinks in the office and she seduces him on the sofa. When Sammy tearfully tells Susannah what happened and how she is madly in love with Max, Susannah feels angry and let down. Max responds by giving Sammy the sack.

July

Susannah doesn't let on to Max that she knows about him and Sammy and quickly reinstates her as a cleaner. She enjoys watching Max squirm. But when Max goes to France to see Patricia, Susannah is furious and takes her revenge by giving all his best clothes to Julia for a charity auction. He returns to the Close to find that Sammy has declared her love for him in front of half the neighbours, many of whom are wearing his shirts. Both Susannah and Max put Sammy in her place but she barges into the restaurant and, in front of the embarrassed diners, tells everyone how Max has used her. Then at a hairshow at Jacqui D's salon, she goes a step further and tells the assembled crimpers that she is pregnant with Max's baby. Later she is forced to admit that there is no baby – she was just looking for a meal ticket for herself and Louise.

Mike hands Lindsey a note he wrote in prison. It asks her to marry him. Choked with emotion, she is only able to nod in agreement. The build-up to the engagement party is marred by an ongoing argument between Jackie and Bev about the buffet. Jackie wants meat; Bev insists on vegetarian food. This erupts into an undignified slanging match at the party itself when Bev spitefully says she'll give Mike and Lindsey three months at the most, at which Jackie accuses her of being jealous.

Sinbad has got two women on the go: Val plus Peter's vivacious sister, Fee Phelan. Juggling his harem so that the two never meet leaves him exhausted and sometimes confused. Mick has been taking steroids to boost his chances in a body-building competition but they are making him extremely bad-tempered, particularly with Leo. Tinhead bullies Danny into doing his homework for him but Danny deliberately supplies him with rubbish so that Tinhead gets hauled before the headmaster. Danny and Leo are forced to flee from Tinhead's gang but, while Danny escapes, Leo takes a beating. An angry Mick marches round to the Simpsons' and physically threatens Danny and Ollie. Sinbad warns Mick to go easy with his temper – advice which makes Mick angrier still. At his wedding rehearsal, the emotionally mixed-up Nat rushes out of church and joins Georgia at the family cottage in the Cotswolds, unaware that Max and Susannah have booked the same cottage for a second honeymoon.

August

The Farnhams return to the cottage from a day's fishing to find Nat and Georgia naked in bed. Max quietly prepares for his and Susannah's immediate departure, leaving Nat and Georgia worried out of their skins as to whether the Farnhams will tell their parents. Not wanting to hurt Jules, Nat goes ahead with the wedding, with 13-year-old Danny as best man. As everyone gathers at the church, Ollie tells Nat that if he's having second thoughts, it's not too late to call it off but he manages to struggle through the ceremony.

At the reception, Jules gushes that it has been the happiest day of her life, which only goes to show what a miserable life she's led. Jules prepares to welcome Nat to the marital bed but he makes an excuse about leaving his wallet in the bar and goes to Georgia's room instead, leaving Jules to sob herself to sleep on her wedding night. The following morning, she tells her family that the honeymoon is off…and so is her marriage.

The Simpsons go home to an even worse reception: Tinhead has burgled their house, with Leo as an unwilling accomplice, and stolen Danny's computer. Meanwhile speculation is rife as to what is wrong with Nat. JC Bradley, Jules's bulldozer of a father, reckons Nat must be gay. Reasoning that this is preferable to the truth, Nat confirms to Jules that he is gay and she slaps him.

In a desperate bid to impress his increasingly grumpy father, Leo takes steroids and tries to lift weights. He ends up with a broken collarbone. Mick comes third in the bodybuilding competition – scant reward for neglecting his kids for three months and pumping his body full of steroids. His aggression remains undiminished and when he argues with Sinbad about his duties as a father, Leo grabs his beloved trophy and whacks him over the head with it.

Unable to find a babysitter, Sammy leaves Louise at home alone while she goes off to work at La Luz. She picks up a fella, Noel, and takes him back home, but when Louise starts crying he is out of the front door faster than Linford Christie. She wins him back by claiming that Louise is her sister's child and soon he invites her to Tenerife on holiday. She plans to get round the small problem of Louise by leaving her with Katie but a breakdown in communications leaves Louise unattended. The tot is spotted crying at the window of the bungalow by the Simpsons and Bel reports Sammy to Social Services. When Sammy lands at the airport, she is arrested by two policemen for abandoning her daughter.

September

Louise is returned to Sammy on the condition that she finds herself a registered childminder; otherwise, she could be taken into care for good. David provides moral and practical support but Sammy, angered when her solicitor advises her to plead guilty at the Crown Court, announces that she intends defending herself. Noel is one of the prosecution witnesses. Sammy tries to get Katie to testify on her behalf, but Katie refuses to lie, even for her sister, and on the stand, Sammy is torn apart, being forced to admit that she didn't phone Louise while she was on holiday. She insists she loves her but in her heart she knows she has lost the case. Sure enough, the jury find her guilty. She is fined £250 but spared a jail sentence. However, Terry then tells her that he can no longer risk employing her while she is still signing on; it could cost him his licence. Sammy leaves the Close, but not before making up with Katie.

Shocked by the news that David wants back the money he lent him for the restaurant, Max plans to make him a sleeping partner. Mike and Lindsey move into the Corkhills' as temporary accommodation before finding a place of their own, but Lindsey becomes irritated that Mike is more interested in making a video about their time in Bangkok than in acquiring a job. Besides, the whole Thailand business brings back painful memories for her.

Mick is full of remorse when he realises

that Leo and Gemma are afraid of him. He gets rid of the weights, throws away the steroids and promises to mend his ways. Sinbad manages to become engaged to two women on the same day and can't decide which one to choose. His hand is forced when Fee spots Val hugging him and he decides to choose Val, but winning her round is no easy matter.

After nearly losing Jackie, Lindsey and Kylie, Jimmy has decided to stay away from drugs for good. He is encouraged to go on a course to become a drugs counsellor and appreciates the opportunity to pass on the benefits of his experience. He then hears that his son, Little Jimmy, needs £1,200 to buy himself out of the Foreign Legion.

October

Worried that the cancer has returned, Patricia travels over to England for a biopsy, accompanied by Jean. Max follows Patricia back to Provence where he meets the new man in her life, Eric. Max is distinctly unimpressed by his Gallic charm and even less by Patricia's assertion that, in the event of her death, Eric should have full custody of Thomas and Alice. Max vows to fight to keep his children, but this gets a frosty reception from Susannah who has no intention of looking after Patricia's kids as well as her own.

The Farnhams aren't the only Brookside residents in France. Jimmy joins Jackie to seek out Little Jimmy. It is soon apparent that Little Jimmy is in big trouble and Jimmy has to rescue him from a gang of heavies. Back in Liverpool, Lindsey sees him with wraps of heroin strapped around his waist. He pleads with her not to tell anyone, claiming that he was an addict once but he's not any more. Lindsey is shocked. When Jackie finds out that her son is a drug addict and a thief (he stole her purse), she wants him out of the house. Jimmy is more sympathetic and tries to help him kick the habit. But when Jackie comes home to find Little Jimmy lying unconscious with the needle next to him, she is horrified at the thought that Kylie could have got hold of it. At breaking point, she seeks comfort from Ron, who is barely on speaking terms with Bev after she has secretly come off the Pill to try for another baby. Before long, Little Jimmy is tracked down by the thugs from France who demand £2,000 … or else.

Sinbad follows Val on her meals-on-wheels round and publicly asks her to marry him. To the delight of her customers, she says yes. The jilted Fee is less thrilled and tips a bucket of whitewash over Sinbad's head to wish him the whitest of weddings. And Mick is elected a school governor.

At the Simpsons', Danny walks in to find Nat and Georgia in bed. In shock, he runs out of the front door and straight into the path of Max's car. With Danny in hospital, Max issues Nat and Georgia with an ultimatum: tell their parents about the incestuous relationship or he will. Danny regains consciousness but remains silent as to why he ran out into the road. However, Georgia, anxious to tell them before Danny does, finally confesses to her parents. The habitually mild-mannered Ollie takes the news particularly badly, slaps Georgia and locks them both in their rooms to keep them apart. Nat tells Ollie he's gone mad; they're not animals, they are adults who love one another. Looking for an explanation, Bel accuses Ollie of abusing Georgia as a child. Ollie is flabbergasted.

November

Danny feels he owes it to Jules to tell her about Nat and Georgia, but regrets doing so when Jules confronts them at a firework display and gives the pair of them a rocket. Feeling she has been made a fool of, Jules takes an overdose. She is rushed to hospital where doctors pump her stomach and JC questions her. When he finds out what made her suicidal, he is on the warpath and reports Nat and Georgia to the police. Meanwhile Bel starts work at the Trading Post with Bev in the hope that opposites may attract. But as the heat builds up with the prospect of Nat and Georgia's exploits being plastered all over the papers,

Bel hits the bottle … of tranquillisers.

At his first meeting as a school governor, Mick addresses the issue of bullying and names the chief culprit as Timothy O'Leary, better known as Tinhead. He confidently states that the boy should be expelled, only to find that Mrs O'Leary is also a parent governor. Like a lioness protecting her cub, she rounds on Mick and accuses him of being the bully.

In the course of extensive rebuilding work at the nightclub, a body is discovered beneath the foundations. Terry's errant dad, Jack, seems unduly concerned about the identity of the corpse which is thought to have been there for at least 30 years. The police suspect foul play. Ron and Jackie continue to use each other as an escape from their own family problems; Ron in particular would like it to go further.

Corkhill father and son turn to crime in a bid to raise the £2,000. Little Jimmy breaks into the Dixons' and Big Jimmy steals Max's car from the petrol station forecourt. When Jackie finds out, she again turns to Ron and agrees to spend a night with him in Southport. After Little Jimmy steals the money his dad has raised and overdoses on heroin, Jackie and Jimmy decide the only way to get him off the stuff is to lock him in the extension, so when he comes out of hospital, they board up the window. Little Jimmy is in a terrible state. Jimmy decides he has no option but to give his son a fix but Jackie spots this and storms off to Ron. Bev is annoyed when Ron takes Jackie in, but for once he stands up to her and tells her to shut up. Jackie is about to run off with Ron when a dishevelled Little Jimmy turns up and accuses his cheating mother of hypocrisy, demanding to know if it is any wonder he turned out to be a robbing, smackhead lowlife with parents like his. In the ensuing struggle, Jackie falls down the stairs.

With Jackie in hospital, Jimmy and Bev find out the awful truth about Ron and Jackie's romance. Bev lingers only to rip the bedding from the four-poster and to deliver a few choice words. When two men turn up at the Trading Post looking for Little Jimmy, Ron assumes it's the drug squad and tells them where he lives. But they are the drug dealers Little Jimmy owes money to. They go straight round to No. 10 and execute him in cold blood.

December

Jimmy initially blames Ron for the death of his son, but, realising he is being unfair, lays all the guilt at his own door instead. Jackie tells Ron that she can't go away with him after everything that's happened, but he continues to live in hope. However, he no longer lives in No. 8 after a mystery arsonist sets fire to the house. Jimmy is arrested but released without charge, and Bev admits to Ron that it was she who, in a fit of bitter jealousy, set fire to Casa Bevron. With no apparent hope of a reconciliation with Jackie, Jimmy plans to make a fresh start in London.

Mike has literary pretensions and shows Ollie a book he has written about his experiences in Bangkok. Ollie is dismissive and Mike gets annoyed when Lindsey suggests some alterations. Susannah surprises Max with a secret nest-egg which she invests in the restaurant. Consequently it now belongs to her and David, but she tells an astounded Max that he'll get half of it back if he marries her. Val is rushing ahead with the wedding arrangements too fast for Sinbad's liking, and he uses Little Jimmy's murder as an excuse to postpone things. Their relationship has fizzled out.

Nat and Georgia are charged with incest and move into the pizza parlour flat. Returning home from a drink one night, Nat suggests they give Max a Christmas message and spray 'Fascist' on the Farnhams' window with aerosol snow. Everyone comes out to investigate the commotion, whereupon a drunken Georgia tells them all about her and Nat. Embarrassed beyond words, Bel and Ollie drag the two of them into No. 9. Ostracised by the neighbours, Nat and Georgia at least learn that they're not going to be prosecuted after all. But then Georgia discovers she is pregnant

and has a secret abortion.

Mick's latest flame is Elaine Davies, whom he met at the school parents' evening. Over Christmas, Elaine brings her family – mum Gladys, daughter Tanya and sister Cassie – to visit. Mick gets on well with them. David turns supersleuth in a bid to unravel the mystery of the La Luz body and draws up a list of possible victims. He is intrigued when Stella Fraser, sister of Henry, one of the names on the list, tells him that her brother was seen arguing with a man on the night he went missing. When dental records confirm it, Jack confesses to Terry that he killed Henry Fraser. And Julia has another surprise for Jack: in the last seconds of the old leap year, she asks him to marry her.

1997

Jack runs off with Julia's money ... Matthew and Emily Farnham are killed in a car crash ... Susannah takes an overdose ... Mick marries Elaine ... Jacqui suffers a horrifying attack ... Mick and Elaine put Gladys out of her misery ... Elaine leaves Mick in the lurch ... Rachel takes revenge on her new husband ... Jacqui agrees to be a surrogate mother ... Barry returns and sorts out Bar Brookie.

January

Jack appears apprehensive about marrying Julia, not least because he is already married. Terry had always been led to believe that his mum was dead but now Jack confesses that she's very much alive. Terry tells him he can't possibly marry Julia – becoming a murderer *and* a bigamist – but Jack doesn't want to hurt her and goes along with Julia's manic wedding plans. Terry goes in search of his mum, Mary, and meets his half-brother Steve. A few days later, his mum comes to see him and reveals that every year she sent him letters on his birthday and at Christmas, but Jack marked them 'return to sender'. Terry angrily warns Jack to call off the wedding or he'll be forced to go to the police.

Jimmy leaves for London and Jackie moves back in with Lindsey. Ron is sorry to see her go but makes a fresh attempt to win her heart now that Jimmy is out of the way. He is devastated when she tells him it'll never work because she doesn't love him. Deep down, she still loves Jimmy. But it looks as if Jimmy wants a clean break for he is planning to sell the house. It would mean the end of 20 years of marriage and, when it comes to signing the contract, he just can't bring himself to do it. Lindsey and Jackie are delighted that they're back together as a family but Jacqui Dixon, who was going to buy the house, is absolutely furious and threatens to take Jimmy to court. Jimmy and Jackie have a heart-to-heart during which she tells him that she never actually slept with Ron.

Mike creeps to Ollie with his revised manuscript and riles Lindsey by taking all the credit for the changes. A publishing house accepts the book, but at the launch Lindsey storms out when Mike again claims that the work is all his. He makes matters worse by insisting that he is her intellectual superior and they split up.

Nat and Georgia also agree to finish, but he still can't bear seeing her with another man, so when he catches her enjoying a drink with Peter, he flies into a jealous rage. Georgia is equally jealous when she sees Nat dancing with Rachel, a situation which also inflames Sinbad who warns Nat to stay away from her: the last thing she needs in her life is another pervert. Tinhead gets drunk on alcoholic lemonade, encouraging Mick to renew his efforts to have him expelled, this time successfully. Mick celebrates by asking Elaine to marry him.

February

Elaine accepts Mick's offer but points out that she can't devote all her energy to him as she has to look after her infirm mum who is awaiting a hip replacement operation. Mick is happy to take on Gladys as well, if it means he can be with Elaine. The wedding must wait until after Gladys's operation so Mick tries to hurry things along by persuading her to abandon her principles and go private. In fact the consultant says there's no need to go private as the operation needs to be brought forward anyway. Cassie Charlton starts work at the Trading Post, to the irritation of Ron who thought he had chosen a white candidate. Bel is none too thrilled either when she returns from a break in the Cotswolds to find that Cassie has taken the place downmarket. But then there's not much call for Bel's line in exotic cheeses in a shop where spaghetti hoops are considered a delicacy.

On his first day as a voluntary worker at the youth club, Jimmy confronts Tinhead about bringing alcohol on to the premises. But Jimmy quickly discovers he has met his match and ends up locked in a storeroom from where he has to be rescued by the organiser. Jimmy's chance to get even comes when the police visit the club in search of stolen booze, but Jimmy refuses to 'grass' and so earns Tinhead's grudging respect.

Nat goes berserk when he sees Peter giving Georgia a facial massage at the salon and lashes out at him. Ollie has to intervene to prevent Peter pressing charges. With everyone condemning his behaviour, Nat finishes with Rachel and starts attending therapy sessions. When the whole family go, Bel repeats her accusation that maybe Ollie abused Georgia in the past.

Despite Terry's warnings, Jack is planning to go through with his Valentine's Day wedding to Julia, so Terry takes matters into his own hands and introduces Julia to Mary. No sooner has Julia discovered that her groom-to-be is already married than he confesses that he is also a murderer. Julia is heartbroken. First Cyril Dixon and now Jack: how does she come to attract bigamists? Terry has simply had enough. He is supposed to be opening the replacement for La Luz, Bar Brookie, in partnership with JC Bradley, but instead he leaves the keys and his debts with his manageress Jacqui and tells her to get on with it. Jacqui makes such a success of it that JC agrees to let her become a partner. Max and Susannah decide they don't want any more children so she suggests he has a vasectomy.

March

Unable to come to terms with the fact that Bel has accused him of molesting Georgia, Ollie packs his suitcase and leaves. He comes back, but only for the sake of Danny. Persuaded to return to the therapy sessions, he is appalled to hear that Georgia had been pregnant with Nat's baby and that they have no intention of giving each other up. Angrily Ollie turns on Tony, the therapist, accuses him of destroying the family and hurls a chair through the two-way mirror behind which the other two counsellors were observing events. Why don't they all join the party?

Katie tries to get back together with Christian but Rachel unwittingly steals him off her, and Julia gives Jack another chance. He moves into her spare room but when she urges him to give himself up to the police, he does a runner with some of her savings.

Kicked out to make way for Elaine and Gladys at No. 5, Sinbad moves into the Corkhills' extension. He may resent the way Mick has treated him but the two do have one thing in common – a dislike of Tinhead which borders on the homicidal. When Tinhead's brother, Ben O'Leary, turns up in Sinbad's shop asking whether anyone has been trying to sell stolen gear, Sinbad tells him the culprit is Tinhead. Later that day, Sinbad gets a brick through his window. It doesn't need Inspector Morse to work out the guilty party.

Jimmy and Jackie learn that the Coroner is finally able to release Little Jimmy's body which means they can give him a proper send-off. But there is a hitch when, to save costs, Jimmy brings the body home in Sinbad's van, which is then stolen while he nips into the bookies to put a bet on a horse called My Son. The good news is, My Son wins. The bad news is, Little Jimmy could be half-way down the M6. Jimmy and Sinbad head off to get another coffin but have to put something in it otherwise Jackie will realise it's too light. So Jimmy has the brainwave of weighing it down with some garden turf which David is laying at the Dixons'. Jackie is fooled by the deception and sits there mourning over the coffin, unaware that Little Jimmy is not inside. Luckily, Sinbad's van is found on the day of the funeral and, after a hasty switch of the coffins, Little Jimmy is buried with due decorum. An emotional Jimmy apologises for being such a dreadful father and wishes he could have a second chance. Jackie tells him he can: she's pregnant.

Gladys's hip operation is cancelled when the doctors discover she has terminal cancer. Gladys takes the news stoically but Elaine worries that she will need a lot of looking after. Knowing she hasn't long to live, Gladys asks Mick to bring the wedding forward.

April

Max isn't exactly looking forward to his vasectomy and, as is his wont, secretly backs out at the last minute. He hasn't the courage to tell Susannah he didn't go through with it. Susannah takes Matthew and Emily out for an open day at the fire station but, on the drive home, the children start fighting and momentarily distract her. She doesn't see a car turn out from a side street and smashes into the back of it. Matthew and Emily are killed and when Susannah's breath test proves positive (but not over the limit), she admits to having drunk a glass of wine in the restaurant before leaving. Susannah blames herself for the tragedy and seems to be heading for a nervous breakdown.

Nat and Georgia's attempts to find a flat in

Hoylake are wrecked by the vengeful JC Bradley, but she then gets a transfer at work with a house thrown in. Bel is genuinely sorry to see them go but Ollie has totally disowned them. David takes over the franchise of the petrol station, to the dismay of Ron who thinks he'll put him out of business. And Lindsey is a hit as Cher in a talent show at the Legion.

Mick and Elaine tie the knot with Gladys bravely managing to walk her daughter up the aisle. At the reception, Mick tries to reassure Gladys that once she's had her treatment, she'll be dancing till dawn, but Gladys has other ideas and says she isn't going to have any treatment. She's not prepared to spend her last days attached to a machine – she wants to go out with dignity. Cassie resents how close Gladys is to Mick and when she hears that her mum is selling the house, she suspects Mick's motives, particularly as he has a pile of money problems. In her eyes, he is trying to take over their family. Gladys's pain gets worse and she reiterates to Mick that she doesn't want to go to hospital and be kept alive with drugs and apparatus but doesn't know how she can stop Cassie or Elaine from sending her to hospital if she becomes very weak. Mick tells her about 'living wills' and Gladys decides to make one there and then, with Mick as her witness.

May

Cassie continues to charge around after Mick like an enraged moose. When she learns that Gladys has sold the house at a knock-down price she blames Mick, saying that he's got Gladys just where he wants her now and that the money from the sale of the house will end up in his pocket. Her suspicions are further aroused when she notices that Gladys's living will is in Mick's handwriting. Gladys reassures her that Mick understands and respects her wishes and hints that she would expect her and Elaine to perform a mercy killing when the time comes. Cassie and Elaine discuss this and both are adamant that, no matter how ill Gladys was, they wouldn't be able to kill her.

Sinbad meets a new woman, Carmel, only to discover to his horror that she is Tinhead's mother. The sight of his old adversary causes Tinhead to run off and squat in the flat above the pizza parlour, where his attempts to steal a washing machine flood the shop. When Mick confronts Carmel, she defends her son to the hilt. Sinbad is sickened by hs behaviour and tells her if Tinhead carries on the way he's going, he'll end up in prison. Mick is forced to accept money from Gladys to rebuild the business.

Susannah allows Max to bring Thomas and Alice over from France to stay, but the experience leaves her more desolate than ever and she can't help admitting she wishes that Alice had died instead of Emily. When the postman brings a parcel addressed to Emily, it tips Susannah over the edge and she takes an overdose. Max reaffirms his love for her and together, with tears streaming down their faces, they take Matthew and Emily's ashes and scatter them into the sea.

Rachel moves in with Christian who soon shows evidence of a possessive streak. But Rachel is certain he is the man for her and when he asks her to marry him, she readily accepts.

Jacqui bumps into a familiar face in Bar Brookie – old schoolfriend Leanne Powell, who is using the place as a base for prostitution. When Jacqui discovers this, she throws Leanne out. Leanne gets violent and sprays something in Jacqui's eyes, leaving her screaming in pain.

June

Jacqui is in hospital, her eyes covered with eye pads, afraid that she will never be able to see again. Once released, she insists on putting on a brave face and going back to work, making full use of Katie who volunteers to be her 'eyes'. But Jacqui is an ungrateful patient and lashes out when she blunders into the bar, later accusing Katie of moving everything around. Katie is fed up with being treated like a servant.

While Christian pressures Rachel into a July

wedding, David takes Tinhead on at the petrol station and is determined to instil a little discipline into him. David's military skills have also put the boot into the Trading Post where sales have slumped alarmingly. Ron decides his days there are numbered and it's time to bring the Moby out of retirement. On the road with Danny on work experience, Ron encounters his doppelganger, Dick Ronson, on his patch and with a Moby almost identical to his. A war of words and deeds breaks out which only ends when Ron knocks Dick's wig from his head. Dick hurries off, vowing revenge.

Ollie meets solicitor Eleanor Kitson in Bar Brookie and they enjoy each other's company. Bel is jealous and, as it becomes clear that Ollie has lost all interest in her, she finds an unexpected source of comfort in Mike. Bel and Mike end up sleeping together and Mike wastes no time in boasting about his conquest to Ben O'Leary. He is more reticent about the fact that he's contracted gonorrhoea as a result of his rash behaviour. Bel and Ollie have an emotional reconciliation and make love. Ollie is soon itching to try again.

Susannah learns that the CPS aren't pressing charges over the accident and goes off on a second honeymoon with Max during which he confesses that he never had the vasectomy. After some deliberation, Susannah announces that she would like more children.

With Gladys in excruciating pain and the doctor refusing to increase her medication, Mick asks Jimmy whether he can get hold of some heroin. Jimmy no longer wants anything to do with drugs but is eventually persuaded to contact one of his old suppliers. After Jimmy has prepared the injection, Mick administers it and watches as Gladys slips into a peaceful, pain-free sleep.

July

Gladys is having trouble swallowing and can't take her liquid morphine, no matter how hard Elaine tries. Seeing the agony her mother is in, Cassie wants to call an ambulance but Mick and Elaine stop her, reminding her that Gladys

made the living will so that she couldn't be hospitalised against her wishes. In a desperate attempt to end her own life, Gladys musters up all her strength to put the pillow over her face. Elaine tries to remove it but Gladys grabs her wrist tightly, pushing her hand down on the pillow. Elaine looks to Mick for help. Knowing they're doing the right thing, he places his hand firmly on top of Elaine's and together they press down hard on the pillow to suffocate Gladys. Cassie rushes back into the room and realises that Gladys is dead, but Mick and Elaine can't bring themselves to tell her what happened.

After a scare at Gladys's funeral, Jackie gives birth to son William. Mick's new chip shop opens for business but dastardly Dick Ronson steals the Moby and has it reduced to a chunk of scrap metal. Ron has to come to terms with the loss of his beloved van and his livelihood.

Ollie is horrified to discover that he's got gonorrhoea, and when Bel asks him where he got it he warns her not to try and blame him. Bel is indignant and Ollie locks himself in the bathroom. It begins to dawn on her that she caught it from Mike, so when he knocks on the door asking for another date, her answer comes in the form of flailing fists. Ollie and Bel have a bitter, accusatory row and while Ollie seeks out Mike, Bel packs her bags and leaves. Ollie decides to start divorce proceedings and he and Bel indulge in psychological warfare to win Dan over to their respective camps. Bel is determined that Dan should come and live with her but when he overhears a slanging match about her fling with Mike, he decides to stay with Ollie.

Christian lays down the law about Rachel's wedding. He insists on a low-key (aka cheap) affair, accuses her of being selfish because she wants to choose her own wedding dress, refuses to postpone the nuptials because Mandy can't make it, angrily rejects Sinbad and David's gift of a honeymoon and calls Rachel a slag on her hen night. Otherwise, everything is fine.

August

Christian continues to tighten his hold over Rachel, resenting the amount of time she spends with her 'unsuitable' friends. The happy couple are hardly back from honeymoon before he's sleeping in the spare room and hiding all the photos of Rachel in a swimsuit. Rachel becomes convinced that she's a dreadful wife.

The operation on Jacqui's eyes is a success but Ron intercepts a letter from JC to Jacqui, telling her he is pulling out of Bar Brookie and that she needs to raise £50,000 or he'll look for another buyer. Afraid that Jacqui will lose everything, Ron prepares to raise the money himself but then decides that rather than lend her the £50,000, he'll invest it and become the new joint-owner. Still shocked by the identity of her new business partner, Jacqui suffers another blow when Leanne is imprisoned for just three years for the attack on her. Jacqui reckons she should have got at least double that.

Armed with forged qualifications courtesy of Danny's computer, Jimmy goes for a job as a swimming instructor at a local pool. All goes well until a child is in trouble in the deep end and Jimmy remembers he can't swim. But Danny has proved his point: Jimmy's fake qualifications were taken as authentic. Lindsey and Peter become friends and Ollie sleeps with Eleanor. Ollie is mortified the following morning when Dan asks whether Eleanor is religious – he's been kept awake listening to her saying 'Oh God' all night!

Susannah is now desperate for a baby and is furious when Max goes off playing cards on one of her fertile nights. He snaps that he is a grieving father, not a walking sperm bank or an emotional crutch, and adds that tonight was the first time that, for a couple of minutes, he forgot to think about his dead children. Stunned by his outburst, Susannah rushes upstairs in tears. They later try to arouse their animal passions by watching an erotic video, which turns out to be a beginner's guide to bestiality. A post-coital Max says they don't need dirty films to make their love life exciting. Susannah agrees.

Watching Cassie struggling to come to terms with their mother's death, Elaine can bear the burden of guilt no longer and tells Cassie that she and Mick helped Gladys on her way. When Cassie realises what Elaine is saying, she is filled with hatred and lays all the blame at Mick's feet. Cassie decides she has no option but to tell the police and Mick and Elaine are arrested for murder.

September

Mick and Elaine are charged and released on bail but, after a holiday in Rhyl, they come home to find that the house has been ransacked and the walls sprayed with graffiti reading 'Murderers' and 'Granny Killers'. The whole business is tearing the family apart. Elaine ends up hitting Tanya and Cassie offers Elaine money so that she and Tanya can run away, leaving Mick to face the trial alone. Sinbad moves in with Carmel and Tinhead is sacked by David.

Fed up with being served muesli for breakfast just because Eleanor prefers it, Dan rebels by skipping school and getting in a stolen car with Tinhead, who later steals Jacqui's bag from Bar Brookie. Jimmy combines working at the chippy with a college course as a trainee teacher and, to help him out, Dan steals the textbooks he requires (for being a teacher, not for serving cod and chips) from Ollie's shop. Although grateful, Jimmy makes him promise never to steal again. Jimmy's first day in temporary charge of a class sees him letting them go for break half an hour too early. He realises there's more to teaching than he had anticipated.

Tinhead and Danny's mini crimewave comes to an end when they are arrested while breaking into Sinbad's shop. They escape with a caution but Ollie, realising that Dan has been feeling neglected, finishes with Eleanor. Tinhead appears remorseful but once he's got off he turns on Sinbad and tells him he wants him out of the house. Jacqui rejects Ben's sudden proposal of marriage and Lindsey is filmed working in the chip shop prior to her appearance on the TV show *Sing Like A Star*.

Persuaded by Christian to pack in her glamorous job at Bar Brookie in favour of a mundane job delivering leaflets door-to-door, Rachel is indecently assaulted while out on her rounds. Far from being sympathetic, Christian presses her about whether she encouraged the man in any way and suggests that she was somehow to blame for the fact that Trevor abused her. The nightmare goes on.

Susannah discovers that she will never be able to have children due to an infection which set in after the accident. She decides to adopt, but she and Max are told they wouldn't be considered yet because they have a lot of problems they must come to terms with before they can think about taking on another family. Instead they are advised to consult a bereavement counsellor. Susannah's state of mind deteriorates until Max suggests that surrogacy could be the solution to their problem. And her sister Lisa could be the perfect surrogate mother.

October

Lisa is appalled at the Farnhams' offer and rejects it out of hand, but Susannah is determined to find someone else and eventually settles on Jacqui Dixon.

Elaine breaks down at the committal hearing and gets home to find that Tanya has locked herself in a cupboard at school and wet herself. Elaine can't take any more and she goes on the run, taking Tanya with her. Eleanor explains to an anguished Mick that the CPS were considering dropping the case against him and Elaine, but there's no chance now that she has absconded. At Sinbad's urging, Mick changes his story, putting all the blame on Elaine. Sinbad also tries to persuade Cassie to change her story, but she refuses.

To toughen up his feet for a field trip, Jimmy soaks them in a bowl of vinegar. Not wanting to waste good vinegar, he pours it back into the bottle for use in the chippy. Later

Ben starts choking on his fish. Jimmy convinces him it's a bone when in truth it's a toenail clipping. Ben is puzzled: it's not as if he was eating fish fingers.

Accompanied by his girlfriend Sharon, Tinhead releases three rockets at the windscreen of an oncoming truck. The driver swerves and ploughs into the O'Learys' house, nearly killing Tinhead's sister Melanie. She escapes with cuts and bruises. Shaken by his actions, Tinhead adopts a more purposeful outlook and decides to join the army. Dan has had enough of his dad moping about the house and urges Eleanor to get back with him. At the custody hearing, he decides to stay with Ollie.

Convinced she is worthless, Rachel receives a visit from Bunty, Christian's mum – a deeply unpleasant woman who treats Christian like dirt. Rachel begins to see where he got his attitude from and tries to show him sympathy after Bunty has gone. But when she makes some innocuous comment about his mother, he viciously rounds on her and says at least his mother never stabbed anyone, leaving them to rot under the patio. Christian then tries to force Rachel into having sex but she pushes him away. Finally, driven to the limit, she locks him in the bathroom without food or water and puts a CD on at full volume to drown his cries for help. She leaves him there for three days, ignoring his pleas, until she and Jacqui release him. He makes one last attempt to attack Rachel before falling to the floor – tired, hungry, filthy and totally humiliated.

When a fight breaks out in Bar Brookie, Callum Finnegan steps in to eject the trouble-makers and explains to a Jacqui that he's in the security business and can sort the bar out with a bouncer. After all, Ron's not exactly a deterrent. Finnegan is soon making veiled threats about what could happen to the place if Jacqui doesn't accept his services, but when he presents her with a contract charging £750 per week, she rips it up. Almost immediately, another fight starts and Mike is beaten up in the toilets. Ron and Jacqui reluctantly sign the contract. To raise the money, Ron moves into the bungalow with David and lets No. 8 to the O'Learys, only for Finnegan to raise his weekly fee to £1,000. Barry Grant returns to the area and soon comes face to face with Finnegan.

November

Finnegan's protection racket is threatening to ruin Jacqui financially, but she has no hesitation in turning down the Farnhams' offer of £15,000 to have a baby for them. Barry starts asking questions about Finnegan and hears that he has the reputation of being something of a headcase – a state of mind with which Barry can readily identify. Barry warns Ron that, unless something is done, Finnegan will bleed them dry, and so he offers his own services to Jacqui: for £30,000 he will get rid of Finnegan. Ron is extremely wary but, when he is menaced by Finnegan and suffers another angina attack, Jacqui realises her dad's health is at risk and agrees to Barry's terms and conditions. Barry wants the money in two instalments and, to raise the cash, Jacqui tells the Farnhams that the surrogacy deal is on after all and, after Max has done his duty, she inseminates herself with a turkey baster.

Barry sets about putting the frighteners on Finnegan but finds him a formidable adversary. Just before he jets off to be hairdresser on a photo-shoot in Bali, Peter asks Lindsey to marry him. Lindsey is non-committal, partly because she is rapidly becoming attracted to the dark, brooding Mr Grant whose idea of living dangerously extends beyond having highlights. Jackie expresses alarm at her daughter being involved with Barry – Peter is such a nice boy – but Lindsey will not be swayed and allows Barry to take her to Norwich for her appearance on *Sing Like a Star*. They are followed there by Finnegan, hell-bent on revenge after taking a beating from Barry. Finnegan doesn't return. When Callum's big brother Alisdair inquires as to has whereabouts, Barry neutralises his potential threat by locking him in a cargo container. All Barry wants now is the money, but Jacqui is struggling to get herself pregnant. If she doesn't pay him soon, he says he'll torch Bar Brookie.

Tinhead is enthusiastic about the prospect of army life and does his first recorded good deed by rescuing Julia from a gang of louts on the bus. He is confident about sailing through his army medical but comes home in tears after being rejected for failing the hearing test. Tinhead's world is shattered. After Ollie has revealed all the Simpsons' sordid secrets, Eleanor surprises him with a skeleton of her own – her long-lost daughter Louise.

December

Ron goes searching for a rich widow who will keep him in the lap of luxury in his remaining years and buys *Country Life* and *The Lady* to seek out the local golf club talent. He quickly spots a birdie in the shape of Molly Marchbank and, in order to impress her, passes himself off as a highly successful businessman.

Lindsey and Peter are engaged, but Lindsey still can't say no to Barry. Jacqui is having second thoughts about the surrogacy deal and, determined to get Barry off her back once and for all, offers Peter a larger stake in the salon in return for £15,000. Peter agrees to pay her in cash but is mugged on his way out of the bank and staggers home £15,000 worse off. The mugger was acting on the orders of Barry, as part of his plan to wreck Peter's relationship with Lindsey. But Barry finds he has got a tougher foe than Peter to overcome when Jackie catches Barry and Lindsey in bed together at No. 10. Jackie lets Barry know precisely what she thinks of him by whacking him across the face in Bar Brookie. Meanwhile, when Jacqui sees how much a baby would mean to the Farnhams, she can't bring herself to back out. Still not pregnant despite Susannah's best-laid plans and with no money from Peter, she tells Barry she can't pay him yet. He responds by charging her £1,000 a week interest.

The police think that whoever mugged Peter must have known he was carrying the money. Lindsey mentions this to Barry – the only other person who knew Peter was going to the bank that day – but he denies any involvement. Jimmy is not so sure and decides to warn Barry off Lindsey. He tracks Barry down to Bliss, his club in Birmingham, and Barry says he'll stay away from Lindsey if Jimmy will do a job for him – steal a lorry-load of beer. Jimmy reluctantly agrees but deliberately leaves the load outside a police station. The other gang members corner him and Barry head butts him to the ground. Jimmy knows he can't stop Barry from seeing Lindsey and, on returning to Liverpool, swears to Jackie that Barry had nothing to do with Peter's mugging. Worse still for Jimmy, Cracker is killed by a van. Jackie decides there have been enough bodies in their garden, so he makes a coffin for his faithful friend and tosses her into the Mersey.

1998

Lindsey finishes with Peter … Mick walks free … Jacqui falls pregnant … Ron gets depressed … Louise makes contact with Marcus … David strikes it lucky with Molly … The Shadwicks buy the bungalow … A gas blast rocks the parade.

January

Just when he thought he'd seen the last of Cracker, Jimmy gets a visit from the police who say she's been washed up at Seaforth Docks. They'd found her address from her identity medal. A grief-stricken Jimmy now gives her a proper burial in the back garden. After an unpleasant encounter with a sleazy club boss, Lindsey decides to pack in singing. She also decides to finish with Peter who immediately accuses her of having an affair with Barry. She denies it and hands him back her engagement ring but, in a fit of pique, 'Scissorhands', as Barry sneeringly calls him, hurls the ring across the Parade before stomping off. He later confronts Barry in Bar Brookie but Barry catches up with him in the toilets and threatens him with a gun, a scene witnessed by Lindsey.

Susannah is becoming unbearably possessive about Jacqui. She is so desperate for a child that her behaviour has lost all sense of reason, as evidenced by her wild over-reaction when she saw Jacqui giving Ben a playful New Year's kiss. Katie warns Jacqui that if Susannah is like this now, what's she going to be like when Jacqui is pregnant? A week later, Jacqui discovers that she is pregnant. Recalling Katie's words, she decides she's had enough of Susannah constantly breathing down her neck and thinks about having an abortion and moving to Spain. Barry is amazed to learn the lengths to which she was prepared to go to save Bar Brookie and makes her an offer she can't refuse. If she signs the bar over to him, she can keep 50 percent of the profits and continue running the place. There's only snag: the deal leaves Ron out in the cold. But that's not enough to prevent Jacqui from signing.

From a photo in his wallet, Lindsey learns that Barry is married. He heads back down south and Lindsey says that from now on she's going to stand on her own two feet. Jacqui can't go through with the abortion and finally breaks it to Max and Susannah that she's pregnant. Barry returns Peter's £15,000 to Lindsey. While Jimmy is thinking of more practical uses for the cash – like a new washing machine – Jackie takes it straight round to Peter.

Louise goes to Reading in search of her biological father, unaware that Eleanor has sent her on a wild goose chase. Far from being a cycle shop owner named Nick, her real dad is a violent jailbird named Marcus. Still, it's an easy mistake to make. Ron takes Molly on an expensive golfing weekend but is horrified to find that she lives in a terraced house. He thinks she's a gold-digger and wants nothing more to do with her. David willingly takes his place.

At his trial, Mick pleads not guilty but then delivers an impassioned speech in which he admits killing Gladys and tells the court that he would do exactly the same thing again if it meant giving someone back their dignity. He is acquitted and he and Cassie make their peace.

February

Max warns Susannah not to say anything about the pregnancy but an overjoyed Susannah says it's OK, she's only told one person – Julia. She might as well have taken out a full-page ad in the *News of the World*. Rachel is mystified by Jacqui's lack of energy until she finally confesses that she is pregnant.

Ron reacts badly to the news that he's no longer a partner in Bar Brookie; he feels he's been treated shabbily by his daughter. Mike reminds Jacqui how Ron bailed her out when JC was selling his share of the bar, but when she makes an effort to apologise he gives her the silent treatment and is later seen sitting in the garden of No. 8 on the cube of metal which was once his beloved Moby. He feels he's lost everything – his family, his business and his health – and is living on borrowed time. He decides to reject the chance of an incapacity allowance from the DSS and instead demands the £50,000 which Jacqui owes him. She tries to reason with him but he is furious when she says he is responsible for his current financial predicament after going behind her back to buy into the bar in the first place.

Following weeks of feeling sorry for himself after the army rejected him, Tinhead gets a job at a builder's merchants where he is soon talked into making extra money by secretly adding a few bags of cement to a customer's order. Tinhead is happy to line his pockets with a fiddle and splashes out on a bunch of flowers for Carmel. On his next day at work, he steals £60 from a driver's jacket pocket and buys a new shirt. He explains away his new-found wealth by saying he's been getting loads of tips. Carmel is delighted; Sinbad is suspicious.

Lindsey pleads with Peter to believe her when she says she knew nothing about Barry's part in the mugging, but he dismisses her contemptuously. He thinks she's pathetic and declares his intentions of leaving Liverpool for good. Lindsey is crestfallen. She had everything anyone could ever wish for and she's gone and blown it.

Against Eleanor's wishes, Louise persists in trying to track down Marcus. She receives a letter from him which suggests that all the years in prison have hardly changed him. Louise is impressed by this but Ollie reminds her that this is the person who almost killed a man.

March

Despite warnings from Ron and Max, David decides to move in with Molly. Ron insists that David is about to make the biggest mistake of his life until he sees Molly's secret country estate, Bressingham Hall, and realises that it is he who has made the mistake. While David toasts his new lifestyle, Ron is in a desperate way. With nowhere to live now that David has gone, he scarcely has a penny to his name. Jacqui offers to pay money into an account for him but he rejects her charity. He suffers the ultimate humiliation when he hasn't got enough money to pay for petrol. Angrily, he tries to siphon it back as half the Close look on embarrassed.

Builder Greg Shadwick expresses an interest in buying the bungalow and David appoints Cassie as the new manager of the petrol station. On his orders, she offers Ron a part-time job, but he again refuses help. Mike is equally put out when Jacqui promotes Rachel over his head at Bar Brookie. He threatens to resign but backs down.

Jacqui and Susannah go for a baby scan. Everything seems fine until it suddenly dawns on Max that they haven't thought the whole thing through properly. What will happen when the baby is born? Where will they live? There's no way they can stay on the Close.

April

Seeing herself as the obvious choice, Susannah becomes upset when Jacqui asks Katie to be her birth partner. Her grief is compounded when, almost a year to the day after the car crash which killed Matthew and Emily, she is driving home and sees a child's teddy lying in the middle of the road following another smash. It all comes flooding back to her.

The Shadwicks buy the bungalow. It clearly isn't large enough to accommodate a family of five, plus their dog Candy, but Greg has ambitious plans for an extension. Peter returns from a trip abroad with a new girlfriend, Helen, in tow. Lindsey's nose is put out of joint, all the more so when Helen slags her off at Ben's birthday party. Peter angrily finishes with Helen: he still cares for Lindsey.

On the day the Shadwicks move in, Peter and Lindsey chat on the Close. Kylie wanders off towards the shops. Meanwhile Ron buys a gas cooker from Sinbad for his new flat and decides to install it himself. The gas soon starts to leak and when he switches on the light, there is an almighty explosion. Ben drags Ron to safety but catches the full force of a second blast and ends up in hospital. Will he ever walk again?

Max and Jacqui are trapped together before being rescued by the fire crews, while Eleanor suffers a pain in the neck. So now she knows how it feels. Sinbad is also trapped by fallen masonry with Kylie beneath him. Kylie is in danger of drowning from flood water, and Sinbad learns that the only way the crews can reach her is to amputate his legs. It is a sacrifice he is prepared to make. His legs are saved and so is Kylie when Peter and Jason Shadwick block off the flood waters. Peter finds the engagement ring he threw away in disgust when he and Lindsey split up and prepares to give her another chance.

Louise writes to Marcus Seddon in prison and arranges to visit him on the pretext of discussing animal rights. Realising she knows precious little about the subject, he demands to know why she has really come. When he spots a photograph of her in the local paper with Eleanor outside the wrecked Parade, she is forced to confess that she is the daughter he never knew he had.

Claire Sweeney

Claire Sweeney is convinced that fate meant her to play Lindsey Corkhill, as she explains.

I had played Lindsey in a few episodes but then I went off to work as a singer on the cruises. When I decided it was time to come home, I lined up a job in the West End and another singing at Blackpool Pleasure Beach and I also wrote to Mal Young, who was then the series producer of *Brookside*, to ask whether there was any chance that Lindsey might return. It so happened that the day he got my letter was the day of a long-term planning meeting at which they were deciding to move the Corkhills back on to the Close. So my timing was perfect. It was just sheer luck.

And I've had a wonderful time playing her – she has had so many terrific storylines. At first, she was naïve and a bit vulnerable but her singing gave her an inner strength. Phil Redmond has stepped in and given Lindsey a bit more oomph and I thank him for that because I think that with everything she has been through, she would have had to acquire a little toughness.

It was interesting when I had the Peter/Barry storyline that all the women I met said go for Barry, he's irresistible, while all the men wanted me to stay with Peter. I think they felt threatened by Barry. I do think Barry genuinely cared for Lindsey. When he saw her all glammed up for her singing, he knew she could do better for herself than working in a chippie. After all, he'd also come up from nothing to make a successful career for himself. She blossomed with Barry and, for my part, it was exciting to be able to take my pony-tail out and get out of my pinny to dress up as Cher.

I remember, the first day the pizza parlour became the chippie, I had a 7am call. They asked me to talk and wrap chips, but I'd never wrapped chips in my life before. So I practised in the corner and now I'm an expert.

That wasn't Claire's first awkward brush with Brookside food. 'On my second day on set, I had a scene where I had to make breakfast for Jackie. Sinbad was there too. I had learnt all my lines in advance so I thought I was well prepared. I had a box of cornflakes which I was supposed to pour into a bowl before emptying it into the bin. But during rehearsals I kept doing it for real – actually tipping the cornflakes in the bin – so that by the time we came to do the take, there were none left. We had to fish them out of the bin! Then I had to pour them and pour the milk without showing the labels on either container. It was really tricky. And when I'd finally mastered that, I put the box of cornflakes down on the table – right in front of Sinbad's face! I thought I'll never get the hang of this…'

Brookside Versus the Press

British soaps used to be cosy affairs. Sure, there was the occasional tragedy such as the shooting of Ernie Bishop in *Coronation Street* and the fire at Crossroads Motel, but these dramatic storylines were very much the exception. *Crossroads* tried hard by making David Hunter a compulsive gambler, giving his son Chris a Saturday morning job as an international terrorist, making Jill a drug addict and Miss Diane an alcoholic, but somehow their hearts never seemed to be in it and they were invariably cured by the following Monday. So for the most part, it was a steady diet of births, romances and weddings.

Then along came *Brookside*. Never afraid of controversy, *Brookside* led the way in tackling such topics as drug abuse, unemployment, rape and lesbianism, and, more recently, domestic violence, incest and euthanasia. As the goalposts were moved, other soaps were forced to become grittier. Without *Brookside*, *EastEnders'* Kathy Beale would never have been raped, Deirdre Rachid from *Coronation Street* would never have ended up in prison and *Emmerdale*'s Zoe Tate would have been chasing every man in the village.

Right from the start, the Press fretted about *Brookside*, primarily because it was so different. Apart from the odd mild curse from Len Fairclough, soap characters didn't swear so the earthy conversations of Damon, Ducksie and Gizzmo came as a nasty shock to sensitive Fleet Street ears. Jonah Jones also fell foul of moral guardians as those unlikely bedfellows, Mary Whitehouse and the *Sun*, attacked the show's bad language. By December 1982, barely a month after the first episode, Liverpool's *Daily Post* confidently announced that *Brookside* was about to be axed. As an accurate prediction, it was on a par with the man who labelled the *Titanic* 'unsinkable'.

Brookside has, of course, gone from strength to strength but controversy has never been far away. The papers had a field day over the incest storyline between Nat and Georgia Simpson which resulted in the Broadcasting Standards Council and the Independent Television Commission directing Channel 4 to broadcast an apology about showing brother and sister in bed during the Saturday omnibus edition. The ruling decreed that the scene was in breach of the family viewing requirements of the ITC Programme Code and should have been edited from the omnibus edition. The ITC added that the scene was 'unsuitable for early evening transmission when large numbers of children may be expected to be watching'. Channel 4 replied: 'We fully accept the ITC's judgement that the scene should not have been shown at 5pm in the omnibus edition. We are pleased that they recognise that this storyline was an appropriate subject for the 8pm weekday showing, in *Brookside*'s tradition of dealing with difficult and important issues.'

'I think at the time we all felt it was going no further than we had gone in the past in that slot,' says Phil Redmond.

Now we are taking the view in hindsight that society has changed slightly. We have to be more careful about what we do show at 5pm. If we had run it before politicians started to whip up a strong moral crusade, I doubt it would have aroused as much publicity. It came under the spotlight because of the political agenda of the day and the morality debate now going on. It's the same with any sensitive issue. Once you step into these areas, you immediately step into public comment and sanctimonious tabloids with rent-a-quote complainants.

We all recognise that incest is taboo and I think the storyline reinforced that view. Incest is taboo, but the dramatising of it isn't. We weren't simply trying to shock. We had to see Nat and Georgia in bed together otherwise we weren't being faithful to the storyline.

I accept that we made a few mistakes with it – I think we got a bit carried away with what that story was all about. It was about incest, not sex abuse, but because it came so quickly on the heels of the Jordaches, lots of papers and moral guardians started to think it was about sex abuse. This wasn't *Brookside*'s 'next big issue' – the thing I was interested in was: what is this switch that occurs in puberty and adolescence which turns off the testosterone and oestrogen between brother and sister? At an age like adolescence, where anything with a pulse will do, why is it that you just hate your brother or sister? And what happens if it doesn't switch off? What happens then?

Looking back, I think part of the problem was that it all went off too quickly. The Simpsons should have come in with their big secret being the sexual harassment case against Bel who had gone off with this young bloke. We should have got to know the Simpsons first and then, after about 9 or 12 months, introduced Nat and Georgia's problems. We fell into the trap of trying to top ourselves – and we did in more than one way!

We had to get people focused on the fact that the audience weren't bothered. We got far more letters at the time about Sammy Daniels leaving her baby, because incest isn't a part of everyday life for most people. The only complaints about the incest were from the papers and professional complainers. And once I had explained what the story was all about – once the papers realised that the nation's brothers and sisters didn't start fancying each other as a result of our storyline – the fuss died down.

Some people criticised us because they felt Nat and Georgia were too good-looking. I felt that was cultural naivety. I made the decision that they had to be equally attractive and that she had to be older than him so that there was no hint of coercion on either side. It was interesting giving the definition of incest to tabloid journalists and hearing the penny drop. It is 'being sexually attracted to a member of your family' – you're not being forced to have sex. And the omnibus rap was about us showing two people in bed together, not about incest.

We don't do everything on *Brookside* to expose a social issue – sometimes we just want to enjoy the drama. To say we are trying to push back the boundaries of what can be shown on television suggests we have some kind of social agenda. It is not like that at all. Our primary aim is to create good drama and entertain people. The whole programme is based on the births, marriages and deaths columns of newspaper pages. Within that, we get the complexity of human relationships.

Another recent storyline which caused a furore was the mercy killing of the terminally ill Gladys Charlton, a case condemned by the Cancer Research Campaign as 'not only unreal, but irresponsible'. Yet in a Teletext poll, four out of five viewers backed *Brookside*'s handling of the subject.

'Euthanasia is a very emotional subject,' says Redmond, 'and the whole horror of painful death from cancer is particularly emotive.'

> The caring agencies and hospices work very hard, but in 1996 the *British Journal of Hospital Medicine* estimated that 25 percent of cancer patients die without adequate pain relief. We were trying to get across this issue of age in society and to show that the problem of lack of care still exists – it's not a perfect system. The level of care is not homogeneous across the country. There are still gaps.
>
> And Mick Johnson was punished. He lost his wife – although that was a case where an artist's contract overlapped with the story. Beverley Hills, who played Elaine, wanted to leave so we had to have Elaine buckling under the pressure. If she had stayed, they might both have gone to jail. It was the same with Beth Jordache when Anna Friel wanted to leave. There was no way we could have got Beth off the charge but we didn't want her to be off-screen in a prison. I know we could have organised a jail-break but that wasn't on. So we killed her.

The entire Jordache story attracted a wealth of publicity. The day after Mandy and Beth were convicted, the battered wives' charity, Refuge, was inundated with calls for help from similarly abused women. And both the Home Office and the Metropolitan Police requested copies of the programme tapes – the Met to train their officers dealing with domestic violence and the Home Office to help probation officers who have to deal with male offenders.

The Jordache case highlighted a favourite *Brookside* casting ploy – that of getting actors to play against type. Bryan Murray was deliberately chosen to play Trevor because he specialised in light, comic roles. That way, the viewers, like the residents on the Close, would at first be lulled into thinking what a nice person Trevor was. It was much the same with casting Brian Murphy of *George and Mildred* fame to play killer virus-spreading George Manners.

Brookside certainly ensured that actress Anna Friel was rarely out of the headlines for, in addition to her part in the murder of dad Trevor, her character, Beth Jordache, also had the distinction of becoming soap's first lipstick lesbian. Her on-screen kiss with the Farnhams' nanny, Margaret Clemence, stirred up the usual hornets' nest but earned praise from the gay community. Beth wasn't introduced with the idea of making her a lesbian – that idea arose from Anna Friel's powerfully confident performance. And the story worked because Margaret was such an unlikely partner.

As the mailbag for Sammy and her baby illustrated, viewers tend to write in about stories which touch on everyday life rather than the more sensational subjects. Thus topics like the teenage Jacqui Dixon demanding an expensive pair of trainers to wear to school and Tracy Corkhill running up huge phone bills on Chatline attracted more letters than, for example, Margaret's affair with Father Derek O'Farrell or the deaths of Sue Sullivan and her son Danny.

Inevitably, the Press lap up any controversy. Discussing the incest storyline in October 1996, the *Observer* crowed: '*Brookside* has already received several censures from the television regulators. The ITC gave it a formal warning over the knife scene where Trevor Jordache was killed by his wife and daughter. The BSC upheld complaints over the same stabbing scene as well as another involving Jordache beating his wife and, yet another, about cocaine.'

Brookside has had its fair share of brushes with authority. Back in the days when Tracy Corkhill was going out with Jamie Henderson, Tracy's dad Billy stumbled across a packet of Durex. The IBA (forerunner of the ITC) complained that the camera lingered too long on the condoms. Asked to respond, Phil Redmond pointed out that the shot was held partly to ensure that viewers got the message about safe sex and also 'because research shows that the people who most need the information are the ill-educated and the illiterate, and research also shows that people who are illiterate get through life by recognising the design of things. As Durex is also a generic term for contraceptives, we immediately put on screen a graphic image that even people who couldn't read would be able to recognise.' The IBA were suitably appeased.

When Sheila Grant was raped, viewers saw her assailant throw his coat over her head and drag her into the bushes. Channel Four decided to edit the scene out of the omnibus edition and so Sheila turned and the camera cut to a shaking bush. Ironically, this supposedly sanitised version attracted three times more complaints than the original.

Last year, *Brookside* was ticked off by the ITC, apparently for transgressing the code regarding bestiality by transmitting a sound track of a woman having sex with a pig! The offending scene occurred while Max and Susannah Farnham attempted to perk up their sex life in the wake of the deaths of their children by watching an erotic video. Phil Redmond gives his point of view:

> That was a really silly judgement. A lot of fuss over nothing. How anybody could work out that it was supposed to be a woman having sex with a pig is beyond me. I think the people who complained probably need a bit of counselling. We should find out what kind of lives they lead! It was nothing more than a bit of ribaldry in an otherwise depressing storyline. In hindsight, I don't think we needed to have Susannah's line, 'But Max, it's a pig.' Her face would have been enough. It still could have been a wildlife video, which was what I thought at first.
>
> It merely highlighted what a farce cultural regulations are. I have far more faith in viewers than regulators as to whether something is within the bounds of taste and decency. Still, there's one thing we've got rid of after 16 years – the Press have given up saying that we'll be axed.

Steven Pinder

Steven Pinder is pleased with the new, slightly more assertive Max Farnham. 'I haven't been called a wimp for some time,' he enthuses.

Max has had a lot thrown at him over the years and I think he's probably had to develop some sort of multi-personality to cope with it. The fact that he seems a bit tougher now probably stems from the fact that he's with Susannah rather than Patricia. Susannah's not as hard as Patricia could sometimes be and so I think Max has been able to have his say.

Of all the pain Max has been through, the Down's syndrome story attracted the most letters. More recently, the loss of the children was particularly traumatic. It was very tiring for me to do as an actor, playing scene after scene with this horrendous cloud hanging over me. There was a lot of pressure on both myself and Karen Drury who plays Susannah. It's not always easy to switch off at the end of the day – not after playing the character for eight hours – and whilst you may not take the part home, you do take the mood home.

I was in Crossroads for three years before Brookside and one of the key things about appearing in any long-running series is not to make it run-of-the-mill. You have to try to make it interesting because if you're not interested in the part, that will communicate itself to the audience. Fortunately with Brookside we have so many hard-hitting stories that there's never time to lose interest.

And there's always the lighter side. I still have a problem playing scenes with certain actors who have a twinkle in their eye. Mickey Starke is my Achilles' heel. He's just very funny and invariably throws me. John Burgess, who played David Crosbie, was another. I remember doing a scene with John where my closing line was, 'I'm sorry, I've got to go to the Jordaches'.' Instead for some reason I said 'Georgeashes'. This was just before lunch so we broke for lunch, came back, tried again and an hour later, we were still on the same scene, trying to get it right. The longer it went on, the worse it became.

And what might the future hold for Max? 'It would be interesting if he married Susannah,' says Pinder, 'so that he would have married two women twice. I'd like to know whether anyone else in the country has ever managed that. And I think he should start dyeing his hair to hide the grey and should be sent to a health farm for three months to get in shape – but a health farm where he can enjoy a good drink!'

TOTAL **BROOKSIDE**

Famous Faces

A number of famous faces made early appearances on *Brookside*. Singer Sonia played an extra; Malandra Burrows played Damon Grant's girlfriend Lisa before going on to play Kathy Bates in *Emmerdale*; Letitia Dean appeared as Dawn in *Brookside* before moving to Albert Square to play Sharon Watts in *EastEnders*; and Jason Orange's twin brother turned up on *Brookside* as a Jason Orange lookalike – casting which was hard to fault. Another former Take That member, Robbie Williams, also claims to have had a minor role in *Brookside*, but it remains a mystery to the production team.

In addition, a number of non-actors have appeared as themselves. Paula Yates was interviewed by Karen Grant as part of the university's rag week, Russell Grant opened the hospital fete back in 1985 and Sonia and comedian Stan Boardman were guests at a function attended by Barry Grant. And there's more…

The Farm

Background: Geoff Rogers is entering a radio competition offering two free tickets to a Farm concert for the first listener who can unravel a series of clues as to where the band are rehearsing. Geoff and Bumper stake out an old church hall.

First appearance: Walking quietly into the hall carrying their instruments, unseen by Geoff and Bumper.

Second appearance: Leaving the hall, brushing past Geoff who is so absorbed at having got the two tickets that he again fails to notice the band.

Third appearance: On the way into the gig, they stop for a burger and a drink with their fans. Yet again, Geoff doesn't spot them even though he's standing right next to them. The band then start chatting to Geoff's girlfriend, Paula, and autograph her bag.

Lines: None.

Musical contribution: Just the sound of distant drums.

And another thing: *Brookside* and *Hollyoaks* scriptwriter Roy Boulter was the drummer with The Farm.

Sarah Greene

Background: Patricia Farnham hires Sarah to compère a charity fashion show which she is promoting.

First appearance: Stepping out of a cab on the Close.

They say: *Seen who that is?* (Katie Rogers)

  What's Sarah Greene doing here? (Jacqui Dixon)

  She hasn't got Phillip Schofield with her, has she? (Leanne Powell)

  Oh…great. (stifling a yawn, Ron Dixon)

Her first big scene: Sipping coffee at the Farnhams'.

Her embarrassment: Max asking her whether she'd ever met Valerie Singleton on whom he had a schoolboy crush.

Her confession: *I was always a* Magpie *fan myself.*

Gerry Marsden

Background: For Frank Rogers' stag night at La Luz, bride-to-be Lyn organises a surprise for him by hiring Gerry Marsden, Pete Best (on drums) and two of the Swinging Blue Jeans to serenade him with a few of his old favourites.

They say: *Is that Gerry Marsden?* (Frank)

Gerry's introduction: *Ladies and gentlemen, we're here tonight in honour of an old mate of ours from the dark and distant past: Frank Rogers of the Scotty Dogs fame…though I'm not sure fame's the right word. Frank's getting married to Lyn next week and Lyn's organised this little surprise for him.*

Highspot of the evening: When Frank joins the band on stage for a rendition of the Scotty Dogs' one and only song, 'Nobody Butters the Toast Like You'.

Audience reaction: *Oh God, he's not going to sing, is he?* (Bev)

Bruce Grobbelaar

Background: A charity night for Tony Dixon at La Luz.

They say: *What do you think the odds are on Bruce Grobbelaar falling in love with me and taking me away from all this?* (Mo McGee)

    Nice to meet you. (Terry Sullivan)

His first awkward moment: Being kept waiting by Ron Dixon.

His second awkward moment: Having his photo taken with Mo.

His finest moment: Pushing over the pile of pennies.

Eamonn Holmes and Lorraine Kelly

Background: Penny Crosbie decides to go on breakfast television to put her side of the story regarding dead husband Clive's suicide, visits to prostitutes and embezzlement.

His opening line: *Hello, Mrs. Crosbie … Eamonn Holmes. Pleased to meet you. I'll be doing the interview with you along with Lorraine later in the programme.*

Was he cut down to size? David Crosbie tells him: *Funnily enough you look much smaller than you do on the television.*

Her opening line: *Now it's time to meet Penny Crosbie, the widow of MP Clive Crosbie.*

How did Max disgrace himself? By getting Mr Motivator's autograph.

Was the appearance a success? Penny bridles when Lorraine brings up the matter of Clive's secret love-child whereupon David marches on set and tries to hijack the interview. A commercial break spares the nation.

Loyd Grossman and Lily Savage

Background: Food guru Loyd Grossman has been hired to perform the opening of Grants restaurant.

The first hitch: Loyd's plane is delayed and he is forced to cancel.

The saviour: Oscar Dean fixes up a local celebrity as a last-minute replacement –
Lily Savage.

The confusion: David Crosbie doesn't realise that Lily is a man.

The second hitch: Loyd manages to make it after all.

The third hitch: As Loyd and Lily bury a time capsule, madman Terry Sullivan turns
up and loudly accuses Barry Grant of being a murderer.

Michael Parkinson

Background: Jackie Corkhill, Patricia Farnham and Jean Crosbie are invited on to a TV
debate, *Loud and Clear* (hosted by Michael Parkinson), to rally support for the
Jordaches.

They say: *Oh my God, it's him ... it's you isn't it ... Michael Parkinson.* (Jackie)

His embarrassment: Jackie reminding him about his encounter with Emu.

His advice: *When you get out there, try and enjoy yourself ... Speak your mind.*

Pre-show drama: Jean gets cold feet and Jackie, who was supposed to be sitting in the
audience, takes her place on stage at Parky's suggestion.

How did he put Patricia on the spot? By asking her whether she would kill her
own husband.

What was her reply? *If he was abusing myself or my children ... Yes, yes I'd kill him ... Yes
I would kill my own husband.*

How did the debate hot up? When Jackie starts laying into James Payne, MP. *Those
two women should've got medals for what they did ... Not prison sentences.*

Parky's summing-up: *Well, it's a subject that certainly brings out the emotions, isn't
it?*

The Magic Rabbits

When it comes to television, the residents of Brookside Close are very particular about what they view. It used to be their favourite soap, *Meadowcroft Park*, but lately it seems that the only programme anyone sits down to watch is a children's romp with musical rabbits. This has not been missed by the audience at large and hardly a week goes by without Mersey Television receiving at least one enquiry about the Magic Rabbits.

Phil Redmond reveals their origins:

> One of the biggest problems we have is copyright. Any music or soundtrack in the background is too expensive because you have to buy it off the rights holders. Years ago, I said why don't we make some of our own programmes for use on screen and Nick Prosser, one of our directors, went off and made these rabbit glove puppets and did this kiddies' shot. The clip just sits in the library until every now and again a director gets out the magic bunnies and puts them on screen. It's almost like a bit of folklore for ourselves. We get letters from people saying the rabbits should have their own show!

Stunts and Explosions

When a huge gas explosion destroyed Sinbad's shop in April, it was the latest in a long line of natural disasters to rock the area around Brookside Close. In fact, it wasn't even the first explosion at that particular shop – the window was blown out courtesy of Barry Grant when Jimmy operated there under the banner of 'Kowboy Kutz'. No. 5 was decimated by Simon Howe's home-made bomb, while there have been fires at No. 8 (and a separate one in the garden shed), No. 9, Manor Park Primary School and the Donnellys' yard, not to mention a chip-pan fire in the bungalow back in the days of Edna Cross.

'We've done car crashes and so on from day one,' explains Phil Redmond.

> One of our biggest stunts was when Bev burned down Casa Bevron. It was all done by a special effects team with gas canisters and the set was dressed in its burnt-out state and it looked really good. But when I saw the rough-cut, I didn't think the explosion looked big enough. And one thing missing was a shot of Ron standing in the middle of the debris, surveying the remains of his house. To me, that was the most poignant shot of all. They had every other shot bar that so I said: 'Where's the shot of Ron? Go and get it. It's the key moment of the whole drama.' The set had been stripped and the house rebuilt so they had to go back and recreate the burnt-out house!
>
> You've got to be prepared to spend money. In a movie, they'll spend 10 million dollars just to get one particular shot, like the *Titanic* tipping up. Without it, nothing else works. The thousands of pounds that it took to go back and get that two-second shot for us was worth it.

Fire may look dangerous and dramatic on screen but it is all carefully controlled on set under expert supervision, with the result that everything invariably passes off without incident. Of all the stunts which *Brookside* has staged, only two have ever given cause for concern. Simon Howe's bomb which ripped apart No. 5 did a lot more damage to the interior of the house than anticipated and, if you look closely on screen, you can actually see the roof of the house lift off slightly. And when Sinbad inadvertently set fire to the Collins' garden shed, the blaze was so fierce that it caused some damage to the exterior of the house.

To blow out the windows for the destruction of No. 5, the crew put air cannons in each of the bedrooms, constructed window frames out of balsa wood and replaced the glass in the windows with sugar glass. The cannons were filled with paper so that when they went off, not only did the windows blow out readily but paper was scattered everywhere to create the illusion of debris. A few strategically-placed smoke machines provided the final touch. Phil Redmond explains the point of this sort of incident:

> We do explosions to give *Brookside* an injection. And they're easy to do on the Parade because it's a controlled area, part of Mersey Television's site. *Coronation*

Street sent Don Brennan's car into the river and I did the *Emmerdale* plane crash, but otherwise the other soaps are all in the studio whereas we can do it outside. And that gives an added dimension to *Brookside*.

We use these major stunts to refocus on the characters. For example, the big gas explosion earlier this year was used to introduce all of our existing characters to the new family, the Shadwicks. And it was an incident which affected the whole community in different ways. As a rule, we don't use explosions to kill characters off – there's much easier ways of doing that. I wouldn't waste an explosion on that!

The Fashion Victims of Brookside Close

O ver the years, there have been almost as many fashion disasters on Brookside as there have been explosions, fires and fatal car crashes. Who could forget Terry and Michelle's matching perms or Roger's moustache which made him look like a cross between Hitler and Ron Mael of Sparks? Then there was Doreen's peroxide job, Mike's beard and the hair transplants which took place between Jacqui and Eleanor. Jacqui quickly settled into life as a redhead but Eleanor's new blonde look stirred up unwelcome memories for Ollie.

Similarly, if clothes make the man, they nearly destroyed Ron. Those loud shirts which Bev encouraged him to wear, coupled with Bev's own highly individual use of bin liners and skirts that were even shorter than her temper, ensured that Casa Bevron was the sort of home likely to be reported to the Style Council.

'The kids in *Brookside* have always been fashion-conscious,' says Phil Redmond, 'but not all of the actors like what they have to wear.'

> I remember Doreen Sloane, who played Annabelle, detested a striped dress we always made her wear, and when Mike Dixon first arrived, Paul Byatt hated the black leather jacket I put him in. We used to make Gaby Glaister wear culottes as Patricia but she hated them so much that one day she sneaked them out of wardrobe, took them home and hid them so that we couldn't put her in them again!
>
> One Brookside actor, who shall remain nameless, lost his job because he refused to wear a T-shirt that had been deliberately shrunk in the wash. He said it made him look stupid – but that was all part of the characterisation – and he walked off the set. So I had no option but to sack him.

Sue Johnston was infamous for having to wear dowdy clothes as Sheila Grant. She tells the story of how she bought a big coat from Oxfam which she thought was great, but when she wore it into work one morning the *Brookside* receptionist said: 'Oh no, what have they put you in now!'

Celebrity Fans

Brookside has a wealth of celebrity fans. Noel Gallagher, Reeves and Mortimer, Bob Monkhouse, Michael Parkinson, Lily Savage, George Michael, Lorraine Kelly, Jasper Conran and Josie Lawrence have all said they are avid viewers. And The Lightning Seeds' Ian Broudie is so hooked on events on the Close that in 1997 he chose the *Brookside* set for the launch of the band's album *Like You Do*. Here are some more celebrity tributes:

Carol Smillie:

'The first thing which hooked me was the Billy/Sheila/Doreen storyline. It was very plausible in that Sheila, although the older woman, was quite sexy and warm and it was great to see this good Catholic woman falling for Billy. Anyway, who doesn't enjoy a scandal, especially a Brookie scandal? Good television should sometimes make you feel uncomfortable and the whole Jordache storyline pulled at the heart strings. Until then, Sinbad had always been seen as a bit of a joke – the cheeky-chappie window-cleaner that nobody took seriously and who dipped in and out of storylines – but the Jordache story changed him. And of course there's Jimmy. I've never experienced drugs so to me *Brookside* was an education. I think it should be shown to every school to show what can happen to your life if you get involved in drugs.'

Les Dennis:

'I watched the very first episode of *Brookside* but it was only when I came to London that I really got hooked. I think it was probably because I needed my Liverpool "fix". I was really paranoid that I might pick up a Cockney accent, so if I didn't go back home I watched *Brookside* to make sure I remembered my roots. I was really gripped by the Jordache story. When Trevor said to Mandy, "Trust me, I've changed", I was sitting there screaming at the telly: "Don't believe him." Those issues have to be dealt with and if someone doesn't like it, they've got a remote. I think it's blinkered people who won't deal with it and that it's up to shows like *Brookside* to make us face these issues instead of running away from them.'

Sian Lloyd:

'I love Jackie Corkhill. Every word Jackie says sounds right, absolutely perfect for her. You don't imagine there being a script or anything – it's all from the heart.'

Loyd Grossman:

'I remember first seeing Gavin Taylor and thinking, what a jerk, but what a riveting jerk! I really wanted to see what happened to him because everything about him was so objectionable. So the first storyline I was gripped by – or should I say irritated by – was Gavin's business of selling reconditioned cookers. He had that winning combination of being a flash git yet terribly unsuccessful. By the time Gavin popped his clogs, I felt I lived in the Close and would have done anything to get rid of him.'

Sarah Greene:

'I'll never forget the enormous dramatic tension when Sheila finally moved into No. 10 nor the whole Jordache story in the same house. The responses of Beth and Rachel were terribly realistic. They almost underplayed it, which of course is far more shocking. I thought, when's Mandy going to snap? But that was accurate. People do put up with it – they hope things are going to change.'

Sarah White

S arah White is unlikely ever to forget her audition as serial husband-stealer Bev McLoughlin. 'Vince Earl, who plays Ron, said to me: "Would you mind having to kiss a man who's old enough to be your dad?" I said: "No, I've just left college and I'll kiss a bear's bum to get this job." We both roared.'

Liverpool-born Sarah was on her way to do a geography degree course at Newcastle University when she suddenly thought, 'I don't want a sensible job – I want to be an actress.' Sarah had performed with local youth theatres but had never discussed her ambitions. 'This yearning to be an actress had been a big secret with me but in the end I realised that if I wasn't careful I was going to end up doing something I didn't really want to for the rest of my life.' She then walked straight from drama school into playing Bev.

Bev was a great character, totally opposite to me. It meant I could be everything I wasn't. And I was so lucky playing opposite Vince. He's a lovely fella. Sometimes I watch TV and see an actress in a similar role and think: 'You poor sod – he looks like he hasn't cleaned his teeth since 1973.' So kissing Vince was no problem. After a few times, it was like kissing the back of your hand.

Vince was sorry to see me go although he said he'd suspected it for a while. He just said to me: 'Go for it.' Leaving Bev was like splitting up with a boyfriend. I'd played her for nearly four years and loved every minute of it, but when your gut tells you it's time to go, you've got to go. I realised at the end of my third year on *Brookside* that if I didn't leave soon I'd get bored and it would show. If I'd had a stint on the dole after leaving drama school, maybe I wouldn't have quit. But I hadn't, and I haven't got kids so I could give it a go. I did agonise about having to give up my comfortable lifestyle but then I reminded myself that having security was not why I became an actress.

At first, it was like stepping out into the unknown. Sometimes I felt panic – I never thought leaving would have affected me the way it did. Basically, I'm just hoping I can make it work.

Brookside Close – house by house

If there's one character who should be making a fortune in Manor Park, it's the boss of the local removal firm. For hardly a month goes by without someone moving house, albeit invariably to another home on the Close or to a flat above the Parade. This game of musical houses means that nomads like Terry Sullivan, Sinbad or Katie Rogers have, at one time or another, occupied virtually all the available accommodation in the area.

Terry started out on the neighbouring council estate and then moved into No. 10 with Michelle Jones. From there, he flitted across to No. 7 (with Pat Hancock) before doubling back to live at No. 9. After the deaths of Sue and Danny, he stayed in Barry's flat above the Parade but when he found God, he moved into No. 5 with the cult. Following the explosion, Terry was back in Barry's flat (this time with Simon Howe), no doubt cursing the fact that there were still two houses on the Close which he had never been able to call home.

Having briefly lived in the garden shed at No. 8, Sinbad first took root on the Close at No. 7 as caretaker for the Chois. He lived in the caretaker's flat above the Parade for a while before moving into No. 10 with the Jordaches. After selling No. 10 to the Corkhills', he continued to lodge there in the extension from time to time but then moved into No. 5 with Mick Johnson. He had the effrontery to move off the Close for a few months to stay at the O'Learys' but has since bought No. 8 with them. So it's back to square one, but this time not in the shed.

Wandering waif Katie Rogers started out at No. 7, moved with the rest of her family to No. 7 and stayed there when Simon and the cult arrived. Having seen through Simon, she fled to No. 8 where the Dixons took her in. The next stop was No. 6 with Jacqui, Rachel and David Crosbie before the three girls shared a flat of their own above Brookside Parade. After the explosion, Katies moved into No. 9 for a few nights with Ollie Simpson and Eleanor Kitson.

And lastly word for a promising newcomer. In her relatively short time on the Close, Rachel Jordache has already clocked up four different abodes. She began at No. 10 but when the going got tough, the Crosbies took her under their wing at No. 6. In the wake of Beth's death, she returned to No. 10 but soon went back to No. 6 to share with Jacqui and Katie. They then moved into a flat above the Parade, only for Rachel to move into a place of her own when she married Christian. After the breakdown of her marriage, it was back to the flat with Jacqui and Katie. It's hardly worth unpacking.

Number 5

The first occupants, from 1982 to 1989, were the Grants but when Bobby and Sheila's marriage fell apart, the Rogers family moved in. After Frank's death in 1993, the cult moved in before Barry Grant bought the old family house. Then at the end of 1995, Mick

Johnson became the new owner. *Deaths:* 2 (The mercy killing of Gladys Charlton by Mick and Elaine, plus Lynn Rogers' miscarriage after being pushed down the stairs by Sammy). *Assists:* 2 (Frank Rogers was killed while at No. 5 and Damon Grant was technically still a resident when he was fatally stabbed in York). *Explosions:* 1.

Number 6

Alan Partridge lived in the bungalow from 1982 until 1984 when Harry Cross moved in, looking for somewhere smaller than his old house next door. Harry stayed, first with wife Edna and then with lodger Ralph Hardwick, until 1990. The Johnsons took up residence until 1993 when financial difficulties forced Mick to sell up. The Crosbies duly moved in but David left the Close with Molly Marchbank early in 1998, allowing the Shadwicks to become the latest occupants. *Deaths:* 1 (Edna Cross). *Assists:* 1 (George Manners died on the drive).

Number 7

Harry and Edna Cross lived there for a year until Harry let the house to tenants, including Sandra Maghie, Pat Hancock, Kate Moses and Terry Sullivan. Frank and Chrissy Rogers bought the house in 1987 but soon switched to No. 5, leaving the way open for the Chois to move in. They remained for a year before selling up to the Farnhams. *Deaths:* 2 (Kate Moses, John Clarke). *Assists:* 2 (Matthew and Emily Farnham died while living at No. 7). *Sieges:* 1.

Number 8

Paul and Annabelle Collins occupied No. 8 from 1982 until 1990. They were succeeded by the Dixons (Ron first with DD, then with Bev) but in 1998 Ron gave way to the O'Learys. *Deaths:* 0. *Assists:* 1 (Tony Dixon was killed while a resident). *Fires:* 1.

Number 9

Heather Haversham lived at No. 9 from 1982 until 1986, initially with first husband Roger Huntington, then by herself, and lastly with second husband, Nicholas Black. In 1987, Jonathan Gordon-Davies and Laura Wright moved in and, after Laura's death, Jonathan took in Terry Sullivan as a lodger. Jonathan finally moved to London in 1990 and the Sullivans bought the house. From 1992 to 1994, it was owned by the Harrisons and from 1994 to 1996 by Rosie and Eddie Banks. Their hasty departure resulted in an auction which saw ownership pass to the Simpsons. *Deaths:* 1 (Laura Gordon-Davies). *Assists:* 4 (Nicholas Black, Sue Sullivan and her unborn child and Danny Sullivan all died while living at No. 9). *Fires:* 1.

Number 10

Gavin and Petra Taylor lived in the Brookside House of Horrors from 1982 to 1983. After Gavin's death and Petra's suicide, the Jacksons (Marie Jackson was Petra's sister) moved in but George's imprisonment forced the rest of the family to relocate to Leeds. The Corkhills arrived on the scene in 1985, the start of a stormy eight-year tenure. Next came the Jordaches until Mandy moved to Bristol, allowing Jimmy and Jackie Corkhill to restore the home to its former splendour. *Deaths:* 3 (Gavin Taylor, Trevor Jordache, Little Jimmy Corkhill). *Assists:* 2 (Petra Taylor committed suicide in Wales, Beth Jordache died in jail). *Headstones through window:* 1. *Bullets through window:* Several.

Playing God

The air at the *Brookside* long-term planning meeting was heavy with thought. The show's 12 writers, plus series producer Ric Mellis, outgoing series producer Mal Young, executive producer Phil Redmond, script editor Sue Mooney and researcher Stephen Byrne, were seated around a long table in October 1996 trying to solve a tricky problem relating to the Farnhams.

It had already been decided at an earlier meeting that *Brookside* would be featuring a surrogacy storyline. Furthermore, it had been decreed that Jacqui Dixon would get her comeuppance. She had been lording it around the Close for too long and would now find herself in dire straits financially, having over-reached herself. Her desperation for instant cash would lead her to agree to be the surrogate mother. So which family on the Close would want another baby and why? The Farnhams seemed the most likely candidates, but with two children of their own already, Max and Susannah would hardly need a third to cement their new relationship.

At that point, writer Barbara Phillips, attending her first long-term planning meeting, piped up: 'Why don't we kill off Matthew and Emily?'

There was a hushed silence as the assembled gathering considered the implications of killing off two children. Everyone waited for Phil Redmond's reaction. Would he like the idea or not? He liked it: Matthew and Emily's death warrants had been signed.

There now remained the question of the small print. How exactly would they die? After further debate, a car crash emerged as the preferred means of disposal – with Susannah driving. To add to her guilt and to give the neighbours something to gossip about, Susannah would have had a glass of wine before getting in the car – not enough to make her drunk but maybe just enough to impair her judgement. So when the kids started playing up in the back seat, she would turn around long enough for her gaze to be averted from the traffic ahead. If she had been stone-cold sober, she might have been concentrating harder. Susannah herself would emerge relatively unscathed from the crash – another factor which would serve to heighten her sense of guilt – but an infection which set in after her injuries would mean that she would no longer be able to have children. Research showed that adoption agencies would not consider the Farnhams while they were clearly still grieving so, with Susannah unable to wait, surrogacy would become the only solution. Enter Jacqui.

The long-term planning meetings on *Brookside* take place twice a year and run over two days. Sometimes they are held at Mersey Television – in the room which has played the courtroom at the trials of the Jordaches and Mick Johnson – or occasionally they will be made into a weekend away in somewhere like the Lake District. These meetings are attended by Phil Redmond, the producer and the 12 writers, and are designed to map out *Brookside* storylines up to a year or so ahead. The team discuss where they want *Brookside* to go and what should happen to the various characters, although this is sometimes determined by the expiry of an artist's contract.

Every four weeks throughout the year, writers and producer meet in Liverpool over a two-day period to plan in detail a month's episodes. These meetings take place four months ahead of transmission. The dozen writers are deliberately selected to represent a cross-section of society. They are split roughly equally between men and women and cover a wide age range and social background. It doesn't take long to work out who identifies with the Farnhams and who identifies with the Corkhills. Similarly, it doesn't take long to discover which characters the writers dislike.

The meetings begin at nine in the morning and often go on for 12 hours each day or more. The only break is one hour for lunch, although refreshments are brought in morning and afternoon to revive weary minds. The debate can be long and fierce as different writers argue the pros and cons of a particular storyline. Although there is plenty of black humour in evidence around the table, what immediately comes across is how passionately the writers care about the show's regular characters and will fight against anything implausible. Peter Cox, who has been writing for *Brookside* since 1986, admits: 'We often seem to spend more time with each other than we do with our families. The arguments can be tough and on *Brookside* we are renowned for being particularly hard on each other. But any criticism is always constructive.'

Sometimes an entire scene is played out first at the monthly writers' meetings. A prime example of this was the split between Frank and Chrissy Rogers. One writer was taking Chrissy's side while another was seeing things from Frank's viewpoint. The exchange between the two writers was so forceful and convincing that the then series producer, Mal Young, urged the script assistant: 'Get all this down because this is the scene!'

The month's 12 episodes (unless there is a special five-nighter) are marked out on a large board, divided among the current families. Artist availability is also taken into consideration, so if an actor is away on holiday during the shooting of a week's episodes, there is not much point trying to write him into the action. Armed with the outline from the long-term planning meeting which indicates the ultimate goals for each character, the writers, under the guidance of the producer, work out the plots for the individual episodes. When the plots are completed, they go through them to decide on the hook for each episode, ensuring that the real cliffhanger comes at the end of the week, on a Friday.

Tuning in to proceedings from the back of the room is researcher Stephen Byrne. If a point requires clarification – it may be medical or legal – he will disappear and make a few phone calls so that he can present the required information to the meeting. There is no guesswork on *Brookside*. Plotlines are determined by authenticity. When Mick Johnson was complaining about the fact that it was nearly always black kids who were suspended or excluded from Brookside Comprehensive, that story was based on official statistics. The figures weren't just plucked out of the air.

The researcher also presents a list of things which will be happening in four months' time, not only in Liverpool but in Britain as a whole – like major sporting events and festivals – so that they can be incorporated into the storylines if necessary. There is also a list of characters' anniversaries and birthdays, culled from the *Brookside* bible. It is not just wedding anniversaries which are noted but anniversaries of significant events in the characters' lives. Thus last spring we saw the Farnhams remembering that it was a year to the day when Susannah had the fatal car crash. Additionally, the writers are issued with reminders of what has happened in previous episodes to ensure consistency of plot. This list may include seemingly trivial events – such as when Mike Dixon first grew his beard – but it is all an essential part of the quest for continuity.

The next step is the commissioning meeting at which the producer commissions the writers who are to script that month's episodes. New writers are broken in with single episodes, then doubles, until finally, if they make the grade, they are given a whole week's episodes. The series producer selects the writers who are most suited to particular scripts. Some writers excel at emotion, others at humour; some may write really well for the Corkhills, others for the Simpsons. At the commissioning meeting, the producer takes the chosen writers through the storylines, reminding them of the various qualities which need to be brought out in the script.

The writer has two weeks in which to produce a first draft of the script which is then dissected by the producer at a first-draft meeting. These can be occasions of considerable blood-letting as writers have to listen to their hard work being ripped to shreds, and have been known to last well into the night. These are not occasions for the faint-hearted. Taking the amendments on board, the writer has a further ten days to come up with a second draft. Assuming that this is acceptable, the artists are then scheduled and a director from the show's pool of seven directors is assigned to each week's episodes. Like the established writers, the directors will be in charge of a whole week at a time. The appropriate directors and writers then get together with the producer for a writer/director meeting at which the producer and the writer explain what they are trying to do with the story. They also give the director the hooks for future episodes.

Then for the writers, with their scripts completed, it is back to the next monthly meeting to start playing God all over again.

TOTAL **BROOKSIDE**

Who's Who

Here are the major characters who have passed through Brookside Close over the past 16 years. Some have even lived to tell the tale.

Bagga (Tina Fairclough) 1989

The hard-nosed bully of Brookside Comprehensive tried to force timid *Katie Rogers* into stealing money for her. Katie's brother Geoff realised what was going on and, together with his pal *Bumper Humphries*, decided to warn Bagga off. But Bagga and her gang weren't easily deterred and, to avoid a beating, Katie stole some money from mum Chrissy. Subjected to further threats, Katie finally heeded Geoff's advice and told one of the teachers, Mr Jenkins, as a result of which Bagga was sent home until after the Christmas holidays. While Katie sobbed out the truth to a sympathetic Chrissy, Bagga vowed revenge. Happily she never got the chance.

Carl Banks (Stephen Donald) 1994–95

Carl Banks's life was one long chapter of mistakes. He got married too young, made a career blunder by joining the army and then tried to rectify the situation by deserting. Reunited with his family, instead of playing the doting father, he preferred to play the field. And he even did that on his own doorstep, first with *Margaret Clemence*, then *Jacqui Dixon*. He managed to throw away his chance of a steady job at La Luz by instigating a dodgy lager scam which ended with him lying in hospital and facing possible manslaughter charges. By the time he finally tried to make a go of his marriage and face up to his responsibilities, it was too late and it came as no surprise when wife Sarah chose not to follow him to his new life in Dubai. Given Carl's track record with women and drink, he's probably a few limbs lighter than when he left Liverpool.

Eddie Banks (Paul Broughton) 1994–96

Factory worker Eddie Banks was a big bear of a man but beneath that grizzly exterior, he was just a soft teddy. He blamed himself for youngest son Lee's joyriding as it was Eddie who had taught him to drive. At home, it was Eddie who invariably acted as peacemaker when wife Rosie was on her high horse. Only as a last resort did he ever put his foot down. Yet Eddie loved her dearly, along with his trade union principles, his Harley-Davidson motorbike and his bendy 'Bully', a legacy of his appearance on *Bullseye*. Unfortunately Rosie misinterpreted Jim Bowen's advice about 'keeping out of the black and into the red' and ran up huge gambling debts. In despair, Eddie found himself thrown into the arms of daughter-in-law Sarah with whom he had always got on well (unlike Rosie, he tried to keep Carl and Sarah together). After the affair with Sarah ended in tears, he and Rosie patched things up and left the Close for new horizons. The man deserved a break.

Lee Banks (Matthew Lewney) 1994–96

Teenage joyrider Lee Banks was painted as a bad lad (across the forehead actually) but it was merely a case of him having fallen in with the wrong crowd. After serving two years in a young offenders' institution, Lee

Rosie Banks (Susan Twist), Jimmy Corkhill (Dean Sullivan), Eddie Banks (Paul Broughton) and Cracker

wanted to show that he had learned his lesson. He was full of remorse but the only person on the Close who would give him the time of day was the equally troubled *Rachel Jordache*. And she got him into more hot water by taking him on a shoplifting expedition. From then on, apart from a crush on *Katie Rogers*, Lee led an increasingly solitary existence, spending an inordinate amount of time in his bedroom with his computer, but he found a new maturity in helping to reunite his mum and dad. They may never play happy families, but it was a start.

Rosie Banks (Susan Twist) 1994–96

Rosie Banks first met husband Eddie when the pair were in the Territorial Army. She later became a traffic warden, an appropriate job for someone whose mission in life appeared to be to make other people suffer. Never slow to voice her opinion, firebrand Rosie was the mother-in-law from hell, forever haranguing Sarah about the upbringing of little Rebecca. It seemed to have escaped Rosie's attention that Carl and Lee were hardly an advertisement for her own prowess as a mother. But then with Rosie, it was always someone else's fault. Her behaviour reached an all-time low during her gambling phase when she was even prepared to frame Lee for the theft of meat from Grants' freezer rather than face the consequences herself. It was only when she had lost everything that she finally realised what a fool she had been. Not that Rosie was without her plus points. On a good day, she could be the life and soul of the party and was a mean darts player. But most of the time she was just mean.

Sarah Banks (Andrea Marshall) 1994–96

Poor Sarah must have broken a few mirrors in her time to account for all the bad luck she endured at the hands of the Banks family. She married Carl in 1990 when she was 16 and pregnant and he was just a year older. They had a miserable marriage, she had a silly fling with Eddie and endured a relationship with Rosie so hostile that a UN peace-keeping force would not have been out of place in the hallway of No. 9. With Rebecca to raise and precious little support from her part-time husband, Sarah cut a lonely, vulnerable figure. But she was still young and pretty and didn't see why she should be stuck at home forever when she had no shortage of male admirers, even though *Mike Dixon*, for one, lost interest when he realised that the package deal included a daughter. The best decision she made was to move away. If only she had married into a nice quiet family, like the Munsters.

Marcia Barrett (Cheryl Maiker) 1990–93

Marcia Barrett spent most of her time in the middle of eternal triangles. As *Josie Johnson*'s best friend, she frequently found her loyalties divided between Josie and Mick, and as the old flame of Mick's slippery brother *Ellis Johnson*, she constantly tried to keep the peace between Ellis and her latest beau, *Sinbad*. Marcia had worked with Josie at the notorious Fourstar Club, an establishment more likely to be featured in the *Police Gazette* than *What's On*. Yet she was essentially a kindly soul who captured the heart of Sinbad to the extent that he proposed to her via the electronic scoreboard at Goodison Park. Nevertheless she accepted, only for the relationship to founder when she revealed she couldn't have children. They got back together but it wasn't easy going. Eventually playing piggy in the middle proved too complicated for her and she dramatically called off the wedding at the last minute. It was just as well. With her history, she'd probably have found herself at the centre of a bitter row between the vicar and the organist.

Nisha Batra (Sunetra Sarker) 1988–90

Teenager Nisha came from a strict Indian background and her parents liked to vet her friends before allowing her out for the evening. Given that one of her best friends was *Sammy Rogers*, they weren't bad judges. Nisha and Sammy met when they worked together part-time at the supermarket and she was a passenger in the stolen car which crashed, killing two lads and leaving Sammy's boyfriend, *Owen Daniels*, in a coma. For her part, Nisha suffered concussion. She and Sammy kept in touch until Nisha was beaten up by racists while out on a foursome with Sammy, Owen and her boyfriend Pete. Fearing further reprisals, Pete finished with Nisha, whereupon she spat in his face. They didn't go out much after that.

Maria Benson (Pauline Daniels) 1991

When the future *DD Dixon* suffered a nervous breakdown and spent 18 months in a mental institution, she became friendly with one of the cleaners, Maria. She and Maria became best friends. DD married Ron and Maria married Charlie Benson. Maria had a sexual appetite which bordered on the ravenous and enjoyed watching erotic films, unlike DD who found *The Sound of Music* quite raunchy enough. Maria later had an affair and asked DD to cover up for her. This put an intolerable strain on the friendship and the two drifted apart.

Adam Black (Tony King) 1986

The youngest son of *Nicholas Black* from his first marriage, Adam was the only one of the Black offspring to welcome his father's relationship with *Heather Haversham*. Mature beyond his years, Adam was a keen cricketer and used to discuss the finer points of the game with *Paul Collins*, who in turn was simply pleased to meet a boy with good manners. Ironically, it was Adam who first hinted to Heather that his father had secrets.

Barbara Black (Brenda Elder) 1986

Nicholas Black's lesbian ex-wife worked at a feminist print workshop where *Heather Haversham* was doing an audit. The two women got on well and when Nick's heroin addiction reared its ugly head, it was the capable Barbara to whom Heather turned for advice. She told Heather not to build up hopes of him cleaning up his act. Her caution was not misplaced for within a few weeks Nick had overdosed fatally.

Heather Black (née Haversham, formerly Huntington)
(Amanda Burton) (1982–86)

Combining brains and beauty, Heather was everybody's dream accountant with a smile that could charm the birds from the trees. Even *Harry Cross* was hard pushed to say a word against her. In her smart suits, yellow Citroen 2CV and neat little house, she epitomised upward mobility. She seemed to have the world at her feet, but there was one fatal flaw in her personality – she was a lousy judge of men. In fairness to Heather, it wasn't easy sorting out the wheat from the chaff when most of the men in the northern hemisphere appeared intent on chatting her up. And sometimes her looks counted against her, especially at work. A spurned boss is not a happy boss. Her first mistake was *Roger Huntington*. She simply wasn't ready for marriage. She wanted a career, he wanted a family. When she devoted all her energies to her forthcoming final accountancy exams, the writing was on the wall. Roger started playing away and, despite his pleas, Heather wouldn't have him back. For she was nobody's pushover and behind that easy smile lay a steely determination. Following the break-up of her marriage, she reverted to her maiden name of Haversham and began to enjoy her new-found independence. But she still couldn't resist a smooth talker. She was even naïve enough to fall for a used-car salesman, *Don Summerhill*, only to discover that he had more than one careful owner – namely, a wife at home. It looked like the real thing with *Tom Curzon*, chairman of Curzon Communications, until she realised that, like Roger, he wanted her to pack up work and concentrate on motherhood. Heather reckoned she was worth more than that and called the wedding off. So it was that, disillusioned by men, she fell for the childlike charms of *Nicholas Black*. It was to prove her biggest mistake of all. Heather ended up fleeing No. 9 in the dead of night to catch a boat bound for her native Northern Ireland, with Nick dead from an OD. The woman who had everything left the Close with nothing.

Nicholas Black (Alan Rothwell) 1985–86

Breezing through the city in his MG Midget, Nick Black braked so sharply that the car behind ran into him. Its driver was *Heather Haversham*. It soon became apparent that architect Nick had designs on Heather and he became a frequent caller to her house, even staying up all night to finish off her decorating. A divorcee with three children, Nick seemed everything Heather wanted in a man. He was gentle, kind and funny and used to leave her cute little drawings to say 'hello' or 'goodbye'. Heather was suitably smitten and, just seven months after they had first bumped into each other, they were married. But Nick's easy-going nature was merely a camouflage for weakness. He became increasingly dependent on his best mate, *Charlie Dawson*, and on their shared secret: heroin. He promised Heather that he'd change but his promise was just empty words. When she hid his cheque book to prevent him paying his pushers, he funded his habit by stealing her ruby pendant. Hopelessly addicted, he tried to get Heather to take heroin – so that she could understand – but she threw him out. He went to Sefton Park, fell asleep on a park bench and died from hypothermia. He couldn't live without heroin and he couldn't live with it.

Ruth Black (Joanne Sidwell) 1986

Ruth was daddy's girl. Spoilt and selfish, she was party to his innermost secret and bitterly resented the arrival of Heather on the scene, fearing that the interloper would come between her and her father. She did everything she could to make Heather feel uncomfortable and certainly wasn't going to tell her about Nick's addiction. By the time

she saw sense, it was too late.

Scott Black (Philip Glancy) 1986

Nick's elder son Scott joined forces with Ruth in treating Heather as a Wicked Stepmother. Like Ruth, he adored his father and saw Heather as a threat – a point that was rammed home when they blamed Heather for Adam's accident. He mellowed towards Heather after the wedding but they were never likely to become bosom buddies.

Cheryl Boyanowsky (Jennifer Calvert) 1988–89

Canadian student Cheryl Boyanowsky and her friend Donna met *Terry Sullivan* and *Jonathan Gordon-Davies* on a skiing holiday in Austria. Jonathan was trying to get over the death of his wife Laura and was thus more miserable than ever, but Cheryl offered a sympathetic ear and eventually won him round. At the time she was engaged to a Canadian divorcee, John Deburau, but gave him up to come and live with Jonathan at 9 Brookside Close. It was an uphill struggle from the start. The ghost of Laura was everywhere and, worse still, there was a physical presence in the form of Terry and his increasingly unstable girlfriend *Sue Harper*. Cheryl found herself in the middle of a battle zone and threatened to leave, particularly as Jonathan was becoming preoccupied with work. By way of an apology, he proposed marriage and talked gushingly about babies and nappies. Cheryl was horrified and was on her way back to Canada faster than Jacques Villeneuve.

Anne Bradley (Faith Brown) 1996

The rarely-seen wife of *JC Bradley*, Anne was a Grade One snob who enjoyed belittling the Simpsons about their decline in circumstances from a spacious residence in Formby to a modest house on Brookside Close. Although she was not exactly shy in

J C Bradley (Ken Sharrock)

coming forward, she was a shrinking violet next to her blustering husband.

JC Bradley (Ken Sharrock) 1996–97

It was more than coincidence that John Bradley liked to be known as 'JC', for he thought of himself as Jesus Christ, Moses and God all rolled into one. The bullying builder was very much a self-made man whose business achievements spoke for themselves – when they could get a word in. Vulgar in his displays of material wealth, his motto was that money could buy anything. He doted on daughter Jules and spoilt her something rotten, insisting on buying her a house as a wedding present. He was never keen on *Nat Simpson* as a future son-in-law and liked to deliver stern warnings as to what would happen if his little girl wasn't treated properly. In the end, Nat surpassed even JC's worst nightmares and the

avenging father-in-law used all his influence to hound him from Merseyside. It would do nothing for his precious Jules, but that didn't matter as long as it made him happy.

Jules Bradley – see Jules Simpson

Sharon Bridges (Hayley Smitton) 1997–

The girlfriend of wayward *Timothy 'Tinhead' O'Leary*, Sharon may look a pushover but appearances can be deceptive. When Tim produced a packet of condoms in the hope of breaking his duck, she expressed her disgust by kicking him where it hurts most. She is well aware of his shortcomings but finds going out with him preferable to staying at home watching telly.

Julia Brogan (Gladys Ambrose)

Julia Brogan (Gladys Ambrose) 1985–

Just as the city centre has CCTV, Brookside Close has Julia Brogan. Able to hone in on gossip faster than a tabloid journalist and with a surveillance technique which makes MI5 look amateurish, Julia is the eyes and ears of the Close. There's not much that gets past her and if she does only manage to pick up bits and pieces of a story, that's no problem. Her fertile imagination will fill in the gaps. In her younger days, Julia had singing aspirations and reckons she could have become the next Doris Day had she not fallen pregnant with 'our Renee'. The Renee in question became *Doreen Corkhill*. Widow of Arthur Brogan, Julia has spent years looking down on the Corkhill clan, even though she herself was not averse to fiddling 'the leccy' in her younger days. But ever since she was wrongly accused of thieving from the till by *Ron Dixon*, Julia has been what she might call 'a pillock of the community'. She is as comfortable with the English language as Little Miss Muffet would be in the insect house at London Zoo and trots out malapropisms as often as other people use verbs. This is yet another reason why most of the residents steer clear of engaging her in conversation. Julia is never backward in offering her opinion and over the years has dished out more advice than Claire Rayner. She has high morals and likes to see that justice is done – in person. So whenever there's a good trial, Julia will be sitting in the gallery with her knitting and a bag of boiled sweets, passing sentence along with the judge. Well, it's a day out and it's in the warm – what more could a pensioner ask for? Julia wears her bus pass with pride and is the most active of senior

Kirsty Brown (Joanne Black)

suffered similar misfortune at the hands of *Jack Sullivan*, but she hasn't given up hope of finding Mr Right. It's just that as each year passes it become increasingly difficult to find a beau with his own teeth.

Shaun Brookes (Richard Trinder) 1995
Mike Dixon's handsome young boss at the video company found himself the object of desire of both *Katie Rogers* and *Jacqui Dixon*. He was supposed to be Katie's boyfriend but Jacqui got her claws into him in the hope that he would lend her £2,000. Guided by his groin rather than his brain, two-timing Shaun fell for the bait, slept with Jacqui and then tried to back out of the deal. But the conniving Jacqui was too smart for him and forced him to pay up. The only revenge he could exact was to sack Mike, so it wasn't all bad news.

Ducksie Brown (Mark Birch) 1983–84
Archetypal scally who used to hang around with *Damon Grant* and *Gizzmo Hawkins*. While the bungalow was unoccupied, the trio used it as a base for their shared interests – smoking, boozing and snogging. Rumour had it he earned his nickname because he was so overweight he used to waddle like a duck. He later surprised many people, including himself, by finding gainful employment.

Kirsty Brown (Joanne Black) 1986–89
Rod Corkhill could hardly believe his luck when he started dating pretty nurse Kirsty Brown. All he could think about was that caring bedside manner, those gentle soothing hands. Little did he know he'd found a nurse who modelled herself on Hattie Jacques in *Carry On Matron*. For if Kirsty was a medical condition, she'd be a migraine; if she was a DIY tool, she'd be a drill; and if she was a pub, she'd be the Nag's Head. Ironically for a policeman, Rod was well and truly under the cosh. Planning for

citizens, forever organising fund-raising events for the over-55s. If she had been in charge of Live Aid, it would have been done in half the time, as long as Queen didn't mind going on at the British Legion, just after the meat raffle. She has always kept her hand in with a number of little part-time jobs, most recently at the hair salon and cleaning for the Farnhams (or 'Farn-hams' as she insists on calling them). She thinks the Farnhams have breeding and so puts on her finest airs and graces in their presence. All that's missing is her tiara. Although she can have a sharp tongue when in full gossip mode, Julia has a heart of gold and will take in any waif or stray…provided it's not Ron Dixon. Not only has she never forgiven him for the unsavoury business at the Trading Post but she was badly let down by Ron's bigamous dad, *Cyril Dixon*. She later their future together virtually from day one, Kirsty kept tight control over the purse strings and interrogated him if ever there was the slightest suspicion that he'd been enjoying himself. Her miserly behaviour eventually drove him into the welcoming arms of WPC *Emma Reid* and Kirsty turned her homemaking instincts to his best pal, PC *Neil 'Tommo' Thompson*. As long as he obeyed her 'no sex on new soft furnishings' rule, they will have got along famously.

Cassie Charlton (Ebony Gray) 1996-

'Opinionated' would be the polite way of describing Cassie Charlton. For she has never been slow to express her views, particularly when sister Elaine took up with *Mick Johnson*. If her actions had kept pace with her mouth, she might have done more to help mum Gladys through her last months, but instead she was happily to leave all the donkey work to Elaine and Mick while she went swanning off around town. In any conversation with Cassie, an argument seemed only a second away, but she has mellowed since Mick's trial and appears genuinely remorseful that she put the family through such pain by reporting Elaine and Mick to the police. She is a conscientious worker although her scowling face must have driven away so many customers it was no wonder the Trading Post went out of business. *David Crosbie* was more appreciative of her efforts and, on his departure, appointed her manager of the petrol station.

Gladys Charlton (Eileen O'Brien) 1996–97

Gladys was an inspirational figure. Widowed after husband Charlie's death, she bore her illness with great fortitude, never complaining or wallowing in self-pity. She didn't want to be a burden to her family but at the same time she had firm views as to how she wanted to spend her remaining weeks. A lifelong socialist, she didn't believe in private health care and wasn't keen on hospitals in general. All she wanted was to die with dignity. For someone who had given so much throughout her life, it wasn't much to ask.

Caroline Choi (Sarah Lam) 1989–90

When Caroline Choi moved to 7 Brookside Close with her brother Michael and his five-year-old daughter Jessica, she was intent on expanding her jewellery-making business. Instead she ended up as little more than a childminder to Jessica. Not surprisingly, Caroline felt that Michael was taking advantage of her good nature and they argued constantly. Hong Kong-born Caroline needed a little light relief and it was provided by *Sinbad* and his performing bucket. He took more of a shine to her than he did to his windows, but much as she liked him, he wasn't really to her taste. When shifty ex-boyfriend *James Markham* appeared on the scene and embezzled from her business to pay his gambling debts, Caroline knew there was nothing to keep her on the Close. Following James's death, she returned to Hong Kong, leaving Sinbad to cry into his chamois leather.

Michael Choi (David Yip) 1989–90

Dr Michael Choi's prescription for happiness was simple: he liked to get his own way over everything. A widower following the death in November 1988 of Meilin, his wife of seven years, in a road accident caused by a drunk driver, Michael wanted only the best for daughter Jessica, as long as other people did the work. If his sister Caroline couldn't look after her, he kicked up a fuss. He demanded that Caroline put Jessica's welfare before her own career, yet on the one occasion that he was forced to take Jessica with him to the surgery, his sense of martyrdom would have done justice to Joan of Arc. Michael's selfishness and his relationship with westerner *Alison Gregory* brought him into

Caroline (Sarah Lam) and Jessica Choi (Anna Sung)

constant conflict with his equally stubborn father, but the Chois did bury the hatchet (not in each other) before Michael, Alison and Jessica headed for a new life in the United States.

Stephen Choi (Kwong Chee Leong) 1989–90

Stephen Choi, Michael's restaurateur father, wasn't so much inscrutable as insufferable. With a look of disapproval never far away, Choi senior was a die-hard traditionalist who frowned upon western culture, although he wasn't too proud to take their money off them on a Friday night. He was particularly concerned about Michael's blossoming romance with a western girl (although given that this was stony-faced *Alison Gregory*, he may have had a point) and instead tried to fix Michael up with Amy Ying, the daughter of an old family friend. When this failed, he attempted emotional blackmail, using Jessica as a pawn in his

little game. For one who prided himself on oriental wisdom, Stephen displayed a distinct lack of intelligence by appointing *Sinbad* as official caretaker to No. 7 in the wake of the Chois' departure.

Karyn Clark (Joanna Phillips-Lane) 1992–93

Karyn was *Patricia Farnham*'s boss at the advertising agency, but when it was taken over by a larger company she lost her job and decided to set up a PR consultancy with Patricia. Their first venture was the charity fashion show hosted by Sarah Greene, and they were soon toasting the future of Farnham Clark Associates. Unfortunately Karyn enjoyed mixing business with pleasure and took a fancy to *Barry Grant* while the pair were discussing plans for the opening of La Luz. Barry's partner, *Joe Halsall*, was angry that Barry had hired Karyn without consulting her first and was unimpressed by her advertising campaign.

So when Karyn and Barry returned from a New Year's trip to Paris, Karyn disappeared to London and hasn't been heard of since.

John Clarke (Robert Pugh) 1985

It was a chance encounter at Alder Hey Hospital Fête which brought John Clarke into the lives of *Kate Moses*, *Pat Hancock* and *Sandra Maghie*. A psychopathic loner, Clarke recognised Kate as one of the nurses who had been on duty at the hospital when his elderly mother died. He blamed the medical staff for her death and took a full and bloody revenge by holding the trio hostage at gunpoint at 7 Brookside Close. The siege ended when Clarke, after shooting Kate dead, turned the gun on himself.

Vicki Cleary (Cheryl Leigh) 1985–87

Glamorous van-hire queen Vicki Cleary crossed swords with *Terry Sullivan* and *Pat Hancock* when the dynamic duo set up in competition. The Clearys sent Pat and Terry off on a number of wild-goose chases, a situation which Pat tried to resolve in the only manner he knew – with his fists. Terry favoured the softly softly approach and not only put an end to the van war, but also won the girl. However, Vicki soon got fed up with Terry's dithering. He eventually decided that he wanted her to move in with him and she agreed, but only on condition that he got rid of Pat, in much the same way that you'd get rid of rising damp. Terry dithered again and by the time he'd made up his mind, Vicki had walked out for good.

Margaret Clemence
(Nicola Stephenson) 1990–94

In a street which frequently made the Bronx look like Budleigh Salterton, Margaret was one of the good guys. She was friendly, kind and conscientious – qualities which naturally brought her nothing but grief. Although she had left her Oldham home at a tender age to work as the Farnhams' nanny, Margaret wasn't very streetwise.

Father Derek O'Farrell (Clive Moore) and Margaret Clemence (Nichola Stephenson)

What little experience she'd had of boys, she didn't like. Indeed one of the reasons she had been so keen to leave Oldham was to get away from her over-physical boyfriend Kieran. She just wasn't sure about that side of a relationship and felt safer playing with young Thomas Farnham. Not that she necessarily received much thanks for it: *Patricia Farnham* could be a moody boss, particularly when feeling guilty about not devoting enough of her own time to Thomas. On such occasions, she would take out her guilt on Margaret, fretting that Thomas would pick up her Oldham accent and might be wearing a cloth cap and racing whippets by the time he was four. Margaret's outwardly sunny nature and

Shane Cochran (Richard Norton)

that he was more bothered about his next fix than his next audience. For Shane was a secret heroin addict and was usually higher than Jack at the top of the beanstalk. When *Gary Stanlow* supplied him with uncut heroin, it was Shane's final curtain-call.

Annabelle Collins (Doreen Sloane)
1982–90

Although Brookside Close came as something of a culture shock to her after the Wirral, Annabelle Collins was not one to bemoan her fate. Instead the former French teacher set about involving herself in the community, standing bail for *George Jackson*, acting as election agent for an old friend, Robin Tate, and forming a local ratepayers' association. Whilst most of her new neighbours found husband Paul, to whom she had been married since 1960, a prickly proposition, the compassionate Annabelle was a different kettle of fish. She thought that life was too short for feuding and spent much of her time soothing troubled waters which had been stirred up by Paul. Despite always being immaculately attired and looking born to twin set and pearls, she never paraded herself around the Close. She had the common touch. And she had plenty of scope for practice on Brookside Close. She dealt sensibly with family problems, but listening to Paul's constant complaining became increasingly tiresome. She needed more to occupy her time. She even took up jogging (Paul thought he'd see her in a body-bag before he saw her in a tracksuit) and started a home catering business, but it was not until she became a magistrate that she felt truly fulfilled. That was partly due to fellow magistrate, *Brian Lawrence*. Annabelle surprised herself by embarking on a torrid affair with him. But when she realised how shallow Brian was, she went back to Paul, although humble pie was not on the menu. Annabelle wasn't willing to spend the rest of her days apologising and Paul wasn't one

willingness to help brought her into contact with young Father *Derek O'Farrell*. She felt safe with a man of the cloth but, as friendship turned to passion, she incurred the disapproval of her mum and took the full force of the wrath that was Derek's zealous sister, *DD Dixon*. Hopelessly confused and still searching for her inner self, Margaret fell into a brief fling with Beth Jordache. It ruined their friendship but at least it made her realise how much she missed Derek and she went off to join him in Bosnia – older and certainly wiser than when she had first arrived on the Close.

Shane Cochran (Richard Norton)
1995–96

Australian soap star Shane Cochran came to Liverpool to star in the Christmas panto in which *Katie Rogers* was a dancer. He caught the eye of *Jacqui Dixon* until she learned to forgive and forget. Eventually they reached an understanding and moved to the Lake District so that Annabelle could care for her sick mother, *Mona Fallon*.

Gordon Collins (Nigel Crowley/ Mark Burgess) 1982–90

Even though money was tight in the Collins household, son Gordon was able to stay on at private school where he furthered his interest in computers and the head boy, *Christopher Duncan*. Gordon was an intelligent lad and was dismayed by the small-minded reaction to his homosexuality, both from his parents and from the cream of Merseyside's youth. Fleeing from a gang of queer-bashers wasn't his idea of the perfect end to an evening out. Gordon hated life at No. 8 – it was so parental – and he developed an unlikely bond with his confused grandmother, Mona, who understood his feelings far better than his parents. Between manning an AIDS helpline and making frequent trips to France on his motorbike, Gordon drifted from one job to another – working at a supermarket, helping Chris restore furniture and acting as a reluctant car salesman for his mother's lover, *Brian Lawrence*. He also developed a taste for fine wine and eventually landed a job with a wine merchant where he became friendly with one of his colleagues, Judith. She had hoped that the relationship might lead somewhere, but when he broke the news that he was gay, they settled for being friends. But she left him the key to her flat in case he ever changed his mind.

Lucy Collins (Katrin Cartlidge/ Maggie Saunders) 1982–90

Lucy Collins was the first wild child of Brookside Close. After enjoying the privileges of private school, she rebelled at having to continue her stuttering education at Brookside Comprehensive where the natives bullied her over her posh accent.

Gordon Collins (Mark Burgess)

But Vlad the Impaler would have been hard-pushed to bully Lucy and by the end of term most of her oppressors were seeking stress counselling. She then skipped her French 'O' level exam to picket a council meeting for CND and ended up getting herself arrested. Annabelle was horrified and packed her off to France to stay with family friends Gerard and Monique Dubois. The change of scenery failed to produce the desired effect. Lucy fell in love with a married man, *James Fleming*, and followed him back to England. He tried to end the affair but the wilful Lucy insisted on a showdown with his wife. Lucy suffered a humiliating defeat, turned to shoplifting and embarked on a hectic schedule of one-night stands. Eventually she teamed up with *Barry Grant* to sell videos. Spiteful to the

Paul (Jim Wiggins) and Annabelle Collins (Doreen Sloane)

end, she wrecked Annabelle's attempts to rehabilitate young offender *Louise Mitchell* before announcing that she was off to manage a restaurant in France. They gave us dead sheep; we gave them Lucy Collins. It was probably a fair exchange.

Paul Collins (Jim Wiggins) 1982–90

An archaeological dig of 8 Brookside Close would have unearthed an old fossil in surprisingly good condition. His name was Paul Collins and he was a throwback to the days when you could hear the words of a song, you didn't eat with your elbows on the table and any haircut other than a short-back-and-sides was grounds for suspicion. Despite being the father of a teenage son,

Paul could not communicate with the younger generation. To him they were an alien race whose sole aim in life was to cause trouble. And their leader was *Damon Grant*. Of all the family, Paul was the hardest hit by his sudden redundancy from Petrochem where he had earned a comfortable living as a production manager. Now, in his early fifties, he found himself on the scrapheap with little prospect of a decent job. No wonder he became frustrated at seeing youngsters idling away their time. He did subsequently find work with a subsidiary of Petrochem – a post which, if nothing else, enabled him to renew hostilities with militant shop steward and undesirable neighbour *Bobby Grant*.

226

Paul enjoyed being able to put one over on Bobby: it gave him a purpose to life and something to talk about at the golf club. When he was once again made redundant, he joined a road safety campaign with such vigour that he was arrested. That was something else for them to talk about at the golf club. Paul was a proud man who was obsessed with keeping up appearances. When he learned that Gordon was gay, his biggest worry was what the neighbours would think. Once he had got over the initial shock, the old stuffed shirt took great delight in telling the world how proud he was of his son. He did have a heart after all. Unfortunately he didn't display it often enough to Annabelle and when she sought solace elsewhere, he was deeply hurt. She was the one person he thought he could always depend upon. Though they patched the marriage up, things would never quite be the same again. But then the world as a whole had changed too much for Paul's liking.

Billy Corkhill (John McArdle) 1985–90

The Corkhills were one of the best-known families in Liverpool. They were known to the police, the council and just about every pub landlord in the city. Between them, they spent more time in court than Perry Mason. The eldest brother, Frankie, had been murdered as part of a gangland feud, and the youngest, Jimmy, had handled more hot property than he'd had hot dinners. Then there was Billy. He didn't want much from life. All he asked for was a job which paid enough for him to support his wife Doreen and kids Rod and Tracy. But somehow the Corkhill name always seemed to hold him back. When Billy first parked his rusty old Datsun in the drive of 10 Brookside Close, he had a steady job as an electrician with a local firm, Pollocks, and things appeared to be looking up … but not for the neighbours. Finding Terry Sullivan's

Billy Corkhill (John McArdle)

stuff still in the house, Billy promptly dumped the lot in the front garden. If that didn't make the Collins' curtains twitch, the erection of naff white shutters on the outside of No. 10 certainly did. Paul argued that Billy hadn't got planning permission. Billy was in a dilemma: he didn't know whether to head butt Paul or chin him. In the end he decided Paul wasn't worth it. Billy had no such qualms over Tracy's lecherous geography teacher, Peter Montague, and, displaying his

Doreen Corkhill (Kate Fitzgerald)

tendency to think with his fists, found himself charged with assault. The resultant publicity cost Billy his job. Billy would do anything for his family, but all that Doreen and Tracy did in return was land him in debt. With nothing but bills coming into the house, Billy started to crack up. He grew angry, bitter and desperate. Any self-esteem he had was torn to shreds by being on the dole. He and Doreen fought so much they made Tom and Jerry look like pacifists. Billy had always tried to avoid becoming part of a reconstruction on *Crimewatch UK* but his plight was now such that he was persuaded to drive the getaway car on a

supermarket robbery. He evaded prosecution, but the lies and deceit drove Doreen out. In spite of everything that had gone on between them, he still loved her and wanted her back, but soon he found comfort in the unlikely form of *Sheila Grant*. Sheila was everything that Doreen wasn't: kind, considerate and God-fearing. Despite Doreen's attempts at sabotage, a JCB digging up the front lawn and Frankie's tombstone being delivered through the glass front door, Billy had never been happier. He and Sheila married and set sail for Basingstoke. Billy Corkhill had achieved respectability at last.

Diana Corkhill (née Spence)
(Paula Frances) 1990–93

It is not uncommon for a lad to fall for a salesgirl at a supermarket, but usually the purchase which sparks the fires of passion is a packet of condoms. In Rod Corkhill's case, it was spot cream. The salesgirl, Diana Spence, was suitably flattered by the attention although Rod had told her he was a trainee supermarket manager. When the truth emerged it created friction between her and her father, *Freddie Spence*. Diana wore a permanently glazed expression. She was a good-natured, trusting girl. She turned out to be illiterate and when she began attending classes, her self-confidence rose considerably, to the detriment of her marriage. For Rod was happier with a meek little wife than an assertive new woman. Eager to find a soul-mate, she became friendly with *Peter Harrison*. But the subsequent rape trial shattered her new-found confidence and the not guilty verdict left her feeling betrayed and vulnerable. Two men she cared about had destroyed her life. It would be a long time before she trusted another.

Jackie (Sue Jenkins) and Lindsey Corkhill (Claire Sweeney)

Doreen Corkhill (Kate Fitzgerald)
1985–90

From an early age, Doreen had wanted to better herself. Curiously, her chosen method of achieving this goal was to marry into the Corkhills. The promised land turned out to be a run-down council estate. Dissatisfied and egged on by her mother, *Julia Brogan*, Doreen left husband Billy in no doubt that she was unhappy on the estate. Ever the soft touch, Billy capitulated and, although they couldn't really afford a house of their own, he agreed on a move to Brookside Close. Impressed by the fact that her new next-door neighbour was a professional businesswoman (Heather) instead of a professional burglar, Doreen set about living up to her heightened social status, and she clocked up huge debts on her credit card, even though there was only Billy's intermittent work and her modest salary as a dentist's receptionist to support them. Her way of dealing with final demands was to hide them. As her grasp on reality grew ever more tenuous and with the family facing repossession, she thought about sleeping with her boss, Mr Howman, in return for the cash. She retained one last shred of dignity by backing out. But she displayed little dignity after walking out on Billy. Absent for 18 months, she suddenly returned to reclaim her man as if he were a prize in a *Reader's Digest* draw. By then, he was heavily involved with *Sheila Grant* and the fur started to fly. Previously just dopey, Doreen now showed the vindictive side to her nature, but Billy called her bluff. Finally she sloped away with her tail between her legs. Doreen's aspirations of grandeur remained spectacularly unfulfilled.

Jackie Corkhill (Sue Jenkins) 1991–

When Jackie first met Jimmy Corkhill back in 1971, she was wearing tight jeans and he bought her the New Seekers' 'Never Ending Song of Love' as a token of his affection.

Twenty-seven years on, she's still wearing tight jeans (even though she's now a grandmother) and has lasted considerably longer than the New Seekers. But that small gift from Jimmy was about as good as it's ever got. For the most part, all he's ever given her is grief by the lorryload. A good friend, loyal wife and devoted mother, Jackie certainly deserves better, but nobody could ever accuse her of being a moaner. Whereas some women want to move home at the first sign of a crack in the ceiling, she has stayed put in a house where there was once a body under the patio, where the front of the house has come under gunfire and where her own son was gunned down in the extension. Even a fresh coat of paint to cover the bloodstains wouldn't have gone amiss. To some, she is a saint for sticking with Jimmy through everything; to others, she is a fool and a hypocrite for repeatedly being taken in by his lies and promises. Of course, they did spend some years apart, but that was when Jimmy was into such trivial activities as sleeping with her sister, *Val Walker*, and being king of the knock-off. When he graduated to murder and drug dealing, she seemed prepared to put up with it. She always protested otherwise – and indeed didn't know about his drug habit for a long time – but the fact is, she always went back to him. Her threats to leave were as empty as Jimmy's promises to change his ways. Life with Jimmy has hardly been idyllic but the physical attraction between them has always over-ridden his criminal activities. Besides, she liked the smart house and nice clothes that he was able to provide for her, even if it was with drug money. Sometimes a dutiful wife just has to turn a blind eye. Even her fling with *Ron Dixon* was half-hearted. Maybe she felt uneasy about sleeping with a man whose son had been killed by her husband. Or maybe it was the recollection that her first moment of passion with Ron had taken place next to a dozen tubs of Pot Noodles and three tins of Spam in the Trading Post stock room. Whatever, it was Jimmy she still wanted. And now that he's going straight, she feels wholly vindicated – even though she can never be sure exactly how long it's going to last.

Jimmy Corkhill (Dean Sullivan) 1985–

Jimmy used to see himself as a loveable rogue – the cheeky patter, the dodgy deals, always sailing close to the wind but never doing any real harm. Brand new Chippendale chair? Jimmy Corkhill's the man. But behind the cocky exterior lurked a sad, lonely figure. Separated from Jackie and disowned by son Little Jimmy following his indiscretion with Auntie Val, the final humiliation came when daughter Lindsey told him she didn't want him at her wedding. Realising how barren his life was, he resolved to win Jackie back. Jackie had always thought of him as a loser. So he reckoned the only way he could put things right was to boost his earning power, to show her he could make something of himself. Crooked crimper *Brian Kennedy* first introduced him to drugs and, from then on, Jimmy was on the slippery road to ruin. He thought nothing of burgling neighbours' houses for drug money and later, in prison, when it dawned on him that taking drugs was a mugs' game but that there was big money to be made from dealing, he justified it by convincing himself that he was doing it all for Jackie. He'd got her back – that was all that mattered. Besides, he reasoned, if kids didn't buy the stuff from him, they'd get it from another dealer. But he's not the hard man he thinks he is. Deep down, he has a conscience, especially where his family are concerned. Desperate to make up for lost time with Lindsey, he reluctantly agreed to give her layabout husband, *Gary Stanlow*, a job with his latest business venture, Korky Kars, which was little more than a front for drug dealing. But the move backfired – literally – with a bullet through the window of No. 10 from an irate drug baron whom Gary had crossed. Horrified at the thought that granddaughter Kylie might have been hit, Jackie left him again and this time Jimmy knew he had about as much chance of winning her back as *Cracker* did of winning the Greyhound Derby … unless he stopped having anything to do with drugs. Unable to bear losing his family again, for once he was as good as his word. The death of Little Jimmy brought home the futility of it all and now Jimmy is Mr Clean, pursuing a worthwhile career as a teacher. He may never escape his past completely but at least he's loosened the shackles.

Little Jimmy Corkhill
(George Christopher) 1991–96

When he was eight, Little Jimmy caught his dad Jimmy in bed with Auntie Val. It scarred his whole life and left him bitter and resentful. He did everything in his power to prevent his mum and dad getting back together and when his efforts failed, he drifted into the murky world of drugs. By the time he contacted the family again, he was on the run from dealers to whom he owed money. His dad desperately tried to make up for lost time by offering support and positive help, but Little Jimmy was well and truly hooked and looked scary enough to give little Kylie nightmares. His hatred of his parents continued until the very end. After such a miserable life, the final bullet was almost a merciful release.

Lindsey Corkhill (née Stanlow)
(Claire Sweeney) 1991–

Lindsey Corkhill is too much like her mother for her own good. Just as Jackie is essentially a decent woman who had the misfortune to fall for a dangerous man, so Lindsey is an impressionable girl who craves excitement. You'd have thought the

Rod Corkhill (Jason Hope)

sight of her mum being given the runaround by Jimmy over the years would have made Lindsey choose a man with a safe job, but the only safe job the Corkhills know is the one Frankie got seven years for. So instead Lindsey too likes to live dangerously. First she married *Gary Stanlow* who was dangerous enough to plant drugs on daughter Kylie's teddy so that Lindsey and *Mike Dixon* were imprisoned in Bangkok. When Lindsey was freed, Gary raped her. She then got a job in the local fish and chip shop. Mike simply wasn't sufficiently dangerous for Lindsey, nor was hairdresser *Peter Phelan* (unless he accidentally left customers under the dryer for too long), but *Barry Grant* definitely fitted the bill. Seduced by his menace, she thought of a life as an international singing star where the only chips she'd handle would be in casinos. But when she and Barry split, and finding out Barry was married, she realised what a mess she had made of things. If only she could turn back the clock with Peter … And when Peter played a heroic part in rescuing Kylie from the debris of the Parade, Lindsey saw her chance to rekindle their romance.

Rod Corkhill (Jason Hope) 1985–93

The white sheep of the Corkhill family, Rod the Plod was a serious-minded lad who seemed to be old before his time. His sole teenage indulgence was supporting Everton. There was no loud music, no under-age drinking and the only magazine he read beneath the sheets was *Police Gazette*. Mind you, with the Corkhills that qualified as an obscene publication. Even his girlfriends – first *Kirsty Black*, then *Diana Spence* – were dull. The only time he appeared to enjoy himself was with the arresting WPC *Emma Reid* – and the redoubtable Kirsty soon put a stop to that. For the rest of the time, he lived in blissful ignorance of all the criminal activity that was going on around him. He could have shared a house with Jack the Ripper and been none the wiser. This did not exactly mark him down as strong detective material. But he was nothing if not conscientious and chose to spend the morning of his wedding to Diana unofficially investigating rent boy Craig and his pimp Eddie. He finished up in hospital instead of church, although Diana did visit him in her full bridal gear to show him what he would have won. They finally got married seven months later, but any happiness was short-lived. When he became caught up in an armed robbery at the hair salon, Diana persuaded him to leave the force. He took a security job in Warrington and the pair drifted apart. He resented her friendship with *Peter Harrison* and a bitter argument – and their marriage – ended with Rod slapping her face. It was the first bit of emotion he'd shown in seven years. He then embarked on a new life in Hull.

Sheila Corkhill (formerly Grant)
(Sue Johnston) 1982–90

The matriarch of Brookside Close for eight years, Sheila was a strong, compassionate woman who believed in sticking to her principles at all costs. Unfortunately for her first marriage, her militant unionist husband *Bobby Grant* was equally proud, stubborn and opinionated, with the result that 5 Brookside Close was frequently a verbal battleground with no prisoners taken. Sheila and Bobby had been married for 24 years and had lived on the same nearby council estate as the Corkhills. Sheila in particular had been anxious to move away for fear that the locals would be a bad influence on eldest son Barry. Little did she know that most of the other residents were moving out because of Barry. Sheila definitely had a blind spot where Barry was concerned. If either Karen or Damon were in trouble, she would come down on them like the proverbial ton of bricks. When she found a card of contraceptive pills in Karen's bedroom, Sheila immediately accused her of sleeping around. But,in Sheila's eyes, Barry could do no wrong. She was no fool – she knew he was operating with at least one foot on the wrong side of the law – but she preferred to bury her head in the sand. At Damon's funeral, Barry delivered a warts-and-all speech about his brother's life. Bobby was furious but Sheila, needless to say, supported Barry all the way. Sheila and Bobby argued about many things, but few subjects were guaranteed to divide the camps as sharply as their number one son. This was partly due to Sheila's guilty secret. For Bobby wasn't Barry's father at all – it was Barry's best friend, *Matty Nolan*. Since Sheila was a devout Catholic, she was used to guilt. She

Sheila (Sue Johnston) and Billy Corkhill (John McArdle)

worked hard to keep the family together but Bobby's vasectomy in the wake of Claire's birth drove an immovable wedge between them. She accused him of political hypocrisy (because he had it done privately) and of going against the Church, and their marriage went downhill from that point, the decline hastened by her rape ordeal. Sheila wanted to spread her wings intellectually and emotionally, but Bobby was one of the old school who expected his wife to wait on him hand and foot. What she needed was a new man. The prospect of the new man being *Billy Corkhill* might have seemed unlikely, but Sheila brought out Billy's sensitive side and the pair were able to enter into a union where Bobby wasn't shop steward.

Tracy Corkhill (Justine Kerrigan)
1985–92

Tracy Corkhill was born miserable. She was miserable to her dad Billy. She was miserable to her mum Doreen. She was

Cracker

kept calling in for a haircut, but she made him so miserable that he threw himself off a building. No sooner had she got a job as a stylist with *Brian Kennedy* than he packed her off to Chester to run his salon there. She didn't say how she felt about leaving, but the rest of the Close were happy.

Lana Costello (Diana Ricardo) 1989

An American friend of *Gerald* and *Mona Fallon*, Lana embarked on a whirlwind romance with *Ralph Hardwick*, much to the dismay of Ralph's friend and landlord, *Harry Cross.* Harry did everything he could to split them up (he was convinced that Lana was only after Ralph's money) but Ralph was smitten and they planned a wedding in Lana's home town of Las Vegas. Lana, who was no gold-digger, tried to act as mediator but the two men refused to speak. Finally, as the happy couple were about to board the train at Lime Street, Harry swallowed his pride and said an emotional farewell. And to show there were no hard feelings, he was best man at the wedding.

Cracker 1995–97

With all due respect to Paul Collins' Lucky, Ralph Hardwick's Rommel and Harry Cross's Monty, Jimmy Corkhill's dog Cracker has been the real canine star of Brookside. Given to Jimmy as part-payment on a drugs deal, Cracker may not exactly have been Cruft's material, but she was a loyal companion and became a celebrity when unearthing a bone from the Jordaches' garden. Usually placid by nature, she took an instant dislike to the fur coat which *Barry Grant* bought Kylie and started snapping at her. Jackie no longer

miserable to her brother Rod. And she was miserable to her equally miserable boyfriend *Jamie Henderson*. She dreamed of being a model but was miserable when a woman photographer, aiming to cash in on Tracy's affair with schoolteacher Peter Montague, suggested she go topless. Instead she signed up for a YTS hairdressing scheme but was so miserable that the salon owner, *Shelley Rimmer*, sacked her after less than four months. To show how miserable she was, Tracy painted her bedroom black. At another hairdresser's, in a case of sexual harassment she won £1,500 for wrongful dismissal. Still she was miserable and made the point by spraying a customer's face with hot water. Miserable that *Sheila Grant* had moved in with Billy, Tracy slept with Sheila's son Barry. She ended up pregnant and was none too happy about it. So she had an abortion. Meanwhile a lad named *Liam Riley* was curiously infatuated by her and

Jean (Marcia Ashton) and David Crosbie (John Burgess)

wanted the dog in the house and that indirectly led to her death under the wheels of a van. The nation mourned.

Carl Crawford (Nicholas McKenna) 1990–91

Carl was a mate of *Mike Dixon*'s who used their friendship as a basis for chatting up sister Jacqui. He tried to impress her by helping Mike get rid of the dangerous *Sinnott* but the relationship never got anywhere – the protective Mike saw to that. Carl also helped Mike in his attempts to rebuild an old banger and together they raided a scrapyard for spare parts. They even took the precaution of taking along some food to distract the guard-dog, only to be mobbed instead by a gaggle of guard-geese!

David Crosbie (John Burgess) 1992–98

David 'Bing' Crosbie is Mary Whitehouse in a blazer. Somewhat hypocritically he appointed himself moral guardian to Brookside Close (a full-time job if ever there was one) and upholder of all that is decent, David pokes his nose in where others fear to sniff. He is a born organiser who sees it as his duty to maintain standards in the community. He fights injustice with the zeal of Superman although he would be quick to point out that a telephone box is strictly for making calls, not for changing one's clothes. Under his leadership, the Brookside Residents' Association (or BRA for short) flourished to become a real force in the land. It was run with military precision, the penalty for desertion being too awful to contemplate. When he and wife Jean first arrived on the Close from Spain to be near their daughter Patricia Farnham, he was that most dangerous of species – a pensioner with time on his hands. A retired pharmacist, he had no intention of letting the grass grow under his feet and threw himself into any noble cause he could find, regardless of whether his help was actually required. Although he can be narrow-minded, pompous and intolerant, he can also be surprisingly caring, particularly if the person needing the care is wearing a skirt. For ever since his 18-month affair with Sandra, the family nanny, some 25 years ago, women have been his Achilles' heel. They simply can't help falling for a dapper, old-fashioned gentleman. He managed to resist the overtures of *Julia Brogan* but briefly succumbed to the dubious charms of *Audrey Manners*, a decision he immediately regretted. Naturally his own indiscretions have not prevented him chastising anybody else who has strayed from the straight and narrow. He was genuinely mortified when Jean left him but quickly set about rebuilding his life, concentrating his energies on running the petrol station opposite Brookside Parade. He was rewarded with the prestigious Golden Pump award for franchise of the month. The target for much jesting from the young (when he got drunk at a party on alcoholic lemonade, *Jacqui Dixon*, *Katie Rogers* and *Rachel Jordache* sprayed his hair orange), he found genuine female companionship with *Molly Marchbank* and left the Close to move into her country pad, Bressingham Hall. He always was cut out to be Lord of the Manor.

Jean Crosbie (Marcia Ashton) 1992–96

Jean Crosbie was always more liberal than husband David, but then so was Oliver Cromwell. For years she had put up with his petty rules and regulations and his exasperating ways, purely for the sake of daughter Patricia. She treated him like a child but he was always so wrapped up in his own little world that he never noticed. Then, on their Ruby Wedding anniversary, she announced that she had once had a relationship with an old schoolfriend, Jane. David could never condone such a thing and he and Jean began to lead separate lives under the same roof. When Jean contracted the deadly virus and David admitted to sleeping with *Audrey Manners*, it was the beginning of the end. He had only told her because he thought she was about to die. Fully recovered, Jean set about spreading her wings, seeing the world before it was too late. She was tired of living in a bubble. She teamed up again with Jane, who was running a holiday painting school in the South of France, and then moved closer to Patricia in Provence. For Jean, there was a life beyond the next meeting of the Brookside Residents' Association – and it was a better one for the absence of David.

Penny Crosbie (Mary Tamm) 1993–95

For 15 years Penny Crosbie, David's sister-in-law, enjoyed the perks of being an MP's wife: the big house in Banbury, the designer clothes, the social standing and the round of functions. But there was one aspect to an MP's portfolio she had reckoned without – the statutory love child (in this case, a boy, Lawrence). When husband Clive got wind of impending tabloid headlines which would expose his shortcomings – notably his romps with a call-girl – he killed himself, leaving Penny to pick up the pieces. When she finally came to terms with the fact that most of Clive's late-night sessions had been with prostitutes, she chose to follow a similar path with Brookside's own bit of rough, *Barry Grant*. For Barry, it made a change to bed a bit of class. She even moved in with him, but made the mistake of issuing him with an ultimatum: choose between mad *Terry Sullivan* and her. To her fury, he chose Terry and went off to Spain. Haughty Penny didn't like playing second fiddle and sought revenge by teaming up

Harry (Bill Dean) and Edna Cross (Betty Alberge)

with *Max Farnham* and *Sam Martin* to oust Barry from Grants. When Barry returned, Penny was out on her ear. But at least she had a nice Christmas with Sam to remember. He was much more her type. Barry was just a novelty act.

Edna Cross (Betty Alberge) 1983–85

All of those years living with Harry had obviously rubbed off on Edna Cross, for she marked their arrival on the Close by upsetting the removal men, who promptly dumped her stuff on the pavement and drove off. No wonder Harry was proud of her. Brookside Close was supposed to be Harry and Edna's retirement home, but he was the only one who ever took things easy. Constantly reminded about Harry's dodgy heart (she wasn't even sure he had one), the long-suffering Edna was obliged to wait on him hand and foot. The arrival of Harry's old colleague from the railways, widower *Ralph*

Hardwick, helped ease the burden, simply because Edna found she had more in common with Ralph than Harry. Ralph liked to laugh; Harry thought it was a mortal sin. Edna's other escape was to have a little flutter on the horses, but all that stopped when she suffered her stroke. She died the following month, leaving Harry to realise what a good wife he had lost.

Harry Cross (Bill Dean) 1983–90

First, God created Adam. Next he created Eve. Then, when he decided that everything in the Garden of Eden was too rosy, he created Harry Cross. If moaning were an Olympic sport (and it probably will be before long), Harry would be a gold medallist every time. He was always complaining about something – his health, the neighbours, the neighbours' health. He trod on so many toes that the entire Close was soon limping. Those who weren't used to his ways took offence but most people just took him with a pinch of salt for they knew that, like his little dog Monty, his bark was worse than his bite. And buried deep down, somewhere beneath the earth's crust, he did have feelings. Harry had worked on the railways all his life. At 18, he had been employed in the sheds at Edge Hill before eventually fulfilling every boy's dream of becoming a train driver. On his retirement, armed with his lump sum and his British Rail pension, he and wife Edna sold their house and bought 7 Brookside Close in what they thought would be a nice quiet cul-de-sac to spend their twilight years. Scotland Road at chucking-out time would have been quieter. Deciding the stairs were a bit much for him, he snapped up the bungalow next door and let No. 7 out to suitable tenants – a contradiction in terms where Harry was concerned. As a landlord, he made Rachman look considerate and, when he wasn't putting up the rent, he was forever snooping around to find an excuse for eviction. Edna's death hit him hard and his lodger, *Ralph Hardwick*, became his constant companion. He was terrified of losing Ralph too which is why he tried to put obstacles in the way of Ralph's romances with *Madge Richmond* and *Lana Costello*. He had an uneasy relationship with son Kevin and simply didn't want to end up a lonely old man. When Ralph and Lana went to live in America, Harry realised there was nothing left for him on the Close and took his garden gnomes and set up home in St Helens. To say he was sorely missed would be a lie, but for all his faults, you couldn't help liking him.

Kevin Cross (Stuart Organ) 1984–89

It was tough being Harry Cross's son. As a youngster, everything Kevin did was criticised and the inevitable result was that, in adulthood, he kept Harry at arm's length and further. He knew that whatever he did would meet with his father's disapproval and so resolved to lead his own life. A teacher in nearby Maghull, he rarely visited and so it came as a bolt from the blue when he announced that he was living with a married woman, *Sally Haynes*, and her daughter. Even then he broke the ice by first telling his more understanding mum. Harry made no secret of his disdain for the fact that Kevin and Sally were living in sin but he mellowed when she presented him with grandson Tim. In Kevin's eyes, it was not before time.

Graeme Curtis (David Banks) 1991–92

Graeme Curtis was sadder than the average trainspotter. Divorced from a wife who didn't understand him (then again, Freud would have been hard pushed to understand Graeme), he found problems communicating with women. Then *Sue Sullivan* joined the law firm where he worked and provided a shoulder to cry on. Sue's innocent gestures were misinterpreted by Graeme who rapidly became obsessed with her. Soon he was driving her to work, driving her home again and driving her to drink. He bought her flowers she didn't want, stole a scarf and a family photograph from her desk and even turned up at her funeral despite the fact that he was the prime suspect. Wrongly convicted of her murder, he killed himself in prison. He may have been seriously deranged but he would never have hurt a fly.

Tom Curzon (Brian Stephens) 1985

When *Heather Haversham* was despatched to go through the books of Curzon Communications prior to their flotation on the Stock Exchange, she was immediately attracted to the company's handsome young chairman, Tom Curzon. Soft-spoken, charming and educated, he seemed Heather's ideal man. After whisking her off to Portugal, he took her crown green bowling. What more could a girl want! She even liked his father, Jim, and soon she and

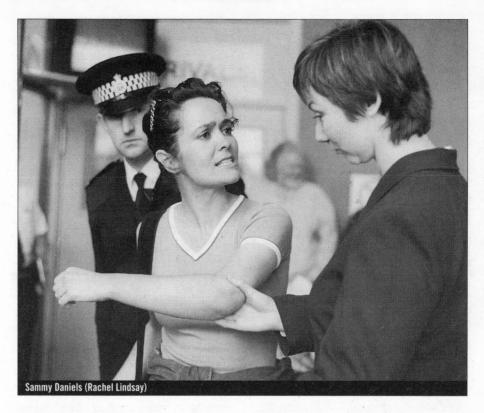

Sammy Daniels (Rachel Lindsay)

Tom were engaged. But, with the bouquets ordered, she began to see another side to Tom – a side she didn't like. There was the fact that he had a secret daughter, Rowena (someone Jim never knew existed) and the nagging feeling that, once they were married, she would be expected to abandon her career to make lots of little Curzons. Tom also made it clear that work always came first in his life. She'd had enough of secrets and saw herself as more than a pretty wifey to impress clients so, although she still loved Tom, she called the wedding off. He was left to himself.

Owen Daniels (Danny McCall)
1989–93

Owen Daniels was natural son-in-law material – well-groomed, courteous and thoughtful. Unfortunately his father-in-law was *Frank Rogers*, who wouldn't have appreciated any of these qualities if he'd run

them over in his lorry. Owen was in the year above Frank's daughter Sammy at Brookside Comprehensive and hatched an elaborate Valentine's Day plot to win her heart, but their romance hit the rocks when Owen was temporarily confined to a wheelchair and Sammy hit the bottle. When they got back together, Sammy ended up pregnant and Owen did the decent thing by agreeing to marry her. He couldn't help thinking that Sammy had engineered the pregnancy and this resentment simmered beneath the surface of their marriage. Owen was a bright lad who wanted to continue his college studies but Frank made it clear that he now had a family to support and should get himself a proper job. Thus poor Owen wound up selling conservatories – although given the number of windows on the Close that get bricks hurled through them, double-glazing would have been a more lucrative concern. He then worked in the

1995

Sharon Bridges (Hayley Smitton), Leo Johnson (Steven Cole), Tanya Davies (Heather Tomlinson) and Timothy 'Tinhead' O'Leary (Philip Olivier)

got drunk and draped herself all over him in front of his girlfriend Grace, who promptly emptied her glass over Sammy. Following the disintegration of her marriage, she again turned to the bottle for comfort and seduced *Max Farnham*. She tried to keep him by pretending that she was carrying his child. When she abandoned Louise for a second time, to go on holiday with her latest pick-up, she managed to alienate everyone on the Close except for *David Crosbie* who supported her through the subsequent court case.

Sammy cut a pitiful figure in the dock as she explained that she loved Louise but just wanted to enjoy herself, to have a bit of fun. She couldn't see anything wrong with that. But that had always been Sammy's problem.

pizza parlour where at least he made a crust. There were more marital problems when Sammy rejected baby Louise and, as Owen began to assert himself more, it came as no surprise when the couple finally split up in 1996. The miracle was they'd stayed together that long.

Sammy Daniels (née Rogers)
(Rachel Lindsay) 1987–96

Sammy liked to live life to the full – full diary and full glass. The only thing she hated was baby Louise's full nappies so she left her at the hospital. Sammy knew what it was like to be abandoned – after all, mum Chrissy cast something of a shadow over Sammy's wedding day by walking out on the family. But the wedding-day blues were just the latest misadventures in Sammy's troubled life, following on from leaving her boyfriend in a coma, becoming an alcoholic and having a disastrous fling with an older man, *Tim Derby*. As with all of Sammy's relationships, it ended in glorious acrimony. Sammy certainly wasn't afraid to stand up for herself. When she decided she wanted Owen back, she

Elaine Davies – see Elaine Johnson

Tanya Davies (Heather Tomlinson)
1996–97

Daughter of Elaine, leggy teenager Tanya had plenty of admirers at school, among them step-brother Leo, although this was possibly because she was the only 16-year-old on Merseyside who wasn't at least a foot shorter than him. She was a constant source of worry to her ever-anxious mother. Whenever Tanya spoke, Elaine rushed to check that Gladys was OK. On Elaine's flight from justice, she took Tanya with her.

Charlie Dawson (Philip McGough)
1986

So laid-back as to be almost horizontal, former lecturer Charlie Dawson was Nick

Black's partner in heroin. The pair were old university buddies and Charlie was best man at Nick's wedding to *Heather Haversham*. Charlie was a natural sponger who liked to hang loose with Nick; as far as he was concerned, he and Nick had their heroin intake completely under control. They weren't doing anyone any harm – they didn't go around beating up old ladies – so what was the problem? The problem was that they hadn't got it under control at all: they were hopelessly addicted. Charlie blamed Heather for Nick's death but continued to hang around the Close in the hope of finding a bed for the night until *Barry Grant* threw him out. And with that, Charlie said 'ciao' for the last time.

Oscar Dean (Ken Campbell) 1993

The eccentric Oscar Dean, who had a liberal attitude towards everything, including drugs, proved a good friend to *Barry Grant*. He ousted *Joe Halsall* as owner of La Luz, got Barry off a charge of attempted murder and immediately made him a junior partner in the club. But Oscar also had a number of business interests abroad and disappeared as quickly and as mysteriously as he had arrived.

Tim Derby (Christopher Blake) 1991

A 39-year-old divorcee with two grown-up children (Chloe and Adam), Tim Derby was boss at the hotel where *Sammy Rogers* worked as a chambermaid. He approved of her idea of room service and they embarked on a passionate fling. To Tim, that's all it was and he got the shock of his life when Sammy turned up on his doorstep with her bags after a big row with her dad. Tim quickly tired of Sammy's immaturity and went away for three weeks. Sammy's parting shot was a brick through his window. At last she had done something to make Frank proud.

Ken Dinsdale (Eamon Boland) 1986

The hot-headed husband of Sally, Ken Dinsdale was a bully who used force to keep his wife in place. And when *Sheila Grant* started meddling in their affairs, his answer was to make a series of anonymous calls to her. With his wife and children staying at the Grants', Dinsdale continued to hover menacingly and became an immediate suspect when Sheila was raped. For all his faults – and there were many – Sally knew her husband wasn't a rapist and begged Sheila to clear his name. Dinsdale didn't deserve such a loyal spouse.

Sally Dinsdale (Kate Riding) 1986

In many ways, Sally Dinsdale was a prototype for *Mandy Jordache*. Having met *Sheila Grant* on a college course, Sally turned to her for help when she was unable to take any more of husband Ken's violence. She turned up at the Grants' battered and bruised and Sheila allowed her and her children to stay, against the wishes of Sheila's husband Bobby who thought she was getting too involved and neglecting their own new arrival, baby Claire. But Sheila wasn't one to turn her back on a friend in need and strongly advised Sally to leave Ken. To Sheila's disappointment, Sally eventually went back to him.

Cyril Dixon (Allan Surtees) 1990–91

Born in the tough Kirkdale are of Liverpool, Cyril Dixon was a staunch Protestant and Orange-Lodger. So he was horrified when son Ron married DD, a Catholic, and took a while to forgive him. It was easier to hammer a nail into blancmange than to pin down Cyril. The wily old fox lived a colourful life and was always on the move, not least because he was a bigamist three times over. Julia Brogan had been hoping to get him up the aisle but was puzzled by his frequent visits to his 'sister' in Wolverhampton. When he finally confessed to his multiple life, Julia pointed that he could get seven years for bigamy … for each offence. Faced with a lifetime in jail, Cyril agreed to get engaged

Ron (Vince Earl) and DD Dixon (Irene Marot)

and Julia invited half of Merseyside to the party. The only person who didn't show up was Cyril himself. When Ron discovered Cyril's secret, he disowned him and before father and son could be reconciled, Cyril died of a massive heart attack, no doubt brought on by trying to satisfy so many women at the same time.

DD Dixon (Irene Marot) 1990–96

Deborah Dixon, known to all as DD, had an unhappy childhood, losing both her parents when she was 17. Her father died from a terminal illness and her distraught mother committed suicide shortly afterwards. At the time, DD was a novice nun, having just left convent school, but the double tragedy made her question her faith. She turned her back on God, quit the convent and ran wild for eight months. Her new God was PJ Proby and her new church was the Top Rank. But the guilt about losing her parents and her faith in quick succession created an

emotional backlash. She suffered a nervous breakdown and admitted herself into a mental institution. After a stay of 18 months, she was on the road to recovery but decided to keep her past a secret. For someone with such firm beliefs and a deep commitment to humanity, it was odd that she chose to marry Ron whose goals were purely materialistic. She refrained from telling Ron about her time in either the convent or the hospital and instead invented a fictitious past for herself. She only revealed the truth when she found herself having to lie about her best friend *Maria Benson*'s affair. DD could be good fun but had a sense of humour bypass during her priest brother *Derek O'Farrell*'s affair with *Margaret Clemence*. Short of flying the Pope over from Rome, she did everything she could to stop the relationship. She eventually gave them her blessing but the entire episode had soured her marriage and she soon had another foe to contend with

– *Bev McLoughlin*, the mouth of the Mersey. In an attempt to keep the family together, or maybe just to get at Bev, DD was even prepared to have Ron back, but he let her down once too often and she left the area. When she returned briefly around Christmas 1996, she was altogether more contented, probably because she had Tom, a much younger man, in tow. They were going to get married. DD had the last laugh after all.

Jacqui Dixon (Alexandra Fletcher) 1990–

From schoolgirl swimmer to hard-headed businesswoman – Jacqui Dixon has come a long way in a short time. She is certainly a chip off the old block, the block in question being dad Ron. She has not only inherited his business acumen (though on a much grander scale), but also his ruthless, single-minded determination. If Jacqui wants something, she gets it – and she doesn't mind who she hurts along the way. She also shares some of his bigotry and was quick to condemn lesbian *Beth Jordache*, even before she knew that Beth had buried her father under the patio. Maybe Jacqui was angry that she hadn't thought of it first because, as a result of their similarities, she and Ron have endured many a spat. Her involvement in Jacqui D's Style House and Bar Brookie has left little time for boyfriends. *Ben O'Leary* did propose despite the fact that he and Jacqui had barely been on a date, but she knocked him back and he didn't even get a drink on the house for his trouble. Many entrepreneurs go into decline after hitting the bottle but Jacqui's troubles started with a bottle of hair colourant rather than whisky. For no sooner did she switch from blonde to redhead than things started to go wrong. Protection racketeer *Callum Finnegan* began leaning on her and she found herself in dire straits financially. Consequently, she was forced to sell the bar to *Barry Grant* and agree to be a surrogate mother. In Jacqui's case, blondes really do have more fun.

Mike Dixon (Paul Byatt) 1990–

Mike 'no fixed abode' Dixon is the flip-side to sister Jacqui. Whereas she has drive, energy and great ideas, he drifts along from one dead-end job to another. For one who has had pretensions – first of being the next Bruce Springsteen, then the next Steven Spielberg and most recently the next Frederick Forsyth – he has spent an inordinate amount of time serving in bars and pizza parlours. Maybe he is like those Hollywood hopefuls who work as waiters in celebrity diners hoping to be discovered. But the chances of a Hollywood mogul turning up at Bar Brookie would appear to be slim. Although he has a university degree and may be big on ambition, Mike is low on achievement, his lack of career success being matched only by his lack of success with women. He even grew a beard to appear intellectual and mature but the truth is, Mike couldn't pull a bird in an aviary. And when he did get to grips with *Bel Simpson*, he gave her more than she bargained for. Dad Ron was swift to capitalise and when Mike appeared with June, an older woman, on his arm, a despairing Ron asked him whether he had learnt nothing from his trip to the VD clinic. June walked off without a word. Devious, lazy, permanently broke and occasionally downright dishonest, Mike remains one of life's losers.

Ron Dixon (Vince Earl) 1990–

If the advancing years precluded him from being one of 'Thatcher's children', Ron Dixon was certainly one of her middle-aged distant relatives. Ron always admired her principles. He had worked for years in a Kirkby factory but joined the great rush for self-employment as advocated by the Prime Minister. With his redundancy

DD (Irene Marot) and Ron Dixon (Vince Earl)

off. Ron did have an unfortunate habit of falling for his employees, although he made an exception where *Julia Brogan* and Cassie concerned. Bev gave him a new lease of life and he started dyeing his hair and wearing shirts so loud they are generally forbidden in a built-up area. Yet it wasn't Bev or DD whom he really wanted to spend the rest of his life with, but Jackie. Alas, she was pledged to another. He has since become increasingly bitter and twisted, his ultimate crime being to lie to the Health and Safety Executive that *Sinbad* fitted the gas cooker which caused the blast on the Parade. But lest history judges Ronald Dixon too harshly, we should remember that he hasn't had an easy life. In the space of a few years, he's lost Tony, Josh, DD, Bev, Jackie, the Moby, the Trading Post and his share in Bar Brookie. But he's still got Mike. Now there's a consolation.

Tony Dixon (Gerard Bostock/ Mark Lennock) 1990–94

As a youngster, Tony Dixon was a right little horror. On his seventh birthday, he drank half a bottle of Martini and had to have his stomach pumped. With his mates Togga and Benno, he got up to all sorts of mischief, revelling in the family feud with the Farnhams. It was Tony who masterminded the collapse of the Farnhams' shed. He was a constant irritation to neighbours and his own family alike, not least because he supported Liverpool and the rest of the Dixons followed Everton. Then suddenly he changed. He became quiet, studious and polite and preferred to spend hours in total silence in his room rather than play with his mates, who had vanished anyway.

money he bought his dream machine – not a Harley-Davidson or a Porsche but the Moby. He was a cross between the Pied Piper and Dick Turpin. He'd drive his mobile shop around the neighbouring estates and all the children would rush out to see it, eagerly clutching their pennies in their hands. Then he'd rob them blind. For Ron, charity not only began at home, that's where it stayed – firmly locked in a cupboard. He was no better when he swapped the Moby for the Trading Post. His meanness as an employer was legendary, his idea of a Christmas bonus to his staff being a tin of corned beef each. Like Ron, the tins were past their sell-by date. However Ron did take a keen interest in training his staff and both *Bev McLoughlin* and *Jackie Corkhill* learnt the art of stocktaking in the back room, with the light

Lesley Donnelly (Sylvia Gatril) 1995

Booze bootlegger Lesley Donnelly was a hard case. So when *Jimmy Corkhill* called time on her deal with *Carl Banks* to supply illegal alcohol to La Luz, there was never any

Gordon Collins (Mark Burgess) and Christopher Duncan (Stifyn Parri)

question of her losing her bottle. Instead she had Jimmy's dog Cracker kidnapped and torched *Barry Grant*'s furniture, thinking that it belonged to Jimmy who had passed himself off to her as Barry Grant. It wasn't one of Jimmy's better ideas. Jimmy responded by petrol-bombing the Donnellys' yard, inadvertently putting Carl in hospital. This was Jimmy's second least bright idea. But with things turning uglier than the World Gurning Championships, Lesley was prepared to call it quits as long as the police weren't involved. So the Corkhill way triumphed again.

Christopher Duncan (Stifyn Parri)
1986–88
The gay head boy at a private school, Christopher embarked on a homosexual relationship with fellow pupil *Gordon Collins*. Christopher was always the dominant one, imposing his forceful personality on the more sensitive Gordon.

Sometimes Gordon took exception to his friend's black humour – such as when their car ran over the inappropriately-named dog Lucky – but for the most part they got on well and worked together for a while restoring furniture. Surprisingly, Gordon's strait-laced father, Paul, quite liked Christopher and the family as a whole had reason to be grateful to him when he exposed the scandal of *Mona Fallon*'s treatment at the nursing home. Nevertheless when 8 Brookside Close became the target for queer-bashers, Paul ruled that Christopher had to go. Gordon went with him but within a couple of months they had split up.

Marianne Dwyer (Jodie Hanson)
1992–94
Londoner Marianne Dwyer first came into *Mick Johnson*'s life after he had presented a petition to the Chairman of the Education Committee against the plans not to rebuild

Mona Fallon (Margaret Clifton) and Annabelle Collins (Doreen Sloane)

did her a favour. She was able to take a good job in Glasgow and never have to look at another pizza again. The fact that she hasn't been in touch since tells its own story.

Gerald Fallon (Bryan Matheson) 1989

Suave pensioner Gerald Fallon was a resident in the same retirement home as *Annabelle Collins*'s mother, Mona. At that age, there's no time for long engagements so after a romance which, if not exactly whirlwind was certainly breezy, they married in April 1989 and set up in home at Mona's house in the Lake District. Sadly, three years later Gerald died of a heart attack.

Mona Fallon (née Harvey)
(Margaret Clifton) 1987–89

Widowed by the death of Jack Harvey, *Annabelle Collins*'s dotty old mother became the bane of Paul's life during her stay at No. 8. She was convinced that her son-in-law was first a police spy and then a poisoner and took to flushing any food prepared by Paul down the loo. Both Paul and Annabelle were compared un-favourably with Mona's dear son Teddy who lived on the Wirral and intended staying there – as far away from Mona as possible. She got in a fearful muddle over grandson Gordon's boyfriend Chris and, thinking it was a girlfriend 'Christine', offered Gordon her wedding ring. Paul tried in vain to explain that Gordon was gay yet when she did finally cotton on, she was much more open-minded about the relationship than Gordon's parents. After falling down a hole in the road, she became so confused that the safest place for her was in a home, but, because of her previous wild accusations, Paul and Annabelle refused to believe her stories that she was being mistreated there. Following her rescue, she married *Gerald Fallon*.

Manor Park Primary School following the fire. Marianne represented the department at a meeting and impressed Mick with her honesty. But it was brother Ellis who made the first move, only for Marianne to leave him standing at the altar, having realised she was about to marry the wrong brother. She duly moved in with Mick but it was never a smooth relationship. Mick was beset by money worries while Marianne was very much a career woman and one who certainly wouldn't have been happy baking pizzas. Nor was she too keen on looking after Mick's children, Leo and Gemma. Much as she loved Mick, she felt that he was holding her back. She got as far as a second abortive wedding day but Mick's arrest for armed robbery probably

Max (Steven Pinder) and Susannah Farnham (Karen Drury)

Max Farnham

(Steven Pinder) 1990–

Max Farnham could go down in history as one of the few men to marry two wives twice! With that bemused 'little boy lost' look, he manages to prove irresistible to women, but he has never quite been able to decide whether he prefers his first wife Susannah to his second-and-third wife Patricia or vice-versa. Not surprisingly, this indecision, for which Max is justifiably renowned, has caused one or two conflicts over the years. He met Susannah when they were both sixth-formers studying for their 'A' levels. They married while they were at Liverpool Polytechnic and Max set the standard for future encounters by getting her pregnant almost straight away. They moved out of her cramped flat and into their first house but the removal van was only just disappearing into the distance when the God of fertility struck again. Susannah thus had little option but to abandon any thoughts of a career in favour of raising Matthew and Emily. But Max got restless and his roving eye began to set off on marathons. En route, he encountered Patricia and soon got her pregnant too, with Thomas. There followed a bitter divorce from Susannah who decided to make Max pay for his adultery with crippling maintenance payments. When he and Patricia got married, his salary as a quantity surveyor was insufficient to keep Susannah happy and they were obliged to move to a smaller house – 7 Brookside Close. But Susannah was never far away and Max was still clearly attracted to her, partly because he felt guilty about the way he had treated her. The ex-wife seemed to understand him so much better than the present one. He and Patricia did get divorced, only to re-marry almost immediately. And when the split came for the second time and Patricia left for France, Susannah was on the doorstep within a couple of days. Since then there has been much heartache – some of it self-inflicted (witness *Sammy Daniels*) –

Patricia Farnham (Gabrielle Glaister) and baby Alice

working hard at her advertising job, only to see the money go towards Susannah's extortionate maintenance payments. Like Max, Patricia saw the Close as something of a comedown. She wasn't as much of a snob as Max and enjoyed pricking his pomposity, but she could be aloof with some of the less desirable neighbours such as the Dixons, the Rogerses, the Sullivans, Jimmy Corkhill, Josie Johnson ... Her attempt to branch out into business with her own shop on the Parade, the Gift Box, was less than successful. The novelties soon wore off. The battle against breast cancer and the birth of baby Alice, a child with Down's syndrome, gave Patricia a new perspective on life and, having caught Max out once, she wasn't prepared to accept his pleas of innocence when he was charged with soliciting. She felt she could no longer trust him and that was no basis for a marriage. So, with a steely determination inherited from her mother *Jean Crosbie*, she left for France. She now lives in Quebec with her French boyfriend Eric.

Susannah Farnham (Karen Drury)
1991–

A Cheshire gal who, by her own admission, was a highly-sexed teenager, Susannah has never stopped loving Max, even when he left her for Patricia. Both Susannah and Patricia have always had the knack of being able to twist him around their little finger, but Susannah really is a supreme manipulator. And she knows that if ever he expresses irritation at her machinations, she can win him round between the sheets. For the sexual chemistry between the two is as strong as it was all those years ago when they first met. Until one fateful day in 1997 everything was rosy in Susannah's garden but the deaths of their children, Matthew and Emily, shattered the Farnham household. Susannah blamed herself for the accident and her subsequent desperation for another child showed Max a side of her

and Max has never been the most supportive of partners. He would argue that when the heat is on, he doesn't get out of the kitchen, in fact quite the opposite. What he fails to mention is that the kitchen in question is his restaurant, Grants – well away from home.

Patricia Farnham (Gabrielle Glaister)
1990–96

Elegant, intelligent, witty – Patricia Farnham seemed to have everything. Yet she was also riddled with insecurity where Max's ex-wife Susannah was concerned. Patricia made no secret of her dislike for Susannah. She not only saw her as a threat to her marriage (not helped by the fact that Max occasionally slipped up and called Patricia 'Susannah') but also resented he had never seen before – vulnerable yet obsessive. Like Patricia, she is an excellent mother – indeed the two love rivals are alike in so many ways. No wonder poor old Max could never make up his mind which one he wanted.

Callum Finnegan (Gerard Kelly) 1997

Scottish hoodlum Finnegan decided to expand his protection racket business to incorporate Bar Brookie, uttering dire warnings of what might happen to the place if *Jacqui Dixon* didn't meet his demands. But when these demands escalated by the minute, she accepted *Barry Grant*'s kind offer to sort Finnegan out. Things turned ugly (in Finnegan's case, they didn't have far to go) and he and his henchmen followed Barry and *Lindsey Corkhill* to that underworld mecca, East Anglia. There, Finnegan terrorised Lindsey and tried to rape her. Barry's retribution meant that Finnegan won't be troubling Bar Brookie again.

James Fleming (Gene Foad) 1985–86

James had an affair with *Lucy Collins* in France and promised to fix her up with a job as a translator back in Liverpool. When that fell through, he fitted her in as a secretary at his office. Lucy was expecting more. James tried to end the affair but Lucy wasn't giving him up without a struggle. She insisted that James was about to leave his wife Penny, but James's body language at work suggested otherwise. He started avoiding her, so the headstrong Lucy decided it was time for a confrontation with the wife. However, Penny stood her ground and Lucy, left in no doubt as to where James's loyalties lay, scurried home to mummy and daddy.

Geoffrey Fletcher (Chris Wright) 1991

Pillar of the local Round Table and habitual thrower of dinner parties for the business-minded, estate agent Geoffrey Fletcher did *Max Farnham* a favour by fixing him up in a job with his firm. He subsequently became Max's confidant regarding the delicate nature of relations between Patricia and Susannah and even agreed to cover up for Max on occasions so that a degree of domestic harmony could be maintained at No. 7.

Joey Godden (Carl Chase) 1990–91

Joey Godden was a hard man. Blessed with one of those rare faces which actually looked better under a stocking mask, the dome-headed thug was a leading light in the Merseyside criminal fraternity. His sworn enemies were the Corkhills who not unreasonably bore something of a grudge because he had been responsible for the deaths of both brother Frankie and cousin Don. When Jimmy sought revenge, Godden didn't resort to fists or firearms but preferred to say it with flowers – in the form of a pre-wedding wreath to Billy and Sheila. In case the message hadn't sunk in, he then delivered Frankie's tombstone through the front window of No. 10. But he met his match in *Barry Grant*, who put the fear of God into Godden by threatening to blow his brains out with a shotgun. And getaway driver Jimmy neatly concluded the vendetta by stranding Godden outside a nightclub after a raid. Honours were just about even.

Jonathan Gordon-Davies (Steven Finch) 1987–90

A former public schoolboy, Londoner Jonathan had met his bride-to-be Laura at Liverpool University where they were both studying law. After qualifying as a solicitor, a profession to which he was drawn by its social status and salary, he joined an established firm in the city centre and the couple moved into 9 Brookside Close in readiness for their marriage. Rugby-playing Jonathan was the archetypal yuppie who liked the trappings of success: the Volvo, the smart house and, one day, the 2.4 children. He loved Laura dearly but the build-up to the wedding was tense, mainly because of

Joey Godden (Carl Chase), Billy (John McArdle) and Jimmy Corkhill (Dean Sullivan)

the constant interference from her parents, the Wrights. But, being professional people, when Jonathan and Laura disagreed it was more of a constant niggle than a full-blooded Brookside barney. Instead of bricks, bottles and fists, their weapons were sarcasm, dramatic irony and alliteration. Jonathan never looked happy. There was a suspicion that his mouth had been put on upside down so that he appeared perma-nently sullen. He had even less to smile about following Laura's tragic death, although he did perk up for a while when he met *Cheryl Boyanowsky*. But he saw her as a Laura substitute and when it became clear that she was in no hurry to start a family, they went their separate ways. Jonathan landed a plum job with a Japanese firm and moved back to London just so that he could

work with his latest girlfriend Helen. They later married and gave birth to two children. Jonathan was happy at last – not that you'd know it.

Laura Gordon-Davies (née Wright)
(Jane Cunliffe) 1987

The ill-fated Laura was a working-class girl made good, to the delight of her parents who were fiercely proud of her. She was very much a modern woman, with a strong streak of independence and a firm sense of justice. Her idealistic approach to the law was in stark contrast to Jonathan, who was pragmatic to the point of being cynical. As a solicitor with a conscience, she was something of an endangered species but, to her, work was more important than anything – and that included Jonathan. So when she became involved in a complex deportation case, she thought nothing of moving out of the house temporarily and postponing the wedding for a month. Jonathan didn't think much of it either. When they did eventually get married – in a marquee so huge it could have doubled as the Millennium Dome – there was still a lot of tension in the house. But this was soon relieved by her dad's electrical repairs.

Mark Gossage (Ian Morris) 1983

According to *Paul Collins*, Mark Gossage was a thoroughly bad influence on his son Gordon. Mark took Gordon into pubs when he was under-age, composed songs about anarchy, went to rock concerts and played darts – clearly an undesirable character. Mind you, Paul did have a point for it was Mark who stole Harry Cross's boxing medals, leading to a fight between Mark and *Damon Grant*. Mark joined Gordon's band, Jugular Vein, but when, after a studio session, Mark delivered a drunken Gordon home with a stolen drum machine, it was the end of the friendship. Paul for one was mightily relieved and looked forward to Gordon making more suitable friends in the future. *Christopher Duncan* wasn't exactly what he had in mind …

Barry Grant (Paul Usher)

Barry Grant (Paul Usher) 1982–

As mixed-up as a box of Smarties, Barry Grant is just about the most complicated character ever to set foot on the Close. He can be ruthless, he can be vulnerable; he can be cruel, he can be kind; he can be cold, he can be passionate. He can be a heartless killer and a doting father. In his younger days, Barry was a joiner by trade but he always had an eye for the main chance, involving himself in all manner of crooked deals. Mum Sheila thought the sun shone out of his wallet but Bobby, the man who thought he was his father and raised him as his son, took a different view and the pair argued bitterly. Not that Barry was ever around for long – a few fights, break a girl's heart and he'd be off to another part of the country to make his next grand. He began to earn a reputation for being able to handle himself and came to the attention of crime barons like *Tommy McArdle* and *Sizzler*. He envied their lifestyle and saw them as living proof that crime does pay. He branched out into the twilight world of acid house parties before hitting the big-time by acquiring the shops of Brookside Parade. Suddenly Barry Grant was a respectable businessman. Perhaps because of his own criminal past, he despised *Billy Corkhill* and couldn't believe that Sheila would marry into such a bent family. Above all, he was jealous. He hated seeing other people happy; it merely served to emphasise his own loneliness and inability to sustain a relationship. Sure, he could get girls into bed for a night or two – no trouble – but when they saw what he was really like, they were out of the door sharpish. So it was that he decided to wreck his best mate *Terry Sullivan*'s chances of happiness with Sue. First, he tried the usual tactics of being deeply unpleasant but when that didn't work, he slept with her. For an encore, he pushed her and little Danny to their deaths. Barry has always maintained that it was an accident and the killings have preyed on his mind ever since but following the episodes with *Simon Howe* and *Callum Finnegan*, he now has a great deal of blood on his hands. What he really wants is a son, but *Tracy Corkhill* had an abortion, *Fran Pearson* took baby Stephen to a place where even Barry couldn't find them and *Anna Wolska* backed out of their baby deal. Now he is married to former beauty queen Pam (Miss Letchworth 1992) with two daughters, but that doesn't stop him wrecking other people's lives, as *Lindsey Corkhill* and *Peter Phelan* can testify. He has money, power, a beautiful wife and a family, but he also has a past from which he can never escape. For that reason alone, Barry Grant will never be truly happy, which is perhaps some consolation to his many victims.

Bobby Grant (Ricky Tomlinson)
1982–88

A big bear of a man, Bobby Grant spent most of his life being grizzly. He was invariably angry about something, whether it was eldest son Barry's general lackadaisical attitude or an incident which had offended his strong trade union principles. Bobby was a crusader who wore his heart on his sleeve and liked to take the high moral ground. Occasionally he was forced to compromise, although he would never admit it. So he told his workmates at Fairbanks Engineering that wife Sheila had made him move to Brookside Close (home-

ownership went against his personal doctrine) whereas in truth he too had been keen to get away from the run-down council estate. He was shattered by the closure of Fairbanks, which left him without a job. Bobby thrived on hard work, but now he felt he had no goal in life. Sometimes it was a struggle just to get out of bed in the morning. But the union, impressed by his commitment during the strike at Fairbanks, came to his rescue and offered him a full-time post. He was elected District Secretary and with it came a brand new Austin Montego. Bobby Grant was back on his feet. He threw himself into the job and 5 Brookside Close staged more meetings than Haydock Park. But the more time he devoted to the union, the less he devoted to Sheila. Bobby may have been happy with his lot but, with the kids grown up, Sheila wanted to expand her horizons. She chose further education. Bobby was not impressed. What if his pie and chips weren't ready when he got in? Soon the split widened into a yawning chasm and Bobby packed his bags. He married a woman named Susan Morgan and they lived in Reading (that familiar *Brookside* bolt-hole) with son Jack. Bobby had had his vasectomy reversed. He could be flexible when it suited him.

Damon Grant (Simon O'Brien)
1982–87

Barry's cheeky younger brother Damon was a bright kid but felt that the education system let him down. In fairness, he wasn't always there to find out, nor was his cause helped by the fact that, from listening to his mother, he must have thought his name was 'R. Damon Grant'. Five years of trying to work out what the 'R' stood for didn't help his progress. He did leave school with an education in life but was soon dismayed at not being able to find a worthwhile job. Although he got into a few teenage scrapes, he was essentially an honest lad who would

Barry Grant (Paul Usher)

have put in a good day's work if only somebody had given him the chance. He joined a YTS scheme as a painter and decorator but was wrongly accused of stealing a vase. That was another obstacle for Damon: he attracted trouble and tended to get the blame whenever anything went wrong. Only his immediate family seemed to have any faith in him. When he fell in love with Debbie McGrath, her father certainly didn't have any faith in him and left Damon in no doubt that he considered him beneath his daughter. Disillusioned, the young lovers ran away together to York, hotly pursued by Debbie's family, only for Damon to attract trouble again, this time in the shape of the blade of a knife wielded by a gang which was trying to burgle the houseboat on which Damon and Debbie were staying. His life was over before it had even begun.

Karen Grant (Shelagh O'Hara)
1982–90

A spirited girl with a steady stream of male admirers, Karen was also the smartest of the Grant children, physically and intellectually. As a clothes-mad teenager, she dreamed of starting up her own fashion business and was blessed with the gift of the gab. She could talk her way out of most situations although she had a nasty scare when boyfriend Duane, thinking he could sleep with her just because she was on the Pill, turned nasty and accused her of being a 'teaser'. The Pill and Karen's decision not to

Joe Halsall (Susie Ann Watkins)

go to church anymore were just two of the issues which put her at loggerheads with mum Sheila. But the two could also be good friends, and when they went to bingo together, Karen won £75. However, Karen wasn't pleased at the prospect of suddenly acquiring a new baby sister and told Sheila how disgusted she was about it. Yet after Sheila's rape ordeal and Damon's death, Karen, more than anyone else, was a tower of strength for her mother. Meanwhile boyfriends had come and gone. Bike-mad Andrew hung around for a while and even persuaded her to go to a bikers' disco, but it was at Liverpool University, where she was taking a course in communication studies, that she met her first true love, *Guy Willis*. She still wasn't sure about having sex but Guy's tenderness won her over and

she lost her virginity. Things didn't work out with Guy but Karen started a new course in London before landing a job as a reporter on an evening paper in Exeter. She came back for Sheila's wedding to Billy and told big brother Barry exactly what she thought of his antagonism towards the nuptials. That's where Karen was different from her mum: she wasn't afraid to stand up to Barry.

Sheila Grant – see Sheila Corkhill

Alison Gregory (Alyson Spiro)
1989–90

A single parent with an eight-year-old daughter, Hattie, research scientist Alison Gregory first encountered *Michael Choi* when they tried to resuscitate an old lady who had collapsed in the street. From such unlikely beginnings, love blossomed but Alison soon met opposition to the relationship from Michael's father, Stephen. Not that she went out of her way to win friends and influence people. She had a manner which, at its most conciliatory, was brusque and an expression which indicated thunder on the horizon. She didn't go out socialising much, partly because of the constraints of her daughter but also because they didn't have many vivisection nights down at The Swan. So when she and Michael left for America, the Close wasn't exactly decked in bunting for a grand farewell. Anyway they split up within six months.

Joe Halsall (Susie Ann Watkins)
1992–93

There may not have been much of Joe Halsall but what there was spelt trouble. She was a tough cookie who, as head of Halsall Leisure, opened La Luz in partnership with *Barry Grant*. She wanted to do things her way and quickly fell out with Barry over his plans to stage rave nights at the club. Her way was less than honest and included fiddling the books, running a dubious 'escort agency' on the side and framing Barry for the attempted murder of doorman *Jimmy Corkhill*. When *Oscar Dean* exposed her little games, she didn't hang about.

Pat Hancock (David Easter) 1984–87

Forget the Liver Building, Anfield or the Anglican Cathedral, Cockney Pat Hancock's favourite view of Liverpool was in the mirror. Blessed with a vanity which would make Narcissus appear self-effacing, Pat saw himself as the answer to every girl's dreams. More often than not, he was their worst nightmare. He set himself up as the local stud but wasn't very successful. Maybe his job as a hospital porter wasn't glamorous enough; perhaps it was his mode of transport, a battered old ambulance; maybe it was the fact that his best friend was a human skeleton. Or maybe it was just Pat himself. For whilst he had good chat-up lines and could be funny and considerate, he could also be childish, sexist and hot-headed to the point of violence. Sharing No. 7 with nurses *Kate Moses* and *Sandra Maghie* seemed like the dream ticket for Pat and after the siege, he and Sandra became an item. But Pat's self-destruct button was soon pushed and he became insanely jealous over Sandra's friendship with *Dr Tony Hurrell*. When Pat started hitting her, it was the beginning of the end. Ever eager to better himself (by now he'd been sacked from the hospital), Pat became involved in a succession of increasingly dubious money-making scams. His one legitimate interest was music and so he jumped at the chance of acting as roadie to Fran and her all-girl group. Inevitably he wasn't satisfied with a minor role for long and blackmailed Fran, Ellie and Trish into letting him be their backing singer. Yet his greatest talent was for upsetting people, and by the time he left the Close he had fallen out with just about

Pat Hancock (David Easter)

everybody. Not that Pat cared. He was off to seek fame and fortune. Nobody was holding their breath.

Grace Hardwick (Ruth Holden) 1984

Ralph and Grace Hardwick were old friends of *Harry Cross* and his wife Edna yet the chance encounter between the two couples at the International Garden Festival was their first meeting for a long time. The Hardwicks were due to go away on a cheap holiday but Grace's health deteriorated alarmingly and they gave the tickets to Harry and Edna instead. When they got back, Harry phoned Ralph to thank him, but there was no reply. A few days later, he called round to say that Grace had died.

Ralph Hardwick (Ray Dunbobbin)
1984–89

Alongside St John, St Paul, St George (but not St Ringo), there should definitely be a St Ralph. Anyone who can work with *Harry Cross* for the best part of 20 years and then share a house with him for another five deserves recognition of the highest order. Nobody would have blamed Ralph if he had taken an axe to the old devil in the middle of the night, yet Ralph not only put up with Harry's moans and groans, he did so with a sunny smile. Ralph was actually closer to *Edna Cross* than her husband, and it was she who suggested Ralph move into the bungalow following the death of his wife Grace. Harry wasn't sure, particularly when Ralph immediately started decorating the entire house. He felt Ralph was trying to show him up. Edna's death hit Ralph almost as hard as it did Harry and, to get over it, the two old railwaymen went on a railway holiday to Wales where they enjoyed a ride on the foot-plate of a steam train on the famous Blaenau Ffestiniog railway. It fulfilled a lifelong ambition for Harry. Another was to learn to drive, so the pair splashed out on a hideous pink Fiesta at auction. Unfortunately, Harry could only drive on rails. Unlike Harry, Ralph was one of life's enthusiasts – another day, another hobby. He took up photography with a fervour until he realised it was impossible to find, let alone capture, Harry's good side. Ralph scrubbed up well and his natural kindness made him attractive to women of a certain age. After the ill-advised liaison with *Madge Richmond*, he found true happiness with *Lana Costello* and they went away to get married in Las Vegas. If anyone deserved to hit the jackpot, it was Ralph.

Sue Harper – see Sue Sullivan

Barbara Harrison (Angela Morant)
1991–93

The eminently sensible Barbara Harrison moved to the Close from Stamford in Lincolnshire to take up the post of deputy head at Brookside Comprehensive, a job which comes with a government health warning. She was very much a career woman with little time for cooking or cleaning and she showed more interest in the problems of one of her pupils, *Katie Rogers*, than she ever did in her own family. Her short stay on the Close was dogged by misfortune. Aside from the standard brick through the conservatory, she and husband John were accused of fraud, he was arrested for shoplifting and son Peter was charged with rape. Barbara's only concern through all this was the effect the publicity might have on her career so when the chance of a new school job came up, she resigned and dragged John off to fresh pastures, leaving Peter to face the backlash of the trial on his own. Must try harder. Four out of ten.

John Harrison (Geoffrey Leesley)
1991–93

John Harrison had never led the most exciting of lives. Not for him the glamour of showbusiness or the adventure of the armed forces – he co-owned a firm which manufactured brass pins for electrical plugs. John ran the engineering firm with his brother Hugh: John was Production Manager and Hugh was in charge of the financial side. But when John suffered late-onset asthma, he decided to take early retirement and he and Hugh closed down the firm. The ever-cautious John put his money into savings while Hugh jetted off to live in Spain. With no job of his own, John was obliged to trail around the country hanging on to the coat-tails of domineering wife Barbara. And while she was out teaching all day, he was left to get on with preparing the meals and doing the housework, knowing full well that if she found a speck of dust on her return, he was likely to be given 100 lines. In view of the humiliation and boredom to which he was subjected, it was hardly surprising that he became a kleptomaniac – at least it broke up his day. But it very nearly broke up his family too.

Peter Harrison (Robert Beck) 1992–93

From the moment he stepped on to the Close, the Harrisons' handsome son Peter made heads turn. At first the Oxford chemistry graduate was very much the young rebel with an interest in radical, left-wing politics, but when he acquired a suit and an office job at Saffron Chemicals, he began to look like the boy next door. Accordingly he became friendly with the girl next door, *Diana Corkhill*, and helped her learn to read. But he misread the signs at a party at the Farnhams' and she accused him of raping her. The subsequent trial made the Harrisons the unwelcome focal point of the Close. While mother Barbara was preoccupied with the new curriculum, father John at least had the decency to stand up for his son and came to blows with both *Jimmy Corkhill* and *Julia Brogan* who were striving to protect the Corkhills' good name. Apart from his father, the only other person who really stood by Peter was the Farnhams' Polish nanny *Anna Wolska* and, when she was sacked after his acquittal, she came to lodge at No. 9. John told Peter that he could stay on in the house until it was sold and soon the perennially homeless *Mike Dixon* had wormed his way in, along with his pal *Keith Rooney*. Anna was very fond of Peter but the rape trial had shattered his faith in women and he wasn't ready for another relationship. When he discovered that she had drifted into prostitution, he was suitably appalled. He did manage to get it together with the new girl next door, *Beth Jordache*, but Jimmy wrecked that romance by telling her about Peter's rape case. Intent on driving him from the Close, Jimmy set out to wage war on Peter. Eventually Peter decided he'd had enough of the hassle and left for Oxford, his reputation in tatters.

Peter Harrison (Robert Beck) and Diana Corkhill (Paula Frances,

Where once he made heads turn, now it was stomachs.

Mona Harvey – see Mona Fallon

Heather Haversham – see Heather Black

Gizzmo Hawkins (Robert Smith) 1982–87

Damon Grant's mate Gizzmo Hawkins fancied himself as a junior sex God. He thought the way to impress girls was to act the hard man, but he became so besotted with Damon's sister, Karen, that he even helped her to do the dishes. He was a new man before his time. Although he wielded a mean tea-towel, Karen wasn't remotely interested. Perhaps he would have stood a better chance if he had washed his hair

Louise Hope (Lisa Faulkner)

wondered what all the fuss was about, she found out on their very first visit to Brookside Close. When Harry met Sally, sparks flew. He didn't try to hide his disapproval of the fact that his son was living with a married woman (and her daughter Jessica), while she wasn't the sort to be trampled upon by an irascible narrow-minded bigot. Daggers remained drawn until Sally became pregnant with Harry's grandchild. He showered the unborn baby with teddy bears and planned to install Kevin and Sally next door in No. 7 once he had got rid of sitting tenants, *Pat Hancock* and *Terry Sullivan*. But Sally would rather have walked barefoot across red-hot coals than live next door to Harry and she wasn't afraid to tell him so. During the bitter row which followed, Sally went into labour. Baby Harriet was born prematurely. Harry's prayers for her survival went unanswered and his granddaughter died. Two years later, Sally did bear Harry a grandchild – Tim. At first, she suffered from post-natal depression and kept her distance from Harry but eventually they began to visit more regularly and Harry was moved when she allowed him to take Tim to visit Edna's grave. Sally had at last been accepted by Harry. It had been a long struggle but both decided it was worth it in the end.

Jamie Henderson (Sean McKee) 1987–89

If ever a relationship was made in heaven, it was that between *Tracy Corkhill* and Jamie Henderson. They had so much in common. Both were surly, lazy and monosyllabic. They could go on a date, barely speak to each other all evening, yet still manage an argument. Tracy first caught Jamie's eye when he was working as a delivery boy to *Shelley Rimmer*'s hair salon where Tracy was – for want of a better word – a stylist. Worzel Gummidge had more style. They also shared a common love of alcohol and used to drown their sorrows by getting drunk

more than once a month. Later he nearly mowed Karen down while cruising the Close on roller-skates, which merely served to reinforce her preference for boys whose mode of transport wasn't strapped to their feet. Gizzmo came from a tough home and if he ever stepped out of line he could expect a beating from brother Eric. Given that Gizzmo spent most of his time hanging around with Damon, Eric did not go short of practice.

Sally Haynes (Roberta Kerr) 1984–89

When *Kevin Cross* first fell in love with married woman Sally Haynes, he kept a dreadful secret from her. It wasn't that he was a serial killer or a multiple bigamist – it was much worse than that. The awful truth which he couldn't bring himself to reveal was that his father was *Harry Cross*. If Sally together. Before long, Jamie was jobless and homeless and Tracy smuggled him into the garage of No. 10. There were so many comings and goings that nobody noticed Jamie. Then again, he was easy to miss. It was thus no surprise that when he went to London to look for the runaway Tracy, he joined cardboard city and fitted in perfectly. Eventually even Tracy came to realise that Jamie wasn't exactly Mr Dynamic and love's young dream slowly fizzled out.

Paula Heneghan (Jodie Draper) 1991

Paula Heneghan was the best-looking girl in *Geoff Rogers*' year at Brookside Comp. So when he received a giant Valentine's card and found out that the sender was the gorgeous Paula, he could hardly believe his luck. Paula told Geoff he reminded her of soap heart-throb Tarquin Tully from *Meadowcroft Park* and was all over him at every opportunity, much to Geoff's embarrassment. He simply wasn't used to such adulation. When Geoff was rejected by Tranmere Rovers, he tried to finish with Paula, believing that he wasn't in the same league as her. She told him not to be so stupid. He was touched by this and for an English essay about the best moment in his life, he wrote about Paula. In the end, it was football which did split them up. For when Geoff was taken on by Torquay United, it was too far to travel for a no-score draw.

Roy Heneghan (David Rooney) 1991

Paula's over-protective father was less than enthusiastic about her friendship with *Geoff Rogers*, especially as their first date ended with her coming home drunk and being sick on the doorstep. When he accused Geoff of 'taking advantage' of his daughter, he incurred the wrath of *Frank Rogers*, who head-butted him. For some reason, this did little to improve relations between the two families. Geoff tried to apologise but Heneghan responded by hurling a full bucket of water at him. Thereafter, Paula

had to avoid Geoff at school in case her 12-year-old brother saw them and told her dad.

Derek Hobbs (Norman Gregory) 1983

As *Roger Huntington*'s solicitor boss, Derek Hobbs reckoned that one of the perks of the job was being able to chat up Roger's lovely wife Heather. Dirty Derek made a pass at her at a Law Society dinner, an offer which Heather rejected with her usual charm, and then tried to woo her with expensive presents and dinner invitations, hinting that unless she played ball, Roger's hopes of promotion were even less than Rochdale's. Hobbs resorted to sending Roger away on overnights so that he could have Heather to himself, but she was always able to keep him at bay. As other men discovered, there was a steely determination behind her easy smile.

Louise Hope (Lisa Faulkner) 1997–

Looking like Liverpool's representative in the UK Body-Piercing Championships, Louise Hope breezed on to the Close as *Eleanor Kitson*'s long-lost daughter. She certainly rattled Eleanor, who had abandoned her as a child and frankly was hoping never to see her again. But without telling her adopted parents, Tom and Joan, Louise left Durham to seek out her real mother. And once she'd done that, she wanted to find her biological father too, perhaps so they could all enjoy a game of happy dysfunctional families. After much probing, she discovered that her dad was animal rights activist Marcus Seddon, who was serving 30 years in jail for GBH and possession of explosives. To find that she was sired by some kind of folk hero came as a pleasant surprise to the impressionable Louise – particularly after Eleanor had originally told her that her father was a bicycle repair man.

Simon Howe (Lee Hartney) 1993–94

When Simon Howe first went to work at the

of the other girls, Caroline. As he took over the house, he disconnected the TV and radios so that no outsiders could poison their minds. He became more and more deranged, recruiting *Terry Sullivan*, kidnapping *Barry Grant* and blowing up the house with a home-made bomb. Having failed to go out with a bang, he chose instead to go out with a whimper, rigging a car exhaust so that he and Terry suffocated. Barry arrived in time to pull Terry to safety but wisely decided to let Simon meet his maker. At least he might get a decent haircut in heaven.

Martin Howes (Andrew Hall) 1988

Solicitor friend of *Jonathan Gordon-Davies* and ex-boyfriend of *Sue Harper* (as she then was), Martin Howes became notorious as the secret father of Sue's son Danny. By the time Sue knew she was pregnant, she had finished with Martin and moved on to *Terry Sullivan*. Sue considered an abortion but backed out and instead chose to let Terry think that he was the father. When Terry discovered the truth he was a shade peeved. He would have engaged Martin in a heated intellectual debate – if he had known how.

Brian 'Bumper' Humphries (James Mawdsley) 1988–91

Tubby 'Bumper' was *Geoff Rogers*' best friend and partner-in-crime. A likeable lad, he was a willing participant in, and often instigator of, practical jokes – whether it was the rooftop relocation of *Paul Collins's* furniture, the giant Easter bunnies which roamed the Close or erecting 'For Sale' signs outside all the neighbours' houses. Bumper didn't have much luck with girls. He worshipped Lisa Jenkins from afar and was gutted when Geoff pulled *Paula Heneghan*, all the more so because he had to give up his ticket for a concert by The Farm so that Geoff could take Paula instead. In fact, he wanted Geoff to drop Paula so that he and Geoff could be single again and have some

Simon Howe (Lee Hartney)

petrol station for *Terry Sullivan*, he seemed a normal enough lad. But the clue was in the haircut. That pudding-basin job had to be the work of someone with a demented mind and so it proved. Seeing himself as the new Messiah, he was soon attempting more conversions than the England rugby team. He began with the vulnerable *Katie Rogers*, still grieving from the death of her father. By listening sympathetically to her problems and putting a comforting arm around her, he persuaded her to allow No. 5 to be used as a meeting-place for the rest of his religious family. He lured her into his bed in an initiation ceremony, promising her that it was Jesus's will, but little did she know that he was also slipping into the room of one fun. Ultimately, Bumper resorted to going out with imaginary girlfriends. They were less trouble and considerably cheaper.

Betty Hunt (Marji Campi) 1988–89

The widowed sister of *Arthur Parkinson*, Betty acquired *Ralph Hardwick* as a reluctant chaperone to the Commonwealth Day celebration. However, *Harry Cross* proved a more willing beau and began courting Betty with his own inimitable – and sometimes invisible – charm. He ingratiated himself by taking up her campaign to allow women to sit on the club committee, a measure which Arthur had hitherto steadfastly resisted. Convinced he was on to a winner, Harry laid on a romantic tea for Betty, only for it to be rudely interrupted by tenant *Frank Rogers* complaining about a broken hot water system. Harry knew it was time to sell No. 7 – he'd had enough of being a landlord. Eventually he plucked up the courage to propose to Betty and was rendered speechless when she turned him down. After that, there was no more tea and scones.

Betty Hunt (Marji Campi)

Roger Huntington (Rob Spendlove) 1982–83

Roger Huntington saw himself as clever, good-looking and upwardly mobile – a man with a future. Others saw him as smug, stuffy and intensely irritating – a pain in the neck. A solicitor's clerk from Salford, Roger married his university lover Heather and waited for the patter of tiny feet. Although their marriage was still in its infancy, his parents were already making noises about the lack of activity on the Mothercare front and Roger, viewing the non-arrival of a son and heir as a slight on his manhood, felt decidedly irked. Heather made it clear that her career was of paramount importance so Roger, who was used to getting his own way, went into a sulk. To take his mind off things, he busied himself around the house but this merely put him in a worse mood. For do-it-

yourself was his Achilles' heel and his unsuccessful attempts to erect shelves, burglar alarms and TV aerials made him the laughing stock of the Close. He was as comfortable with a drill as *Bobby Grant* was in an apron. Roger was keen on keeping up appearances. To stay in shape, he decided to take up jogging, but after an unpleasant early-morning encounter with a dog, he accepted Heather's suggestion that badminton might be a safer form of exercise. Soon he found an infinitely more pleasurable way of exercising in the shape of client *Diane McAllister*, but when Heather found out about the affair, she dumped him and his briefcase on the street. Despite the efforts of Roger's father Syd, there was no going back. Heather had no qualms about being alone. She wasn't afraid of being left on the shelf – unless it was one of Roger's.

meet regularly at No. 7, sifting through evidence, to the exclusion of Pat who became convinced they were having an affair. At that stage, the relationship was perfectly innocent, but Pat's violence drove Sandra ever closer to the dishy doc. And when Tony was warned off pursuing the Cribbs-Baker case and decided to leave Liverpool, his farewell to Sandra saw them end up in bed for the first time. Swept off her feet by Dr Hurrell's bedside manner, Sandra agreed to start a new life with him in Scotland. Pat decided he had been right all along.

Gary and Little George Jackson
(Allan and Steven Patterson) 1983–85

The terrible twins of Brookside Close led parents George and Marie a merry dance. There was nothing malicious about them – they were just boisterous and adventurous – but they were forever getting into scrapes at school. In a bid to curb their excesses, Marie tried to enrol them in a private school but the headmaster decided he'd rather have the Kray twins than the Jacksons.

George Jackson (Cliff Howells)
1983–85

George Jackson epitomised firefighters up and down the land – a modest hero who saw saving lives as just part of his job and who liked to unwind at his local with a pint and a pub quiz. It was down at The Swan that George was engaged in conversation by *Tommy McArdle*. George innocently relayed details of a tricky warehouse fire he had fought but the next thing he knew he had been arrested for burgling the place. *Barry Grant* and *Terry Sullivan* knew George had been fitted up faster than a Hygena kitchen, but the jury were not privy to such information passed to them by Victor and George, a nervous figure on the stand with an unconvincing alibi, got 18 months. Determined to see that justice was done, Marie launched a 'Free George Jackson'

George Jackson (Cliff Howells)

Dr Tony Hurrell (Martin Wenner) 1986

Whereas Pat Hancock was a disciple of the 'wham-bam, thank-you, ma'am' school of courtship, Dr Tony Hurrell preferred to woo *Sandra Maghie* with the softly-softly approach. The highly personable Dr Hurrell first came into contact with Sandra when they were investigating a possible case of malpractice against a leading surgeon at the hospital, Mr Cribbs-Baker. They began to campaign. Terry was puzzled: why would anyone want a free George Jackson? But the campaign fizzled out under pressure from Tommy, and when George was transferred to a prison near Leeds, Marie and the twins moved to Yorkshire so that visiting would be less onerous. Thus George Jackson went down as the first great Brookside martyr – jailed for a crime he didn't commit.

Marie Jackson (Anna Keaveney)
1983–85

Short in temper and stature, Marie Jackson was nothing if not a fighter. A graduate of the school of hard knocks, she had raised younger sisters Petra and Michelle almost single-handedly after their mother died when Marie was 12. The sisters' drunken father, *Davy Jones*, was about as much use as a chocolate teapot. When Petra went missing and with their own house being refurbished by the council, the Jacksons moved into No. 10. Marie was convinced that she had psychic powers. Just by looking at the tea leaves in the bottom of a cup, she could tell the dishes needed doing. She tried in vain to contact Petra, but then had a foreboding dream. Later that day, Petra's body was found. With nothing to keep them on the Close now that their house was once again fit for habitation, Marie thought about leaving. As ever in moments of doubt, she consulted a clairvoyant who told her to stay, promising that things could only get better. Marie should have asked for her money back. She enjoyed nothing more than a good barney and found a willing participant in *Sheila Grant*, who gamely defended Barry from Marie's verbal assaults. But it was George's wrongful imprisonment which presented Marie with her biggest battle. She lobbied Downing Street and attracted so much publicity that the real culprit, *Tommy McArdle*, started to get decidedly nervous. Threats were issued to Marie, followed by a brick through her window. The twins were taunted at school.

Marie was forced to back off. For the first time in her life, she had to admit defeat.

Elaine Johnson (née Davies)
(Beverley Hills) 1996–97

Elaine was a born worrier. Understandably, she worried about her infirm mum, *Gladys Charlton*, but she also seemed to take the problems of the world on her shoulders. She worried about the treatment of black children at Brookside Comprehensive, as a result of which she met *Mick Johnson*. Then she worried about whether to accept Mick's proposal of marriage and how he would cope with her devotion to Gladys. When she was with Mick, she worried that she should be with Gladys and when she was with Gladys, she worried that she should be with Mick. And when she was with sister *Cassie Charlton*, she worried that nobody was with Gladys. After she had helped put Gladys out of her misery, she worried about the consequences, particularly whether or not to tell Cassie. Given Cassie's reaction, perhaps she should have worried a little more. When she and Mick were arrested, she worried about going to jail. She probably also worried about why the petrol station wasn't built on a through road and why Mick's son Leo suddenly sprouted a new head. In fact, the only thing she didn't appear to worry about was doing a runner and leaving poor old Mick to carry the can by himself.

Ellis Johnson (Francis Johnson)
1991–93

Rather like a rat at a banquet, Ellis Johnson was bad news. Trouble followed him around as surely as night follows day and John Major follows Chelsea. Ellis was the complete opposite to older brother Mick. Whereas Mick is honest, conscientious, shy with women and perpetually broke, Ellis had no scruples, was an incorrigible Lothario and always seemed to be able to conjure up money from somewhere. But it

Marianne Dwyer (Jodie Hanson) and Ellis Johnson (Francis Johnson)

with the consequences. So they saw Mick as dull, staid and boringly responsible – old before his time. When he suddenly reappeared in Mick's life in a flash car and designer clothes, Ellis succeeded in losing him his livelihood as a cabbie, putting him in deep debt in the pizza parlour and nearly marrying the woman he loved, *Marianne Dwyer*. So as Ellis for once played the part of the unlucky-in-love brother and made a hasty exit from Liverpool, it was hardly surprising that Mick didn't shed too many tears.

Gemma Johnson (Naomi Kamanga)
1990–

Mick's daughter Gemma is a quiet, polite girl with an inquisitive nature. This has landed her in the odd spot of bother, as when she nearly drowned in *Harry Cross*'s garden pond or the time she went missing for a few days. Generally she is happy and contented although, like elder brother Leo, she feared Mick's wrath when he was going through his steroid phase.

Josie Johnson (Suzanne Packer)
1990–93

Mick's ex-wife Josie was about as reliable as a railway timetable. She'd flit in and out of Mick's life as she pleased, vacillating between him and her exciting lover Tony, seemingly disregarding the effect it had on her children, Leo and Gemma. One day she overheard Leo saying he wished his mum and dad could get back together so she uprooted them and descended on Mick, who at the time was lodging in *Harry Cross*'s bungalow. She immediately set about doing up the place. She got a part-time job in a DIY shop and also worked at the infamous Fourstar Club with her best mate *Marcia Barrett*, but still ended up buying most of the stuff out of a catalogue. When the family returned from a Christmas break with Josie's parents, the Christies, in Cardiff, they were greeted with a furniture bill for £2,500,

was best not to ask too many questions about how he came by it. He could also be snide and condescending, as when he discovered that his ex-girlfriend *Marcia Barrett* was going out with *Sinbad*. Ellis did everything he could to make Sinbad feel small – something which no amount of dieting has ever managed – but, after a bit of wavering, Marcia made it clear that the man with the damp cloth got the nod over the man in the sharp suit. Mick tried his best to look after Ellis – indeed as a teenager he had acted as a second father to Ellis after the first one had done a vanishing act – but he never really forgave Ellis for having introduced his first wife Josie to Tony, the guy for whom she kept on leaving Mick. The trouble was Ellis and Josie were two of a kind. They both liked to have fun and to hell

Leo Johnson (Steven Cole)

courtesy of Josie's 'spend now, think later' policy. She further incurred Mick's wrath when she 'borrowed' the cabbies' collection money for his forthcoming assault trial and used it to buy knock-off children's clothes from that reputable supplier, *Jimmy Corkhill*. Mick always knew that one morning he'd wake up to find Josie gone and sure enough she soon went back to Tony. She made a last-ditch attempt to win Mick back at Ellis's non-wedding, but Mick had finally got wise to her. Anyway, he was in love with *Marianne Dwyer*. Josie was left to crawl the well-worn trail back to Tony.

Leo Johnson (Leeon Sawyer/ Steven Cole) 1990–

From the moment he was cast as the black king in the school nativity play, Leo has been subjected to sporadic racial abuse from his classmates. As a result, school has been something of a struggle and Mick has been obliged to seek extra help

with his son's education. Unfortunately, his first helper was Leo's deranged teacher *Jenny Swift* and the second tutor was *Jimmy Corkhill* – he of the forged qualifications. Jimmy's idea of maths tuition was to have Leo working out betting odds. Apart from a brief dalliance with shoplifting, Leo has largely managed to steer clear of trouble and is a loving brother to Gemma, but this hasn't stopped Mick being exceptionally hard on the lad. Mick is fiercely proud of him but sometimes expects standards which Leo struggles to live up to. If Mick isn't careful, he's going to lose him.

Mick Johnson (Louis Emerick) 1989–

For years, Mick Johnson had the reputation of being the nicest – and also the unluckiest – guy on the Close. In view of the fact that his rivals in the first category included *Barry Grant, Jimmy Corkhill, Harry Cross, Frank Rogers* and *Trevor Jordache*, maybe the

Mick Johnson (Louis Emerick) and Jenny Swift (Kate Beckett)

opposition wasn't too stiff, but there was no doubting that he was a deserving case for sympathy. For someone who would rather be closed down by the Health and Safety Executive than short-change anyone, he has spent an inordinate amount of time in police custody. Doting father, loyal but exasperated husband, hard-working provider, he has needed more patience than BUPA to cope with the catalogue of misfortune which came his way. He ended up in hospital after being attacked in his cab; he was prosecuted for using physical force to apprehend a burglar who was trying to break into the children's bedroom; he lost his livelihood and his wife through no fault of his own; he was reported as an illegal immigrant by racist *George Webb*; he was wrongly arrested for armed robbery on his wedding day, as a result of which the bride-to-be walked out on him; and he was the victim of a crazed stalker. Even when he met a pretty girl while out on a singles' night

with *Frank Rogers*, Mick finished up having to walk home *Julia Brogan* instead. But beneath the surface there was always the suspicion that the Gentle Giant had a darker side and this certainly manifested itself when he entered a bodybuilding competition and started taking steroids. He became aggressive with everyone who crossed his path, hitting Leo and pinning his best mate *Sinbad* against the wall. Maybe he thought lifting Sinbad off the ground would be a good test of his upper body strength. Even now that he's off the steroids, Mick still displays a harder edge to his personality. Having switched his culinary talents from pizzas to chips, he has become a tougher businessman, less inclined to do favours, as *Mo McGee* found out when he gave her the push. Nobody takes advantage of Mick anymore; he has learnt from bitter experience that it doesn't pay to be soft.

Alun Jones (Norman Eshley) 1986

Sheila Grant's college tutor was more interested in furthering her sexual education. At the time, she was going through a rough patch with Bobby and was happy to go to The Swan one evening to discuss her course with Jones. But there Jones poured out his true feelings for her. Having rejected his overtures, a shocked Sheila headed home but was raped on the way by her taxi driver. Jones briefly became the prime suspect but was soon cleared. Sheila did not rejoin the course.

Davy Jones (Ian Hendry) 1984

The father of *Marie Jackson, Petra Taylor* and *Michelle Jones*, Davy Jones was an old seadog with a fondness for the bottle. After having nothing to do with the family for years, he suddenly turned up on the doorstep of 10 Brookside Close, hoping to cash in on Petra's death. Only the twins were pleased to see him. In the absence of a will, he claimed that, as the next of kin, the house was rightfully his. Displaying no compassion, he tried to evict his two surviving daughters, only for his plans to be scuppered when a will was produced. Not surprisingly, Petra left him nothing. He decided not to hang around where he wasn't wanted but on his way out helped himself to Michelle's catalogue money. It stayed in his pocket until he reached the nearest off-licence.

Michelle Jones (Tracey Jay) 1983–85

The recipient of a tidy sum of money from *Petra Taylor's* will, Michelle, the youngest of the three sisters, set about furthering her ambition to be a beautician. Then she bumped into someone crying out for a makeover – *Terry Sullivan* – and love blossomed. At first, Michelle was suspicious of Terry, mainly because of his friendship with *Barry Grant* whom Michelle and elder sister Marie both blamed for Petra's suicide. Michelle took great pleasure in treating Barry with contempt, while Marie was one person he was genuinely frightened of. Terry promised Michelle he'd stop seeing Barry but even then, Ba' seemed to exert a hold over him. Marie reckoned Terry was only after Michelle's money – until she found a pair of Terry's Y-fronts in Michelle's bed and realised there was more than one thing he was after. With their matching perms, Michelle and Terry looked like bookends, and she showed her belief in him by investing into his and Barry's tool-hire business. To reciprocate, Terry asked her to marry him. They moved into a flat together and then into No. 10 but Michelle grew bored. To relieve the tedium, she attended dance classes and fell for her instructor, *Richard de Saville*. When Terry caught him teaching her a few steps between the sheets, he threw the mattress out of the bedroom window and began hacking it to pieces. Sensing that their relationship was over, Michelle wisely decided to join Marie in Leeds.

Beth Jordache (Anna Friel) 1993–95

Considering everything she had been through in her young life, it was a miracle that Beth Jordache turned out as well-balanced as she did. Raped by her father when she was 13 and a witness to his abuse of her sister and his countless vicious attacks on her mother, it wasn't surprising that she had doubts about her own sexuality. What was remarkable was that these experiences hadn't drained every ounce of energy or self-respect from her. Instead they seemed to endow her with an inner strength, a determination to succeed and a definite self-confidence. From the moment the evil Trevor reappeared on the scene, Beth wanted him out and went to stay at the Harrisons' rather than sleep in the same house as him. Even though mother Mandy was wavering, Beth refused to believe his stories that he had changed. Where Mandy was weak, Beth was strong.

Brenna Jordache (Gillian Hanna)

comfortable in the relationship. Not only was the sex great but Chris, who was 12 years older, treated her like an adult and listened to her opinions. Nevertheless, Beth was anxious to keep it from her family. It wasn't that she was ashamed of her sexuality so much as a feeling that her mother wouldn't understand and had enough on her plate anyway with the constant worry over whether Trevor's body would ever be found. This time, however, Beth wasn't the dominant partner and ended up being badly hurt by Chris. Suddenly Beth Jordache appeared lonely and vulnerable. She had to put up with a lot of jealousy and spite from *Jacqui Dixon*, but Jacqui's brother Mike proved a surprisingly good friend even when he realised he wasn't going to get anywhere with her. The murder trial verdict left her emotionally and physically shattered but, with her imminent release a distinct possibility, she died in her cell from a hereditary illness. Trevor had exacted a full revenge.

Brenna Jordache (Gillian Hanna) 1993–95

Trevor's unmarried, shrewish sister Brenna had never liked Mandy. All she saw in her brother was a gentle, caring man with sparkling eyes – never a hint of violence. As far as Brenna was concerned, if Trevor had hit Mandy, she must have driven him to it by making his life a misery. Brenna stayed as close to Trevor as prison would allow but, when he went missing after being released, breaking the terms of his probation order, she became suspicious, all the more so when she found that the local window-cleaner had moved in with Mandy. Even Brenna wasn't that house proud! Sinbad thought that Brenna would soon give up the hunt but Mandy knew better and went through with the sham funeral in the hope of getting Brenna off her back. When the truth finally emerged, Brenna was suitably apoplectic. She sent the family hate mail

Whereas Mandy was afraid of doing anything to upset Trevor, Beth told him to his face what she thought of him. Mandy may have delivered the fatal blow but Beth had to do all the tidying up afterwards. Mandy would have simply frozen and left Trevor's body lying in the kitchen waiting to be discovered. It was the same with relationships. Beth was not afraid to take the lead. Things didn't work out with *Peter Harrison* – they couldn't when she learned that he too was a possible rapist – so she decided to bring her feelings for *Margaret Clemence* out into the open. Beth made all the running and when Margaret came to the conclusion that she really did prefer men, the pretty medical student took up with her gay university lecturer, *Chris Myers*. Beth felt

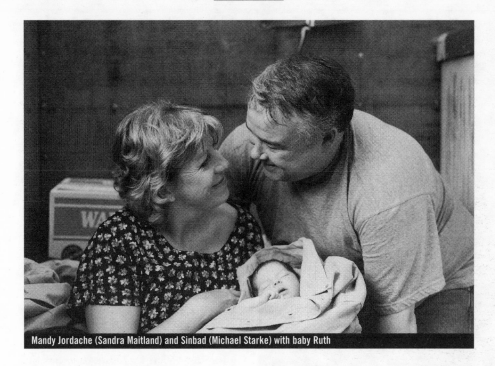

Mandy Jordache (Sandra Maitland) and Sinbad (Michael Starke) with baby Ruth

and tried to poison Rachel's mind against her mother and sister. Like Trevor, Brenna could be a convincing liar and managed to persuade the released Mandy that she had turned over a new leaf. Instead she was trying to poison her. It may not be every bride's dream to have her stomach pumped on her wedding day, but Mandy didn't press charges. Perhaps she felt Brenna deserved pity rather than prison.

Mandy Jordache (Sandra Maitland)
1993–95

When *Trevor Jordache* started beating his wife Mandy, he not only left her battered and bruised, he also left emotional scars which would never heal. Mandy was an empty shell, stripped of her dignity, her confidence, her self-respect. She lived in fear, knowing that Trevor couldn't be kept behind bars forever and that one day he would come looking for her. She was relieved when the Shackletons found her, Beth and Rachel a 'safe' house at 10 Brookside Close, little knowing that nothing

on Brookside Close is ever safe ... and that includes cars, washing, doors, windows, furniture, children, dogs and garden gnomes. She'd have been safer on an anti-drugs march in Bogotá. Rarely venturing out, she tried to keep herself to herself, but that can be difficult with the likes of Julia Brogan in the vicinity. In a bid to wipe Trevor from her memory, Mandy told her new neighbours that he was dead, so there were puzzled faces when he suddenly turned up looking very much alive. He used every ounce of his charm to persuade her that he was a new man and, as her resistance crumbled, he managed to worm his way back into the house. No sooner had he done so than the beatings started again. Mandy didn't want to kill him but acted in self-defence to protect her herself and her daughters. It has to be said that Mandy was gullible and weak, something which Trevor and later his old cell-mate *Roy Williams* and loan shark *Kenny Maguire* were both quick to exploit. *Sinbad* was the only man who treated her with respect. Still an emotional

Rachel Jordache (Tiffany Chapman)

Rachel Jordache (Tiffany Chapman) 1993–

Rachel has been through enough traumas to keep her in therapy for life yet she has proved to be a survivor. For years she was unable to accept the fact that her father had done anything wrong to her. She loved him so much that she could never think of him as some kind of monster. Like all little girls, she just wanted to please her dad. She was upset when he mysteriously disappeared and grief-stricken when he was apparently found dead in the woods, yet she managed to bottle up her emotions and coped with the loss as best she could. So when she finally learned the truth – that her mother and elder sister had killed him – she despised them, not only for what they had done, but also because they had lied to her. She resented the fact that Mandy had confided in Beth, but not in her. She felt left out. Spurred on by Auntie Brenna, she ostracised her mum, which hurt Mandy deeply. These days, mother and daughter are much closer although Rachel was disappointed when Mandy couldn't make it to her wedding to *Christian Wright*. Perhaps she knew something, for Christian was anything but Mr Right. He made Rachel feel utterly worthless and at one point in their brief, unhappy marriage she contemplated taking a leaf out of her mum's book – or at least a knife out of her drawer – and terminating the union by force. In the end, she settled for subjecting him to gross humiliation. Despite all she has been through, Rachel remains cheerful and friendly, very much a party animal. She has always had a generous spirit; even when she went shoplifting, it was to buy presents for the family. She is blessed with the same determination as her late sister, and it is to be hoped that she can put both Trevor and Christian behind her.

Trevor Jordache (Bryan Murray) 1993

To those who didn't know him, Trevor

minefield, she found it difficult to express her feelings for him and nearly lost him on more than one occasion. After killing her husband, losing one daughter and being estranged from the other, all in the space of a couple of years, there was a suggestion that she was rushing things by agreeing to marry Sinbad. In the end, the wedding postponement, caused by Brenna's poisoned porridge, did Mandy a favour. She realised that her true vocation lay in helping other battered women and left Liverpool to work at a refuge in Bristol. Sinbad was devastated – he'd not only lost Mandy but also their baby Ruth – but for the first time in her tragic life, Mandy Jordache had made a decision which suited her.

Jordache was a typical Irish charmer. But he was a Jekyll-and-Hyde character: in a split second, that friendly smile could disappear and his expression be contorted into one of snarling aggression. The outside world only saw the gregarious, affable Trevor. The hate-filled venom was reserved for his wife Mandy. When he wasn't sleeping with his daughters, he was beating Mandy black and blue. He was bad enough when he was sober, but when he'd got a few drinks inside him he was positively demonic. Mandy used to cower in bed or under the stairs, dreading his return from the pub, knowing that whatever she said or did would probably provoke a violent reaction. Prison did not mellow him. If anything, it left him more bitter than before – livid that the woman over whom he thought he had complete control should have dared to report him to the police. Released on parole, he immediately set about tracking down Mandy and the girls. The neighbours thought he was a decent chap – so polite – but no sooner had he got his feet over the threshold than he had crept into Rachel's bed and back into Mandy's. When he threatened Mandy that he'd kill all three of them, and then himself, if anyone was told about his past, there really was only one place for him: under the patio.

Brian Kennedy (Jonathan Caplan) 1992–93

When fresh-faced Brian Kennedy took over the franchise of the hairdressing salon following the hasty departure of *Angela Lambert*, he was quick to make his mark with the locals. *Tracy Corkhill* thought he was the hairdresser from heaven when he first took her on as a stylist and then promoted her to one of his salons in Chester. And her gran, *Julia Brogan*, was delighted when he offered her a job sweeping up, making tea and generally gossiping with the customers. It was what Julia did best. He caught *Patricia Farnham*'s

eye too while she was going through a rough time with Max and always gave the impression of being a perfect gentleman as well as a successful businessman. But you don't get to run a shop on Brookside Parade without having some dark secret – and his was drugs. When he heard from La Luz doorman *Jimmy Corkhill* that there was drug-taking on the premises, Brian encouraged Jimmy to try an Ecstasy tab. Tempted by the cash he needed to win Jackie back, Jimmy began supplying Brian with drugs to order via the cabbies who operated outside the club. Jimmy envied Brian's lifestyle and wanted in on the big deal Brian was talking about. But it all went pear-shaped, leaving Brian a guest of Her Majesty and Jimmy on the road to destruction. The Home Office won't confirm which prison Brian is currently held in, but it's the one where all the officers have bouffants.

Eleanor Kitson (Georgia Reece) 1997–

Some people can brighten up a room just by walking into it. Eleanor Kitson can brighten up a room just by leaving it. For whilst the young solicitor is attractive, she is also permanently gloomy. She became embroiled with *Ollie Simpson* following his split from wife Bel. At first, Ollie's son Danny resented the relationship but gradually he came round, and she agreed to give up her flat and move in to No. 9 where she and Ollie soon immersed themselves in intensely serious conversations, completely forgetting that they were supposed to be enjoying each other's company. When Eleanor had her hair dyed blonde, it brought back unpleasant memories for Ollie of incest-scandal daughter Georgia. He could hardly bear to look at the new-look Eleanor and, in order to explain what was wrong, was obliged to reveal the whole sordid Simpson family history. Eleanor justifiably pointed out that his keeping such a secret was hardly a promising start to their relationship, but almost immediately it transpired that she too came with more baggage than Concorde – in the form of a hitherto unmentioned daughter, *Louise Hope*. Bit by bit, Eleanor revealed details of her own sorry past. At university, she had been an animal rights activist and had fallen pregnant to the charismatic Marcus Seddon. When he was jailed for 30 years, she had the baby adopted. Now Louise has come back to haunt her. Between bouts of philosophising over the meaning of life with Ollie, Eleanor occasionally finds time to work from her new office on the Parade where *Katie Rogers* has proved a capable assistant.

Angela Lambert (Hilary Welles)
1991–92

Angela Lambert was the first occupant of the hair salon on Brookside Parade. A stylish lady who had two young daughters and was separated from husband Colin, Angela soon stirred *Barry Grant*'s interest. But she was more than a match for him and wasn't going to be swept off her feet by his dubious charms. She told him that if he wanted her, he'd have to take the kids on board as well. One day Colin suddenly turned up and announced that he had a solution to her babysitting problems: he wanted to move in with her, sell the house and split the proceeds. But when she discovered that he was heavily in debt and had remortgaged the house, she suspected that the only reason he was keen to get back together was to save his business from going down the pan. To reduce the risk of losing her, Barry secretly paid off one of Colin's debtors. But then Barry did one of his disappearing acts and, a few months later, the hair salon was the subject of a vicious armed robbery during which one of Angela's daughters was threatened. The experience so traumatised Angela that she sold up – the only person to quit hairdressing because of the dangers.

Brian Lawrence (Vincent Maguire)
1988–89

Going through a mid-life crisis which saw her tire of husband Paul, *Annabelle Collins* threw herself into an affair with fellow magistrate Brian Lawrence. Used-car dealer Brian first got a close-up of her bodywork on a course in Shewsbury and carried on when they got back to Liverpool. When Paul found an incriminating ring – a present from Brian to Annabelle – he invited Brian round for drinks on Christmas Day and confronted the pair of them. Brian, who compared unfavourably with a ferret, quickly made his excuses and left. Realising that her beau was only interested in saving his own skin, Annabelle dropped him and returned to the bosom of her family. If Brian thought he'd got off lightly, he was wrong, for Annabelle's son Gordon, who was working at the showroom, took his pound of flesh by selling off Brian's cars at giveaway prices. Satisfied with his day's work, he then quit … seconds before Brian sacked him.

Diane McAllister (Rosie Clayton)
1983

Wealthy femme fatale Diane McAllister was the attractive client who lured *Roger Huntington* away from the marital bed. Not that he needed much luring – a carrot on a piece of string would probably have done the trick. He viewed an affair as an essential step in his progress up the legal ladder and Diane was only too willing to comply. After one particularly fulfilling business trip to Birmingham, she presented Roger with a tie pin which he only just remembered to remove before greeting Heather. When Heather eventually discovered it, she realised what was going on and kicked him out. Roger rushed straight round to Diane's flat, only to hear that Diane was jetting off to Barbados the next day. The party was over.

Mrs McArdle (Peggy Shields) 1986
The mother of arch villain *Tommy McArdle*

appeared at first glance to be one of those dotty old gangsters' mums who have no idea what their darling sons are up to. So when Tommy asked *Terry Sullivan* and *Pat Hancock* to accompany her to Barbados, it seemed a routine enough job. In fairness, Terry did suspect that her senility was just an act, but Pat was too preoccupied with tour guide Avril to worry about anything else. Acting as Tommy's courier, Mrs M. had no trouble in outsmarting the boys – admittedly not the most onerous of challenges – and got an unwitting Terry to smuggle an envelope back to England. Her job done, she went home and had a nice cup of tea.

Tommy McArdle (Malcolm Tierney) 1984–86

He was kind to his mum, he bred budgies and he only ever hurt those whom he thought he deserved it. Tommy McArdle was a gangster with old-fashioned morals and, in many respects, likened himself to a modern-day Robin Hood. He sorted out Dutton, the taxi-driver who raped *Sheila Grant*, and promised to take care of *George Jackson*'s family if the fireman went down without a whimper. Mind you, Tommy's interpretation of taking care of somebody was just as likely to involve a knee-capping as an arm around the shoulder. Operating from a chain of outwardly legitimate clubs, the camel-coated businessman was involved in all manner of criminal activities and recruited the services of no-hopers like *Terry Sullivan* and get-rich-quick merchants like *Barry Grant*. They knew that if they fouled up, Tommy would be round asking for a favour in return. These requests were non-negotiable. It really was best not to cross Tommy McArdle – unless you enjoyed the taste of hospital food.

Don McAteer (Freddie Boardley) 1994

Jimmy Corkhill's Scottish cell-mate ran a flourishing drugs empire from inside prison, getting smack off his girlfriend, stashing it in the kitchens and selling it to his fellow inmates. He encouraged Jimmy to take some to ease his troubled mind, but overdid one session and ended up dead in his bunk in the morning. After the officers had searched the cell and found nothing, Jimmy, seeing an opportunity too good to miss, sought out the hidden stash and set up as a dealer in his own right. It's what Don would have wanted.

Mo McGee (Tina Malone) 1993–

Rosie Banks's sister Mo first appeared as a barmaid at La Luz. When *Jacqui Dixon* started up Bar Brookie, Mo was deemed surplus to requirements and finished up working for a while at Mick Johnson's fish and chip emporium. Mo has always been a reliable employee and a good worker, often being obliged to cover for less conscientious staff like *Sammy Daniels*. Kind-hearted Mo loved Rosie dearly but was appalled at her gambling addiction and tried to talk some sense into her. Rosie responded with predictable venom, leaving Mo deeply hurt. A larger-than-life figure, Mo enjoys nothing more than a night on the town, particularly if there is a chance of pulling an unsuspecting fella. So far her closest encounter was with Kevin, landlord of the pub where the Brookside Ladies' darts team played, but she got so drunk that she couldn't prevent him making his escape. Men beware: she's still looking.

Debbie McGrath (Gillian Kearney) 1986–88

Schoolgirl Debbie met *Damon Grant* at a New Year's Eve party. He had just finished with the dreaded Gail so he was delighted to meet someone whose idea of a fun day out went beyond looking at soft furnishings. Damon liked Debbie a lot, but her disciplinarian father took a different view. He wanted only the best for his daughter and didn't see a cheeky scally who couldn't

Bev McLoughlin (Sarah White)

hold down a job as much of a catch. Damon's mum Sheila was equally fond of Debbie but even she expressed her misgivings about the relationship. Debbie was very young. Mr McGrath tried to nip it in the bud but Damon, determined to prove himself to be a suitable suitor, found a job as a door-to-door salesman. It was a disaster and he packed it in. Then McGrath had a better idea and, convinced that if he put a few miles between the young lovers the romance would fizzle out, offered Damon a job in Ipswich. With Damon away, Debbie went through a miserable time. Her mother left home and her father became increasingly fractious. On his return from Ipswich, Damon spotted a bruise on her neck. She passed it off as a sporting injury but finally admitted that her father had hit her. Damon and Debbie ran off together but the dream ended in tragedy. Following

Damon's murder, Sheila grew closer to Debbie – they had both loved and lost Damon – but Bobby unjustly blamed Debbie for Damon's death. Later Debbie found that she was pregnant with Damon's baby. Debbie was a diabetic so there was a risk that the baby might be deformed. Her father wanted her to have an abortion (the thought of which horrified Sheila) but word subsequently reached Bobby that she had suffered a miscarriage. However, just over a year after Damon's death, Debbie turned up holding Simon, Sheila's grandson. Sheila was overjoyed and was left to reflect what a smashing daughter-in-law Debbie would have made.

Bev McLoughlin (Sarah White)
1993–96

On Bev McLoughlin's tombstone the inscription will read: She had a gob on her.

274

When Bev first arrived on the Close, most of the women, including her elder sister Lyn, despised her because they reckoned she was after their husbands. And by the time she went in a blaze of glory three years later, nothing had changed. She had upset so many people with her brash behaviour and tactless comments that nobody was sorry to see the back of her. Bev was the Queen of Tack. Her house was tacky, her clothes were tacky and her whole approach to life was tacky. She had always been trouble. She had an abortion at 14 and later wrecked her sister's marriage by sleeping with Lyn's husband *Steve Matthews*. So when Bev turned up on the Close, Lyn immediately warned her off her groom-to-be, *Frank Rogers*. But Bev could sniff out married men like a Jack Russell in a rabbit warren. She preferred older men because they were experienced and usually grateful. Also, they knew how to treat a lady. Her craving for old married men was satisfied when *Ron Dixon* offered her a job at the Trading Post. When he realised that she fancied him, he could hardly believe his luck, pulling a bird half his age. For her part, she got a kick out of stealing Ron from his wife DD and soon had him wrapped round her little finger. At first, he was just another married bloke to add to her collection, but then she made the fatal mistake of falling in love with him. Ron was similarly besotted and the lust-driven fling developed into something more serious. Although Ron tried to compensate for the age difference by dyeing his hair and wearing younger clothes for the fuller figure, there were numerous rows and walk-outs, partly because Ron felt guilty about the way he was treating DD. During one of these brief separations, Bev decided to get back at Ron by sleeping with his son Mike. The result, baby Josh, delivered the final blow to Ron's marriage. Installed in their own love nest, Casa Bevron, everything seemed rosy until the novelty began to wear off. With his dicky heart, Ron wanted to take things easy,

Kenny Maguire (Tommy Boyle)

while Bev still wanted to party all night. When another long-admired shop assistant, *Jackie Corkhill*, came on to the market, Ron made a move on her and ditched Bev. The biter had been well and truly bit and her revenge was to set fire to Casa Bevron. Even when she confessed to the arson attack, she pleaded with Ron to take her back, insisting that she'd only done it because she couldn't bear the thought of him being with Jackie Corkhill. This time, he didn't want to know. She'd burned too many bridges ... not to mention her house.

Sandra Maghie (Sheila Grier) 1984–86

Fiery Scottish nurse Sandra Maghie shared 7 Brookside Close with *Kate Moses* and *Pat Hancock*, no more than a twitch of the curtains away from their prying landlord, *Harry Cross*. Sandra considered herself to be fairly streetwise but she suffered a nasty shock when she was attacked by radiographer Jimmy Powell. She turned on Pat, who, to her disgust, had hired a 'naughty nurse' outfit for his kissagram service, and accused him of encouraging men to attack women. Her estranged husband Ian had been wanting a divorce for some months and one day he drove down from Glasgow to press his case. When she refused to consider it, he hit her, forcing Pat to intervene. Ian then announced that he would cite Pat as co-respondent. Her relationship with Pat was always a love-hate affair, never more so than after the siege. They turned to each other for comfort and wound up in bed together. But, as a frustrated Sandra discovered, Pat could never make anything last long and when she became professionally involved with *Dr Tony Hurrell*, a jealous Pat began hitting her. By now, Sandra had seen quite enough of Brookside Close and, when Tony took a new job in Edinburgh and asked her to join him, she didn't hesitate. At last she had the chance to settle down in a relationship where she wouldn't be used as a punch-bag.

Kenny Maguire (Tommy Boyle)
1994–95
Kenny Maguire was the ultimate coward – a small-time villain who made his living out of preying on the defenceless. Taking over the Jordaches' loan, Maguire raised the payments to an intolerable level. But his charm convinced *Mandy Jordache* that it was all above board and, without reading the small print – or indeed anything, she signed the contract. Seeing what an easy target she was, he later coerced her into repaying him in kind. Mandy went along with it but forgot to ask for a receipt. He also tried his luck with the spineless *Max Farnham* (although he did draw the line at sleeping with Max) but had reckoned

without Max's slightly more forthright business partner, *Barry Grant*, and his access to a cement-mixer. In the end, it was Barry who saw that Maguire received a beating of such ferocity that he would never be tempted to bother Mandy again. The loan was repaid.

Audrey Manners (Judith Barker)
1994–95
Audrey 'bad' Manners was the overbearing matriarch of the over-55s club who took an instant shine to *David Crosbie*, the man she called 'the Major'. She made no secret of her desire to get him into bed. As far as David was concerned, it was a regrettable episode best forgotten, but Audrey was hungry for more and began resorting to blackmail. Worse still, when her boiler packed up she moved in with the Crosbies. Salvation was at hand in the form of her long-lost husband George, a man whose very existence she had previously denied. George brought Audrey a holiday present from Kenya – a deadly virus which wiped them both out. As a few unchivalrous thoughts entered his head, David was almost relieved … but not for long.

George Manners (Brian Murphy)
1995
After years of marriage to Audrey, the hen-pecked George went out one day and never came back, taking all of her jewellery with him. Little wonder that when he suddenly turned up on the Close selling timeshare holidays, she initially passed him off as her brother. George was a none-too-smooth-talking conman who nevertheless quickly succeeded in parting half of the Close from their money. But before he had a chance to spend it, he was fatally struck down by the virus he had brought back with him from Kenya.

Molly Marchbank (Diane Keen)
1997–98

With his habitual pulling pad, the Trading Post, shut for good, *Ron Dixon* had to cast his net further afield in his quest for female company. Deciding to move up-market and hunt out a wealthy widow, he took *David Crosbie* along to the local golf club where he was immediately captivated by the glamorous Molly Marchbank. He was even keener when he heard her family history, for her late husband Norman, who had suddenly dropped dead the year before, was not only an ex-captain of the golf club with a tournament named after him, he had also expanded the Marchbank chain of butcher's shops throughout the 1970s, making him a millionaire. Ron quickly made his move and, abandoning the principles of a lifetime, spent some money on her. But when he found her house wasn't exactly on millionaire's row, he dropped her, allowing David to slide in smoothly and take his place. Little did Ron know that, to deter gold-diggers such as himself, Molly had pretended to would-be suitors that her mother-in-law's modest terraced house was really her own. Only when she was convinced that David was the genuine article did she reveal her true abode – a sumptuous Cheshire estate, Bressingham Hall. Ron could only reflect on the one that got away.

James Markham (Tom Mannion)
1989–90

The smarmy ex-boyfriend of *Caroline Choi*, James Markham was on the run from heavy gambling debts when he turned up on the Close in the hope of gaining access to both Caroline and her lucrative jewellery-making business. With his fast tongue and his fast car, he swiftly saw off the challenge of *Sinbad* (whose very participation had been a bit like a donkey entering the Derby) and asked for Caroline's hand in marriage. He then appointed himself her business manager, from which position he proceeded to have fake stones inserted in her merchandise. Caroline didn't suspect a thing – even when she learned about a pile of video nasties in the boot of his car – until presented with irrefutable evidence that Markham was behind the fraud. He continued to lie in a bid to save his skin, finally stealing her car in a desperate move to stay one step ahead of his pursuers. He perished in a car crash in Aberdeen. Like Markham himself, it was highly suspicious.

Sam Martin (John Harding) 1994–95

Considering that the first time he met *Penny Crosbie* he was dressed as a fairy on board the Round Table Christmas sleigh, it was a minor miracle that Sam Martin won her heart. The divorced property developer was approached by Penny and by his Round Table colleague *Max Farnham* to help buy out *Barry Grant* from the restaurant. He expressed an interest in the deal and also in Penny, who came to spend Christmas with him at his grand country house. But when Barry got back from Spain and discovered what the gang of three had been up to behind his back, Sam got a thump in his pretty face along with his marching orders.

Alison Matthews (Jenny Beaver) 1993

There are many things teenager Alison Matthews had dreamed of in life, but acquiring *Frank Rogers* as a stepfather was not one of them. So when mum Lyn announced that she intended to marry the truculent trucker, Alison registered her disapproval in the strongest possible terms. Frank tried to win her round by buying her a new computer but Alison was singularly ungrateful. Complaining that she was being neglected, she ran away, thus jeopardising the entire wedding. But Frank refused to bow to her pressure and won her over with his musical virtuosity: when dad Steve failed to turn up for her school concert, Frank couldn't bear to see her alone on stage with her violin, so he grabbed a guitar and climbed up to join her.

Lyn Matthews – see Lyn Rogers

Steve Matthews (Lawrence Mullin) 1993

A drummer with a band, Steve had wrecked his marriage to Lyn by getting his kit off with her brassy sister, *Bev McLoughlin*. Steve, whose high opinion of himself was shared by few others, still fancied Bev and, on learning that she was pregnant and living with geriatric gigolo *Ron Dixon*, advised her to get rid of the baby and Ron and to join him on a forthcoming cruise job. Ron reckoned the cruise was the Mersey Ferry. Seized by the glamour of it all, Bev was about to accept the offer when Steve, as unreliable as ever, told her that someone else had got the job. While Bev slunk back to Ron, Steve went off to chat up the talent on the cruise. Some of them liked him so much they put their teeth in specially.

Louise Mitchell (Jenny Hesketh) 1989–90

Young offender Louise Mitchell had run away from a children's home when she turned up unannounced on the doorstep of magistrate *Annabelle Collins*, asking for help. Against the better judgement of husband Paul, Annabelle allowed Louise to stay. They took pity on her after discovering that she had been abused at the home by brother Gary, but thoughts of adoption foundered as a result of her persistent thieving. She just couldn't help herself. Matters deteriorated further when *Lucy Collins* returned from France and began treating Louise like dirt. To try and impress her, Louise told Lucy about Annabelle's affair with *Brian Lawrence*. Paul felt betrayed and realised that Louise was trouble they didn't need at their time of life.

Lisa Morrisey (Amanda Nolan) 1997–

Susannah Farnham's younger sister Lisa offered a shoulder to cry on following the car crash which killed Matthew and Emily and promised that she would always be there to help. Consequently she was Susannah and Max's number one choice for prospective surrogate mother. However, their case was not helped by a clumsy presentation which sounded as if they were proposing a threesome and, even when Lisa realised what they were driving at, she made it clear that she was horrified at the suggestion. It was back to the drawing board … and *Jacqui Dixon*.

Kate Moses (Sharon Rosita) 1984–85

Young West Indian nurse Kate Moses was the quiet member of the trio who rented No. 7. But next to *Sandra Maghie* and *Pat Hancock*, Ruby Wax would have seemed reserved. A single girl, Kate was diligent and hard-working and was quite prepared to land Pat in trouble when she uncovered a food-selling scam he had been running at the hospital. She would surely have gone a long way in nursing but for the intervention of mad gunman *John Clarke* whom she met at the hospital fête. It was to be a fête worse than death. During Clarke's siege, Kate was the only one able to get through to him. While Pat fell to pieces, Kate became more assured by the minute and looked set to bring the episode to a peaceful conclusion. But in the end she was too compassionate for her own good. For when Clarke announced that he was going to kill himself, she tried to stop him. The outcome was that he shot her and then himself. At Kate's funeral, her sister Debbie blamed Pat for her death, saying he should have been the one to take control, not Kate. Deep down, Pat knew she was right. He and Sandra had let Kate down.

Darren Murphy (Matthew Crompton) 1992

Teenager Darren Murphy led his gang on a crime wave around the Close, vandalising property, breaking into schools, mugging *Julia Brogan* and ultimately setting fire to Manor Park Primary. *Jacqui Dixon*, who had been hanging around with Darren, was almost killed in the fire and father Ron sought retribution. For messing with Darren, Ron had a stolen car dumped outside his house, his shop window smashed and received a punch on the jaw from Darren's equally loutish father. The Harrisons' conservatory met a similar fate after Barbara Harrison had become involved. The residents responded by setting up a vigilante patrol of which *Frank Rogers* and Ron were slightly more enthusiastic members than *Max Farnham*. Eventually Jacqui, seeing younger brother Tony being threatened by Darren, decided to shop her boyfriend to the police and Darren's little spree was over.

Chris Myers (Maria Francis)

Chris Myers (Maria Francis) 1994

After experimenting over her lesbian leanings with *Margaret Clemence*, *Beth Jordache* went all the way with her 30-year-old gay university lecturer, Chris Myers. Outgoing and supremely confident about her sexuality, Chris swept Beth off her feet and made her realise that there was nothing to be ashamed of in being gay. She took Beth to gay bars and soon Beth was feeling comfortable. But when sister Rachel spotted them cuddling on a day trip to New Brighton and then an outraged *David Crosbie* discovered them kissing at the Farnhams', it was only going to be a matter of time before Beth's mum Mandy found out. When she did, Beth moved into Chris's flat. Beth thought it was a great idea but Chris was beginning to cool and, when Mandy threatened to report her to the education authorities, Chris put self-preservation before any romantic feelings.

Beth, angry and hurt, scurried back to the Close and Chris accepted a new post in California.

Matty Nolan (Tony Scoggo) 1982–92

Bobby Grant's best mate at Fairbanks Engineering, Matty was part of the great cover-up in the Grant household. Barry had always thought of Bobby as his father but it was only years later that he discovered that his real father was Matty. Likeable scouser Matty (real name Patrick) had always been close to Bobby's wife, Sheila, which was partly why she was so angry when he had an affair with fellow mature student Mo Francis. Matty was equally angry at Sheila's interference and the resulting argument made him a suspect when she was raped. Following the suicide of his wife Teresa, Matty was rejected by his son Stephen and it took him a while to put his life back in order. More than anyone, he worked to try

Teresa was rocked by a double blow. First, Matty told her that he had been having an affair and then she saw him arrested on suspicion of raping Sheila. When she heard that a man had been charged and there was no sign of Matty, she put two and two together and assumed that it was him. In fact, he was on his way home after being released, but arrived to find a suicide note from Teresa. Thinking she had nothing to live for, she had jumped off a ferry into the Mersey.

Derek O'Farrell (Clive Moore) 1990–94

Like many before him, serious-minded young priest Derek O'Farrell was ill-prepared for the dramatic chain of events which would overtake him once he set foot on Brookside Close. He arrived as *DD Dixon*'s God-fearing younger brother – a man dedicated to the Church and all it stood for. The only temptations he had encountered had been on DD's *Motown Classics* LP. Derek had a friendly word for everyone – no easy task on the Close – and his affability, not to mention good looks, were picked up on by the Farnhams' nanny *Margaret Clemence*. Margaret was an outsider in the community, like Derek and was looking for a friend. Able to spot a prospective Church helper at 100 paces, Derek roped her in to assist on various projects. With her enthusiasm, patience and hard work, he reckoned she had all the makings of a first-class flower-arranger. But Margaret wanted more than the promise of fresh freesias for life and set about defrocking the priest. She began spending every available minute with him. At first, it was innocent enough, but when he realised that she had feelings for him, he tried to back away. He knew he couldn't get involved in a relationship, and if he did forget for a second there were plenty of people around – including DD and his boss Father Thornton – to remind him. But Margaret persisted and eventually Derek succumbed.

Matty Nolan (Tony Scoggo)

and save Bobby and Sheila's marriage, but it would have needed superglue to keep those two together. He later landed a job at the newly-opened pizza parlour, but when it was temporarily closed down by the health authorities after an outbreak of food poisoning, Matty found himself out of a job.

Teresa Nolan (Ann Haydn Edwards) 1983–86

Matty's wife Teresa was one of *Brookside*'s most tragic figures. A good friend of *Sheila Grant*'s, she was always popping round for a gossip while the men talked about the constant fear of unemployment which was gripping the community. Then in 1986,

Torn between his love for the Church and his love for Margaret, he briefly considered suicide as the only answer before finally deciding to relinquish the priesthood. They became engaged and he accepted a voluntary job with Catholic Aid for Overseas Development, first in Romania, then in Bosnia. After her initial reluctance to leave one war zone (the Close) for another, Margaret joined him and they continued to perform good deeds for mankind in general as well as for each other.

Ben O'Leary (Simon Paul) 1997–

Fireman Ben is the acceptable face of the O'Leary family. Following the death of his father, Ben took over as the man of the house, attempting in vain to keep younger brother Tim on the straight and narrow. It proved an impossible task, particularly as he received little support from their gullible mother Carmel. Ben likes to work hard and play hard and, to further his chances in that direction, moved into a flat with *Mike Dixon*. Ben had been smitten with Mike's sister Jacqui but she rejected his proposal of marriage even after he had dressed up in a white tuxedo to pop the question. She thought he was very sweet but ... So now, with his own pad, Ben was intent on playing the field. Mike could only watch and learn. But Ben's world was shattered by the gas explosion which shook the Parade. He bravely rescued *Ron Dixon* but suffered terrible injuries when caught in a second blast.

Carmel O'Leary (Carol Connor) 1996–

Carmel has had it tough bringing up three kids virtually single-handedly. She has tried to do her best for them but Tim, otherwise know as Tinhead, has consistently taken advantage of her leniency. Seeing any criticism of him as a criticism of her own capabilities as a mother, she steadfastly refuses to hear a bad word said against him. At a Brookside Comprehensive parent-governors' meeting, she bridled at *Mick Johnson*'s demand for Tim's exclusion on grounds of bullying, claiming that whenever anything went wrong it was always her poor boy who got the blame. She found love in the ample shape of *Sinbad* (perhaps he thought her name was Caramel) but the relationship was thrown into jeopardy when he discovered that her son was the bane of his life. Sinbad's attempts to instil a little much-needed discipline into the lad were constantly rebuked by Carmel, who accused him of picking on Tim for no reason. Only when she was presented with over-whelming evidence was she able finally to admit that perhaps Tim wasn't exactly whiter than white. Consequently her relationship with Sinbad got on a surer footing. But Tinhead remains the cause of virtually every argument in the O'Leary household.

Melanie O'Leary (Elizabeth Lovelady) 1997–

The sister of Ben and Tim, Melanie had a lucky escape when Tim's firework prank caused a lorry to crash into the house. She escaped with a few cuts and bruises, which was more than could be said for the house. Mel might not be Brain of Britain but at least she's leading a more productive life than one of her brothers.

Timothy 'Tinhead' O'Leary (Philip Olivier) 1996–

Having lost his father when he was young, Tim, known to friends and enemies alike as 'Tinhead', has gone badly off the rails. A one-man crime wave, he has graduated from being a school bully with a taste for under-age drinking to burglary, theft and joyriding. The only time he appeared to be getting his act together was when he thought he was joining the army. At last his life seemed to have a purpose – he could get into all sorts of scrapes and be paid for it. So it came as a shattering blow when he failed his hearing test at the medical. He retreated into his shell at home, lounging around with girlfriend *Sharon Bridges* or spending hour upon hour aimlessly watching daytime television. Nobody deserves such punishment. He returned to his old insolent ways, particularly towards *Sinbad* whom he saw as an inadequate father substitute. Sinbad did his best to win him round – even covering up for him on occasions – but all he received in return was sneering contempt. There is a good side to Tinhead, as seen when he rescued *Julia Brogan* from a gang of youths. But the receipt of a bravery award made him curl up in embarrassment. It didn't fit his hard-man image. Sinbad isn't the only person who has tried to help him. *David Crosbie* gave him a job at the petrol station but he soon abused the privilege, and when he landed a job at a building suppliers, the first thing he did was get involved in a fiddle. At this rate, he'll end up being sacked more times than Rome. With his eye for making fast money regardless of the consequences, Tinhead has all the makings of being the next *Barry Grant*.

Joe O'Rourke (Christian Rodska) 1990

When daughter Sammy began staring at life through the bottom of a glass, *Chrissy Rogers* booked her in to see Dr O'Rourke. Whereas husband Frank could only rant and rave about Sammy's alcoholism, Joe O'Rourke listened sympathetically. Chrissy was impressed and, when she got home, began quoting the doctor to Frank. This was like a red rag to a bull. The only expert Frank trusted was John McCririck and he was quick to pour scorn on the doctor's ideas. Over the ensuing weeks, Chrissy and Joe grew progressively closer. She could have a real conversation with him, he seemed to understand, even when Sammy wet her bed. The sexual attraction between Chrissy and Joe was growing fast. They went to the cinema, had lunch together and seemed all set to embark on an affair. He offered her a job as his receptionist – the perfect cover for out-of-hours liaisons – but she couldn't go through with it. It had been exciting while it lasted but, for the time being at least, she went back to Frank.

Andrea Parkin (Jane Morant) 1986

Andrea Parkin ate men for breakfast and spat them out afterwards. The middle-aged but well-preserved wife of local amateur football club chairman Bernie Parkin, Andrea drove around in a flash sports car on the lookout for toy boys. *Pat Hancock* and *Terry Sullivan* both played for the club and it was Pat, on the rebound after *Sandra Maghie*'s departure to Scotland, who was lured into Andrea's web. Terry warned Pat to be careful because, whilst Bernie was apparently prepared to turn a blind eye to his wife's indiscretions provided she didn't get too carried away, he also employed some gorillas who would think nothing of burying Pat head first in the centre circle. But Pat wouldn't listen and was soon scoring more regularly than Gary Lineker. However, when he overstepped the mark and started getting possessive, Andrea dumped him pronto and went on the prowl for her next victim.

Arthur Parkinson (Edward Clayton) 1988–89

As secretary of the Commonwealth and Empire Club, Arthur Parkinson (brother of *Betty Hunt*) ruled the roost with a rod of iron. A stickler for the rule-book, he wouldn't give a dying man a glass of water unless it had been passed by the committee. Under his jurisdiction, both *Harry Cross* and *Ralph Hardwick* were elected to the committee, but Harry fell out with Arthur in a big way when he discovered that the grave of his late wife Edna had been moved and that Arthur was responsible. To make his point, Harry paraded outside the club wearing a sandwich-board proclaiming Arthur to be a grave-robber. However, when

Harry was shown Edna's new grave and saw how peaceful the setting was, he agreed to drop his protest.

Dil Parmar (Gordon Warnecke) 1995

The shopkeepers on Brookside Parade had been used to life's little hiccups – like the occasional armed robbery or explosion – but even they were ill-prepared for the sudden appearance on the scene of eligible Asian businessman Dil Parmar. Announcing that the absent *Barry Grant*, whom he had met a number of times on business in the Midlands, had put him in charge of his various business interests, the quietly-spoken Dil (short for Dilip) proceeded to make all of the staff at La Luz redundant before re-appointing them on lower wages. Dil was not going to win any popularity contests. Indeed the only person who seemed to have any time for him was *Susannah Farnham*. They became firm friends, much to the concern of ex-husband Max who was worried about losing children Matthew and Emily if Susannah went abroad to live with Dil. The opportunity never arose because the man of mystery disappeared as suddenly as he had arrived following the return of *Terry Sullivan* who revealed that it was now his turn to be placed in charge of Barry's businesses. The first thing Terry did was to put up all the rents. Nothing much had changed.

Alan Partridge (Dicken Ashworth) 1983–84

Alan Partridge (aha!) was the computer buff to end all computer buffs. A megabore about his megabytes, the portly Partridge could rattle on for hours about hard drives and floppy disks. His problem was finding anyone prepared to listen. Fittingly, he worked as a freelance computer programmer, and with such distinction that he had been advised to spend some of his earnings before the taxman got his grasping little hands on them. So he moved out of his mother's house and into 6 Brookside Close, bringing with him the sort of junk which once graced the Steptoes' yard: old engine parts, bigger chests than you get on *Gladiators*, plus a stack of computer software and even a boat. He stored most of this under an ungainly tarpaulin at the side of the bungalow although he later redeemed himself by constructing a suitably eccentric Japanese garden. Alan didn't believe in doing things by half. In addition to being one of life's great enthusiasts – about rugby as well as computers – he was also an eternal optimist and was convinced that his beautiful girlfriend Sam would one day agree to marry him. He proposed on a regular basis until he finally wore down her resistance. He was over at least three moons but his joy was to prove short-lived when Sam hurried out of the registry office, saying she couldn't go through with the wedding. In despair, Alan turned to drink and an old girlfriend, Liz. But she landed him with a charge of plagiarism and, at his lowest ebb, he lurched out onto the Close one night, rolling around and screaming alcohol-fuelled abuse at the neighbours. It was like an advert for Save the Whale, sponsored by Johnnie Walker. Alan continued to pine for his mate until he heard that Sam was working at the International Garden Festival. Without further ado, he cornered her and begged for another chance. Although he again slurred his words so much he was barely comprehensible, she felt sorry for him and agreed to become Mrs Partridge. They married in July 1984 and immediately left together for Kuwait where Alan had been offered an exciting new job in computers. Well, it was exciting to him …

Molly Partridge (Hilda Braid) 1984

With son Alan about to marry Sam (first time around), his overbearing mother Molly moved into the bungalow to supervise last-minute preparations. So that Molly wouldn't

Fran Pearson (Julie Peasgood) and baby Stephen

Samantha Partridge (Dinah May)
1983–84

One of the great mysteries of life is what blonde, leggy ex-model Sam saw in roly-poly computer nerd Alan. The truth of the matter was, she was fed up with those shallow wine-bar gigolos with their flash cars and predictable chat-up lines so she thought she'd go for someone who was kind, sincere and went to the same tailor as Patrick Moore. Sam was working as a systems demonstrator when she met Alan at a computer fair (where else?). He wanted to get married virtually straight away but she was in no hurry. However, to keep him sweet, she agreed to move in with him and, in doing so, created a thousand teenage fantasies in the minds of *Damon Grant* and his pals, most of them unprintable in a family publication. Finally she agreed to marry him but, on the build-up to the wedding day, she received a succession of phone calls from her agent offering her the glamorous job of a lifetime in Los Angeles. She said no, on the grounds that she was getting married, but the calls set her thinking. Was marriage to Alan what she really wanted at this stage of her life? She came up with the answer at the registry office, and ran out in the middle of the vows. Later she explained that she still loved him, but just couldn't marry him at the moment. She knew how much she had hurt Alan and started missing him more than she ever thought possible, so when he tracked her down to the garden festival, she agreed to try again. This time she didn't feel she was being pressurised into marriage and the whole thing went smoothly. And the beautiful princess and the tub of lard lived happily ever after.

Fran Pearson (Julie Peasgood)
1991–93

Vivacious blonde divorcee Fran Pearson followed a well-worn path around Liverpool by falling for *Barry Grant*. But she went

know they had been living together, Alan got Sam to pack her things and move back into her flat until after the big day. Molly arrived in a sports car like a whirlwind and immediately set about feeding what she saw as her under-nourished baby. The term 'mollycoddling' could have been invented for her. So after her big baby's heart was broken by the wicked Samantha, Molly let her have it with both barrels when she tried to call round and explain. Molly continued to wrap Alan in cotton wool, even refusing to allow him to go out and drown his sorrows with *Barry Grant* and *Terry Sullivan*. 'Mother knows best' was her motto and when Alan dared to disagree he was forced to apologise. So his relief was tangible when she announced that she was returning home.

further than most by getting pregnant by him. Fran worked at the same solicitors' office as *Sue Sullivan* and it was through Sue that she met Barry. She could see straight away that Barry fancied Sue but when Sue made it clear that the feeling was not mutual, Fran stepped in. As a single girl with no ties, Fran enjoyed a full social life and kept on urging Sue to get out more. Not surprisingly, Sue found the prospect of going for a drink after work with Fran more appealing than going home to husband Terry. Although it was Fran who found the incriminating family photo of Sue with Terry and son Danny cut out in *Graeme Curtis*'s desk, she never believed that he was responsible for Sue's death. She sensed that lover-boy Barry was involved and relations between the two soured further when she caught him flirting with hairdresser *Angela Lambert*. To get her own back, Fran told Terry that Barry had slept with Sue, although Barry subsequently forced her to issue a retraction. Pregnant and petrified, Fran hid away in Birkenhead but kept in touch with Terry. When Barry kidnapped baby Stephen, she decided she needed to go even farther afield than the Wirral and, with Terry's help, mother and son fled for Greece. But she'll always be looking over her shoulder in case Barry tries to reclaim his son.

Peter Phelan (Samuel Kane) and Lindsey Corkhill (Claire Sweeney)

Fee Phelan (Jackie Downey) 1996

Big-hearted Fee Phelan suffered one of life's great indignities – to be rejected by *Sinbad*. The sister of hairdresser *Peter Phelan*, Fee was given the opportunity to start up a beauty salon above Jacqui D's Style House. Sizing up the available men from her lofty vantage point, she plumped for Sinbad, little knowing that he was seeing another woman – *Val Walker*. All that summer Fee fattened him up with romantic picnics, run off with games of tennis. Sinbad couldn't bring himself to tell her about Val because not only was he genuinely fond of Fee but

also she would probably have put him in a half-nelson. Eventually, after a nice holiday away together, she misinterpreted his intentions and came to the conclusion that they were engaged … minutes after he had also accepted Val's proposal of marriage. Forced to choose, Sinbad picked Val. Fee was heartbroken and too embarrassed to hang around. So the signs went up at the salon: 'No Fee'. It did wonders for trade.

Peter Phelan (Samuel Kane) 1995–

Jacqui Dixon returned from one of her exotic holidays with a new business partner – hair stylist Peter Phelan. With his sunny disposition and tremendous vitality, he was an instant hit with every woman from *Bev McLoughlin* to *Julia Brogan*, and because he seemed camper than a row of tents, nobody saw him as a threat. He certainly injected some life into the salon, beginning with the hiring of Julia, the only person who could out-gossip him … although Jacqui was none too thrilled with the appointment. He promised to consult her in future. His extrovert personality particularly appealed to Bev, who was beginning to notice the age difference between her and Ron. Like Bev, Peter wanted to go to nightclubs; Ron was more at home in a Darby and Joan club. Peter liked Bev a lot and wanted to be more than just mates, but, much as she was tempted, she loved Ron and made sure Peter knew exactly how far he could go. As far as the ever-suspicious Ron was concerned, anywhere Peter went wouldn't be far enough away. Following Bev's spectacular exit, Peter teamed up with *Lindsey Corkhill*. Again they started out as friends, but this time there were no obstacles in the way – at least, not at first. Peter helped Lindsey with her singing career, dreaming of the day when he would see a photo in the papers of her with her idol, and beneath it the caption 'Cher and Cher alike'. But just when things were going well, the eternal bad penny, *Barry Grant*, turned up and swept Lindsey off her feet. The engagement was called off and Peter's plans for the future were wrecked. All he was left with was a wave of sympathy. He returned from a trip abroad with a new girlfriend, Helen, but deep down he still loved Lindsey. It took Kylie's brush with death to bring them closer again.

Gina Philips (Gill Brassington) 1991

When *Chrissy Rogers* was going through something of a mid-life crisis, she turned for support to her old student friend Gina Philips, or Gina Brookes as she had been at university. In a bid to get husband Frank out more, Chrissy suggested a foursome with Gina and her husband Nigel. They met for dinner at a smart restaurant – a marked departure for Frank who had never before ventured beyond a Happy Eater. During the evening, as they reminisced about old student days, Chrissy realised just how boring her life had become. What made it more marked was that back in the old days Gina had always been the boring one. Frank felt totally left out of the conversation, but at least had the decency to pay the bill. Gina and Chrissy went on another girls' night out where Chrissy told her about the near-miss with *Joe O'Rourke* and how she was worried about daughter Sammy making the same mistakes she had. Gina was a good listener – one thing Frank had never been accused of – but the nights out stopped when Frank began kicking up a fuss, telling Chrissy that she should be looking to her daughter's future, not her own past. Having made his point, he sifted through his collection of old Scotty Dogs' memorabilia …

Emma Piper (Paula Bell) 1994–95

Short of a caterer for his housewarming, *Barry Grant* was relieved when Legion compère *Ray Piper* offered the services of Emma, his daughter from his first marriage. Emma had been forced by her father to do ballroom dancing as a child and had won medals for it. She then sampled hairdressing but couldn't find enough work and so took up catering as a nice little earner. She proved extremely capable and efficient but when Barry insisted on giving her a hard time, she upped and left. *Penny Crosbie* was impressed, however, and offered her a waitressing job at Grants. Barry began to see Emma's single-mindedness as a challenge and asked her out. The two were hardly compatible. She was a virgin who didn't believe in sex before marriage and who also abhorred violence, having once been out with a fist-happy bouncer. Sex and violence were Barry's two main hobbies. Yet, against all the odds, Emma and Barry became unofficially engaged and she moved in with him … in separate bedrooms, of

Jacqui Dixon (Alexandra Fletcher) and Leanne Powell (Vickie Gates)

course. Then Barry disappeared off the face of the earth amidst rumours that he was in financial trouble and Emma, tired of waiting for him to return, packed her bags and left. She was way too good for him anyway.

Ray Piper (Duggie Brown) 1994

To *Ron Dixon*, Emma's father Ray was public enemy number one. First he had the temerity to challenge – and defeat – Ron for the coveted position of compère at the Legion, and then he turned his smooth line in patter towards Ron's partner, *Bev McLoughlin*. As Bev responded to his flattery, Ray scored more brownie points by telling her what a great voice she had. Ron just thought she had a voice which grates. And when Ray fixed it for her to win a talent contest at the Legion, he hoped she would show her gratitude in the time-honoured showbiz fashion. So, telling her she should get herself an agent, he offered to take some professional photos of her. She turned up at

the studio in her talent night gear but Ray wanted to take topless shots. When he made a pass at her, she slapped him across the face and marched out. It came as a bitter blow to learn that he hadn't wanted her for her singing voice after all.

Mark Potter (Paul Crosby) 1991

Rod Corkhill's colleague Mark Potter liked being a police officer because it gave him a feeling of power. Rod's sister Tracy certainly fell under his spell and soon the two were going out together. But Mark's sinister side began to show through. First, he was unnecessarily cruel to Rod's fiancée Diana and then Rod found him using excessive force on a lad he caught trying to steal his car. The jealous *Barry Grant* also took an instant dislike to the cocksure young copper and deliberately scratched his key along the side of Mark's precious car. Mark threatened revenge and started harassing Barry, stopping his vehicle whenever the opportunity arose. The result was an unseemly brawl with Tracy throwing them both out of the house. The next time Mark called round, he tried to rape her. She fought him off and Rod strongly advised him to get out of the force. He took the hint and obtained a transfer.

Leanne Powell (Vickie Gates) 1992–97

Teenage temptress Leanne Powell lived in a fantasy world. She fantasised that *Owen Daniels* fancied her and invented a story that they had slept together. In truth, he wouldn't have touched her with the proverbial barge-pole. Indeed she boasted to schoolfriend *Katie Rogers* that she'd been with lots of boys, whereas the reality of the matter was that she was still a virgin. When she did seduce a lad – a casual ex-boyfriend of *Jacqui Dixon*'s named Paul – she fell pregnant and spun a tale to *DD Dixon* that her parents were so awful that she would kill herself if they ever found out. DD arranged an abortion, only to discover afterwards that Leanne's parents weren't two-headed monsters at all. Leanne didn't learn from her mistakes and moved into prostitution, using Bar Brookie as her base. There she propositioned *David Crosbie*, so business was obviously slack. When Jacqui discovered what she was up to on her premises, she threw her out but, as a parting gesture, Leanne squirted a corrosive liquid in Jacqui's eyes. Despite looking a picture of innocence in court and pleading remorse, Leanne was sentenced to three years in prison. Jacqui reckoned she should have got twice that. Having pinched Jacqui's fella and nearly blinded her, it is doubtful whether Leanne will be celebrating her eventual release in Bar Brookie.

Emma Reid (Tricia Penrose) 1988–89

Worn down by the perpetual nagging of girlfriend *Kirsty Brown*, *Rod Corkhill* was flattered when, at his mate Tommo's party, sexy WPC Emma Reid asked him to accompany her to the bedroom. When Kirsty later saw the scratch marks on his back, he had to come up with a convincing alibi. Emma remained ready and willing, eagerly waiting for her chance, and the opportunity arose on Rod's 21st birthday trip to Blackpool. Kirsty cried off through work so Rod invited Emma to take her place. But then Kirsty turned up unexpectedly and, seeing Rod and Emma in each other's arms, laid into them. Rod was devastated but recovered his composure some weeks later to ask Emma out. To his surprise, she turned him down, saying she was fed up with his part-time interest in her. Exit Emma.

Madge Richmond (Shirley Stelfox) 1986–87

Missing his late wife Edna, *Harry Cross* decided to advertise for a lady companion in the local freesheet. Along with a few cranks, a promising reply came from a refined lady from Birkenhead. Her name was Madge Richmond. With Harry's friend *Ralph Hardwick* tagging along to lend moral support, Harry arranged to meet Madge at the Walker Art Gallery. Panicking because there was no sign of Madge, Harry approached the wrong woman, who assured him she did not come to an art gallery to be touched up. Meanwhile Ralph had made contact with the real Madge and the two were getting on famously. Harry quickly found himself out in the cold as Ralph put on his best Wirral accent to woo the seemingly charming Madge. Together with *Julia Brogan*, they made a foursome for a trip to Torquay and, on a clifftop stroll, Madge reminisced about her GI sweetheart Tony Cagliorani. Ralph lapped it up, but Harry had his suspicions, particularly when Madge appeared to have two birthdays. She shrugged it off as a misunderstanding and whisked Ralph away to Spain where, due to a mix-up over travellers' cheques, she had no money and was thus unable to pay for anything. Ralph did put his hand in his pocket, however, to buy Madge an expensive engagement ring. When Julia told Harry she spotted Madge with another man outside the art gallery, Harry was more convinced than ever that Madge was taking Ralph for a ride. Donning heavy disguise, Harry arranged to meet Madge at the gallery and, true to form, she turned up in the hope of adding another to her collection of suitors. Harry exposed her as a gold-digger and Madge was forced to admit that she was six-timing Ralph. Obliged to come clean and call off the engagement, Madge, brazen to the last, spun Ralph a yarn about still grieving over her late husband and Tony Cagliorani. Ralph blamed Harry until Julia put him in the picture about the art gallery fake. Only then did Ralph realise that he'd been framed.

Liam Riley (Adam Sunderland) 1990

Lonely teenager Liam Riley developed what turned out to be a fatal crush on *Tracy Corkhill*. As a customer at the hair salon, Liam was impressed by her friendliness and decided to reward her accordingly. Usually the only tip Tracy got was: learn some manners. He bought her flowers and gave her a holiday photo of himself, much to the annoyance of the brooding *Barry Grant*. At first, Tracy was flattered but, as Liam continued to pester her and started declaring his love for her, she grew more alarmed. And when he presented her with an engraved bracelet and tried to kiss her, Barry threw him out. Tracy wanted to let Liam down gently but reckoned the only way to put him off was to tell him the truth – that she was pregnant. Liam didn't take the news too well and jumped to his death.

Shelley Rimmer (Lesley Nicol)
1986–87

Salon owner Shelley Rimmer was given the thankless task of trying to educate YTS employee *Tracy Corkhill* in the art of hairdressing. It would have been easier teaching *Sinbad* ballet. From the outset, Shelley attempted to show Tracy that there was more to the job than just cutting hair – it was a question of making the customer feel good. But Tracy was to customer relations what Julie Andrews is to rugby league, and she soon succeeded in antagonising virtually everyone who came under her dryer. Despite Tracy's attitude and skiving, the patient Shelley persisted with her for four months before finally sacking her for being rude to one customer too many.

Penny Riozzi (Linda Rooke) 1988

Of *Barry Grant's* countless sexual assignations, the one with glamorous Penny Riozzi was potentially the most hazardous. It was instigated by the crooked *Sizzler* who wanted to get his hands on a chain of betting shops owned by Penny's husband Franco. To achieve this, Sizzler gave Barry the keys to a hotel room and told him to get to work on Penny. Very much the archetypal rogue's wife, with plenty of time and money and an unquenchable sexual thirst, Penny was an easier pushover than The Swan's pile of pennies. But she and Barry had a nasty shock when Sizzler walked into the room brandishing a tape of their romp and blackmailed her into letting him have the unofficial accounts from the betting shops. Terrified of what her volatile husband might do if he found out about her and Barry, Penny had no choice but to meet Sizzler's demands. Sizzler duly told Franco that if he didn't sell up, he'd reveal the fiddles that were going on to the tax inspector. So Sizzler got what he wanted and Barry, who had developed a soft spot for Penny, managed to acquire the incriminating tape, thus sparing Penny's blushes, not to mention her features. Nevertheless, for Penny it had been an expensive evening.

Chrissy Rogers (Eithne Brown)

Kathy Roach (Noreen Kershaw) 1988–90

Anyone whose idea of an exciting secret lover was *Jimmy Corkhill* was perilously close to certifiable. So downtrodden Kathy Roach, who already had a husband of her own, must have been a glutton for punishment to allow Jimmy to make her his mistress. The attraction for Jimmy was obvious: Kathy worked at a local bookie's. And whilst his irresponsibility drove her to distraction, she couldn't help laughing at some of his antics. And laughter, as Jimmy knew only too well, is a powerful aphrodisiac. It was a stormy relationship, punctuated by rows, fist-fights and walk-outs. Kathy's husband Dave had already thrown her out (hardly surprising since she decided to tell him about Jimmy) and she faced the additional dilemma of knowing that if Jackie gave him another chance, Jimmy would have gone running back to his wife. When *Doreen Corkhill* moved out, Kathy came to stay at No. 10 and persuaded Billy to put up her best friend, *Sheila Grant*. Kathy turned a blind eye to Jimmy's petty thieving but when he became involved in the violent feud with *Joey Godden*, she had seen enough and walked out for good. She thought she deserved better. She was probably right.

Sean Roach (Derek Hicks) 1989–90

Kathy's strapping son Sean was a dangerous customer. He put his physical strength to use as a soldier in Ulster before deserting from the army. On the run, he turned up at the Close and attacked *Sheila Grant*. Even Sheila's son Barry was wary of him. Kathy, who had earlier been left battered and bruised by Sean, was frightened what he might do next but couldn't bring herself to turn in her own son. However, Sheila made her realise that she had no option and that it would be for Sean's own good to be caught before he got into even bigger trouble. So, with great reluctance, Kathy shopped him.

Adrian Roache (John Basham) 1993–94

Nicknamed 'Cock' by his colleagues (on account of his locust-like behaviour rather than his sexual prowess), low-life tabloid journalist Adrian Roache was the man who brought the newly-widowed Penny Crosbie face-to-face with her dead MP husband's favourite call-girl. After months of patient probing, he finally persuaded Penny to grant him an interview. She was reasonably pleased with it and granted him a second audience, only to find that the follow-up article revealed all about Clive's long-term mistress, Sandra Pennington, and ten-year-old love-child Lawrence. Penny felt obliged to appear on breakfast television to put the record straight.

Chrissy Rogers (Eithne Browne)
1987–93

Chrissy Rogers' life was a catalogue of unfulfilled dreams. As a young student, her head was full of ideas about how she was going to make the world a better place. She wanted to be a teacher, to spread knowledge, to communicate. It was what she did best. Then she met Frank. He came from a poorer, working-class family but he had the gift of being able to make her laugh. Against all the odds, she fell in love and then fell pregnant. Almost overnight, her dreams were washed away in sea of nappies as she devoted all her energies to baby Sammy. Two more children, Geoff and Katie, followed and by the time Chrissy came up for breath, her life was half-over. But Chrissy wouldn't take it lying down and, mustering that old fighting spirit, she battled for Frank to be given an office job, for Geoff to be diagnosed as dyslexic and given a proper education, and for Sammy to have treatment for alcoholism. In each case, Frank thought she was making a lot of fuss about nothing; his apathy was one of the many things which were forcing them apart. By now, she and Frank were rapidly falling out of love. They had precious little in common and she began to think about what might have been if she hadn't made a mistake so young in life. The chance discovery of an old photo featuring her student friend *Gina Philips* prompted a reunion and more reminiscing. When Frank overheard Chrissy expressing her regrets at not having pursued a teaching career, he accused her of being selfish. Slap in the middle of a mid-life crisis, Chrissy nearly embarked on an affair with understanding doctor *Joe O'Rourke*, but her abstinence was merely delaying the inevitable. She and Frank could hardly agree on anything. She despised the way he had

allowed himself to get into a rut and told him it was time he came out of the Stone Age. As the argument escalated, she blurted out something about Dr O'Rourke. She assured Frank that she hadn't slept with the doctor but Frank didn't want to know and threw her out. She and Katie stayed with Gina for a few days but Katie was desperately unhappy and, against her better judgement, Chrissy agreed to go back to Frank. A month later, she learned that Sammy was pregnant and was planning to get married as soon as possible. Seeing history repeating itself, Chrissy warned Sammy not to throw her life away. Frank, on the other hand, was all in favour of Owen making an honest woman of his daughter. The wedding went ahead but Chrissy couldn't take any more and quietly left home during the reception. She suspected that Frank wouldn't even notice she'd gone until he wondered where his breakfast was. Making up for lost time, she attended teacher-training college and then, after Frank's death, returned to challenge his widow Lyn over the children's rights to the house – a fighter to the last. She is currently living in Japan.

Frank Rogers (Peter Christian)
1987–93

Frank Rogers struggled to come to terms with the requirements for a modern husband. Frank believed that women should be seen and not heard and was quite happy for them to be chained to the kitchen sink, as long as they could also reach the oven. But although he was a dinosaur, he was a dedicated family man who genuinely did his best for his children. Frank's own childhood was marred by the fate of his father, tortured to death by the Japanese during the war. To compensate for his own lack of parental guidance, Frank became a strict disciplinarian with his own children. Chrissy favoured a more understanding approach. The result was conflict. Seeing Frank in middle age, it was hard to imagine him as a player – albeit a bit-part one – in the Sixties' Merseyside scene. His band, The Scotty Dogs, might not have been snapped up by Brian Epstein but 'Nobody Butters he Toast Like You' became a cult classic in the pubs and clubs of Liverpool. Fame was such that Frank's name was known as far afield as St Helens. Throughout the rest of his life, Frank loved to hark back to the Sixties. He drove an immaculately-preserved maroon Cortina and cherished a guitar strap given to him by Billy J. Kramer. He was less proud of a conviction for actual bodily harm. Frank continued to solve arguments by force, rarely bothering to think things through. Indeed the only time he used his head was to butt someone. He was happy with his job as a long-distance lorry-driver (he had also worked 'on the lump' in the Sixties) but Chrissy was adamant that he should better himself with a desk job. Frank just wanted a quiet life. It was the same with the kids: whilst ruling their social lives with a rod of iron, he wasn't bothered about what they achieved academically. He reasoned that he'd never had much of an education and he hadn't done badly, although quite how Katie would have coped as a lorry-driver remains a mystery. But Chrissy always demanded more – in his view, unreasonably. The parting of the ways was inevitable. After Chrissy's departure, Frank was lucky enough to pick up a new bride, Lyn. But his luck ran out on his wedding day at the hands of *Jimmy Corkhill*.

Geoff Rogers (Kevin Carson/ Stephen Walters) 1987–93

Known to his friends as 'Growler', Geoff was the apple of Frank's eye. Not that he didn't love Sammy and Katie too, but he'd always wanted a son, someone through whom he could realise his own sporting dreams. Heaven help Geoff if he'd wanted to be a dancer! Consequently, Frank wasn't particularly bothered that Geoff was

diagnosed as dyslexic; his sole concern was that Chrissy's campaign was singling the boy out for unwanted attention at school. For, although he could be cheeky, Geoff was basically a sensitive lad who just wanted to blend in with the crowd. His talent was football and Frank encouraged him all the way. Both were delighted when he was accepted by Tranmere Rovers, although the appearance of football groupies on the Close proved a huge embarrassment to Geoff, all the more so when it turned out to be a case of mistaken identity. There was further grief when Frank learned that Geoff was being picked on by a bigger boy at the club. Frank demanded that the coach take action. When it suited him, Frank could be just as interfering as Chrissy. But Geoff's world fell apart when Tranmere showed him the door. In despair, he walked out of his school exams, but cheered up on landing a YTS placement at Torquay United. However, just before Frank's wedding to Lyn, Geoff came home, saying that the team didn't have a game. He was sullen and evasive and eventually admitted that he had walked out of the club because he wasn't even good enough to get into Torquay United Reserves. Scarred by rejection, Geoff was going downhill fast and angered sister Katie by selling Frank's records and clothes after his death because he needed the money. Chrissy had always wanted him to get an education because she knew how precarious a footballing career could be. Frank had had no such reservations. Now with nothing to fall back on, Geoff was left to ponder which parent he should have listened to.

Katie Rogers (Debbie Reynolds/ Diane Burke) 1987–

Waif-like Katie, the youngest of the Rogers clan, has always been a serious-minded girl. Psychiatrists could probably trace her sadness back to the time she was chosen to play a sheaf of corn and not the Virgin Mary in the school nativity play. A quiet, unassuming child, she always had a strong sense of morality and once boycotted a firework display on ecological grounds. She may have been a friend of the earth but even that forgot her birthday. Indeed, until the arrival of *Jacqui Dixon* she had few close companions and cut a lonely figure at school. She was bullied by the snarling *Bagga* and when she tried to impress her science teacher Mr Molyneaux, on whom she had a crush, she fell into a polluted river and was rushed to hospital suffering from a form of toxaemia. If nothing else, it made sure that he noticed her. Things were no better at home, where she had to listen to her parents arguing night after night – except when they were cowering from her dreadful trumpet-playing. She didn't so much hit notes as bludgeon them. Then, when Chrissy moved out and Frank was killed, poor Katie was left with nobody. At her most vulnerable, she was easy prey for bible-basher *Simon Howe*. She took to wearing sensible shoes and cardigans as she fell under his spell. By the time she came to her senses, she had lost her virginity and very nearly her marbles. Dancing should have been her salvation, but her self-worth was so low that she became bulimic. Sharing with Jacqui and *Rachel Jordache* brought Katie out of her shell a little and she landed a steady job as secretary to solicitor *Eleanor Kitson*. She's still not exactly the life and soul of the party but she is just about the most sensible person around. And after everything she's been through, that's no mean achievement.

Lyn Rogers (née Matthews)
(Sharon Power) 1992–94

Lyn, her brother Nick and younger sister *Bev McLoughlin* were shattered by the death of their father when they were all still children. When their mum Betty later acquired a boyfriend, Bev in particular resented the intruder. Lyn was more tolerant, but then

Lyn Rogers (Sharon Power)

she soon left home to embark on a career as a professional dancer, in the course of which she met and married musician *Steve Matthews*. The birth of children Alison and Gavin forced her to curtail her hoofing trips abroad and she finished up with the less glamorous job of doctor's receptionist. Her marriage hit the rocks after Steve slept with Bev, and that blow was followed by Nick's death in a lorry crash. He had been doing a favour for workmate *Frank Rogers* who, racked with guilt, felt that it should have been him. The nation agreed. United by grief, Frank and Lyn became an item and then, in the autumn of 1993, Frank suffered a minor heart attack at the wheel. As Lyn nursed him back to health, he realised how

Greg Salter (Paul Barber), Rosie Banks (Susan Twist) and Marianne Dwyer (Jodie Hanson)

important she was to him and proposed. The wedding day was spoilt somewhat by the death of the groom, for which Lyn was pilloried by Frank's family. She further antagonised them by stating that she fully intended staying on in the house. As Frank's possessions were carved up, Lyn was involved in an unseemly struggle with *Sammy Daniels* over Frank's prized guitar. Lyn tumbled down the stairs and lost the baby she was carrying – Frank's baby. Sammy backed off and Lyn decided to sell the house.

Sammy Rogers – see Sammy Daniels

Dick Ronson (Bill Cookson) 1997

Dick Ronson was *Ron Dixon*'s mysterious double – a man who behaved like Ron, owned a Moby just like Ron and had a full head of hair like Ron. The only difference was that Dick's was a wig. When the two men's paths crossed for the first time, they realised that they had been operating on the same patch. Both accused the other of muscling in on their territory. Dick's tyres were let down and sugar was put in his tank, but he had the last laugh by stealing Ron's Moby and having it reduced to a chunk of scrap metal. Even Quasimodo didn't stoop that low.

Keith Rooney (Kirk Smith) 1991–93

A schoolmate of *Mike Dixon*'s, Keith came on to the scene as drummer in Mike's band. A polite, friendly lad with artistic talents (it was he who did the artwork outside the pizza parlour), he nevertheless incurred the displeasure of *Ron Dixon* for dating his daughter Jacqui. Keith's crime was to be black, and Ron's objections enabled Jacqui to see her father in a new light. Keith was always on the lookout for a girlfriend but, with Mike as his partner on the prowl, his chances were strictly limited. He did hit the bullseye with *Margaret Clemence* but that was just a one-night stand designed by her to spite *Beth Jordache*, and shortly afterwards Keith left Liverpool to work in Turkey.

Carol Salter (Angela Walsh) 1993–94

It was quite appropriate that Carol Salter used to work in a chip shop because the biggest chip of all was on her shoulder. Admittedly, she'd had a tough life. She had son Garry when she was 16 and, in the absence of her wayward husband Greg, who did a runner when the boy was still a toddler, raised him single-handedly for 13 years. She fought for Garry all the way, taking on his teachers, the police, and anyone who had the effrontery to put him down. But she was so inarticulate and pushy that her ceaseless complaining rarely had the desired effect. When Garry started disrupting *Mick Johnson*'s football sessions, Carol bullied Mick into giving her son a chance. For once, she found a sympathetic ear, but then mistook Mick's concern for something more romantic and, after talking her way into a job at the pizza parlour, set about replacing *Marianne Dwyer* in his life. She won over Leo and Gemma but Mick proved a tougher nut to crack and, when he realised what she was up to, put her straight. It obviously came as a nasty shock, for almost immediately Carol was confined to a hospital bed.

Garry Salter (Stephen Dwyer) 1993–95

Written off academically even though he was quite bright, Garry concentrated his energies on boxing instead. He was a big lad for his age, and his size, coupled with his vociferous mother Carol and his ever-present ghettoblaster, tended to land him in trouble. As a result, Garry developed an attitude problem and it was only when *Mick Johnson* took him under his wing that the more caring side to his personality emerged. He soon began to see Mick as his second father, but the peace was shattered by the return of his first one. When Garry found out that Greg had framed Mick for the armed robbery at Litrotech, his loyalties were sorely divided. In the end, he realised how much he owed Mick and persuaded Greg to confess. But, just as things were looking up for Garry, fate dealt him a cruel blow on his first day at work at the leisure centre where he fell into the pool, the first victim of the killer virus.

Greg Salter (Paul Barber) 1994

Garry's dad Greg had done more porridge than the Three Bears, and no sooner had he arrived in Manor Park than he was looking for a job to pull. He settled upon a wages delivery to Litrotech, in the process incriminating poor old *Mick Johnson*, the man who had been decent enough to give employment to an ex-con. Greg seemed perfectly happy to let Mick take the rap until Garry began exerting emotional pressure, and for the first time in his life, Greg did the decent thing and told the police the truth. Garry was almost proud of him.

Richard de Saville (Robert Dallas) 1985

In search of a career where he could pull a better class of woman, bricklayer Albert Duff decided to reinvent himself as dancing instructor Richard de Saville. Among his pupils was *Michelle Jones*, who was soon taken in by his sequins and flattery. It was only a matter of time before she was tangoed. But when her boyfriend, *Terry Sullivan*, caught them in bed he went berserk, forcing Richard to glide through the front door and out of the Close.

Greg Shadwick (Mark Moraghan) 1998–

After working for Cammell-Laird, Greg Shadwick decided to join the great flood of the self-employed and, together with son Jason, started up Shadwick and Son – Builders. Soon the jobs were piling in and they even got round to finishing some of them. When *David Crosbie* announced that he was selling the bungalow, Greg, who had earlier done an estimate for him on a conversion, wasted no time in putting in an offer. Unfortunately, moving-in day coincided with *Ron Dixon*'s attempts to fit his own gas cooker.

Jason Shadwick (Vincent Price) 1998–

The 'son' of Shadwick and Son, 20-year-old Jason added another to his collection of fans

Georgia Simpson (Helen Grace)

Bel Simpson (Lesley Nightingale)
1996–97

Bel Simpson managed to get up more noses than a Vick inhaler. Her kids were tired of her, her husband was certainly fed up with her and, by the time she left the Close, few of the neighbours were too sorry to see her go. She was forever moaning about her lot in life even though she alone was responsible for the family's reduced circumstances. For the Simpsons had lived in a smart house in Formby, with a lifestyle to match, until Bel got the sack from her well-paid job for jumping into bed with a younger colleague. With no references to land a new job, she became a neurotic wreck who couldn't get through the day without taking tranquillisers. It didn't take much to start her off again so the news of her children's incest sent her into orbit. Predictably, she tried to put the blame on husband Ollie, as good as accusing him of sexually abusing daughter Georgia as a child. That marked the end of their marriage but, for good measure, Bel took another toyboy, this time *Mike Dixon*. But she got more than she bargained for, in the form of a sexually-transmitted disease. When she then had a final fling with Ollie, he was soon itching to get away. She was prepared to fight all the way for custody of younger son Danny, but he was so appalled by her sleeping with Mike that he preferred to stay with his dad. She moved back to Formby where she found a flat and a new man, Patrick.

Danny Simpson (Andrew Butler)
1996–

Young Danny Simpson is wise beyond his years, but that's hardly surprising given the amount of growing-up he's had to do. Coming from a family background which redefined the term 'dysfunctional', Danny has had to cope with warring parents, sex-charged siblings and the delights of Brookside Comprehensive where his posh

when he bravely helped stem the flow of water to facilitate the rescue of little Kylie Stanlow from the Parade gas blast. A hard-working lad, he nevertheless envisages a more glamorous occupation than being a builder all his life. But he got a nasty shock when girlfriend Katrina told him she was pregnant.

Margi Shadwick (Bernadette Foley)
1998–

A mother of three – Jason, Nicky and Emily – Margi works in a food-processing factory and is a strong trade unionist. She is not afraid to speak her mind and incurred the wrath of Emily by coldly depositing the collar of dog Candy (killed in the explosion) in the bin. Emily may have thought Candy deserved a better send-off but Margi is not one to wallow in sentimentality.

accent stands out like Brian Sewell at a dockers' meeting. He has coped admirably with all the slings and arrows of outrageous misfortune, apart from briefly being led astray by *Tinhead O'Leary*. Even then, he was a reluctant participant in Tinhead's orgy of crime. Computer buff Danny is a brainy kid and relished the challenge of forging *Jimmy Corkhill*'s educational qualifications as a stepping stone to the latter's unlikely teaching career.

Georgia Simpson (Helen Grace) 1996–97

When the Simpsons' daughter Georgia arrived on the Close having split from her husband Martin, all of the family were delighted to see her ... except the one person who mattered – brother Nat. You could cut the atmosphere between the pair with a knife, to the puzzlement of Bel and Ollie who thought their two eldest were indulging in some silly squabble. They urged Nat and Georgia to kiss and make up, little realising that they'd been doing plenty of kissing over the past few years. Like Nat, Georgia knew that the relationship was wrong, but was powerless to do anything about it. No matter how hard they both tried, they couldn't keep away from each other. Nat may have been about to marry Jules, but Georgia knew that it was her that he really wanted. When the news finally got out about their incestuous affair, she decided to let the whole neighbourhood in on the secret with a drunken tirade on the Close. Still, it was nice to see her letting her hair down for a change. Worse was to come when she became pregnant and had a secret abortion. She started to drift away from Nat and, with no shortage of admirers, turned to *Peter Phelan* for support. But she knew she was only kidding herself and Nat's fits of jealousy showed her that he felt the same way too. Eventually she got a new design job in another part of the country with a cottage thrown in – the ideal place for her and Nat, where nobody would know about their past

and where even the vengeful *JC Bradley* wouldn't be able to find them. As they passed themselves off to their new neighbours as husband and wife, they seemed the perfect young couple.

Jules Simpson (née Bradley) (Sarah Withe) 1996

If ever a woman drove a man to sleep with his sister, it was gormless Jules. Beloved daughter of *JC Bradley*, she somehow succeeded in hooking *Nat Simpson*, only to drive him to distraction with her incessant whining. There must have been times when Nat wanted to crown Jules. Left to pick up the pieces of her life after being abandoned by her new husband on her wedding night, she scuttled around in ever decreasing circles trying to get to the root of the problem. Against all reason, she still loved Nat and would have given him another chance, but the hammer blow came when she found out that he was in love with Georgia. When she confronted them on bonfire night, sparks flew and, in despair, Jules rang the Samaritans. However she slammed the phone down and attempted suicide by taking an overdose. Her cry for help was heeded by her father, who encouraged her to grab her pound of flesh by reporting Nat and Georgia to the police. On learning that they weren't going to be charged, she threatened to expose them until Ollie pointed out that she would be caught up in the attendant publicity. Although she tended to come across as pathetic rather than sympathetic, Jules did have her good points: she was loyal, she was kind to her parents and she left the area quickly.

Nat Simpson (John Sandford) 1996–97

It could be argued that architecture student Nat got off lightly for having designs on sister Georgia. He escaped prosecution and, better still, he escaped a lifetime of misery from being married to Jules. Where

Georgia was concerned, Nat was rarely in control of his emotions. His heart ruled his head. He kept trying to back off, but to no avail. The lure was too strong. He hated what the incestuous affair was doing to them both and he also hated what he was doing to Jules. Sex between Nat and his fiancée had never been that great since he had moved into 9 Brookside Close. And Georgia's presence simply made things worse. But, in spite of everything, he still cared deeply about Jules and genuinely didn't want to hurt her. He couldn't bear the thought of her finding out why he had really walked out on her and so played along with the idea that he was gay. But Jules knew he wasn't – too much had passed between them. If he had ever thought things might be easier if they were out in the open, he was sorely mistaken, as condemnation not witnessed since Maradona's 'Hand of God' goal descended upon his shoulders. He just about rode the storm and became friendly with *Rachel Jordache*, who had had problems of her own. But his heart wasn't in it and, after everything they had been through together, Nat couldn't bear to be separated from Georgia. And so they left to start a new secret life. But he will always be wondering whether the next knock on their door is the man from the *News of the World*.

Ollie Simpson (Michael J. Jackson) 1996–

Ollie Simpson used to infuriate his wife Bel. For while she would be ranting and raving, flinging her arms in the air like a windmill in a tornado, he would remain calm and rational, almost to the point of being comatose. Laid-back and liberal, Ollie believed in giving his kids plenty of rope, little suspecting that the two eldest would use it to hang themselves. In the Sixties, he helped set up a small publishing company and now runs an independent bookshop in

the city even though he rarely seems to venture into work. Very much a middle-class trendy, he favours a pasta diet which he eats only with his fork . All knives have obviously been banished from the house for fear of a repeat of the unfortunate incident next door with *Trevor Jordache*. Ollie believes in good living, but his legendary patience was tested when he learned about Nat and Georgia. Strangely, it was Bel who was better able to accept the relationship. Ollie couldn't handle it at all and, despite repeated requests from them for a reconciliation, wanted nothing more to do with either Nat or Georgia. He didn't want much more to do with Bel either. Furious about her wrongful accusations that he may have abused Georgia in the past, his decision to split was confirmed by her infamous liaison with *Mike Dixon*. As the grasping Bel started to lay claim to at least half of everything, Ollie petulantly began sawing the dining-room table in two. Dignity was at a premium. Having got rid of Bel, he replaced her with solicitor *Eleanor Kitson* who immediately had her hair dyed so that she looked a dead ringer for Georgia. Ollie found it deeply disconcerting. Between serious discussions about the meaning of life, Ollie and Eleanor enjoyed great sex, but it soon emerged that, like him, she had more skeletons than the Royal Liverpool Hospital. What Ollie really needs is a woman to put a smile on his face. There's always *Julia Brogan* …

Sinbad (Michael Starke) 1984–

When *Ruth Sweeney* was 17, she fell pregnant on a day-trip to Blackpool. She only knew the lad as 'Figgy' and never saw him again. Her God-fearing parents were horrified and packed her off to stay with relatives, where the baby was passed off as a late child of her mother's before being put into a children's home. The baby's name was Thomas Henry Edward Sweeney, but years later, when he was cleaning windows on Brookside Close, everyone knew him as

Sinbad (Michael Starke) and Marcia Barrett (Cheryl Maiker)

Sinbad. This was because he treated a window as if it were the circular porthole of a ship: he cleaned the centre bit but left the corners dirty. In spite of his deprived childhood, Sinbad always had a smile on his face in those days and was invariably up to some scam, whether it involved unplaced racing bets, dirtying windows or live turkeys. His best mate was *Jimmy Corkhill*, which explains a lot. Sinbad had never enjoyed much luck with women and it was no different with *Caroline Choi*. Two things

came between them: his stomach and her unpleasant boyfriend, *James Markham*. Then he moved on to *Marcia Barrett*. While he was hunting out his birth certificate prior to obtaining a passport for a holiday in Spain, Marcia sneaked a look at it, since they had only ever known him as Sinbad. When she saw his real name, she wanted to know about his family background and encouraged him to track down his long-lost mother. Sinbad wasn't too keen, but Marcia was like a dog with a bone. If it was a shock finding his mother after all those years, it was also a shock losing Marcia to whom he had got engaged. But suddenly, with a middle-age confidence to match his middle-age spread, Sinbad was proving irresistible to the opposite sex. His next port of call was *Mandy Jordache*, for whom he perfected the art of building a patio. Her husband Trevor helped with the foundations. When Mandy became pregnant by Sinbad, it seemed as if he had finally found the stable family life which he had been craving, but Mandy decided that her heart lay with battered women and took baby Ruth to live in Bristol. Sinbad was left alone again … naturally. He didn't let the grass grow under his feet for long, however. He started keeping in shape and swiftly found himself engaged to two women – *Val Walker* and *Fee Phelan*. In the end, he ditched Fee and things just fizzled out with Val. Having abandoned his window-cleaning round due to a bad back, he opened up a 'white goods' shop on the Parade. His chief tormentor there was the delinquent *Tinhead O'Leary* so, ever the glutton for punishment, Sinbad set up home with Tinhead's mum, Carmel. Sinbad is a lot more serious these days, but after taking on the O'Learys and seeing his world – well, his shop – come crashing down around his head, that's hardly surprising. It's enough to make him yearn for the times when he was up a ladder in freezing weather cleaning *Sheila Grant*'s windows.

Sinnott (Neil Anthony) 1990–91

As a teenager, *Mike Dixon* was always fiercely protective of sister Jacqui, so when he found her sick and frightened in her bedroom following a party, he wanted to catch the culprit. It turned out to be a fellow sixth-former, Sinnott, who had spiked her drink and Mike took his revenge in a flurry of fists, for which he was suspended. Sinnott fought back by causing Mike and

Jacqui to be arrested in possession of drugs, and the feud escalated to dangerous levels when Mike spiked Sinnott's cola, as a result of which he hurled himself through a window. Sinnott survived, and then accepted Mike's challenge to a car race for a £100 bet. This time, Mike ended up in hospital and he and Sinnott called it quits. But Sinnott had one last trick up his sleeve. His girlfriend Tina was the singer with Mike's band and, for their debut gig, Sinnott doped Tina up to such an extent that she was out of her head on stage and began stripping off. Whilst the audience enjoyed the impromptu show, Mike felt it did little for his musical credibility.

Sizzler (Renny Krupinski) 1987–88

Between them, *Tommy McArdle* and Sizzler had Liverpool's underworld sewn up. Tommy, with his air of calculated menace, made people an offer they couldn't refuse. Hollow-cheeked Sizzler looked like a skeleton in a suit and that's how anyone who seriously crossed him would end up. It wasn't so much what he said as what he didn't say. *Barry Grant* got into his bad books after bedding a girl named Ursula. It was only when Sizzler returned unexpectedly that Barry realised she was Sizzler's girlfriend. Barry escaped in Sizzler's bathrobe, which Sizzler called round to reclaim the following day. Fortunately for Barry, Sizzler was in a forgiving mood, provided Barry did him a small favour in return. *Sinbad* had inadvertently stolen a car being used by Sizzler as a getaway vehicle on a job and, with it, some valuable miniature paintings which he had then sent to an autumn fayre. Barry and Sinbad managed to retrieve the miniatures and return them to Sizzler, but by then they were too hot to handle. Sizzler was impressed by Barry's ingenuity and continued to employ him from time to time – first on the *Penny Riozzi* case and then to buy out Ma Johnston. When Barry drew the line at killing her dog and delivering its head to her, he knew he owed Sizzler another favour. Luckily, a judge reckoned Sizzler owed Her Majesty 10 years.

Diana Spence – see Diana Corkhill

Freddie Spence (Peter Corey) 1991

Diana's beefy father had not been a great fan of the boys in blue – ever since his wife ran off with one when Diana was four. So when Diana broke it to him that her fiancé, *Rod Corkhill*, was a policeman, his reaction was decidedly frosty. He snapped that, unless she finished with Rod, she was no daughter of his. Diana tried to convince him that not all policemen were the same but, just as he appeared to be wavering, he was introduced to Rod's mate *Neil 'Tommo' Thompson* and suddenly realised he was surrounded by coppers! Eventually, Rod won Freddie round and he was the proudest man in church on their wedding day. Unfortunately Rod was otherwise detained in the toilets at Lime Street station. Freddie might have known what would come of marrying a copper.

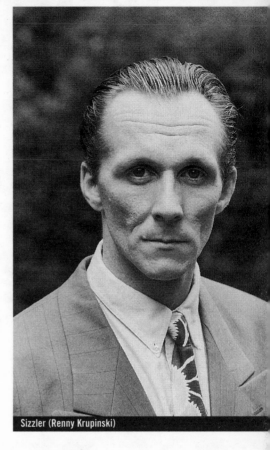

Sizzler (Renny Krupinski)

Gary Stanlow (Andrew Fillis) 1995

The phrase 'baby-faced assassin' could have been invented for Gary Stanlow. On the face of it, he looked perfectly innocent, almost cherubic, but this masked his true colours: for when pushed, he could be aggressive to the point of violence. The only thing Lindsey and Gary had to show for four years of marriage was daughter Kylie. Gary was a waste of space, bone idle, never able to hold down a job for more than five minutes. Finally Lindsey decided she'd had enough, left him and went back to live with Jimmy and Jackie. Gary followed her, begging to be given a fresh chance, promising her that he was a reformed character. Jimmy had no time for Gary – he reminded him too much of how he had been at that age – but agreed to give the errant son-in-law a job at his

latest business enterprise, Korky Kars. When Gary realised it was a front for drug-dealing, he wanted in on the action. But Gary didn't have even Jimmy's brains and contrived to mess up big time. He was hopelessly out of his depth. He knew that he'd blown it with Lindsey but couldn't stomach seeing her and Kylie head off to Australia for a new life with *Mike Dixon*, so he slipped some smack in Kylie's teddy and waited for customs to do their worst. Unfortunately, he had calculated without the plane stopping over at Bangkok where the penalties for drug trafficking are just about the most severe in the world. Any remorse he might have shown quickly evaporated: he agreed to help secure Mike's release only on condition that Lindsey and Kylie came back to live with him. Gary wanted to play happy

Jack Sullivan (William Maxwell) and Julia Brogan (Gladys Ambrose

families, but Lindsey didn't want him near her. Night after night, she made excuses as to why she couldn't have sex with him until, frustrated and angry, he raped her. When Jackie found out, she had a quiet word with drug baron Big Davey (whom Gary had crossed) and Gary suddenly ceased to be a problem ... or so it seemed.

Lindsey Stanlow – see Lindsey Corkhill

Mike Stevens (Saul Jephcott) 1987

Kiln builder Mike Stevens lodged briefly at No. 7 with work colleague Mick. Whereas Mick was scruffy, kept an annoying parrot and burnt the toast, Mike was a clean-cut smoothie. But given that the only woman he fancied on the Close was *Doreen Corkhill*,

he shouldn't have been allowed near anything sharp, let alone a trowel. A mean card player, Mike's appeal to *Terry Sullivan* and *Pat Hancock* waned when landlord *Harry Cross* realised they were hiding a joker in the pack, and the two builders moved out shortly afterwards.

Jack Sullivan (William Maxwell) 1984–97

For years, Jack Sullivan never bothered much with son Terry. Between various money-making schemes, most of which bordered on legality, trips to the bookies and supping pints at The Swan, he would occasionally pop round to see how his offspring was doing, but usually only because he wanted something. Then, at the end of 1996, he suddenly turned up again after a body had been unearthed beneath La Luz. Jack's worst fears were realised when it turned out to be that of Henry Fraser, a man Jack had killed in an argument some 30 years earlier. He wormed his way out of that one but didn't find it as easy to hide his wife, Mary. Her very existence came as something of a surprise to Terry since Jack had told him she had died years ago. These developments naturally put a bit of a strain on Jack's engagement to *Julia Brogan*, but she nobly stood by him and was prepared to go through with the wedding as long as Jack went to the police about Henry Fraser. This was all too much for Jack and he vanished into thin air with Julia's savings.

Sue Sullivan (née Harper) (Annie Miles) 1987–91

A deceiver, liar, manipulator and two-timer, she was also utterly selfish. If anyone on the Close deserved to leave a head imprint on the new concrete outside Brookside Parade, it was her. She was working as secretary to *Jonathan Gordon-Davies* at his legal firm when she started dating *Terry Sullivan*. Her black moods soon surfaced when Terry made a fuss of the Canadian girls he and Jonathan had met in Austria, but she temporarily overcame her jealousy to lure Terry towards matrimony. Finding she was pregnant by former boyfriend *Martin Howes*, she instead passed the baby off as Terry's because she needed a father for the child. Once they had married and she had given birth to Danny, the cold, calculating Sue thought about easing what little guilt she was experiencing by planning a second baby, this time with Terry. Unable to conceive, she became depressed and when Terry took a sperm test, he discovered that he couldn't father children. Terry wasn't the brightest but it didn't take Einstein to work out that he wasn't Danny's dad. Following a series of blazing rows, the Sullivans were reconciled in the wake of the sudden death of Sue's mother. Terry gave her another chance and went into hospital for an operation, at the end of which he was declared fertile. At last, Terry could become a real father, but Sue was concerned only with her own feelings. Back working at the legal firm, she enjoyed her new-found social life with colleague *Fran Pearson* and calmly informed Terry that she had decided not to have another baby just yet. Terry went ballistic and smashed all the plates. *Barry Grant* called round and thought it was Greek night. Sue had always despised Barry but the moment he turned on the charm, she was stripped and ready for action. It was the final kick in the teeth for Terry, though she would probably have delivered more had she not wandered round to meet *Graeme Curtis* on the Parade that fateful morning …

Terry Sullivan (Brian Regan) 1982–97

Terry Sullivan was the chameleon of Brookside Close. Over the years, he changed from Mr Dependable who just wanted to settle down, to Mr Nasty who wanted to fight the world, to Mr Zombie,

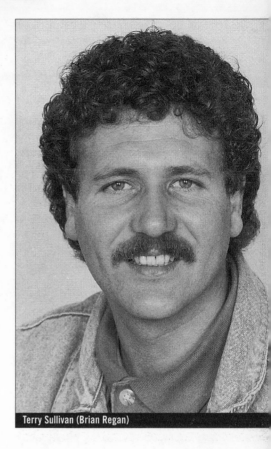

Terry Sullivan (Brian Regan)

dutiful disciple to *Simon Howe*, and finally to Mr Businessman, the budding entrepreneur. Terry used to live on the same council estate as his mate *Barry Grant* and when the Grants moved to the Close, Terry popped round from time to time. Barry's mum, Sheila, almost treated him like another son. Girls liked Terry. He may not have carried Barry's air of danger, but he was kind-hearted and reliable. However he did possess a temper, as witnessed when he butchered the mattress at No. 10 on which his girlfriend *Michelle Jones* had slept with her dance teacher, *Richard de Saville*. Terry would have plenty of opportunity to lose his rag in years to come. He moved into No. 7 with *Pat Hancock* and began dating *Vicki Cleary*. That too was doomed to failure. His next move took him back across the Close to No. 9 as lodger with the newly-widowed

Jonathan Gordon-Davies. It was through Jonathan that he met *Sue Harper*, the woman who was to cause him so much grief. The one positive aspect to Terry's tempestuous marriage to Sue was that he finally saw his old mate Ba' in his true light. Not one to condemn a man without a fair trial, Terry nevertheless concluded that anybody who was prepared to sleep with his best friend's wife, kill his best friend's wife and kill his best friend's son wasn't really much of a mate at all. With the money from the sale of the house, Terry bought the pizza parlour, but was too drunk to notice. When he got bored with that, he took over the petrol station where a shot of Redex became his favourite tipple. An increasingly sad and lonely figure, he wanted to enter into a marriage of convenience with *Anna Wolska* until good old Barry sent her fleeing from the country. This setback plunged Terry into an even deeper depression. He grew a bushy beard and found God, a remarkable achievement for someone who had hitherto struggled to find the Parade. Following the death of his guru, Simon, Terry took to wandering aimlessly around the kitchen at Grants, looking very much like the Chef's Surprise. But a recuperative spell away did wonders for his sanity and he reappeared, without beard, to announce that he had taken over Barry's business interests. Suddenly he was in charge of La Luz and behaving as if he knew what he was talking about. However, just when his life seemed a little more settled, he discovered that his dad was a killer and that his dead mum was still alive. The news threatened to tip Terry over the edge again and he walked out on La Luz to re-invent himself once more.

Don Summerhill (Jonathon Barlow) 1985

Following the acrimonious split from husband Roger, *Heather Haversham* cheered herself up going out to buy a new car, and bumped into an old flame, used-car salesman Don Summerhill. Like many dodgy car dealers, Don was keen to turn back the clock, but just as Heather was about to fall for his sales patter, the doorbell rang to halt their progress to the bedroom. It was his wife. Don had forgotten to mention that he was still married. Heather had no time to protest her innocence as Mrs S. laid into her, branding her a marriage-wrecker. As Don was frog-marched home, Heather resolved never to trust a second-hand car dealer again, even if she did admire his bodywork.

Ruth Sweeney (Mary Healey) 1992–94

Deciding to trace his long-lost mother, *Sinbad* located a certain Ruth Sweeney in Runcorn but, on visiting the woman, he and girlfriend *Marcia Barrett* found her abrupt and evasive. However, Marcia tried again – this time alone – and the woman admitted that she was Ruth Sweeney, but that she was Sinbad's sister. It was only after another visit that Ruth finally confessed that she was Sinbad's mother and poured out the sad tale of how she had been forced to put him in a children's home. As a parting gesture, she presented him with his baby wristband. Now that Sinbad had met his mum, he didn't want to lose touch and the softly-spoken librarian came to stay at No. 10 with Sinbad and the Jordaches. However, she always felt she was in the way and when the chance came to move to Australia to join her brother Jake, she seized it. But she had one last present for her son. She sold her house for £45,000 and gave the entire proceeds to Sinbad. It was by way of an apology.

Jenny Swift (Kate Beckett) 1995

Jenny Swift was everybody's favourite teacher. She taught English and history at Brookside Comprehensive where she was popular with pupils, fellow members of staff and parents. She was pretty, friendly and had tremendous enthusiasm for her chosen subjects, coupled with a genuine care for pupils of all abilities. *Leo Johnson* could certainly never be described as 'teacher's pet', but even he liked Miss Swift. The feeling was mutual, so that when Leo, still traumatised by the death of his friend *Garry Salter*, became afraid of swimming, Jenny offered to help him overcome his fear. For his part, Leo's dad Mick was delighted that his teacher was taking such an interest. What Mick didn't quite grasp at the time was that Jenny was seriously unbalanced. She quickly became obsessed with Mick and started asking him out for a drink. He politely declined, but she used her feminine wiles to lure him back to her flat. When he came out of the loo, she was standing there stark naked except for his jacket wrapped around her shoulders. Mick had never experienced this with any of the other teachers at the school – not even the headmaster, *Mr Thornton*. Jenny continued to press for extra-curricular activities and, despite receiving no encouragement whatsoever, was soon telling *Rosie Banks* that she and Mick were engaged. She even laid on a secret party. Mick went spare. Seeing her shrine to him in her bedroom, he realised he was dealing with a stalker, but whenever he confronted her, she simply apologised sweetly or fainted or pretended she was suffering from a terminal illness. She came up with more stories than *Jackanory*. After falling down the stairs, she agreed to attend counselling sessions. Ever the gentleman, Mick offered to take her, but just when he thought he was finally free from her mad clutches, she spotted him kissing *Bev McLoughlin*'s friend Janice and held him hostage at gunpoint. In the wake of the Gunfight in the Flat above the Pizza Parlour, Jenny got three years in prison. As she was taken down, she screamed at Mick that she'd get even with him. He knows she means it.

John Swift (John Line) 1995

Respectable solicitor's clerk John Swift was a keen target shooter and unwittingly provided the pistol with which Jenny menaced Mick and shot PC Coban in the arm. John Swift could not comprehend daughter Jenny's behaviour. It seemed so out of character. Therefore he was convinced that everything that had happened was Mick's fault and told the court that Mick had ruined her life. His antagonism towards Mick was reinforced by the severity of Jenny's sentence.

Gavin Taylor (Daniel Webb) 1982–83

Gavin Taylor was Brookside Close's answer to Del Trotter. His business was wheeling and dealing, ducking and diving, anything to make a dishonest bob. The original wide boy (although not quite as wide as *Bobby Grant*), Gavin had set his heart on making his fortune from gas cookers, and so when he and wife Petra moved into No. 10, a mountain of 13 greasy cookers preceded them, dumped in the garden. Style and Gavin were rarely mentioned in the same breath. True, he drove a brand new silver BMW but rather spoiled the illusion with windscreen stickers bearing the names 'Gav' and 'Pet'. Next-door neighbour *Roger Huntington* boiled over about the cookers and was livid when burglars stripped the Close of virtually everything ... except Gavin's ovens. Realising there was no reasoning with Gavin, Roger fired off a letter to the City Planning Officer and Gavin was given a week to get rid of his cherished goods. His retaliation was to erect a multi-coloured shed made from old doors. Gavin also had other things on his mind since Petra was desperate for a baby and he was seemingly unable to oblige. He resented the fact that Petra was casting aspersions on his manhood – or lack of it – and their marriage became increasingly turbulent. Then one day, Petra went upstairs and found Gavin dead in bed. At only 26, he had suffered a brain haemorrhage. Shortly afterwards, Petra learned that she was pregnant. Gavin was a man after all.

Petra Taylor (Alexandra Pigg) 1982–83

Sulky Petra Taylor was not exactly enamoured with life on Brookside Close – and most of her misery stemmed from husband Gavin. A typist at an insurance office, she disapproved of his chosen career, but was even more frustrated by his apparent inability to give her the baby she so desperately wanted. And then he had the nerve to die on her! Her subsequent pregnancy made Gavin's loss all the more poignant and she began to realise how much she had loved him. She was already friendly with *Barry Grant*, who shared similar philosophies to Gavin and who had carried out some building work at No. 10, and now, with Gavin conveniently out of the way, Barry set about stepping into his shoes. He took the young widow off to the Isle of Man for the TT races, but on the boat trip back Petra felt unwell and miscarried. Barry didn't even bother visiting her in hospital. Against the advice of her elder sister, *Marie Jackson*, Petra continued seeing Barry but their arguments became more prolonged until they merged into an ongoing hostility. It was just like being married to Gavin again. When Barry stormed off the Close after one particularly unpleasant fracas, it reminded her of her final row with Gavin. No matter how hard she tried, she couldn't get Gavin out of her mind and one day, while out looking at new cars, she saw a man standing next to a BMW. Convinced it was Gavin, she rushed over to him, only to run off in tears when she realised her mistake. Things got worse. When an innocuous stranger chatted her up in a pub she fled hysterically, while a trip to the supermarket ended with the manageress comforting her and arranging for her to be taken home. Barry opted for the quiet life in London and, unable to take any more, Petra packed her bags and moved out, leaving no clue as to her destination. Five months later, she was found dead in a Llandudno guest house, having committed suicide.

Carol Thompson (Gerldine Griffiths) 1985–86

Starting up her own catering business from home, *Annabelle Collins* decided to hire a cleaner. She chose Carol Thompson, a no-nonsense woman who had seen it all before. At least that's what she thought until *Paul Collins*, unaware of the existence of a new employee, stepped out of the shower wrapped only in a towel and walked straight into Carol, who was cleaning his bedroom. For once, Paul reasoned that a handshake was not an appropriate means of introduction. Carol soon made herself at home and impressed Annabelle with the way she dealt with *Sinbad*, who had been helping himself to stuff from the freezer in the garage. In return for not reporting him, Carol made him clean their windows for nothing. However, when Carol discovered that the Collins' son Gordon was gay, her prejudices surfaced. Fearing that she would catch AIDS from cleaning their toilet, she quit and Paul felt obliged to defend his son in the face of her narrow-mindedness.

Neil 'Tommo' Thompson (John O'Gorman) 1988–92

The best mate and police colleague of *Rod Corkhill*, Tommo used to rib him mercilessly about how girlfriend *Kirsty Brown* had got him under her thumb. Yet ironically when Rod and Kirsty split up, Tommo started dating her. Rod and Tommo looked out for each other but Rod foolishly chose to disregard Tommo's warning about getting involved with rent boy Craig. Tommo knew it would lead to trouble – and he was right. Earlier, Tommo had been sent to break the news to *Sheila Corkhill* that son Damon had been killed.

George Webb (Kenneth Macdonald) and Ron Dixon (Vince Earl)

Mr Thornton (Graham Seed) 1995–96

The ineffectual headmaster of Brookside Comprehensive favoured the ostrich approach. Whenever a complaint was made, he would bury his head in the sand and insist that nothing untoward ever went on at his school. As far as he was concerned, Brookside Comprehensive had no bullying, no under-age drinking and no truancy. It was left to *Mick Johnson* to enlighten Thornton by introducing him to *Tinhead O'Leary*. Mind you, in view of the fact that Thornton's predecessor thought *Jenny Swift* was perfectly normal, Thornton was only following in an ignoble tradition.

Sarah Townes (Julianne White) 1989–90

Overlooked for a partnership at the legal firm, Sarah Townes suggested to colleague *Jonathan Gordon-Davies* that they set up in independent practice. They started seeking new clients, but events overtook them when Simon Jackson offered Jonathan a large account on condition that he and Sarah left

immediately. But the new business got off to a shaky start when the account turned out to be a dud. As a result, Sarah was forced to seek legal aid work, something which did not go down well with Jonathan, who wanted them to pursue commercial law. Despite the attempts of their secretary Coral to do a spot of matchmaking, Sarah and Jonathan kept their relationship purely on a business footing. Sarah managed to escape the confines of the office when she clinched a trip to the Virgin Islands with a wealthy client, Guy MacLeish, head of the MacLeish Jersey Corporation. She never returned. Even by lawyers' standards, it was a long lunch.

Val Walker (Pauline Fleming) 1996

Jackie Corkhill's sister Val must have been a desperate woman. Not only did she have sex with *Jimmy Corkhill* in days gone by (a scene witnessed by his son, Little Jimmy) but she later rejected *Mick Johnson* in favour of *Sinbad*. She was heavily into body-building at the time but must surely have realised that Wimpey's had already done a pretty good job building Sinbad's body. Her romantic inclinations may have lain with Sinbad, but she introduced Mick to weight-training and steroids, although she counselled against their use. By then, Mick was too hooked on competition to listen. Whatever her faults, Val was certainly a cut above her secret love rival, *Fee Phelan*, but when she finally got Sinbad to herself the relationship seemed to die – this despite the fact that she did a meals-on-wheels round, something which proved an instant attraction to her new fiancé. Without the thrill of the chase, Sinbad lost interest. She would have found it easier to fix a date with Leonardo DiCaprio than to fix a date for her wedding with Sinbad and, just before Christmas, they decided to go their separate ways. It had been fun while it lasted.

George Webb (Kenneth Macdonald)
1992

Racist George Webb took over as manager of the petrol station opposite Brookside Parade and immediately began a vicious vendetta against the Johnson brothers. First, it was stickers, insults and graffiti but when these failed to have the desired effect, Webb reported them as illegal immigrants. *Mick Johnson* had always preached caution but hot-headed brother Ellis was all for running Webb over. Sadly his brakes were too efficient. But when Webb's war escalated into petrol bombing, *Max Farnham* and *Barry Grant* realised they had a duty to look after the Parade. A quick word with Webb's bosses and the nasty piece of work was booted out of the garage and Manor Park.

Charles Weekes (Tony Armatrading)
1993

Charles Weekes was so oily he was a danger to sea birds. He had the nickname '9^1/$_2$' but only in his dreams. As *Marianne Dwyer*'s boss, he started sexually harassing her and, when she made it clear that she wasn't interested and threatened to report him, he alarmed her boyfriend Mick by telling him that they were having an affair. Charles was so smug, so confident that Mick didn't know who to believe. Charles began to make Marianne's life hell and never missed an opportunity to undermine Mick, constantly chipping away at him, preying on his doubts. When Mick finally accepted Marianne's word, he decided to wipe the smile off Charles's face by knocking him to the ground. It had the opposite effect. The devious Charles announced that he was bringing a private prosecution for assault against Mick unless Marianne dropped her sexual harassment charge. With Mick's track record, it was a threat to be taken seriously. Marianne backed down but exacted sweet revenge by secretly taping Charles's sexual comments and playing them back at an important presentation. Charles didn't wait to be fired.

Nikki White (Michelle Byatt) 1988–92

Nikki was *Tracy Corkhill*'s colleague at the hair salon and a firm friendship was cemented when she agreed to give evidence against her boss Gerrard who was sexually harassing Tracy. The girls went on holiday together to Rhodes and embarked on the statutory holiday romances, Nikki with Sam, Tracy with Aki. Back in Liverpool, Nikki and Tracy both agreed that it was the best holiday they'd ever had. When Tracy worked her way up to salon manageress, she gave Nikki a job, but reluctantly had to sack her because of her attitude. Something about people in glass houses springs to mind ... But Nikki wasn't bothered – she soon got a job with the Giro – and the two remained friends. Indeed Nikki even moved into No. 10 for a while, all the time dreaming of making it on to *Blind Date*.

George Williams (Doc O'Brien)
1983–86

Union convenor George Williams was a more frequent visitor to the Grant house than the milkman, sometimes to the consternation of *Sheila Grant* who repeatedly found her lounge being commandeered for union business. Impressed by *Bobby Grant*'s commitment in trying to save Fairbanks Engineering from closure, George urged him to stand for a full-time union post. Bobby took him up on the offer and was duly elected. George was very much a moderate and sometimes had to curb Bobby's more militant streak, but the two men were always working towards the same goal.

Ronnie Williams (Claire Robinson) 1989–91

A keen clubber, teenager Ronnie was a friend of *Sammy Rogers* and *Nisha Batra*. The three used to go off together in search of unsuspecting lads, but it all turned sour the night they bumped into Kav and Tony. Ronnie was particularly keen on Kav and was mortified by his death in a high-speed car crash. The subsequent inquest led to a falling-out between Ronnie and Sammy and it was another couple of years before they met up again. Ronnie was all for going bowling and having some fun, but Sammy was going out with *Tim Derby* at the time. And nightclubs weren't really Tim's scene – unless they served Horlicks.

Roy Williams (Adam Kotz) 1994

On 2 February 1994, *Mandy Jordache* received a visit from a stranger, Roy Williams. He said he was Trevor's prison visitor and expressed his shock at his friend's death, but, once inside, he admitted that he had been in jail with Trevor. Williams continued to hang around like a bad smell and demanded £500 which he claimed Trevor owed him. He took to squattting in the Harrisons' until he saw the opportunity to catch Mandy alone. Desperate to get rid of him, she gave him £500 from the *Tony Dixon* collection, but Williams wanted more and threatened to tell the world what Trevor

did to Beth. Mandy duly coughed up another £200. Realising he was on to a good thing, Williams materialised again in her kitchen two days later. He turned violent in his desire for money, but *Sinbad*'s arrival stopped him in his tracks. Making his escape, Williams knocked Sinbad unconscious, but the window-cleaner came round again – which was more than the ex-con did.

Guy Willis (Ian Michie) 1986

Starting her communications studies course at Liverpool University, *Karen Grant* was immediately impressed by a fellow student, middle-class Guy Willis. Guy was a cut above most of the lads Karen had hung around with and the two got on so well that it wasn't long before his thoughts began to turn to matters of the flesh. However, Karen was still a virgin and was afraid of sex. But Guy was patient and, after a couple of abortive attempts, he finally helped her overcome her inhibitions. Karen was mightily relieved. There was no holding the two young lovers now and they moved into a grubby flat together. Her parents, Sheila and Bobby, came on a tour of inspection and, although they weren't exactly impressed with the accommodation, they raised no objections. But there was no room for Karen to breathe in the flat. She needed a degree of freedom, and Guy was becoming increasingly possessive. In the end, she realised it wasn't working and left for London to further all aspects of her education. But she never forgot her first tutor.

Anna Wolska (Kazia Pelka) 1992–93

A native of Stupsk in Poland, Anna Wolska was a good Catholic girl who came to Britain to study English. However, she couldn't afford to stay at college so she got a job as a waitress before turning to nannying. It was in this capacity that she arrived on the Close, hired by *Max Farnham* as successor to the love-torn *Margaret*

Anna Wolska (Kazia Pelka)

British husband. She hoped Peter would oblige, but the first offer she got was from *Terry Sullivan.* This was a bit of a come-down for Anna. Despite her predicament, Anna retained her iron will. She came to her senses in time to reject Terry but promptly lost them again when she agreed to marry *Barry Grant* instead. Then she went off Barry, tried to renege on the deal to provide him with a baby, and decided it was Terry she wanted after all. But Barry wasn't going to play second fiddle to anyone – least of all Terry – and spiked the wedding plans by shopping her to the Immigration Department. She was forced to flee the country, but only after ascertaining that none of the customs officers wanted to marry her either.

Joey Woods (Chris Darwin) 1994

Joey Woods and *Eddie Banks* were the Little and Large of Litrotech. Joey was Eddie's best mate at work, but he was angry that shop steward Eddie didn't seem to be supporting the men in an unofficial strike. Joey organised a picket but management warned that unless the men were back at work by the end of the day, they'd be sacked. Eddie nervously passed on the news to Joey who reluctantly returned to work. Joey wasn't at all happy with Eddie's softly-softly approach and told him he didn't think he was doing his job properly. When Eddie challenged Joey to stand against him, Joey took him up on the offer and balloted the men. Eddie lost and trudged home defeated, angry that Joey had done the dirty on him. Joey quickly realised he had bitten off more than he could chew and the next day sheepishly asked Eddie for advice. But Eddie wanted nothing more to do with him. Joey was on his own.

Christian Wright (Philip Dowd) 1995–97

Three years ago, Christian Wright was a slim dancer, a member of the same troupe as

Clemence. She stepped straight into a political minefield since Max's wife Patricia knew nothing about her appointment and was keeping the vacancy open for Margaret. In the early weeks, Patricia was colder than Frosty the Snowman, but thawed slightly when it became apparent that Margaret wouldn't be returning to her job in the foreseeable future. Anna felt lonely on the Close until the arrival of *Peter Harrison.* Unfortunately it was at her party, while the Farnhams were away in Spain, that Peter was accused of raping *Diana Corkhill.* Anna took Peter's side, to the fury of Patricia, who did what she had wanted to do all along and sacked her. With no job, Anna found the going tough and drifted into escort work and prostitution. She confessed that she was an illegal immigrant and needed a

Katie Rogers. He was Katie's first real boyfriend, but after they slept together she became afraid that she might have given him AIDS, as a result of her ill-fated liaison with *Simon Howe*. Christian was none too pleased that Katie had failed to mention this before they climbed into the sack and the relationship came to an inevitable conclusion. After an absence, he returned on the scene as Mr Potato Head. He had given up dancing, which was hardly surprising as he now looked like the entire Young Generation rolled into one. He landed a sedentary job at Bar Brookie and set his sights on *Rachel Jordache*. He proved to be an evil manipulator and a control freak, a legacy of the fact that he came from a broken home after his father had walked out on Christian's overbearing mother Bunty. Under Christian's command, Rachel wasn't allowed to look at another man, let alone smile at one – a difficult job when you're serving behind a bar. He made the poor girl feel dirty and, as soon as they were married, set about prising her away from the bar to a safe job delivering newspapers. At least, it should have been safe, but Rachel was touched up at a bus stop. Christian blamed her for leading the man on. He steadily separated her from her friends and encouraged her to lead an existence which the average nun would have found restrictive. But she went along with everything he suggested because she loved him and trusted him. It was only when he started to get violent that she began to question his methods and locked him in the bathroom to die. She didn't quite go through with it, but it was enough to teach Christian a lesson he would never forget and to get him out of her life.

Dorothy Wright (Jacqueline Morgan) 1987–88

The mother of the tragic *Laura Gordon-Davies*, Dorothy Wright echoed husband Geoff's concerns about their new son-in-law. In their view, *Jonathan Gordon-Davies* wasn't grieving enough about their daughter. They even began to consider the awful possibility that he might somehow have been responsible for her fatal fall, little knowing, of course, that it had been Geoff's lack of DIY skills that had sent Laura plunging down the stairs. When Laura was finally declared brain dead, the Wrights initially resisted the idea of organ donation before coming round to Jonathan's way of thinking. But they remained suspicious, all the more so when Geoff discovered that Jonathan had a new woman living under his roof: *Cheryl Boyanowsky*.

Geoff Wright (Arthur Kelly) 1987–88

Geoff Wright was an irritant of the first order. In the build-up to his daughter Laura's wedding, he was forever popping round uninvited to do painting, decorating and fixing. He did more little jobs about the house than an incontinent terrier. He thought he was being helpful but Jonathan saw him as a complete pain. Yet for a perfectionist who prided himself on being right about absolutely everything, he was a lousy handyman, particularly when it came to electrical repairs. Distraught in the wake of Laura's death, he vented his anger on the unfortunate Jonathan whom he had never truly accepted into the fold. He kept making veiled threats about ordering a new inquest, hinting that Jonathan had something to hide. For his part, Jonathan continued to bite his lip, quite an achievement considering how low it usually drooped. If only Jonathan had told him exactly what he was hiding …

Laura Wright – see Laura Gordon-Davies

Rachel Wright – see Rachel Jordache

Michael Starke

Sinbad didn't look happy trapped beneath a mountain of fallen masonry, facing up to the possibility that he might lose his legs, but Michael Starke relieved the pain by cracking jokes with the design department. 'It was very uncomfortable stuck in that hole for three 12-hour days,' he says, 'eating dust and with bits falling on me. There was dummy concrete to restrict my movement so I felt really hemmed in. It was pretty harrowing stuff to do and quite a strain, so the only way to lighten things up was to have a laugh.'

As his fellow actors will testify, that is something Starke is very good at.

They try not to put Steven Pinder [Max Farnham]and me in scenes together now because we set each other off. It was the same with John McArdle [Billy Corkhill]. I remember a scene where I had to call at Billy's wearing a Father Christmas outfit. John and I just couldn't look at each other without creasing up. The moment they shouted 'Action!' and he saw that red sleeve with the white cuffs through the glass door, he was gone. It was only a 90-second scene, but two hours later we were no nearer getting it done. We were rolling around on the grass, screaming with laughter, totally helpless. By now the crew were getting fed up with us so when we took a tea-break, John and I sat down and said: 'Look, we're behaving like a couple of kids. We know the lines – we've got to get the scene done.' We went straight back on and were going great – no laughter – until a boom crept into shot and we had to start again from the top. That was it – we cracked up again. Our only chance had gone. In the end, they had to rewrite the scene so we weren't together!

I have a lot of fun on set. I've had some great scenes with Louis Emerick [Mick Johnson]and Dean Sullivan [Jimmy Corkhill], although Dean and I were a bit worried about the stuff where Little Jimmy's coffin went missing. We thought we might be pushing the boundaries of taste and we didn't want to offend anyone. After all, I live in Liverpool and I'm approachable – I take my kids to school and go shopping – so I don't want to upset people.

Sinbad always gets a good reaction from people and he's been a great character to play, building him up from virtually nothing. Originally, he was only in for a couple of episodes, and for the first four or five years he was just in and out. I think the scene of which I'm proudest was where Beth and I had to dig up Trevor's body to retrieve the ring. It was a night

313

shoot and the floor manager told me: 'You won't see the crew or the cameras.' It was a still, quiet night and, because it didn't feel like a set, it was very eerie. It seemed for real. We did it in one take and the tears I shed were genuine. I had some tearstick [the menthol-like substance they use for inducing tears] on my finger in case I couldn't cry, but I didn't need it. Then when they said 'Cut!' I forgot myself and wiped my eyes with my finger … and I ended up crying all night!

Where are they now?

Have you ever wondered what happened to some of the actors in Brookside? If so, read on ...

Dicken Ashworth (Alan Partridge)

The Yorkshire-born actor has enjoyed a fruitful career since leaving *Brookside*, appearing in TV productions such as *Scab, Making Out, Gentlemen and Players, The Bill, Inspector Morse* and *The Riff Raff Element*. He also returned to soap to play Blackpool resident Jeff Horton, maternal grandfather of Tommy Duckworth, in *Coronation Street*.

David Banks (Graeme Curtis)

A former cyberleader in *Doctor Who*, David Banks combines a three-way career as actor, writer and director. Since Graeme Curtis committed suicide, David has written a novel, *Iceberg*, appeared in the mini-series *A Time to Dance*, played Gavin in *EastEnders* and Max in the Live TV soap *Canary Wharf*.

Paul Barber (Greg Salter)

Following a lifetime of supporting roles, Paul Barber has suddenly become a household name as one of the stars of *The Full Monty*.

Robert Beck (Peter Harrison)

Voted Sexiest English Star by *Playgirl* readers in 1993 and Best Looking Man on Television by *TV Times* readers in 1994, Robert Beck has gone on to appear in *The Upper Hand, Thief Takers, Dangerfield, Princess in Love* and, in a role alarmingly similar to Peter Harrison, as a date rapist on *The Bill*. So perhaps Diana was right after all. He currently lives in the USA.

Eithne Browne (Chrissy Rogers)

After 'peeling a lot of potatoes as Chrissy', Eithne has been concentrating on stage work. She played Beverley in a tour of *Abigail's Party* and Rita in *Educating Rita*. 'I was 42 and playing a 26-year-old so it was a bit of a cheek. I didn't go down the front much!' She also appeared as a particularly unpleasant Fairy Godmother in panto with Norman Collier at Billingham. 'I think I was the first fairy to be booed ...' Eithne has also starred in stage productions of *Shirley Valentine* and *Billy Liar* and been a guest presenter on BBC Radio Merseyside.

Mark Burgess (Gordon Collins)

Mark Burgess has worked mainly in the theatre of late, including *Much Ado About Nothing, Wuthering Heights* and a tour of *The Glass Menagerie*. Other roles have been as diverse as a McDonald's commercial and playing Edgar in the film version of *King Lear*, directed by Brian Blessed.

Amanda Burton (Heather Huntington/Haversham/Black)

A real *Brookside* success story, Amanda Burton is one of the nation's most sought-after actresses. Her first major role after *Brookside* was as Margaret Daily in *Boon* and she followed that with parts in *Inspector Morse, Van Der Valk, Stay Lucky, Lovejoy* and *Minder* before nursing the population of Derbyshire as Dr. Beth Glover in *Peak Practice*. Since then, she has starred as pathologist Sam Ryan in the BBC series *Silent Witness*. Amanda says of Heather: 'I have very happy memories of my time on *Brookside*. It was very exciting being in right from the outset but I knew that once I'd made the decision to leave, I would never go back. It was like leaving school. I emptied my locker and drove off into the future with my car loaded with flowers. I never once looked back.'

Jennifer Calvert (Cheryl Boyanowsky)

Canadian actress Jennifer Calvert came to Britain in 1984 and since *Brookside* has appeared on TV in *Spotz*, *Come Home Charlie and Face Them* and *Westbeach*. Her stage roles include a national tour of *The Philanthropist*.

Katrin Cartlidge (Lucy Collins)

Katrin Cartlidge has enjoyed a blossoming film career since saying farewell to the rebellious Lucy Collins. In 1994, she was voted European Actress of the Year at the Geneva Film Festival for her role as Sophie in Mike Leigh's *Naked*. In 1997, she earned a Best Actress nomination from the London Film Critics Circle for *Breaking the Waves* and won the Best Actress prize at the Evening Standard Film Awards for her role as Hannah in another Mike Leigh production, *Career Girls*.

Carl Chase (Joey Godden)

Carl Chase played the Joker's goon in the Hollywood blockbuster *Batman*, an evil pirate in *Cut-Throat Island* starring Geena Davis and another baddie in *Aliens³*. His most recent film was *The Mummy* with John Hannah. TV credits include *BUGS* and the Channel Four comedy *Slap! Love, Lies and Lipstick* and he is also the new face of Smirnoff.

Peter Christian (Frank Rogers)

Peter Christian has been working mainly in the theatre since Frank's sad demise with roles at the Everyman Theatre, Liverpool, in *Can't Pay, Won't Pay* (adapted by Jimmy McGovern) and C*loud Nine*.

Jane Cunliffe (Laura Gordon-Davies)

Since her death in *Brookside,* Manchester-born Jane has worked on TV in *Hale and Pace, Hollywood Sports, Shoot to Kill, Boon, Trouble in Mind* and as the voice of Catherine Kovalic in 20 episodes of the French soap *Cheateauvallon*, dubbed specially for the UK.

Bill Dean (Harry Cross)

Bill Dean is now semi-retired after a long and distinguished career. Since *Brookside*, he has appeared in *The Young Indiana Jones Chronicles, Clarissa, Skallagrigg, Heartbeat, The Liver Birds* and as a personnel officer in the controversial TV film *Hillsborough*, thus reuniting him with Jimmy McGovern, the writer who penned so many of Harry Cross's finest scenes.

Ray Dunbobbin (Ralph Hardwick)

These days Ray Dunbobbin concentrates on writing rather than acting. He specialises in corporate videos (which he also edits and directs), his recent works including a history of the Boy Scout movement. He is also writing a novel.

David Easter (Pat Hancock)

David Easter is now a regular in the Channel 5 soap *Family Affairs* as the show's Mr Nasty, Pete Callan, a character who used to beat up his ex-wife Maria, played by another former *Brookside* star, Annie Miles.

Norman Eshley (Alun Jones)

Bristol-born Norman Eshley's post-*Brookside* TV credits include *The Ruth Rendell Mysteries, Achilles Heel, Taggart* and *Cadfael*. On stage he has appeared in *Lady Chatterley's Lover, Way Up Stream* and *The Exorcism*.

Kate Fitzgerald (Doreen Corkhill)

Kate Fitzgerald has recently been seen in

episodes of *Casualty*, *The Bill* and *Peak Practice*. She made a guest appearance on *The Lily Savage Show* and played Ma Cavannagh in Jimmy McGovern's drama serial *The Lakes*. She has also performed in two productions at the Everyman Theatre, Liverpool – playing Kath in *Scouse* and Norma Kelly in *The Knocky*.

Paula Frances (Diana Corkhill)

The reading tuition which Diana Corkhill received from Patricia Farnham obviously worked wonders because one of Paula Frances' first roles since departing from the Close was as an office secretary in a BBC educational film, *20 Steps to Better Management*. She has appeared in various other training films and played Sue on a national tour of the stage play *Rita, Sue and Bob Too*.

Anna Friel (Beth Jordache)

Since leaving Brookside, Anna Friel's career has gone from strength to strength. On television, she has starred in *Cadfael*, *Tales from the Crypt* and as Bella in the acclaimed BBC adaptation of Dickens' *Our Mutual Friend*. She has also made her mark in the film world with roles as Hermia in *A Midsummer Night's Dream* (alongside Michelle Pfeiffer, Kevin Kline and Rupert Everett) and as Lisa Leeson in *Rogue Trader*, the story of Nick Leeson and the Barings bank collapse.

Gabrielle Glaister (Patricia Farnham)

In the short time since saying goodbye to *Brookside*, Gabrielle Glaister has been extremely busy, playing a doctor in the BBC comedy *Get Well Soon*, appearing in two episodes of *The Heart Surgeon* with Nigel Havers and in *Gayle's World* with page three stunna Gayle Tuesday. She also found time to appear in two plays, *Dead Funny* (with which she went on tour) and *Elton John's Glasses*.

Sheila Grier (Sandra Maghie)

Since surviving the siege of Brookside Close,

Scottish actress Sheila Grier has appeared in *Taggart*, *Bookie*, *Emmerdale* (where she was the barrister defending Kate Hughes), *Heartbeat*, *Making Out* and *Invasion Earth*.

Gillian Hanna (Brenna Jordache)

In addition to numerous stage roles, Gillian Hanna has become something of a TV regular since incurring the nation's wrath as Brenna. Her post-*Brookside* credits include *Drop the Dead Donkey*, *Casualty*, *The Heart Surgeon* and *Dangerfield*.

Jodie Hanson (Marianne Dwyer)

Currently based in the United States, Jodie's post-*Brookside* credits include television appearances in *Do the Right Thing*, *Casualty* and *The Bill* plus stage roles in *Romeo and Juliet* (in Manchester) and *Baths* (at Bolton).

Jason Hope (Rod Corkhill)

Jason Hope has quit acting and was last known to be working in his family's hairdressing business.

Cliff Howells (George Jackson)

Cliff Howells' post-*Brookside* credits include *Emmerdale* (he played a plumber), *Sherlock Holmes: The Boscombe Valley Mystery*, *A Very British Coup*, *G.B.H.*, *Coronation Street* (as Terry Seymour) and the odious fire chief Scase in *London's Burning*.

Sue Johnston (Sheila Grant/Corkhill)

Sue Johnston has been one of the country's busiest TV actresses since leaving *Brookside*, appearing in such productions as *Medics*, *Goodbye Cruel World*, *Hetty Wainthropp Investigates*, *Inspector Morse*, *A Touch of Frost*, *Full Stretch*, *Luv*, *Duck Patrol* and as the older Pat Phoenix in *The Things You Do For Love*. She also starred in the film *Brassed Off!*

Gillian Kearney (Debbie McGrath)

Among Gillian Kearney's recent credits are Agnes in the West End production of *School For Wives*, directed by Sir Peter Hall and starring Eric Sykes and Peter Bowles, the film *The Ruby Ring* and, on television, *Heartbeat*, *Hetty Wainthropp Investigates* and *The Things We Do For Love*.

Anna Keaveney (Marie Jackson)

Runcorn-born Anna Keaveney has gone on to play Jeannette in the film *Shirley Valentine* and has appeared on TV in *Widows*, *Stay Lucky*, *Birds of a Feather*, *Emmerdale* (as April Brooks), *The New Statesman*, *Casualty*, *The Bill* and many others.

Roberta Kerr (Sally Haynes)

Roberta Kerr is one of those rare actresses who has enjoyed regular roles in three different soaps. After leaving *Brookside*, she went on to play Ken Barlow's lover, *Wendy Crozier*, in Coronation Street and when that affair fizzled out, she turned up as baby-snatcher Jan Glover in *Emmerdale*.

Justine Kerrigan (Tracy Corkhill)

Justine hasn't done much acting work since Brookside as she has been busy raising a family.

John McArdle (Billy Corkhill)

Like his Brookside spouse Sue Johnston, John McArdle has been much in demand since Billy moved to Basingstoke. His TV appearances have included roles in *Gallowglass*, *Spender*, *Prime Suspect V*, *Born to Run* and the BBC medical drama *Out of Hours*.

Danny McCall (Owen Daniels)

Since Owen stopped serving pizzas, Danny McCall has found a more lucrative career in musicals, playing Billy Fury in *The Sound of Fury* and Rory Storm in *The Need for Heroes*. He also enjoyed a hit single with 'Whose Heart Is It Anyway'. On TV, he has presented *Saturday Disney* and *Going Live* and appeared in *And the Beat Goes On* and *Cone Zone*.

Philip McGough (Charlie Dawson)

Philip McGough has made guest appearances in countless TV series, most recently in *Jonathan Creek* and as the judge at Ian and Cindy's custody hearing in *EastEnders*.

Irene Marot (DD Dixon)

For one who played such a religious zealot in Brookside, it is appropriate that Irene Marot's recent credits include the play *Once a Catholic* and the film *Nuns on the Run*. She has also appeared in an episode of *Cracker*.

Dinah May (Samantha Partridge)

Dinah May decided to give up acting a few years ago.

Annie Miles (Sue Sullivan)

Annie Miles can currently be seen in the Channel 5 soap *Family Affairs* in which she plays Maria Simons, owner of The Lock. With echoes of Sue Sullivan, her character has been known to have the occasional affair.

Clive Moore (Derek O'Farrell)

Those who think Derek is in Bosnia will have been shocked to see Clive Moore still offering a helping hand to those in need as a paramedic in *EastEnders*. He has also appeared in *The Painted Lady* with Helen Mirren and in stage productions of *The Resistible Rise of Arturo Ui* and *Hobson's Choice*.

Simon O'Brien (Damon Grant)

Since Damon's untimely death, Simon O'Brien has carved out a niche for himself as a presenter on shows like *Night Network*, *I Can Do That*, *Move It*, *Fraggle Rock*, *Power Club Plus*, *The Brookside Guide* and the soccer programmes *Standing Room Only* and *Planet Football*. His principal acting role has been in the Central TV sit-com *Young, Gifted and Broke*.

Shelagh O'Hara (Karen Grant)

Shelagh O'Hara's whereabouts remain something of a mystery. After leaving *Brookside*, she went on a cruise with her boyfriend, but her last known acting credit was in a radio play back in 1991. She has been spotted occasionally in Liverpool but is presumed to have given up acting.

Suzanne Packer (Josie Johnson)

The sister of Olympic hurdler Colin Jackson, Suzanne has recently been seen on TV in *All Good Friends*, *Lifeboat*, as Miss Foster in *Grange Hill*, *Porkpie*, *Casualty* and as Maria in *Tiger Bay*. She has also been working in the theatre, including a West End role in *Once on this Island* and a US tour of *Measure for Measure*.

Stifyn Parri (Christopher Duncan)

Stifyn Parri has been working mainly in the theatre in his native Wales although he took *Les Miserables* to the West End. He also starred in the West End as Emlyn Williams in *George ... A One Man Play*. An accomplished singer, Stifyn has performed in concert at the London Palladium and on various radio shows.

Kazia Pelka (Anna Wolska)

Since Anna fled the country hotly pursued by the immigration authorities, Kazia Pelka has slipped across the Pennines to North Yorkshire to play district nurse Maggie Bolton in *Heartbeat*.

Tricia Penrose (Emma Reid)

Following roles in *Albion Market*, *Boon*, the Anita Dobson comedy *Split Ends*, *Medics*, *Coasting* and *Emmerdale*, Tricia Penrose has become a familiar figure behind the bar of the Aidensfield Arms as Gina Ward in *Heartbeat*.

Alexandra Pigg (Petra Taylor)

Born Sandra McKibbin, Alexandra Pigg made a big impact soon after leaving *Brookside* when she played Elaine in the film *Letter to Brezhnev*, a role for which she won the Evening Standard Outstanding Newcomer Award. Subsequent films have included *Strapless* and *Chicago Joe and the Showgirl* while among her TV credits have been *Smart Money*, *Making Out* and *Murder East, Murder West*.

Steven Pinner (Jonathan Gordon-Davies)

Now known as Steven Finch (his real name) to differentiate him from Steven Pinder, who shares the same agent, he has appeared in many series since *Brookside* – among them *Crown Prosecutor*, *Agent Z and the Penguin From Mars*, *The Bill*, *The One*, *The Jump*, and the US science-fiction thriller *Worlds Beyond*.

Brian Regan (Terry Sullivan)

With Terry doing a runner just as Bar Brookie was about to open, Brian Regan has been able to concentrate on new projects. To date, he has appeared in the Nick Berry pilot *Paparazzo* and a Welsh TV show, *Cyw Haul*.

Alan Rothwell (Nicholas Black)

Alan Rothwell has had a tough time in soaps. As David Barlow (Ken's younger brother) in *Coronation Street*, he was killed in a car crash and in *Brookside*, he was found dead on a park bench. Recently he appeared in *Emmerdale* as John Kenyon, Steve Marchant's father. Alan's other post-*Brookside* credits include *All Creatures Great and Small*, *The Adventures of Sherlock Holmes* and *Medics*.

Tony Scoggo (Matty Nolan)

Tony Scoggo has turned his attentions to politics and is now a local councillor with Knowsley Council. He still finds time to do some acting and played Freddie Boswell in the stage tour of *Bread*.

Alyson Spiro (Alison Gregory)

Alyson Spiro can be seen in *Emmerdale* as Sarah Sugden, a role she took over from actress Madeleine Howard. Her *Emmerdale* character is every bit as miserable as her one in *Brookside*.

Shirley Stelfox (Madge Richmond)

Since *Brookside*, Shirley Stelfox has appeared in *Bergerac*, *King and Castle*, as Carol May in three series of *Making Out*, *Stay Lucky*, Rose in the first series of *Keeping Up Appearances*, *Civvies*, *Get Back* and *The Bill*. She also played a prostitute in the film *1984* and Shirley in *Personal Services*.

Nicola Stephenson
(Margaret Clemence)

Nicola has played both comedy and drama on television since leaving *Brookside*. Her comic roles have been Lizzie in *Nice Day at the Office* and Gail in *My Wonderful Life* while in a more serious vein, she has appeared in *Wokenwell*, *Kiss and Tell* and as Lucy Shore in the police series *Out of the Blue*. She also played Ethel in Ken Russell's film of *The Rainbow* and performed in *A Patriot For Me* for the Royal Shakespeare Company.

Mary Tamm (Penny Crosbie)

Mary Tamm has scarcely had time to draw breath since leaving *Brookside*. She has appeared in *Loved By You*, *Heartbeat*, *Crime Traveller*, *CI5 – The New Professionals* and, for American TV, *The New Adventures of Robin Hood*. Recent film roles include *The Darkening* (with John Hurt) and *Night Swimming*. She is also a regular in the Carlton soap *London Bridge*, playing beauty salon owner Jan Bishop.

Malcolm Tierney (Tommy McArdle)

Malcolm Tierney is another familiar face on television. Since *Brookside* he has appeared in such diverse productions as *Lovejoy*, *Room at the Bottom*, *Doctor Who*, *Hannay*, *A*

Bit of a Do and *House of Cards*. One of his most recent appearances was as a gangland villain in *The Bill* – shades of Tommy McArdle.

Ricky Tomlinson (Bobby Grant)

A northern drama series is barely complete these days without the inclusion of Ricky Tomlinson somewhere in the cast. The latest in a long line of credits include running roles in the oil-rig drama *Roughnecks*, as the police chief in *Cracker* and as the women's football team owner in Kay Mellor's *Playing the Field*.

Susie Ann Watkins (Jo Halsall)

She may have played a mean customer in *Brookside* but much of Susie Ann Watkins's work is in comedy. To illustrate the point, her post-Brookside credits include Sandra in *The 10%ers*, Theresa in *The Upper Hand*, Carol Marsham in *An Actor's Life for Me* and Mrs Robinson in *Birds of a Feather*.

Daniel Webb (Gavin Taylor)

Now known as Danny Webb, he has recovered from Gavin's death to enjoy a fruitful career in TV productions such as *Cardiac Arrest*, *Our Friends in the North*, *Murder Most Horrid*, *2point4 Children*, *A Perfect State* and *A Woman's Guide to Adultery* as well as films like *Aliens3* and as Captain Will in Kenneth Branagh's *Henry V*.

Jim Wiggins (Paul Collins)

Jim Wiggins's recent credits include television roles in the Granada serial *Families*, *The Bill* and *Dangerfield* plus Sir Jasper in the national tour of *Me and My Girl*.